In the
Eagle's Shadow

Brooks D. Simpson
ADVISORY EDITOR

IN THE EAGLE'S SHADOW

The United States and Latin America

SECOND EDITION

Kyle Longley
Arizona State University

Harlan Davidson, Inc.
Wheeling, Illinois
60090-6000

Library of Congress Cataloging-in-Publication Data

Longley, Kyle.
 In the eagle's shadow : the United States and Latin America / Kyle Longley. — 2nd ed.
   p. cm.
 Includes bibliographical references and index.
 ISBN 978-0-88295-271-0 (alk. paper)
   1. Latin America—Foreign relations—United States. 2. United States—Foreign relations—Latin America. I. Title.
 F1418.L665 2009
 327.7308—dc22

                                                              2009006282

Cover photo: U. S. President George W. Bush meets Mexican President Vicente Fox at the beginning of meetings between the U. S., Mexico and Canada at Baylor University in Waco, TX, 3/23/05. White House photo by Krisanne Johnson.
Cover design: Linda Gaio

Manufactured in the United States of America

11 10 09 1 2 3 VP

Contents

Maps

Preface and Acknowledgments

IN 1985, THE SUDDEN RESIGNATION OF A PROFESSOR only a few days before the start of the fall semester sent me scrambling to enroll in a new course. As a mathematics major at Angelo State University, I wanted to take a good elective that might prove interesting. My father, a social science teacher, spoke highly of a course in Mexican history he had taken back in his days at Texas Tech University. As luck would have it, there was such a course offered that term and its time slot fit into my existing class schedule. That is how I came to sign up for Dr. Dempsey Watkins's History of Mexico. By the end of the semester, I became a history major who had decided to pursue a Ph.D. in the study of some aspect of Latin America.

From that time until my graduation from Angelo State in 1987, I studied history. My instructors, especially Dr. Watkins and Dr. Shirley Eoff, recognized my enthusiasm and provided me wonderful instruction inside and outside of the classroom. They recommended extra readings on one of the most controversial issues of the time, U.S.-Central American relations. One book in particular, *Inevitable Revolutions* by Walter LaFeber, changed my life. After reading it, I knew I wanted to concentrate on the relationship between the United States and Latin America. Because of my own ignorance regarding the historical conditions that underlay that intricate and ongoing relationship, I wanted to learn much more about it and hoped one day to educate others.

For more than twenty years now, I have studied and learned and taught about the United States and Latin America. Many people have helped in the process. I had excellent instructors at the graduate program in history at Texas Tech University, including Allan Kuethe, James Harper, and Robert Hayes. While doing doctoral work at the University of Kentucky, David Hamilton, Jeffrey Wasserstrom, and Francie Chassen-López greatly helped broaden my knowledge. Most important in my development was my dissertation adviser, George Herring. He is one of the most knowledgeable and generous mentors in the field of U.S. foreign relations. Today, he remains one of my closest friends and a role model.

Since earning my doctorate in 1994, I have had the great pleasure of making many fine associates in the historical field, persons who have helped shape this book. At Arizona State University, Asunción Lavrin, Edward Escobar, Arturo Rosales, Catherine O'Donnell, Gayle Gullett, Peter Iverson, and Linda Wood have been wonderful colleagues and stimulated my intellectual development. Those within the field of U.S.-Latin American relations have made substantial contributions to this work, including friends such as Michael Krenn, Mark Gilderhus, Jürgen Buchenau, Jason Colby, Joseph Smith, Lester Langley, Stephen Webre, Darlene Rivas, Elizabeth Cobbs Hoffman, Michael Conniff, Randall Woods, Richard Immerman, Monica Rankin, Michael Donoghue, William Walker, Stephen Rabe, Larry Clayton, Eric Roorda, Thomas Paterson, Steven Streeter, and Helen Delpar. I owe a particular debt of gratitude to Thomas Leonard, Thomas Schoonover, Jim Siekmeier, Michael Weis, Irwin Gellman, and Brad Coleman, each of whom read sections of the manuscript and made recommendations for improving it. And since this work is a synthesis, I gratefully acknowledge all those who have contributed to the historiography of U.S.-Latin American relations. Finally, I want to thank Admiral Jim Stavridis, U.S. commander of the Southern Command, and Colonel Jorge Silveira for their support during the preparation of this second edition.

A special thanks for developing this book goes to Andrew Davidson, who personally took the time to copyedit the manuscript. He is an accomplished editor and has provided nothing but positive input throughout the publication process. I am indebted as well to the two scholars who read the manuscript of the first edition for Harlan Davidson, Inc., both of whom made insightful comments that led to necessary revisions. Members of the staffs at the National Archives, the Library of Congress, and the presidential libraries helped me gather essential materials, especially the photographs.

I also must thank those persons closest to me for their understanding and patience during the two years that I spent writing the first edition. My parents, Joe and Chan, have always encouraged my endeavors. I could not have selected better parents—even had I been given the opportunity. My wife Maria has been especially supportive; she took on much of the burdens around the house as I hid in my office, typing away on the keyboard.

Finally, I am grateful to my young sons, Sean and Drew, who many times sat in my office playing quietly, waiting for their father to finish concentrating on persons and events far away in time and space.

I dedicate this book to the three people who helped me find my career: Dr. Dempsey Watkins, Dr. Shirley Eoff, and Dr. Walter LaFeber. While students sometimes take their professors for granted, I will never do so. I will ever be appreciative of the time and energy they devoted to me, and of the examples they set. I hope to live up to their models in that my work, too, might help others arrive at a better understanding of the world.

Kyle Longley

Introduction

THE HISTORY OF U.S.-LATIN AMERICAN RELATIONS reads like an epic novel. Heroes and villains abound, as do larger-than-life characters such as Antonio López de Santa Anna, William Walker, Smedley Butler, Theodore Roosevelt, Fidel Castro, and Ernesto "Che" Guevara. Palace intrigues, Byzantine plots, assassinations, revolutions, and wars fill the pages, their descriptions unveiling covert operations to hire spies to place explosive seashells in favorite diving spots, hit men to snuff out political rivals, and mercenaries to drop bombs out the windows of airplanes.

Then tales of human beings versus nature develop. In the jungles, mines, and guano fields, millions of lives changed forever. Persons undertook massive projects to build railroads and canals through jungles and rain forests, creating both enormous wealth and untold devastation. Simultaneously, great people who dreamed of freeing others from their bondage arose, as did dictators and elites equally as concerned with maintaining feudal systems. Everywhere society evolved with the human conditions of poverty, injustice, and inequality. In many cases, the stories seem too weird to be true. Yet they are, and they compose an intricate tapestry that has characterized the interaction of the United States and Latin America.

This book provides a good, concise overview of U.S.-Latin American relations. It seeks to explain in straightforward language the complexities of the important relationship between the United States and its southern neighbors. While primarily a narrative, it incorporates various interpretations from leading scholars of U.S.-Latin American relations to prompt additional investigation and discussion.

Major Themes in U.S.–Latin American Relations

This book underscores several basic themes in U.S.-Latin American relations in order to help the reader contextualize the historical process. Hopefully, these recurring themes will help you realize continuities in your own understanding of this multidimensional and ongoing relationship. First, the author notes that each Latin American nation is an independent entity with unique demographic and geographic conditions that foster a distinct society. For example, Argentina is very different from Mexico, a fact borne out in the nature of the relationship of each country with the United States. Nevertheless, certain similarities hold the larger story together.

Asymmetrical Interdependence

Since the eighteenth century, the destinies of the peoples of the Western Hemisphere have been interwoven. Their geography and relationships with European colonial powers pushed them together. Over time, they became economically and politically interdependent. Although development began on a fairly equal basis, it became more stratified as the United States industrialized and grew into one of the world's largest economic and political powers. This created an asymmetrical relationship on interlocking levels:

1. **Economic**—Once the Spanish Empire opened its colonies to trade in the late eighteenth century, the fledgling United States and Spain's New World colonies became more integrated economically. The United States needed markets for its goods, and the Latin American nations provided good ones. In turn, the Latin American countries supplied raw materials not readily available in the United States, such as coffee and sugar. Over time, the Latin Americans became more dependent on U.S. finished goods and technology. An unbalanced exchange of resources arose over time, one in which the United States generally gained at the expense of Latin America.

By the early twentieth century, that economic interdependence deepened. American bankers and entrepreneurs often replaced their British counterparts as the primary source of capital and technology in Latin America. At the same time, the United States relied on Latin American raw materials to fuel its factories and feed its people. The imbalance increased as the United States became an industrial power and Latin America remained essentially the producer of raw materials. The chief industrial nations, including the United States, typically set the prices, and the economic asymmetry worsened in favor of the United States. Still, as the North American Free Trade Agreement (NAFTA, 1994) and other present-day economic policies demonstrate, the process continues.

2. Political and diplomatic—During the nineteenth and twentieth centuries, the United States and Latin America also developed a political and diplomatic interdependency. They shared many of the same concerns, principally keeping the Europeans from returning to the Western Hemisphere and protecting national sovereignty. Issues of trade, peace, and foreign intervention often unified the region.

By the early twentieth century, the United States had become the dominant power. Yet it still relied on Latin American nations as it prepared for hemispheric defense, first against the Nazis (in World War II) and then the Soviets (in the Cold War). Over the course of the twentieth century, the nations constructed a hemispheric community through the Pan American Union (PAU) and, after World War II, the Organization of American States (OAS). Furthermore, Americans and Latin Americans often cooperated in the United Nations (UN) on major issues, with Washington frequently depending on regional support for its initiatives. This interdependence remains strong and is not likely to dissipate, as contemporary issues including regional stability, commercial trade, the production of and traffic in illegal narcotics, and immigration demonstrate.

The U.S. Drive to Hegemony

Stemming from this interdependence is another consistent theme in U.S.-Latin American relations: the U.S. drive to establish hegemony in the Western Hemisphere. Political scientist Guy Poitras characterizes hegemony as "a preponderance of power of one state over other states," something far more serious than "inequality among states."

Several factors explain this development, including a desire for markets and raw materials, a hunger for new lands, and racism and paternalism. In the first half of the nineteenth century, the United States seemed most interested in Mexico, Central America, and the islands of the Caribbean. As the United States grew more powerful, its influence spread throughout South America. By the mid-twentieth century, the United States used its political and economic power to become, according to Poitras, "not only hegemonic (i.e., dominant) in the Americas but so preeminent that no other center of power in the Americas could dare challenge it."

The extent of U.S. hegemony has ebbed and flowed to different degrees among individual countries. Many factors shape the depth of U.S. hegemony in individual Latin American nations. Proximity to the United States has played a significant role. For example, Mexico, Central America, and the Caribbean nations outside the French and British possessions experienced the earliest and greatest amount of U.S. attention while the degree of U.S. influence in South America took significantly more time and the development of better technologies.

Furthermore, the comparative economic, military, and diplomatic power vis-à-vis the United States affected the extent of U.S. hegemony. For example, in the nineteenth century, Brazil, Colombia, and Chile sustained relatively comparable power in relation to the United States, especially when contrasted with countries such as Haiti, the Dominican Republic, and Costa Rica. The comparative advantages of certain nations has continued into the twentieth century as population, wealth accumulation (related to lucrative natural resources such as oil), and other factors have continued to play a role. Still, the degree of U.S. hegemony has deepened after World War II and particularly in the aftermath of the Cold War.

The United States employed many kinds of tools in establishing its hegemony, including:

1. Military force and covert action—The crudest tool of establishing hegemony is the use of military force to secure territory or crush perceived challenges. In the course of U.S.-Latin American relations, the United States has employed this method many times, from the war with Mexico of 1848 and continuing through 1994, with the invasion of Haiti. In the initial stages, a war of conquest drove U.S. policy toward Latin America. Later, it was a desire to prevent European or anti-American governments from seizing power anywhere in the Western Hemisphere. In the process of its military invasions, the United States strengthened its hegemony in Latin America by removing foreign competitors, both economic and political, and tying the leadership it left in power to Washington, a process borne out later when the United States undertook covert actions in countries such as Guatemala in 1954 and Chile in 1973. Finally, over time, the threat of force became a powerful tool that Washington used to shape the domestic politics of certain Latin American nations. In some cases, merely stationing U.S. ships offshore forced compliance with Washington's demands.

2. Politics and diplomacy—While military interventions have garnered the most attention, the United States established its hegemony through other avenues. These include the use of diplomatic recognition, which the United States could extend or cut off at its whim. This tactic allowed Washington to control political exchanges, the severing of its formal recognition tantamount to diplomatic ostracism. Tied to this was the use of other coercive tools, including economic sanctions and boycotts, as well as U.S. policies prohibiting American business executives and those of U.S. allies from trading with a particular nation. In addition, Washington could also withhold military equipment, food, loans, grants, and other forms of aid. The effectiveness of these tactics rested on the amount of dependence facing the Latin American nation in question. While it required patience, economic pressure could significantly affect the domestic politics of a particular nation by emboldening opposition groups, making them beholden to Washington should they seize power.

3. Economic dependence—Another tool of creating hegemony was the long-term creation of economic dependence. Over many years, private U.S. companies established a preponderant place in many economies throughout the region, making central governments reliant on them for revenues from taxes they paid. U.S. markets also became the dominant supplier as well as buyer of local goods, making it difficult for certain nations to break ties with the United States without serious economic dislocation. In the process, the United States became a major player in determining the prices of the raw materials Latin America produced. It often used its position in Latin America to destroy competition with U.S.-made goods there.

As the United States industrialized in the late nineteenth century, the safeguarding of the capitalist system, the uninterrupted flow of raw materials, and the protection of markets for U.S.-made goods became priorities. This meant that those nations who challenged U.S. business interests often faced military intervention, and that strategic areas such as the Panama Canal were zealously guarded. With each military occupation, U.S. businesses seized a larger percentage of the targeted country's trade, partly because the occupying U.S. force helped build infrastructure and commercial plants on which the host nation then depended, partly because the U.S. government imposed favorable tariffs on the occupied nation's government.

Over time, Latin America's economic dependence on the United States grew deeper. As U.S. bankers took a significant role in the development of many Latin American countries, U.S. power levels only increased. This trend intensified in the 1930s, as the Great Depression dried up potential investment funds and the U.S. government became an international lending agency, expanding from the Export-Import Bank through the International Monetary Fund and World Bank. Washington largely used these institutions to force Latin Americans to follow U.S. models of development. When a country deviated from that model, Washington withheld needed loans until it fell back in line.

4. U.S. dominance of regional and international organizations—Another way the United States established and maintained its hegemony over Latin America evolved through efforts to control regional and international organizations. From the mid-1880s forward, the United States built on the ideas of Simón Bolívar of creating a unified Western Hemisphere. Americans promoted inter-American meetings with the creation of the Pan American Union and local organizations such as the Central American Court of Justice. In the case of almost every such pan-American body, Washington became the headquarters, and U.S. representatives dominated the group. This pattern would extend to the establishment of the OAS in the 1940s. At several junctures, the United States forced the OAS to support U.S. policies as a useful "cover" for U.S. actions, as would be demonstrated in the Dominican Crisis of 1965.

The same trend continued in the larger international organizations, in which the United States sustained a preponderant position along with the other core industrialized powers. The best example is the UN, headquartered in New York City. Within that organization, the United States retained a position on the Security Council, providing it a veto over almost any measure with which it disagreed. It also maintained a lion's share of the power on most of the UN's lending and aid groups. While the Latin Americans had many UN delegates, the United States often worked hard to win their support, thereby undercutting any clear division of power.

5. Cultural imperialism—Finally, certain forms of cultural imperialism worked to establish and maintain U.S. hegemony in Latin America. On one hand, this was the promotion of U.S. political and economic models. Many Latin Americans chose democracy and the U.S. constitutional model. In turn, Washington often promoted its form of government as the answer to Latin America's problems. Equally as important, U.S.

leaders pushed a particular capitalist model of development, one that would maintain open markets and its access to raw materials, often to the detriment of the Latin Americans. Accompanying this was advancement through many venues of mass consumerism and the American way of life. Any deviations often prompted severe criticism and sometimes direct intervention.

There were many levels to the cultural dominance that created strong ties between Latin America and the United States, including sports, the arts and literature, and technology, all of which highlighted U.S. ingenuity and, to a large degree, a perceived superiority. Indeed, U.S. technology permeated the everyday life of Latin American peoples and had a profound effect on their cultures.

Latin American Resistance to U.S. Hegemony

While the United States became the preponderant power in the Western Hemisphere by the early twentieth century, the Latin Americans hardly proved passive actors in the process, and they developed various methods of resistance to protect their own interests. The amount of that resistance differed from nation to nation, depending on comparative strength, availability of valuable resources, location to strategic sites, and historic relationship with extrahemispheric powers. Methods of resistance include:

1. **Violent resistance**—In the most recognizable and well-studied form of resistance, violence plays a significant role in the history of U.S.-Latin American relations, beginning with that waged by Mexicans against the United States in the war of the 1840s and later during the Mexican Revolution of the twentieth century. It continued through the guerrilla wars of the early twentieth century in Haiti, the Dominican Republic, and Nicaragua. The most successful violent resistance to the will of the United States has been waged by Cuba's Fidel Castro, who defeated U.S.-backed revolutionaries at the Bay of Pigs in 1961 and has maintained the sovereignty of the island nation in the face of extreme pressure from the United States for nearly five decades.

2. **Economic resistance**—In the economic realm, Lain American nations have tried to break U.S. dominance by employing tariffs, subsidizing native industries, and, in the most extreme case, nationalizing the holdings of foreign companies. Others have banded together in cooperative economic units to challenge U.S. companies for a larger share of profits. Often, economic resistance has included intense negotiations through

which U.S. companies have compromised and diverted more funds and profits to the host nations.

3. Foreign assistance—From the beginning, the Latin American nations have used their relations with other core industrialized nations as counterweights to U.S. power and influence. In the earliest days, the British and the French provided Latin America markets and sources of income and investment. Over time, the Germans, Spanish, and Soviets became important players in Latin America. Again, Castro provides an excellent case study. He developed relations with the Soviet Union to secure subsidies, markets, and military supplies, thereby breaking a century-old dependence of Cuba on the United States.

At other points, the Latin Americans have worked within the international community to undermine U.S. efforts to maintain its hegemony over the region. They have relied on international public pressure and appealed to international organizations including the World Court and the UN, wherein they have found other member nations equally dissatisfied with U.S. policy. Latin Americans have also benefited from the actions of international non-governmental organizations such as Amnesty International and the Nobel Peace Prize Committee. At different junctures, the international community has significantly affected U.S.-Latin American relations.

4. Cultivating American allies—The Latin Americans also have proven very skilled in fostering important relationships within the United States. This has run the full gamut, from the hiring of lobbyists and public relations firms to shape U.S. public opinion, to cultivating friendships with individual Americans who shared ideas regarding regional economic and political development. Many such connections extended into the White House and Congress and developed from cultural exchanges among prominent Latin Americans in the United States. These friendships have proven significant at important junctures.

5. Cultural resistance—At another level, Latin Americans also have employed cultural tools to assist their resistance to U.S. hegemony. This has differed from the glorification of native cultures and the outright rejection of U.S. values, to promoting alternative views of important issues of development and diplomacy. Cultural resistance can be quite subtle, often coming as it does in the form of sarcasm and irony in novels and poetry to create negative images of the United States and unify various national groups against their pushy neighbor. While seemingly negligible, it is nevertheless an important element of resistance.

Latino Americans

Another long-term trend this book highlights is the significance of the Latino contribution to the United States. What started with the assimilation of the Mexicans in the conquered territories of the Southwest has continued to the point that Latinos have become the largest and one of the most influential minority groups in the United States. Latinos are a diverse group, composed of many different cultures—the largest being Mexican, Cuban, and Puerto Rican—but they share many traits, such as a dominant religion and language and a tendency to reside in the fastest-growing regions of the United States.

Latinos have made significant contributions to United States history, from helping develop the West to serving in large numbers in the U.S. armed forces. They have left an important imprint on American culture in all areas, including the arts, music, food, and language. As their numbers grow, they continue to bring different perspectives to the mainstream. Furthermore, their cultural and political influence will increase and focus domestic politics more closely on issues of family, religion, immigration, and economic opportunity. They have already created a new "America" in the borderlands, one inextricably linked to Mexico, Cuba, and Puerto Rico. Obviously, understanding this trend is an increasingly significant part of U.S.-Latin American relations.

The history of the relationship between the United States and Latin America is a long and complex one, but it is one well worth understanding. That relationship continues to evolve and, as you will see, affects the lives of all who call the Americas home.

SUGGESTIONS FOR ADDITIONAL READING

There are many good surveys of U.S.-Latin American relations. They include Samuel Flagg Bemis, *The Latin American Policy of the United States* (1943); J. Lloyd Mecham, *A Survey of United States-Latin American Relations* (1965); Federico Gil, *Latin American-United States Relations* (1971); Demetrio Boersner, *Relaciones internacionales de América Latina* (1975); Gordon Connell-Smith, *The United States and Latin America: An Historical Analysis of Inter-American Relations* (1975); Graham H. Stuart and James L. Tigner, *Latin America and the United States* (1975); Lester D. Langley, *America and the Americas: The United States in the Western Hemisphere* (1989); Lars Schoultz, *Beneath the United States: A History of U.S. Policy toward Latin America* (1998); Don M. Coerver and Linda B. Hall, *Tangled Destinies: Latin America and the United States* (1999); and Mark T. Gilderhus, *The Second Century: U.S.-Latin American Relations since 1889* (2000).

Some surveys of individual countries include, for Mexico, Josefina Zoraida Vásquez and Lorenzo Meyer, *The United States and Mexico* (1985); Lester Langley, *Mexico and the United States: The Fragile Relationship* (1991); and W. Dirk Raat, *Mexico and the United States* (1992). For Central America, they include Walter LaFeber, *Inevitable Revolutions: The United States and Central America,* 2nd ed. (1993); Thomas M. Leonard, *Central America and the United States: The Search for Stability* (1991); John H. Coatsworth, *Central America and the United States: The Clients and the Colossus* (1994); John E. Findling, *Close Neighbors, Distant Friends: United States-Central American Relations* (1987); Karl Berman, *Under the Big Stick: Nicaragua and the United States since 1848* (1986); and Michael L. Coniff, *Panama and the United States: The Forced Alliance* (1992). For South American countries, they include Stephen J. Randall, *Colombia and the United States: Hegemony and Independence* (1992); Sheldon Liss, *Diplomacy and Dependency: Venezuela, the United States and the Americas* (1978); Kenneth D. Lehman, *Bolivia and the United States: A Limited Partnership* (1999); Lawrence A. Clayton, *Peru and the United States: The Condor and the Eagle* (1999); Judith Ewell, *Venezuela and the United States: From Monroe's Hemisphere to Petroleum's Empire* (1996); William F. Sater, *Chile and the United States: Empires in Conflict* (1990); and Joseph S. Tulchin, *Argentina and the United States: A Conflicted Relationship* (1990). Finally, for the Caribbean area, they include Louis A. Pérez, *Cuba and the United States: Ties of Singular Intimacy* (1990); G. Pope Atkins and Larman C. Wilson, *The Dominican Republic and the United States: From Imperialism to Transnationalism* (1998); and Brenda Gayle Plummer, *Haiti and the United States: The Psychological Moment* (1992).

CHAPTER ONE

A New World Created

For nearly three centuries, European explorers, adventurers, and settlers streamed into the New World. Spain and Portugal dominated the
southern lands while Great Britain and France controlled the north. The
colonies the various European peoples implanted in the Western Hemisphere flourished and provided their respective mother countries with great
quantities of minerals and agricultural goods. Distinct societies shaped by
Europeans and the indigenous peoples with whom they interacted evolved
throughout the New World. For more than 250 years, the colonies remained
tied to their mother countries. Yet, by the late eighteenth century, marked
changes in those relationships had occurred. From 1775 to 1823, U.S. and
Latin American leaders began throwing off the colonial chains and establishing independent, republican governments. Despite dramatic cultural
differences on the surface, the leaders of these New World republics shared
similar visions of the future.

A Tale of Two Empires

The Spanish Model
The cry of "God, Glory, and Gold" rallied the Spanish conquistadors who
stormed the Americas in the sixteenth century. Steeled by years of fighting the Moors in Spain, the conquistadors turned their attention to the
New World after Columbus's voyage in 1492. Over time, they subdued the
great empires of the Aztecs, Mayans, and Incas. For Spain and themselves,
the conquistadors captured great quantities of gold, silver, emeralds, and
diamonds. They settled on the land and enslaved the indigenous peoples,
forcing some of them into mines and fields to extract the vast wealth.
Catholic priests accompanied the conquistadors, converting the natives
and adding hundreds of thousands of souls into the Church's fold. By the

San Francisco

Santa Fe

San Diego

St. Louis

Washington D.C.

UNITED STATES

VICEROYALTY

San Antonio

New Orleans

Pensacola

St. Augustine

AUDIENCIA OF GUADALAJARA

OF

Gulf of Mexico

Havana

CUBA

NORTH

NEW SPAIN

Vera Cruz

Mexico City

SANTO DOMINGO

ATLANTIC

JAMAICA

OCEAN

AUDIENCIA OF MEXICO

Guatemala

Port-au-Prince

Santo Domingo

El Salvador

AUDIENCIA OF GUATEMALA

Caribbean Sea

Granada

San Jose

Cartagena

Portobelo

Panama

La Guaiara

Caracas

TRINIDAD

AUDIENCIA OF SANTA FE

Bogota

VICEROYALTY

OF

NEW GRANADA

Quito

AUDIENCIA OF QUITO

Guayaquil

Sao Luis

VICEROYALTY

OF PERU

BRAZIL

Recife

AUDIENCIA OF LIMA

Lima

AUDIENCIA OF CUZCO

PACIFIC

Cuzco

AUDIENCIA OF CHARCAS

OCEAN

La Paz

Chiquisaca

Brasilia

VICEROYALTY

OF LA PLATA

Rio De Janeiro

AUDIENCIA OF CHILE

Asuncion

Spanish America
circa 1800

Mendoza

Valparaiso

Santiago

Cordoba

Santa Fe

BANDA ORIENTAL

Buenos Aires

Montevideo

SOUTH

Concepcion

AUDIENCIA OF BUENOS AIRES

ATLANTIC

OCEAN

0   500   1000 Kilometers
0   500   1000 Miles

PATAGONIA

FALKLAND ISLANDS

end of the sixteenth century, Spain had vibrant and productive colonies in the New World.

Through the nature of its conquest and heritage, Spain established the social, economic, and political system that dominated its American colonies for three centuries. Determined to exploit fully the Americas, the Crown established a multilayered control system. Chief administrative duties resided in the Council of the Indies, which made decisions on legislative, judicial, and commercial matters, including the monitoring of local officials and collecting patronage for the Catholic Church. Located in Seville, Spain, the Council relied heavily on the court-appointed, Spanish-born viceroys to administer its edicts in the New World colonies. From the capitals of their respective provinces, the viceroys commanded the armies and maintained the public administration. Each area under the purview of a viceroy was administered by a local *audiencia,* composed of an executive head and board of control. The Crown-appointed officials of the audiencias typically were Spanish born. They reported to the viceroy and administered government mandates. Finally, beneath the audiencias were *corregimientos* and *alcaldes* who controlled political life at the district and city levels. Typically purchased from the Crown and held in perpetuity by a family, these civic positions were highly influential throughout New Spain. The men who held these offices controlled city lots and garden areas and provided for the maintenance of public works through leases, fines, and taxes.

In the eyes of the Crown, Spain's New World colonies existed to help fuel the economic development of Spain. In the fifteenth and sixteenth centuries, Spain practiced mercantilism, a system whereby colonies produced raw materials, especially precious metals and agricultural goods, and served as a market for the finished products of the mother country. The Crown monitored trade by granting trade monopolies to Seville's *consulados* (merchant guilds). The consulados relied on a fleet system to transport olive oil, wheat, slaves, and other European goods to the New World. There, they arranged contracts with merchants in Lima, Mexico City, and elsewhere to conduct trade fairs when their ships reached port. At these fairs, Spanish officials also collected taxes on imports and exports. This method allowed Spain to ensure maximum profit and taxes while excluding foreign competition. For more than three hundred years, the Spanish system sustained this insular economy.

To maintain this economic system, the Spanish relied heavily on native labor for the production of raw materials. In the initial stages, the conquistadors depended on the *encomienda,* a program that required Indians on captured lands to serve involuntarily. Over time, the Spanish replaced this brutally exploitative system with requirements that Indian communities provide rotational labor drafts to pay for government expenses and the tithes. The Spanish administrations of New World communities forced their native inhabitants to work in Spanish mines, textile mills, farms, and cattle ranches. Finally, in many areas, the Spanish relied on African slaves to complement the native labor force and, later, a form of debt peonage to maintain a stable workforce.

The political and economic system in Spain's American colonies guaranteed a polarized and racially segregated society. At the top level were the native-born, white Spanish, known as the *peninsulares.* Beneath them were the New World–born people of Spanish descent, the *criollos.* After these elites, a racially ordered group evolved distinguished by amounts of Spanish, Indian, and African blood. This process created a *mestizo* class, one characterized by Spanish interrelationships with natives and slaves. Finally, at the bottom lay the full-blood Indians and African slaves. Colonial authorities made many distinctions in census and other records to differentiate the color of persons. In Mexico, there were sixteen different racial classes, in Peru, twelve. As a prominent social scientist has argued, in many areas where there were "not really classes but . . . rather races. . . . Race went hand in hand with certain modes of production and consumption . . . and came to determine the economic position [class] of settlers."[1]

To maintain order in the stratified societies, the Spanish relied on several institutions, one of the most important of which was the Roman Catholic Church. The separation of church and state was not a concept known to sixteenth-century Spain, as the Crown collected tithes for the Church and the Church administered many civil duties, including the issuance of birth and death certificates and marriage licenses. Many high Church officials held government positions and most education lay in Church hands. In return for its allegiance, the Church, especially its high officials, supported the Spanish Crown. Many Church leaders came from the elite class and fostered the continuation of a system of government that maintained the privileges exclusive to their own class. In return, the Crown granted *fueros* to the Church, which prevented civil and criminal actions against clergy-

---

1 The issue of race in Spain's colonies and Portugal's Brazil, where colonists imported slaves to work on plantations, would have a long-term impact and significantly shape the societies.

men, who could only be tried by their own. In most cases, the relationship between the Crown and Church remained strong and helped sustain the colonial system.

To maintain stability and obedience to its directives, the Crown also relied on the military. The fighting caste of the conquistadors had conquered Spain's New World empire, and their families retained power in many areas. While the military leaders in New Spain lost ground to civil bureaucrats over time, the military remained vital for several reasons, one of the most important of which was the fear of internal insurrections by slaves, natives, and discontented criollos, who tired of seeing special privileges awarded the peninsulares. In the coastal and island areas, and along New Spain's far-northern border in what is now the southwestern United States, foreign threats from French, British, and Dutch raiders and privateers prompted the Crown to raise armies.

Generally, however, these Spanish armies were never very large, for they were expensive to maintain. Therefore, the Spanish tended to rely on local militia commanded by Spanish officers to protect New World settlements. Nevertheless, the military remained an important political player. To recruit servicemen, the Crown also granted special fueros to military officers. Throughout most of the colonial era, the officers remained primarily peninsulares or criollos. This created strong ties between the elites and the military, giving the latter a personal stake in maintaining the colonial system and making them very willing to participate in political matters. When colonial uprisings occurred in the seventeenth and eighteenth centuries, the military brutally crushed them. The threat of force and its occasional use deterred many revolutionaries.

The British Model

The structure and the organization of Great Britain's American colonies differed significantly from those of the Spanish. Historian Bernard Bailyn has written: "England's entry into the Western Hemisphere was the very opposite of Spain's. Where Spain had been swift, England was slow; where Spain had been deliberate and decisive, England was muddled in purpose. For Spain, America almost immediately yielded immense wealth. For England, America created more losses than profits, at least at the start."

Bailyn correctly appraised the differences. Spanish discoveries in the New World had prompted the British Crown to dispatch explorers to search for gold and a shorter passage to India. Yet, the British lacked the resources and sufficient interest to settle in the New World, focusing most of its energies on conquering Ireland. One century after the Spanish established colonies in the New World, the British followed suit, in 1607. Britain's first attempts to colonize the Americas were small enterprises, and throughout the seventeenth century, the few British settlements in mainland North America lay in tideland areas near the Atlantic coast.

Those British settlers who traveled to the New World differed in many ways from their Spanish counterparts. First, the economic system they knew was very different. The majority of the British colonists were small farmers or craftsmen who relied primarily on subsistence farming and bartering for existence. Over time, commercial fishing and whaling and the export of certain agricultural products, including wheat and tobacco, developed, creating more reliance on the mother country for finished goods and markets. Ultimately, this created a thriving merchant class, which sparked the rapid growth of Britain's American colonies. By the early eighteenth century, New York City, Philadelphia, and Boston had become important centers of commerce. The only region of the British colonies that bore a resemblance to the Spanish model was the South, where an agro-export industry (rice, cotton, indigo) built on plantations evolved, one that became reliant on slave labor. While the British Crown exerted certain controls, the economy of its American colonies evolved with much fewer restrictions than did that of New Spain.

Because British settlers found relatively few exploitable minerals or products, the British government maintained only a passing interest in its North American colonies, a policy sometimes referred to as "salutary neglect." The early colonial administrators in the seventeenth century were leaders associated with the original settlers, such as the Puritans and the families who had received proprietary land grants. Over time, the Crown began appointing governors and administrators to collect taxes and ensure the colonists followed Crown and Parliament rules, but these British officials had limited powers and often exerted little direct control over the lives of the colonists.

Unlike in the Spanish colonies, in North America a semblance of self-rule existed. The legacy of the English political system included the *Magna Carta* and the establishment of a constitutional monarchy that divided power between the Crown, the House of Lords, and the House of Commons. The British citizens in the New World transferred several similar institutions. Virginia, for example, set up a House of Burgesses. In other areas, town halls served as public forums. By the mid-eighteenth century, when the Crown and Parliament tried to impose stricter controls, a pattern of self-rule was already well established in the North American colonies.

The economic and political systems in the British colonies created a different set of social relations there. For one thing, the rate of intermarriage between native peoples and settlers remained low. Driven by an Anglo-Saxon sense of superiority and racism, the British focused on the annihilation of or forced resettlement of the native peoples living in and nearby their American colonies. The Anglican Church and other denominations, unlike the Catholic Church, rarely tried to integrate the natives into society. In addition, the absence of large concentrated groups (such as the Incas or Aztecs) made exploitation of Native Americans difficult. In turn, the lack of integration prevented the development of the rigid racial distinctions (outside of the American South) that characterized the Spanish colonies.

The social system in the British colonies also featured substantially different major institutions. One of the most important was religion. The Anglican Church was the official Church of England and headed by the king. Yet, in North America, only the elites maintained a close relationship with it. Indeed, the Puritans and the Pilgrims had left England to escape the Anglican Church, arguing it was too political and corrupt. Other settlers had different backgrounds, including the Presbyterians and the Quakers. Finally, new Protestant denominations such as the Baptists and Methodists, who emphasized the relationship between the individual and God, developed on the frontier. The result was a heterogeneous religious patchwork that diffused religious power. A tolerance for different denominations and a separation of church and state developed over time, although discrimination against Catholics continued.

This religious development also affected international relations. Religious foundations, especially those of the New England area, fundamentally shaped the colonial peoples. In particular, the Puritans emphasized the special nature of the New World, stressing that they had fled an autocratic and corrupt Europe. They believed that their good fortune demonstrated that their way of life was superior, and that God had predestined Americans to shape a new order. Massachusetts Bay Colony governor John Winthrop was representative of that frame of mind. In 1630, in a sermon titled, "City on the Hill," he declared: "the Lord will be our God and delight to dwell among us, as his owne people and will command a blessing upon us in all our ways, so that we shall see much more of his wisdom power goodness and truth than formerly we have been acquainted with." He added: "for we must consider that we shall be as a City upon a Hill, the eyes of all people are upon us; so that if we shall deal falsely with our god in this work we have undertaken and so cause him to withdraw his present help from us." Later, these ideas would coalesce with the concepts of democracy and capitalism to underpin Americans' perceived exceptionalism.

In addition to religious distinctions between the Spanish colonies and North American mainland colonies, several other differences characterized the colonial period in the Americas. In the British colonies, the formal military was significantly less important. While some fortune-seeking soldiers joined the first waves of New World immigrants, most who colonized North America were family men accompanied by their wives and children. Usually, these settlers conquered the countryside themselves in militia and community self-protection groups, as the British Crown sought to avoid large expenditures for wars of conquest and defense. Indeed, the Crown rarely built large-scale fortifications in America, for in most cases, the peerless British Navy easily defended the coastline and the native peoples posed few direct threats. In addition, the absence of potential uprisings from large native populations made the presence of large armies in colonial America unnecessary. Thus, no large-scale military presence existed in the colonies until the European wars of the mid-eighteenth century.

The role of the military in British society of the seventeenth and eighteenth centuries therefore differed significantly from that of its counterpart in Spain. Unlike Spain, Britain had never had to endure anything similar to the *reconquista* (the nearly seven-century-long battle to reclaim Spain from the Moors), which had created a permanent military class in Spain. The British also placed the army in a different position within society. Over time, a tradition had developed whereby the military subordinated itself to the civilian and royal leaders and rarely played a direct role in politics. These traditions would transfer to Britain's American colonies.

Finally, the British colonists in America developed a strong dislike for the military during the mid-eighteenth century, especially as the conflicts in Europe among England, France, and Spain spilled over into the New World. During the French and Indian War (1753–63), the British stepped up its troop levels in the North American colonies. This led to arbitrary acts, such as forcing colonists to house British soldiers and pay higher taxes to help defray the cost of the mother country's imperial wars. This generated among colonists a strong dislike for the military, especially the foreign mercenaries serving in the British Army, and contributed to many of the grievances that caused the American Revolution. All these added up to a uniquely American military tradition, one that continued to evolve after the war of independence. It would help shape the new republic and provide a significantly different political culture from that which developed in most Latin American nations after independence.

Worlds Apart

The dissimilar manner of European conquest and settlement in the New World created disparate cultures in North and South America. Different forms of social, economic, and political societies evolved throughout the three centuries of European rule. For future relations between North and South America, this was significant because it helped foster deep-seated suspicions. That distrust would create obstacles for cooperative relations between the nations that won independence in the eighteenth and nineteenth centuries.

The mutual animosity arose from many years of war and competition and distinct cultural differences. Spain and England inoculated their colonists with suspicions of each other, assuring ethnocentrism and racism. An example from the English side was Thomas Gage. An English Catholic, he had become a Dominican friar who served for more than seven years in Guatemala. In 1642, he returned to his homeland, right at the height of the struggle between Oliver Cromwell and King Charles I. Gage publicly renounced Catholicism in a fiery speech at St. Paul's Cathedral in a sermon, "The Tyranny of Satan." Building on the criticisms of Martin Luther and others who believed the Catholic Church to be a corrupted institution, Gage became a bitter critic of the Catholic Church and its Spanish allies.

For decades, Gage devoted himself to educating England and its colonists about the Spanish. In 1648, he published a book, *The English-American, His Travail by Sea and Land:* or, *A New Survey of the West Indias.* It portrayed the Spanish, as one historian observes, "as indolent and lascivious rulers who had whipped their Indian laborers into submission." Gage told of wonderful, exotic places desperately in need of the guidance of English Protestants to develop fully their potential. His writings inspired Cromwell and others to send armies to the New World to conquer Spain's colonies, although they failed miserably in the expedition.

Despite the failure of the English to conquer new territories in the New World, Gage's view of the Spanish and their colonists became commonplace in the British worldview. According to this perception, the Spanish rulers were corrupt and exploited the natives for personal gain, not devoting the hard work and sacrifice upon which true success depended. The intermarriage of the natives and the Spanish created a bastard race that the English delighted in pointing to as inferior. Finally, Gage asserted, the Catholic Church contaminated the world with its idolatry, paganism, and corruption of basic Christian principles. By the late eighteenth century, the majority of British and Americans held these viewpoints.

On the other side, the Spanish developed equally negative stereotypes of the British and their colonists. To the Spanish, the heresy of the Protestants placed the British at the level of barbarians determined to destroy modern Christianity. The brutality of the wars of the Reformation and succeeding wars in the eighteenth century further confirmed in the Spanish world the avarice and corruption of the Anglo-Saxon race. Most Spaniards looked on the British as nothing more than a nation of greedy merchants lacking the spirituality, polish, and refinement of the Court in Madrid. The absence of great cathedrals and palaces in British lands and the relative poverty of the British people further confirmed the superiority of the Spanish and their allies. Over time, many people began to transfer these stereotypes to the American colonists, whom even many British viewed as brutish and unpolished. Needless to say, the culture divide was quite wide when the peoples of the New World began seeking their independence.

The Seeds of Discontent

Revolutionary ideas laid the groundwork for the independence movements in the New World. In the seventeenth and eighteenth centuries, in a period often characterized as the Enlightenment, new thoughts regarding politics, social relations, and economics evolved. Great thinkers led by Francois-Marie Arouet (Voltaire), John Locke, Charles-Louis de Secondat (Montesquieu), Adam Smith, Immanuel Kant, David Hume, and Cesare Beccaria began challenging traditional European institutions. Most important, they emphasized the happiness and self-interest of the individual, leading one historian to note that these values "would inevitably corrode the old social order, which was based upon principles of self-sacrifice and corporate identity."

Many of the Enlightenment philosophers focused on the political and social systems. Locke argued that intolerance and exploitation originated in societies dominated by absolutism and elitism. Montesquieu promoted a political system based on checks and balances within govern-ments to eliminate despotism and corruption. Voltaire focused on the Catholic Church, challenging its ability to honor "truths" not based on scientific facts. Many joined the attack and called for freedom of religion and toleration of human differences. Others, like Beccaria, pioneered work in legal reform that advanced equal rights under the law, protec-tion from torture, an end to capital punishment, and a respect for basic human rights.

In the economic realm, the Enlightenment philosophers challenged prevailing systems, with the work of Scottish economist Adam Smith prov-ing the most influential. He assailed state imposed monopolies and unfair tax policies that benefited the wealthy and stymied the individual entre-preneur. In his famous work, *The Wealth of Nations* (1776), Smith called for governments to cease interference in private economic activity. His famous doctrine became known as *"laissez faire, laissez passer"* (let it be, let it go). His economic theories gained acceptance and dominated many debates in the eighteenth and nineteenth centuries.

Throughout Europe and the Americas, elites read books, articles, and pamphlets written by Enlightenment philosophers. Young men such as Thomas Jefferson, James Madison, Simón Bolívar, and Francisco Miranda pondered these works and pushed to instill the new ideas into their own cultures. The ideological ferment would serve as a basis for rationalization for the wars of independence and political, economic, and social experi-ments of the late eighteenth and early nineteenth centuries.

The Shot Heard Round the World

For two centuries after conquest, the English colonies remained loyal to the Crown. Yet discontent simmered in many areas and had begun to boil over by the 1760s in the North American colonies. Attempts by the British government to strengthen its ability to control and tax its Ameri-can colonists through legislation such as the Proclamation Act of 1763, the Sugar Act, Stamp Act, Quartering Act, and Coercive Acts inflamed colonial passions. Colonial leaders such as Benjamin Franklin and Samuel Adams helped establish committees of correspondence and ultimately the Continental Congress to express their grievances with the mother country. By the mid-1770s, fighting occurred in Massachusetts, as colonial forces attacked British regulars at Concord and Lexington in April 1775.

Despite the battles, most colonists opposed a separation from Great Britain, but the minority that called for independence was a particularly vocal one. And one of the most vocal of that independence-minded group was Thomas Paine. In January 1776, he published *Common Sense*. One historian declared that Paine, a recently arrived immigrant from Scotland, "belonged to no country, lived by his pen, and saw his role as the stimulator of revolutions." Indeed, in his incendiary pamphlet, Paine labeled King George III a "Royal Brute" and called for American independence. To achieve the goal, he argued that the colonies should band together in a confederation for common protection. Recognizing the need for foreign assistance, Paine promoted opening American ports to ships of all nations' flags, believing that France and Spain would covet the economic opportunities as well as the chance to repay the British for their wars of conquest. He concluded that there was not "a single advantage that this continent can reap by being connected with Great Britain." *Common Sense* sold more than 300,000 copies, the equivalent of one copy for every ten Americans.

Ultimately, millions read Paine's work, including Spanish subjects in the New World. Contemporaries recognized the importance of Paine's ideas in the larger scheme of global politics. After reading *Common Sense,* Adam Smith stated that "from shopkeepers, tradesmen, and attorneys" Americans would "become statesmen and legislators . . . contriving a new form of government for an extensive empire, which, they flatter themselves, will become, and which, indeed, seems very likely to become, one of the greatest and most formidable that ever was in the world."

Following on the heels of Paine's famous work was another revolutionary statement that became an important American legacy. In July 1776, Thomas Jefferson released the "Declaration of Independence," in which the young, well-educated Virginian wrote: "We hold these truths to be self-evident, that all men are created equal; that they are endowed by their Creator with certain unalienable rights; that among these, are life, liberty, and the pursuit of happiness. That, to secure these rights, governments are instituted among men deriving their just powers from the consent of the governed. . . ." He went on to warn that if rulers betrayed that trust, "it is the right of the people to alter or to abolish, and to institute a new government."

The document focused on colonial grievances against King George III, although most people recognized Parliament's primary role in having sparked the protests. Jefferson underscored that the king "refused to assent to laws the most wholesome and necessary for the public good," that he had dissolved representative bodies, obstructed the administration of justice, levied taxes without the consent of the people, and crippled international trade. Therefore, Jefferson concluded that only America's independence would suffice to remedy the situation.

The audacious Declaration would serve as a model for many other revolutionaries. Relying on the principle that the monarchy had violated the peoples' trust, Jefferson had constructed a persuasive argument for the independence of any colony. In an era of divine right monarchy, he had firmly imprinted the concepts of the Enlightenment into the popular consciousness of generations of Americans, Latin Americans, and Europeans. As a biographer noted: "In America in 1776, the human race took a new direction, and Thomas Jefferson pointed the way."

Spanish Discomfort

While many Latin Americans supported the Americans in their war for independence, the response of the Spanish Crown was ambivalent. On one hand, it enjoyed the misfortune then befalling Great Britain. On the other, it feared the precedent. The Spanish foreign minister, the Conde de Floridablanca, regarded the Declaration of Independence as political heresy. Consequently, when U.S. officials sought an audience with him, he initially refused them.

Still, the Americans had an ace in the hole. The French, primarily the French foreign minister, Charles Gravier, the Comte de Vergennes, wanted to see the Americans prevail, for he sought revenge for France's devastating defeat by Britain in 1763 and lost territories. The French began covertly aiding the Americans through a dummy corporation, Rodrigue Hortalez and Company, run by the French playwright Pierre Augustin Caron Beaumarchais, author of the *Barber of Seville.* Spain halfheartedly followed France's lead but resisted making a commitment to the Americans.

Throughout most of the American Revolution, the Spanish followed a course historian Lester Langley describes as "winning the fruits of victory without making an official commitment to the American cause." While covertly aiding the Americans, Madrid secretly negotiated for the return of Gibraltar. When King George III rebuffed their attempts, the

Spanish formally joined France in an alliance sealed by the Treaty of Aranjuez. In return for their assistance, the Spanish wanted Gibraltar and the Floridas, although Madrid refused to commit itself to American independence.

During the period 1779 to 1783, the Spanish provided substantial assistance to the Americans. Still, as Langley observes, "what the British and later the Americans perceived as duplicity was more accurately a trait of Spanish diplomacy that called for treating both friend and foe with considerable wariness." U.S. envoy John Jay arrived in Spain in 1779 and requested a formal alliance. The Spanish ignored him, leading one historian to note that "only the lice in Spanish inns gave him a warm welcome." In the next two years, foreign minister Floridablanca occasionally met with Jay and gave him a small amount of money on which to live. By 1781, when Jay heard from the French ambassador that Madrid had encouraged Paris to reclaim the trans-Appalachian region, he left, disillusioned and suspicious of the Spanish Crown.

Throughout the conflict, the Americans believed the Spanish desired lands legitimately theirs. In the treaty that concluded the war, Spain received Florida and other western territories of the North American mainland. "As in previous New World conflicts, the Spanish, in protecting territory rightfully claimed or conquering territory previously lost," one historian comments, "were judged as duplicitous, untrustworthy, and undeserving. Trusting neither enemy nor ally, they were not trusted." While the Spanish contribution to the American cause was substantial, Spain's diplomacy caused hard feelings and contributed to future conflicts. More important, as one historian underscores: "The Revolutionary War . . . flung the unfortunate Spain across the path of [American] progress."

Another important consequence of the American victory was that it inspired Latin Americans. In 1783, during the peace negotiations that formally ended the American war for independence, the Spanish foreign minister, the Conde de Aranda, recognized the Americans' right to revolution against the British Crown. In the Spanish colonial empire, those who wanted independence looked northward. Francisco de Miranda, an independence fighter from Venezuela, visited the United States in 1784 and declared: "Good God. What a contrast to the Spanish system." Thomas Jefferson received a letter from a Brazilian that declared: "Nature made us inhabitants of the same continent and in consequence in some degree patriots." Many criollo elites would look to Jefferson and Paine for guidance. Yet, many battles remained for the peoples of both regions.

The Rumblings of Discontent

Despite the North American example, most Latin Americans remained under Spanish control for another forty years. Some uprisings occurred in Venezuela in 1749 and Ecuador in 1765, but they were quickly suppressed. One major rebellion occurred in Peru in 1780 led by Tupac Amaru II (José Gabriel Condorcanqui). Disenchanted by the brutality, corruption, and exploitation of the Spanish, some criollos and Indians united in an uneasy alliance. The fighting was ferocious, taking more than 100,000 lives as the Spanish violently crushed the insurrection and executed its leaders. The long-term significance of the rebellion was that it raised fears among many whites about the consequences of another move for independence and the difficulties of maintaining the loyalty and support of the Indian and mestizo population. Nevertheless, Spain's suppression of the rebellion undermined calls for independence in Peru and elsewhere.

Other factors weakened revolutionary fervor. Throughout the late eighteenth century, the Bourbon kings of Spain had strengthened the colonial bureaucracy and military, undermining challenges to their authority. The Crown also abolished most of the commercial monopolies and opened trade between its colonies and the other European countries and the United States. This action defused some discontent, especially among the merchant classes in Mexico, Peru, and New Granada.

Still, the seeds of ferment had been planted. The criollos remained envious of Spanish-born elites who held important government and military positions. The Crown also aggravated the criollos by expelling the Jesuits in 1763, sending roughly one thousand criollo family members away with the order. The new economic freedom also had significant results. It created new wealth in the colonies, building a class that would resist future attempts by the Crown to reimpose control. Equally as important, free trade opened the Spanish empire to new ideas. Criollo elites, royal administrators, and clerics began to acquire Enlightenment tracts deemed subversive by the Crown. In addition, contacts developed between the citizenry of New Spain and European and American travelers, merchants, and scientists who extolled the virtues of modern republicanism. Intellectual societies dedicated to republican principles arose in cities such as Quito, Caracas, Bogotá, and Buenos Aires and helped disseminate revolutionary ideas.

The American Model Flounders

While the Latin American independence movement evolved in the Spanish colonies, the newly formed United States found its experiment in republican government under attack, and itself unable to assist its southern neighbors. In 1781, the states adopted the Articles of Confederation. The Articles organized a Congress that could request troops and funds for national defense, establish a monetary system, and administer foreign relations. Fearing authoritarian rule, the Articles created no executive branch or federal judicial branch. To limit centralization of power, the Articles called for a nine-state majority to pass legislation and required all thirteen states to approve any change to the Articles.

While a major step toward republican government, the Articles had severe shortcomings. Important powers of commercial regulation and taxation remained with the states, creating many problems. In foreign affairs, the absence of a standing federal army and diplomatic corps ensured difficulties, namely that Great Britain failed to evacuate the Northwest Territories and Spain refused to recognize American claims in the west and south. Finally, when internal rebellions arose, Congress had no way to suppress them. In 1786, Daniel Shays and 2,000 debtor farmers in Massachusetts seized local courts and prevented the foreclosures of their properties. State leaders asked Congress for assistance but received none. Although the farmers eventually surrendered, Shays's Rebellion highlighted the weakness of the Articles.

Consequently, leaders of the respective states called for a convention to draft a new federal constitution, one that became the model for many democratic governments. Meeting in Philadelphia in the summer of 1787, the delegates to the constitutional convention debated many issues regarding the sovereignty of the state and the power of federal governments. Led by James Madison, George Washington, and George Mason, those convened framed a document that instituted a national republic. It established three branches of government, an executive, legislative (bicameral body), and judicial branch. The legislative branch had the right to levy and collect taxes, coin money, borrow for expenditures, and regulate commerce. The strong executive branch would be headed by the president, commander-in-chief of the nation's armed forces and its chief diplomat. Finally, the constitution mandated a federal judicial branch. Ultimately, and after much debate, the framers of the Constitution added to the main body a Bill of Rights, which guaranteed certain civil rights such as freedom of speech, religion, and the press.

The U.S. Constitution incorporated the fundamental ideas of the Enlightenment but reflected elite ambivalence regarding the nature of man and government. It had a system of checks and balances and emphasized individual rights. At the same time, the framers feared placing too much power in the hands of the masses, fears expressed by the establishment of the Electoral College to select presidents, and the election of U.S. senators by state legislatures. Finally, paradoxes existed. The framers promoted freedom for all but maintained legal slavery. Despite its complexities and contradictions, the U.S. Constitution was a radical document, one embodying a revolution of ideas that shaped the United States as well as many of the future republics of Latin America.

Europe in Flames

Shortly after the promulgation of the U.S. Constitution, a revolution in France reshaped views of self-rule. In 1789, revolutionaries overthrew King Louis XVI and promoted their ideas in the "Declaration of the Rights of Man and Citizen," which proclaimed: "Men are born and remain free and equal in rights. Social distinctions may be based only on common utility." While radical, it still acknowledged that property was "sacred and inviolable." Two years later, the French adopted the Constitution of 1791, which created a constitutional monarchy. Following the British model, the king of France now reported to an elected parliamentary body. The Constitution stressed equality before the law, abolished titles of nobility, outlawed slavery in the colonies, and placed restrictions on the Catholic Church. Limitations existed, however, as only propertied men could vote. Still, the French revolution marked a dramatic departure from the old regime and provided the world with another new revolutionary model.

The French Revolution went through several stages. While the revolutionaries originally focused on liberty, in the second stage, which began in 1792, they stressed equality. Spearheaded by urban workers and the poor, new demands went out for universal manhood suffrage and popular democracy. After King Louis XVI resisted, he met his fate at the guillotine in January 1793. Outraged, the European monarchies declared war on France. In response, the Jacobian party led by Maximilien Robespierre ruled France with an iron hand. Ironically, to Robespierre and others, the good of the general public outweighed individual rights. Robespierre's "Reign of Terror" and the ensuing civil war caused nearly 250,000 deaths.

The radical stage of the French Revolution ultimately collapsed under its own violence. By the late 1790s, Napoleon Bonaparte took power and reestablished a monarchy. Nevertheless, the French Revolution's influence on the Americas was significant for many reasons. The notions of the rights of man and property became a cornerstone for the ideologies of many Latin American revolutionaries, who from this point forward debated issues such as anti-clericalism and democratization of the lower classes. In addition, the violent end of the king underscored the diminishing popularity of monarchies.

At the same time, the French paradigm helped delay revolutions in Latin America by raising the suspicions of the elites. The excesses of the French had convinced many of the dangers attendant to the revolution, especially the loss of stability and order. When revolutionaries talked of independence, especially those pushing the rights of Man and universal suffrage, reactionaries raised the specter of another France occurring in Latin America. Still, the ideas of the French Revolution spread throughout the region and gave support to certain calls to throw off the yoke of Spain.

Gobbling Up the Spanish

While the independence movements in Spain's American colonies matured, the United States grew stronger. By the mid-1790s, the young republic began to address its long-standing boundary disputes and pursue territorial expansion. As early as 1768, a French diplomat predicted that the United States "will emancipate itself from the Crown of England, but that in the course of time it will invade all the dominions that the European powers possess in America, on the main land as well as in the islands."

The Spanish recognized the American potential, and throughout the 1780s they tried to contain it. Led by Baron de Carondelet, they promoted, according to Lester Langley, to "tolerate a few . . . suborn [bribe] their leaders, and give them minimal protection." Spanish officials in New Orleans especially employed such a strategy. In 1784, the Spanish closed navigation of the Mississippi River and denied the use of markets in New Orleans to the 50,000 Americans who had crossed the Alleghenies to peddle their wares. Soon thereafter, the Spanish dispatched Don Diego de Gardoqui to Washington to negotiate a treaty in which the Americans would surrender their right to navigate the Mississippi for twenty-five years in return for the privilege of trading at New Orleans. Uproar arose among westerners, who allied themselves with southerners to sink the proposed treaty. In the debates, Patrick Henry denounced the treaty: "To seel [sic] us and make us vassals to the merciless Spaniard is a grievance not to be borne." Westerners would not forget the Spanish plot, especially new migrants to Tennessee and the Mississippi Valley, including Andrew Jackson.

By the 1790s, the American government had grown more powerful under the Constitution. And the American population was growing quickly, especially in Tennessee, Kentucky, and parts of the Northwest Territory. The Spanish watched warily, but a costly war in Europe diverted attentions. Desperate to appease the Americans, Madrid now negotiated a treaty with U.S. envoy Thomas Pinckney. In Pinckney's Treaty (1795), the Spanish permitted navigation of the Mississippi River by U.S. citizens and their right to deposit goods at New Orleans for shipment. In addition, it agreed to stop attacks by southeastern Indians and pushed the boundary of West Florida down to the 31st parallel. The United States had won a significant victory. On the other hand, Spain had lost ground and set the stage for further American encroachments in the early 1800s.

Cracks in France's Imperial Foundation

By this time, revolution and war in Europe provided certain advantages to the United States and simultaneously inspired rebellions in the New World. The first major uprising after the American Revolution began in the early 1790s in Haiti, where the values of the French Revolution and thinkers such as Montesquieu, who wrote, "sugar would taste much sweeter if the cane did not require the work of slaves," sparked a rebellion. By the mid-1790s, the Haitian rebellion had degenerated into a race and class war between common Haitians and the French overseers and their landowner allies. The fighting was ferocious and included atrocities, as soldiers of both sides decapitated victims, murdered civilians, and raped women. External forces helped unify the Haitians, such as when the British invaded in an effort to prevent the rebellion from spreading to their slave populations in the Caribbean, especially Jamaica. Haiti's Toussaint Louverture rallied his people and expelled the British, who signed a treaty with the Haitians that promised no invasions in return for a pledge not to export their revolution.

The new government officially swore allegiance to France, but it abolished slavery and promulgated a constitution that extended some civil liberties. It also proclaimed Louverture governor-general for life and officially recognized Catholicism as the official religion. Fearful of economic ruin, Louverture imposed government control of labor and forced freed slaves to work on the sugar plantations, although new laws prohibited the use of the whip and required profit sharing. Overall, he still viewed his own people suspiciously, encouraging the taskmaster on the very plantation on which he had been a slave to "be just and unbending, make the blacks work hard, so as to add by the prosperity of your small interest to the general prosperity of the administration of the first of the black, the General-in-Chief of St. Domingue."

Americans in Haiti and the United States watched the new government apprehensively. The violence struck fear in the hearts of southerners. In 1799, during congressional debates on expanding trade with Haiti, Thomas Jefferson wrote: "we may expect therefore black crews, and supercargoes and missionaries thence into the Southern states. . . . If this combustion can be introduced among us under any veil whatever, we have to fear it." Congressman Albert Gallatin, warned: "Suppose that island, with its present population, under present circumstances, should become an independent State. . . . If they were left to govern themselves, they might become more troublesome to us [and] might become dangerous neighbors to the Southern States, and an asylum for renegades from those parts."

Not all Americans viewed the situation in Haiti negatively. In 1799, some Americans had provided the rebels arms and support during the thick of the fighting. In addition, early abolitionists praised Haiti's experiment, believing it signaled the final demise of slavery in the New World. Others sought trade with the formerly closed French colonial possession. "The cultivators . . . have been recalled to their respective plantations," newly appointed U.S. consul Edward Stevens reported from Haiti, "the various civil administrations reorganized and the most effective measures adopted for the future peace and good order of the department."

The Second War of Independence in the New World

While some stability developed in the late 1790s, problems plagued Haiti. The wars of the decade had decimated society, and Louverture's authoritarianism further alienated persons of all colors and classes. His generals were corrupt and amassed great personal fortunes at the expense of the people. Outbursts of racial conflict and uprisings against Louverture's government continued. Most important, on the horizon arose the greatest threat to the new black society, Napoleon Bonaparte.

After Napoleon took control of France in 1799, Louverture tried to maintain a healthy relationship with the former mother country. He sent his two sons to France for an education and pledged his devotion to the French republic. Still, Napoleon schemed to reintroduce French dominance into the New World. In 1801, he signed a peace treaty with England and pressured Spain to cede all of Louisiana to him. Soon thereafter, he initiated plans to retake Haiti and the rest of the island of Hispaniola. He dispatched an army under the command of his brother-in-law, Charles Victor Emmanuel Leclerc, to occupy the island. Believing in European superiority, Leclerc predicted an easy victory.

Leclerc's optimism proved misguided, for the Haitians proved a formidable opponent. They waged a bloody guerrilla war, relying on a scorched-earth policy. Many observers watched in horror. "One cannot form an idea of those cannibals; they not only murder the white race without consideration of age or sex," one New York correspondent stressed, "but they also direct their barbarity on some . . . who show . . . interest for the fates of the whites." The French responded viciously, murdering prisoners of war and civilians—even creating a crude gas chamber in the hold of a French ship. In 1802, the French momentarily gained the upper hand when they lured Louverture into a trap. They sent him to a French prison where he died a year later from exposure.

Despite the death of Louverture, the revolt continued. The French made the costly mistake of employing black Haitian mercenaries who initially proved a loyal and effective force. But the French soon alienated even their most loyal black supporters when they reinstituted slavery. In response, a Haitian general, Jean Jacques Dessailines, defected and became the leader of the Haitian resistance. In the meantime, American smugglers rearmed the rebels, who proceeded to decimate the enemy. Yet the Haitians' greatest ally was disease, principally malaria, which killed many Frenchmen, including

Leclerc. By 1803, France and England had returned to war, ensuring a British blockade of all ports in the French Caribbean. In November 1803, the French fled and on January 1, 1804, the Haitians declared independence and established the second republic of the New World.

Throughout the fighting, the United States remained very cautious and ambivalent. Since independence, Americans had become more conservative regarding revolution. They shared the common dream of independence for their neighbors but worried how such turmoil might affect their commercial and strategic positions. In the case of Haiti, Americans, particularly southerners, feared the precedent of slaves rebelling against their owners and establishing their own republic. Other than the occasional rhetoric in support of the war of liberation and the arms unofficially provided by smugglers and domestic supporters, the United States never provided direct assistance to the Haitian rebels. This would be a pattern repeated many times.

The issue of race had significantly shaped the U.S. response to the Haitians. Washington refused official recognition of the new republic. In the early 1820s, President James Monroe argued "the establishment of a Government of people of color in the island . . . evinces distinctly the idea of a separate interest and a distrust of other nations." That mistrust extended beyond Washington to others, including Simón Bolívar, who opposed Haiti's participation in regional summits in the 1820s. Haiti remained a pariah despite calls for recognition from prominent American leaders like Henry Clay, who feared losing economic opportunities there. His pleas fell on deaf ears in the United States for more than five decades.

Benefiting from European Disasters

The United States consistently benefited from European mistakes and infighting. The Haitian disaster actually aided the United States by causing Napoleon to abandon his grand strategy for a French empire in the Americas. Soon after withdrawing from Haiti, Napoleon sought to discard Louisiana, despite having promised not to transfer the Louisiana Territory to anyone besides Spain. The death of Leclerc led him to exclaim: "Damn sugar, damn coffee, damn colonies." Instead, as one historian emphasized, Napoleon "wished to get back to his glorious drums and trumpets, his drilling and killing of the fittest youth in Europe."

Now that Napoleon had decided to rid himself of Louisiana, he hoped that the United States would want it. Ever since the French had taken over

Louisiana, Washington had condemned the transfer, fearing the French would not honor Pinckney's Treaty concerning the use of the Mississippi River and New Orleans. Determined to continue to conduct trade in the city, westerners threatened to take the city by force. Jefferson, typically known for his French sympathies, suddenly reversed course and received congressional approval for troop deployment to the vital port.

Napoleon's need for money to finance a new European war made the impasse easily negotiated. On April 11, 1803, Napoleon announced to his finance minister: "I renounce Louisiana. It is not only New Orleans that I will cede, it is the whole colony without any reservation." After weeks of haggling, the Americans offered France $15 million for the entire territory, and the French accepted it. The French foreign minister, Charles Maurice Talleyrand, when asked about boundaries, replied: "you have made a noble bargain for yourselves, and I suppose you will make the most of it." While Jefferson's political opponents criticized the Louisiana Purchase, most people hailed the addition of 828,000 square miles of land, bought at three cents an acre, as a great accomplishment.

From the Louisiana Purchase, the United States had nearly doubled its size, despite Spanish protests that the deal was null and void because the French had failed to honor their agreement with them. The event was significant for many reasons. It endowed the Americans with vast natural resources and land that spurred the development of the United States into a world power. The purchase also created disputes between the United States and Spain, who would challenge the western and eastern boundaries until 1821, when a newly independent Mexico inherited the issue. With one signature, the United States had increased its potential as the preponderant power of the Western Hemisphere. Napoleon had foreseen this fact and remarked: "This accession of territory affirms forever the power of the United States, and I have just given England a maritime rival that sooner or later will lay low her pride." Indeed, not only would the move create the potential for the United States to lay the British low, but many other countries as well.

Throwing Off Spain's Yoke

Events in Europe in the first decade of the nineteenth century also helped ensure independence for the Latin Americans. Once more, Napoleon took center stage. Soon after ceding Louisiana to the United States, he swept across Europe. After defeating the Prussians and Austrians, he pressured the

British to sue for peace. However, he lacked a sufficient navy and materials to invade England, and instead sought to isolate the British with his "continental system" of 1806, which prohibited trade with England throughout his enlarged empire.

Part of his strategy to defeat Great Britain was to detach Portugal and Spain. When the Portuguese refused to declare war on England in 1807, French troops drove the Portuguese monarchy into exile in Brazil. Next, Napoleon focused on Spain and lured Spain's new monarch, Ferdinand VII, to Bayonne, France. There he imprisoned Ferdinand, then forced his abdication in favor of his brother, Joseph. Most Spaniards offered resistance, forcing Napoleon to dispatch 350,000 troops to suppress the rebellion. In response, the Spanish municipalities formed a central junta in Seville, which in turn called for the formation of a *Cortes* (parliament) to draft a constitution. In September 1810, the Cortes convened and established a constitutional monarchy. Two years later, it promulgated a new constitution that dramatically shifted power to the Cortes, including the authority to set public expenditures and taxes. As several historians have noted, "the constitution provided for a new unitarian state that eliminated many features of the old regime."

The French occupation of Spain opened the door for independence throughout the Spanish New World. The first revolution occurred in Buenos Aires and the surrounding region known as the Rio Plata. In 1806, the British, eager to torment their enemy Spain, attacked the Argentine city. After the Spanish leaders fled, the people of Buenos Aires successfully repelled the British invaders. Several years later, they declared independence and established a republic. While turmoil reigned for a decade in South America as the new leaders fought for control, republics evolved in Argentina, Uruguay, and Paraguay. Despite internal divisions, the first successful effort to discard Spain's control had occurred, and it inspired many others.

Precursors to Independence

Other South American nations tried to emulate the success at Buenos Aires. Perhaps the most violent such revolt occurred in Mexico. In September 1810, disenchanted criollos in the wealthy mining region of the Bajío rebelled under the leadership of a parish priest, Father Miguel Hidalgo y Costilla. He called for an end to corrupt Spanish rule and raised the

banner of the Virgin of Guadalupe, the most important religious symbol
of the Mexican lower classes. Within a month, Hidalgo's army captured
Guanajuato and massacred the town's peninsulares. As one historian has
noted, "this was a class and race war more than a struggle over the political
future of Mexico."

The rebellion was short lived. Some limited statements regarding independence and social reform evolved, but not enough to unify the disparate
groups involved. Hidalgo's forces reached the outskirts of Mexico City, the
capital of New Spain, but at this point, fearing another massacre of civilians, the priest turned his army away. Now the government forces regrouped
and overtook the rebel armies, defeating them. They defrocked Hidalgo
and executed him, placing his head in a parrot cage in Guanajuato, where
it remained until 1820 as a warning to potential revolutionaries. While the
rebellion never completely died, the harsh reprisals it engendered stymied
Mexico's independence movement for a decade.

Soon after royalist forces suppressed Hidalgo's rebellion, another rebellion occurred in New Granada (comprising modern-day Colombia and
Venezuela). The two primary leaders of the movement were Francisco de
Miranda and Simón Bolívar. Miranda, a professional revolutionary, had
lived in exile in England and the United States. A great admirer of the
ideas of the Enlightenment, he had encouraged European powers and the
United States to assist Latin America's independence movements. In the
late 1790s, he wrote a Venezuelan: "Two great examples lie before our eyes,
the American and the French revolutions. Let us discreetly imitate the first;
let us carefully avoid the disastrous effects of the second."

Miranda's chief ally in the early independence movement was Bolívar,
who became the symbol of Latin American revolutionaries. Born the son
of a wealthy criollo in 1783 in Caracas, he received an excellent education in Spain by private tutors who taught him about classical Rome and
Greece and the Enlightenment. When he was only sixteen years old, he
argued with the Spanish viceroy of New Spain regarding independence
of the colonies. By 1804, he made a famous vow atop Mount Aventin in
Rome that he would never rest until Spain's colonies were free. He traveled to the United States and continued agitating for the independence of
Spain's New World colonies until the opportunity for direct action presented itself.

Bolívar and Miranda received their wish in 1811. That year, they returned
to Venezuela and presided over a government in power since April 1810.

The ruling junta reduced taxes, established free trade, and abolished the slave trade, although slavery remained. Ultimately, a three-person executive committee replaced the junta, and a Congress penned a federalist constitution. The government proved short lived, however, as local royalists savagely counterattacked. Even nature appeared to be against the republicans. In March 1812, a massive earthquake struck. Pro-Spanish priests called it God's judgment. Soon thereafter, the royalists drove Bolívar into exile and imprisoned Miranda. By 1815, Spanish troops completely controlled the region, with the exception of the Rio Plata.

Friendly Neutrality

As the revolutions swept Latin America, Washington officially remained neutral, although privately friendly toward the Latin Americans. Some U.S. officials wanted trade and highlighted similarities between the shared struggles against European monarchs. At the same time, other factors restrained U.S. leaders. Many Americans feared the spread of anarchy that had accompanied the early rebellions, especially the class and racial warfare in Mexico and Venezuela. Some wanted to avoid antagonizing the Spanish, especially when new chances to negotiate for additional lands in Florida and the Southeast appeared. What resulted was neutrality, although one favoring the revolutionaries.

One American group that openly supported the rebellions was composed of merchants and businessmen who saw new opportunities in the making as Latin Americans worked to establish republics in the Rio Plata, Venezuela, and New Granada. President James Madison dispatched consular agents to the republics, giving them instructions that the "United States cherish[es] the sincerest good wills towards the People of Spanish America as Neighbors" and that this would "coincide with the sentiments and policy of the United States to promote the most friendly relations, and the most liberal intercourse between the inhabitants of this hemisphere." They carried this message to the Latin Americans, who heartily sought Washington's approval.

Other U.S. actions demonstrated general sympathy with the Latin Americans. At a public dinner in Nashville, one person received an enthusiastic response when he toasted: "The patriots of South America: palsied be the arm that would wrest from them the standard of liberty for which they have so nobly struggled. Six cheers." With such attitudes dominant, U.S. officials rarely enforced existing neutrality laws. Latin American agents, working mainly in New Orleans, Baltimore, and Philadelphia, collected donations, negotiated loans, and bought arms and munitions for the revolutionaries. In one case, those in Buenos Aires purchased 1,000 muskets and 372,050 flints. In addition, Americans provided other aid. When the earthquake struck Venezuela in 1812, Congress appropriated $50,000 for relief for survivors.

While more restrained, U.S. officials remained generally sympathetic, a posture one historian describes as "neutral friendly." President Madison conducted correspondence with several rebel agents, giving implicit support and recognition. The administration also allowed South American ships to dock in U.S. ports, regardless of what flag they flew. In November 1811, Secretary of State James Monroe wrote to John Quincy Adams, currently the Minister to Russia, that he favored the revolutions in Spanish America. Nevertheless, he reported that "as yet a formal recognition of a minister from neither [new republic] has been made, nor has it been urged."

At the congressional level, other Americans openly championed the Latin American revolutions. In response to the Declaration of Independence in Venezuela in 1811, the House of Representatives created a "Committee on the Spanish American Colonies." In December of that year it urged Congress to recognize the new republics. Raising the banner of "hemispheric solidarity" and a community of republican institutions, its pronouncement was the first official statement by U.S. representatives in support of the Latin Americans.

Such statements encouraged rebel leaders. In December 1813, Bolívar wrote a colleague about the congressional resolution that "it was the intention of that government to recognize our independence as soon as independence had been proclaimed in New Granada and the other regions that were preparing to do so and then to enter into negotiations with the independent governments." He complained that Venezuelan defeats had undermined recognition, but argued that once the Venezuelans won independence, Washington would provide formal recognition and other assistance.

The Reluctant Eagle

Despite the best efforts of American allies, Washington withheld formal diplomatic recognition of and direct military assistance to newly independent Latin American nations. Influential Americans opposed formal recognition of any of the republics "either because they distrusted the self-governing talents of the Spanish Americans or else because they

opposed all such intervention in the domestic affairs of other people,"
historian Arthur Whitaker observes. They looked on the failures in Mexico and Venezuela and agreed with John Randolph of Virginia in 1816
who emphasized: "You cannot make liberty out of Spanish matter."

Other issues undermined direct U.S. assistance to the Latin Americans. For one thing, Washington wanted Florida. As long as Spain held
the region, Washington moved cautiously for fear of alienating the Spanish
and weakening its own negotiating position.

More important, the United States found itself at war with Great Britain in 1812 after having clashed with that nation repeatedly over its navy's
impressments and trade embargoes. As one historian comments, "one of
the chief victims of the war of 1812 was the Latin American policy of the
United States." During the hostilities, President Monroe instructed U.S.
agents "not to interfere in the affairs of those provinces, or to encourage
any armaments of any kind against the existing government." While not
a direct threat, Washington feared Madrid would offer the British bases
in Florida or Cuba. Nevertheless, covert aid flowed southward, as many
federal authorities turned a blind eye to arms smuggling and the outfitting
of rebel privateers in U.S. ports.

During the two-year war, the United States fought for its survival. In
1814, the British burned Washington, D.C., yet they never truly drove
home their advantage thereafter. War weary and low on funds, the British
negotiated a peace treaty with the United States in 1814. This settlement,
combined with the stunning victory of Andrew Jackson over a superior
force at the Battle of New Orleans—waged in January 1815, shortly after
the Treaty of Ghent formally ended the war—gave the Americans some
sense of pride and accomplishment that they had maintained their independence by again standing up to the world's greatest power.

The New and Improved Friendly Neutrality

"After remaining in a state of suspended animation during the war of 1812,
the interest of the United States in Latin America revived quickly at the
end of the war," Whitaker emphasizes. The end of the war inspired a new
expediency in U.S. policy towards Latin America. Meanwhile, back in
Europe, the defeat of Napoleon at Waterloo ensured the restoration of the
Spanish monarchy under King Ferdinand VII, who immediately annulled

the Constitution of 1812 and prepared large armies to suppress the Latin American wars of independence.

Now, a vocal group within the United States championed the Latin American struggle against European authoritarianism. Many of these persons were merchants or had friends among the Spanish American revolutionaries. They worked closely with rebel agents to propagandize the struggles for independence. A representative example was Hezekiah Niles of the *Baltimore Register.* In 1815, he wrote: "The freedom of Mexico alone, is indeed, fifty times more important to the United States than the rescue of Spain from the hands of Napoleon was." Most supporters stressed the kindred spirit of republicanism and economic opportunities. Still, others emphasized that the return of Ferdinand would endanger U.S. interests and spark renewed conflicts in contested territories of the western United States.

After the War of 1812 officially ended, some Americans more forcefully supported the Latin Americans. In 1815, the Treasury Department allowed revolutionary ships into American ports without restrictions. U.S.-Latin American trade, interrupted by the British navy during the war, began increasing, even to loyal Spanish colonies such as Cuba. American veterans began volunteering for service in Latin America. Merchants in Philadelphia and Baltimore purchased 30,000 surplus army muskets to resell to the insurgents. In several ports, U.S. ship owners sold their wartime privateers to rebel leaders. Throughout the process, U.S. officials made few efforts to stop the private activities.

The lack of U.S. neutrality translated into Spanish condemnations of Britain's failure to crush the Americans. In 1815, the chief Spanish agent in the United States, Luis de Onís, rebuked the British. "Now . . . the United States is going to become a great nation, full of pride, presumption, and the ambition to conquer," he wrote, "and the only hope that it will be checked lies in the absurdity of its constitution." He warned his superiors that the Americans wanted "mountains of gold" and would take Texas and Florida to forward "their ambitious design of dominating the whole continent."

While possibly foreseeing their loss, Spanish officials vigorously tried to protect their North American possessions. Onís consistently complained of Washington's lack of neutrality and bias toward insurgents, arguing that the United States had failed to adopt a "good neighbor" policy. In response, he encouraged the Crown to levy heavy tariffs on U.S. goods and punish severely any Americans aiding the rebel cause.

The Dominoes Begin to Fall

The Spanish could not check the revolutionary tide. Even as Ferdinand sent additional troops to strengthen royalist forces, the rebels continued mobilizing and fighting. Soon, new cracks in the royal foundation appeared. One of the first provinces to fall was Chile, where a group of dedicated Chileans labored tirelessly to win independence. Working from Buenos Aires, José de San Martín and Bernardo O'Higgins organized a small, well-disciplined army. In early 1817, it crossed the Andes, captured Santiago, and declared Chilean independence.

In Venezuela, the rebels also took the offensive. Returning from exile in Jamaica, Bolívar marshaled his forces. Alexandre Pétion, the president of Haiti, proved a valuable ally by sending arms and supplies in return for Bolívar's promise to abolish slavery should he prevail. Bolívar also forged an alliance with the southern llaneros led by José Antonio Páez, who provided the patriots with a skilled cavalry. Once united, the rebel forces won victory after victory. Ultimately, they captured Caracas and later New Granada, declaring independence and establishing a unified government of Gran Colombia.

Speaking Out of Both Sides of the Mouth

During the height of the fighting, 1816–19, President James Monroe officially stated a policy of "impartial neutrality." The debate over official recognition and aid to the rebels centered around two individuals. Those calling for active involvement in Latin America continued to find their champion in Kentucky congressman Henry Clay. Rising on the floor of the House in 1816, Clay condemned the secret negotiations of the European monarchs at the Congress of Vienna. He asked: "Do we know whether we shall escape their influence? . . . Under these circumstances, I am not for exhausting the purse of the country of the funds necessary to enable it to vindicate its rights at home, or, if necessary, to aid in the cause of liberty in South America." "I consider the release of any part of America from the dominion of the Old World as adding to the general security of the New," he bellowed.

On the other side, supporters of stricter neutrality lined up behind Secretary of State John Quincy Adams, who argued that the United States should concentrate on negotiations over Florida and pacify Spanish demands for noninterference. A New Englander with ties to the Boston merchants, Adams also feared the loss of trade with Spain should the United States act too rashly. Finally, Adams worried that the European monarchs would ally against the United States if Spain chose war to punish American actions. Therefore, Adams wanted existing neutrality laws enforced and stated that the United States would not recognize the Latin American republics unless the chance for Spanish recovery appeared "utterly desperate."

Clashes between the two groups continued for several years. Monroe and Adams continued to negotiate with Onís over Florida, emphasizing "impartial neutrality." The Spanish, however, complained that the rebel privateers and arms merchants worked unobstructed. Even Adams recognized the problem, emphasizing that many federal officials were "fanatics of the South-American cause."

In 1818, the two parties sparred again. First, Clay and his allies tried to pass a congressional resolution calling for formal recognition of the Latin American republics. On the House floor, Clay proclaimed that the region had the "most sublime and interesting objects of creation." "We behold there a spectacle," he commented, "still more interesting and sublime—the glorious spectacle of eighteen millions of people, struggling to burst their chains and to be free." Despite Clay's eloquent pleas, the Monroe administration remained unconvinced and attacked the measure. Ultimately, the administration defeated it resoundingly.

However, a major obstacle to recognition and assistance to the Spanish American revolutionaries disappeared in 1819. Throughout his service in the State Department, Adams had continued negotiating on the issue of Florida. He worked with the chief Spanish official, Onís, of whom Adams observed: "I have seen slippery diplomatists, but Onís is the first man I ever met who made it a point of honor to pass for more of swindler than he was." Despite his disdain for his counterpart, Adams desperately wanted Florida, while the Spanish sought favorable boundaries in the New Spanish area of Texas and promises not to assist the revolutionaries.

The issue of Florida peaked in 1818. Andrew Jackson, under instructions from Monroe, marched 3,000 troops to the Florida boundary. Jackson, who despised the Spanish for many reasons, had instructions to punish the Seminole Indians for attacks against American settlers. The Tennessean took his mission seriously, crossing the border and capturing St. Marks and Pensacola. A loud uproar arose from Madrid. Onís vigorously protested, barging into Adams' daily Bible study and demanding indemnity and Jackson's punishment. Adams refused, blaming Spain's failure to secure its borders. After much posturing by both sides, Madrid signed the Transcontinental Treaty, which gave Florida and lands westward to the Sabine River to the United States. In return, the United States agreed to pay $5 million to American citizens who had claims against the Spanish. It said nothing about the United States and the Latin American revolutionaries. "Americans . . . believe that their dominion is destined to extend, now to the Isthmus of Panama, and hereafter over all the regions of the New World. . . . They consider themselves superior to the rest of mankind," Onís warned.

The Final Offensive

Soon after the signing of the Transcontinental Treaty, events unfolding in Spain aided the Latin American revolutionaries. In early 1820, Spanish troops led by Major Rafael Riego forced Ferdinand to share power with a parliament as mandated by the Constitution of 1812. Many republican exiles returned to Spain. Once home, they implemented further changes, including the reduction of church and military privileges. These were important because New World elites, especially in Mexico and Peru, began to fear Spanish republicans and call for independence, hoping to protect their status. Throughout the empire, royalist forces after 1820 discovered significant fractures in their ranks.

The Riego Revolt also affected U.S. policies. Washington moved forward toward recognition of the Latin American republics. U.S. officials increasingly ignored blatant violations of the neutrality laws. A groundswell of support among the American public and Congress arose for recognition and aid to the rebels. The cry became even stronger when the Mexicans declared independence in September 1821 and established a monarchy under Augustín Iturbide. The Central American nations followed Mexico's example, even joining Iturbide's union for a short period. With the exception of Peru, Cuba, and some possessions in the Caribbean, the Spanish had been ousted from their American colonies.

The Portuguese colony of Brazil followed the Spanish colonists' example. Since the Portuguese Court and royal treasury had fled to Brazil in 1808, King João VI had ruled from his colony. Under pressure from a liberal parliament that had taken power in 1820, the king and 3,000 members of the court returned home in 1821, leaving his twenty-three-year-old son,

Pedro, to run the colony. Soon thereafter, the Lisbon government ordered him to join his father. With the support of the Brazilian elite, Pedro dramatically threw his sword into the ground and shouted: "Independence or death!" With British assistance, his forces easily defeated the royalists. By December 1822, he had become emperor of Brazil. Thus, the largest colony in the New World had thrown off its European chains.

Despite the victories, some prominent Americans argued against formal recognition of the newly independent nations. Men such as John Randolph, congressman from Virginia, contended that those in the United States had little in common with the Latin Americans. He predicted, "the struggle for liberty in South America will turn out in the end something like the French liberty, a detestable despotism." "We have no concern with South America; we have no sympathy, we can have no well founded political sympathy with them," editor Edward Everett wrote in the *North American Review*, "We are sprung from different stocks, we speak different languages, we have been brought up in different social and moral schools, we have been governed by different codes of laws, we profess radically different codes of religion."

Even some Latin American patriots shared American apprehensions. In 1798, Miranda wrote: "As much as I desire the liberty and independence of the New World, I fear the anarchy of a revolutionary system. God forbid that these beautiful countries become . . . a theatre of blood and of crime under the pretext of establishing liberty." Bolívar also expressed his fear of the masses, telling an audience in 1819: "We are not Europeans, we are not Indians. We are but a mixed species of aborigines and Spaniards. . . . We are disputing with the natives for titles of ownership, and at the same time we are struggling to maintain ourselves in the country that gave us birth against the opposition of the invaders." The differences in attitudes and histories appeared to some elites as insurmountable.

Still others expressed different concerns. Adams warned against U.S. involvement, especially direct intervention. On July 4, 1821, he cautioned: "Wherever the standard of freedom and independence has been or shall be unfurled, there will [the United States'] heart, her benedictions, her prayers be. But she goes not abroad in search of monsters to destroy. She is the well-wisher of the freedom and independence of all. She is the champion and vindicator only of her own." He feared that once the United States intervened directly, that "the fundamental maxims of her policy would insensibly change from liberty to force. . . . She might become the dictatress of the world. She would no longer be the ruler of her own spirit."

Despite such misgivings, businessmen and idealists like Henry Clay succeeded in persuading President Monroe to recommend to Congress the recognition of the Latin American republics (La Plata, Chile, Gran Colombia, Mexico) in March 1822. The president predicted that Spain's chances of retaking its former colonies were "most remote" and the United States needed to comply with "an obligation of duty of the highest order." Within two months, Congress easily approved Monroe's request and appropriated $100,000 to establish diplomatic missions in the Latin American republics. While Spain protested vigorously, its statements were ignored.

Strange Bedfellows

Despite the euphoria over recognition, the new relationships created many worries for U.S. policymakers. The most significant was that Spain now might send massive forces against the newly established republics. In Europe, the monarchies in France and Russia united with Spain in the "Holy Alliance." Rumors persisted that the Europeans planned to launch a major offensive against the Latin American republics. The specter of the return of the British also manifested itself. London sought to monopolize Latin American trade, already having strong footholds in Brazil, Chile, and Argentina. Another problem was how to deal with the new governments. In particular, Mexico presented difficulties. Iturbide's government had asked members of the European royalty to take Mexico's throne. Monroe and like-minded persons despised monarchies and condemned Iturbide's efforts. Many Americans now called for concrete actions to protect U.S. interests in Latin America and create order and stability in the region.

While the Monroe administration sought to develop a more coherent strategy for dealing with Latin America, the fear of European intervention heightened after French troops helped Ferdinand VII regain power in 1823. Some Americans worried aloud about Spain and its allies returning to the New World. Other problems arose over Russian efforts to force the United States from the Northwest Territories. U.S. officials found an unlikely ally in the British, who shared their concerns about the "Holy Alliance." In August 1823, U.S. minister to Great Britain, Richard Rush, had an informal conversation with British foreign secretary George Canning. Canning proposed that the United States and Great Britain make a joint proclamation warning the "Holy Alliance" against interfering in the Americas.

The British proposal shocked the Americans. President Monroe immediately opened discussions on how to proceed. He consulted former presidents Jefferson and Madison, who encouraged him to accept Canning's offer, with Madison stating, "with British cooperation we have nothing to fear from the rest of Europe." Cabinet members generally supported the combined statement, with the exception of John Quincy Adams, who fought for a unilateral course. The Anglophobe Adams feared that any joint statement would require the United States to surrender future claims in the West. In a cabinet meeting, he argued: "It would be more candid as well as more dignified, to avow our principles explicitly to Russia and France, than to come in as a cock-boat in the wake of the British man-of-war." When asked about the possibility of direct U.S. intervention to protect Latin America's independence, Adams responded: "I no more believe that the Holy Allies will restore the Spanish domino upon the American continent than that the Chimborazo [Andean mountain exceeding more than 20,000 feet] will sink beneath the ocean."

Going It Alone

After much debate, Monroe sided with Adams. On December 2, 1823, he sent his annual message to Congress, which contained the "Monroe Doctrine."[2] It was a two-part statement. In the first section, Monroe focused on the Russians in the Northwest. "The American continents, by the free and independent condition which they have assumed and maintain," he contended, "are henceforth not to be considered as subjects for colonization by any European powers." Monroe clearly intended the statement to extend to other European powers as well.

The second part of the manifesto related more specifically to the Latin American republics. "The citizens of the United States cherish sentiments the most friendly in favor of the liberty and happiness of their fellow-men on that side of the Atlantic," Monroe wrote, adding, "In the wars of the European powers in matters relating to themselves we have never taken any part, nor does it comport with our policy to do so." He then attacked the authoritarianism of the Holy Alliance and noted that the whole of the

---

2 Only after 1844 did it receive the title, "The Monroe Doctrine."

United States was devoted to "the defense of our own, which has been achieved by the loss of so much blood and treasure, and matured by the wisdom of their most enlightened citizens." Next, he warned that "we should consider any attempt on their part to extend their system to any portion of this hemisphere as dangerous to the peace and safety: With the existing colonies or dependencies of any European power we have not interfered or shall interfere." "It is impossible that the allied powers should extend their political system to any portion of either continent without endangering our peace and happiness; nor can anyone believe that our southern brethren, if [left] to themselves, would it of their own accord," he concluded.

A final, albeit important, part of the Monroe Doctrine was implicit. Earlier in 1823, Adams received reports that the British wanted Cuba. In April he wrote the Spanish: "There are laws of political as well of physical gravitation; and if an apple severed by the tempest from its native tree cannot choose but fall to the ground, Cuba, forcibly disjoined from its own unnatural connection with Spain, and incapable of self-support, can only gravitate towards the North American Union, which by the same law of nature cannot cast her off from its bosom." This concept of "no-transfer" would become integrated into the Monroe Doctrine's non-colonization principle.

The Lukewarm Reception

There were many different responses to Monroe's declaration. Most Americans supported the decree, particularly the blustery warning to the European monarchs. Others delighted at the opportunity to thumb their noses at the British. Still, a small minority expressed some reservations. The *Boston Daily Advertiser* asked: "Is there anything in our Constitution which makes our Government the Guarantors of the Liberties of the World? of the Wahabees? the Peruvians? the Chilese? the Mexicans and the Colombians? . . . Could the black, red, yellow and white populations of the Southern Continent return the favor if we were attacked? Did we mean to make that act [recognition] equivalent to treaties offensive and defensive? I hope not."

The Latin American responses were mixed. According to Whitaker, "some of the Latin Americans eyed [Monroe's pronouncement] with a detachment verging on dislike." These people included Mexican conservative leader Lucas Alamán and Bolívar, who believed friendship with Great

Britain and its protection were more valuable than Monroe's pronouncement. Others expressed more optimistic opinions. Chile and Colombia
immediately sought an alliance with the United States, but Washington
hesitated. In most cases, the Latin Americans showed less interest as the
United States failed to take concrete action in support of Monroe's words.

The Monroe Doctrine remains a hotly debated issue among historians.
Some have argued that it served as a vehicle for later American imperialism.
Others question whether the Latin American exhortations for independence were the basis for the doctrine or whether Monroe merely elucidated
long-held ideas of American diplomacy. Nevertheless, the Monroe Doctrine was the first explicit statement by the United States regarding views
of the Western Hemisphere. Rightly, historians and contemporaries have
underscored the fact that the British navy and Latin Americans themselves
had stopped Spain's return, not U.S. threats. Nevertheless, Monroe's declaration laid the foundation of U.S.-Latin American relations well into the
twentieth century.

Final Victory, First Confrontation

For several years following Monroe's bold statement, the Spanish threat
remained, although the Latin American rebels achieved victory after victory. In late 1824, the forces of Bolívar and rebel leader José de Sucre won
the battle of Ayacucho, which ensured Peru's independence. Soon thereafter, Sucre's forces marched southward and defeated the remaining Spanish,
establishing Bolivia. By 1825, with few exceptions, the Spanish had been
completely expelled from the Americas.

Now Bolívar sought to organize the newly independent nations into a
confederation. In 1825, he called the Congress of Panama. On the issue of
disorder, in 1824 he wrote: "I foresee civil war and disorder breaking out in
all directions and spreading from country to country. I see my native gods
consumed by domestic fire." He wanted a federation of states with strong
executive branches that would become "a temple of sanctuary from criminal
trends" and common defense against Europe. In the labors of the Panama
Conference, Bolívar believed, "will be found the plant of the first alliances
that will have marked the beginning of our relations with the universe."

The U.S. response to the Panama Conference helped establish a trend
in U.S.-Latin American relations. Bolívar initially had opposed inviting
the United States to the conference, fearing its intentions. Several years

later, he stated: "The United States appears to be destined by Providence to plague America with misery in the name of Liberty." After much debate, he relented under pressure from several states that believed the United States could provide a potent ally against European aggression.

The invitation sparked a fierce debate in the United States. The newly elected president, John Quincy Adams, and his new secretary of state, Henry Clay, debated the issue internally. Adams was cautious, while Clay remained consistent in his support of the Latin Americans and encouraged Adams to dispatch U.S. representatives to Panama. After receiving promises that the Latin Americans intended to discuss trade, Adams changed his mind. He recommended that the United States participate and asked Albert Gallatin, the dean of American diplomats, to represent the country. Soon thereafter, the president made a fateful mistake by deciding to ask the Senate for approval of his selection of delegates and the House for appropriations to finance the diplomatic venture.

The efforts to persuade Congress went badly. Adams incorrectly believed that his choice of appointments (Gallatin declined), Richard Anderson and John Sergeant, would receive Senate support without significant opposition. He had underestimated the animosity that the contested presidential election with Jackson in 1824 had created. The Tennessean's supporters saw the nomination as an opportunity to attack Adams on foreign policy. Southern senators also rose to protest the possible presence of the Haitians in Panama. Senator Thomas Hart Benton stated: "I would not go to Panama to 'determine the rights of Hayti and the Africans' in the United States."

For four months, debates raged in Congress. Various senators complained that the Latin Americans would become economic competitors, especially in raw materials, while others denounced the Latin Americans for organizing the Congress in the first place without input from the United States. The partisanship was rife and became personal. John Randolph called the Adams-Clay alliance a "coalition . . . between the Puritan and the blackleg." This led to a duel in which Clay barely missed his mark after Randolph fired in the air. Despite the bitter divisions, the Senate finally approved the delegates, and the House appropriated money in the spring of 1826.

Circumstances doomed the mission. Before the delegates left, Clay provided a sixty-four-page list of instructions that pushed for liberalized trade, an agreement on no colonization, and an end to the "exclusive" right of the Catholic Church. Clay's instructions prohibited Anderson and Sergeant from going outside of the guidelines, especially regarding the defensive alliance. It was all for naught. The American delegates never participated in the Panama Congress. Anderson died on the way to it, and Sergeant arrived after the meeting had adjourned.

As historian Walter LaFeber notes, the U.S. response to the Panama Conference "revealed not only the deep divisions between North and South America, but also within U.S. politics." The conference itself produced no substantial gains, as only Mexico, Central America, Colombia, and Peru participated. Bolívar's allies pushed through a strongly worded defensive alliance that only three other delegates supported; only Colombia approved. Participants called for future meetings, but none materialized for six decades. Despite the failures, one historian stresses that "while it is true that the immediate achievements of the Congress [Panama Conference] were nil, the moral effect of merely having made the effort was great."

On a hemispheric level, the Panama Conference had both short- and long-term effects. First, the British representatives in Panama noted the U.S. absence and general lack of interest in the meeting. The British also highlighted that Washington wanted new territories and that Latin Americans should fear an expansionist-minded United States. Since the United States had no representative present, it could not formally challenge the British claims. The vacant seat also demonstrated to many Latin Americans that despite the promises of solidarity, the United States would pursue an independent course that protected its own needs first.

In the long run, however, the Panama Conference was important. Bolívar's dream of a united hemisphere to challenge foreign interests and his hopes for regional solidarity on issues of trade and law never died. (Bolívar himself would die soon thereafter, of tuberculosis, in 1830.) While the concept of unification took many years to accomplish, U.S. and Latin American policymakers would make progress toward it by the end of the nineteenth century. The United States would eventually support hemispheric solidarity, although many problems would plague the effort to achieve it, including American and Latin American nationalism. As historian Thomas Bailey notes regarding the Panama Conference: "The roots of the Pan American ideal, which was later to assume major significance, were definitely planted."

Continuities

While significant cultural differences, shaped by the different colonial experiences, existed, numerous similarities created interdependence between
the United States and Latin America. As early as the late eighteenth century, the economies of the region became more intertwined, as the Spanish
opened their colonies to foreign trade. Wheat, corn, and other goods flowed
southward in exchange for rum and sugar, as American and Latin American merchants increasingly became trading partners. While the Europeans,
principally the British, remained the strongest powers, groundwork had
been laid for more commerce in the post-revolution era.

With trade came cultural exchanges, including the ideas of republicanism and independence. While negative stereotypes existed, the leaders
of the independence movements shared many ideas and tried to support
each other. Washington's desire for land and geopolitical realities regarding
Europe often produced only lukewarm efforts on the part of U.S. officials
to aid Latin American independence movements. But individual Americans like Henry Clay helped the revolutionaries with arms and loans and
often provided moral support. They shared a spirit of independence and
republicanism and had a desire for economic growth, momentarily setting
aside prejudices to work together.

The U.S. drive for hegemony began in this period, although at the
time, many of the future Latin American republics compared favorably in
economic and military potential. Still, U.S. growth and expansion—and
power—increased significantly in the period. While far from being able to
enforce its edict, the release of the Monroe Doctrine in 1823 definitely signified to the Latin Americans and Europeans the intentions of Washington.
Bolívar and others identified the threat from the northern Anglo-Saxon
nation and tried to unify the Latin Americans to limit U.S. influence, with
varying degrees of success. The competition was far from over.

SUGGESTIONS FOR ADDITIONAL READING

For more on the Spanish colonial development, reference Mark A. Burkholder and
Lyman L. Johnson, *Colonial Latin America,* 3rd ed. (1998), and Leslie Bethell, ed.,
Colonial Latin America (1984).

For the move toward revolution among the Spanish colonies, see Richard Graham,
Independence in Latin America, 2nd ed. (1994); John Lynch, *The Spanish-American*

Revolutions, 1808–1826, 2nd ed. (1986); and Jorge I. Domínguez, *Insurrection or Loyalty: The Breakdown of the Spanish American Empire* (1980).

There is not a significant body of work on the early relationship between the United States and the Latin American nations. However, there are some very good works, including Lester Langley, *The Americas in the Age of Revolution, 1750–1850 (1996);* Arthur P. Whitaker, *The United States and the Independence of Latin America, 1800–1830* (1941); James E. Lewis, Jr., *The American Union and the Problem of Neighborhood: The United States and the Collapse of the Spanish Empire, 1783–1829* (1998); John Johnson, *A Hemisphere Apart: The Foundations of United States Policy toward Latin America* (1990); Harry Bernstein, *Origins of Inter-American Interest, 1700–1812* (1956); Peggy Liss, *Atlantic Empires: The Network of Trade and Revolution, 1713–1826* (1983); C. C. Griffin, *The United States and the Disruption of the Spanish Empire, 1810–1822* (1937); and Frank L. Owsley, Jr. and Gene A. Smith, *Filibusters and Expansionists: Jeffersonian Manifest Destiny, 1800-1821* (1997).

For more information on the United States and its relationship with Spain through the wars of independence, reference Samuel F. Bemis, *Pinckney's Treaty: A Study of America's Advantages from Europe's Distress, 1783–1800* (1926); Philip C. Brooks, *Diplomacy and the Borderlands: The Adams-Onís Treaty of 1819* (1939); and Reginald Horsman, *The Diplomacy of the New Republic, 1776–1815* (1985).

Some of the best monographs on the Monroe Doctrine and European and Latin American responses include Dexter Perkins, *The Monroe Doctrine* (1927); Albert Bushnell Hart, *The Monroe Doctrine: An Interpretation* (1916); and Ernest R. May, *The Making of the Monroe Doctrine* (1975).

CHAPTER TWO

The Turbulent Era

IRONICALLY, THE DEMOCRACY THAT FLOURISHED in the United States in the early nineteenth century, historian Lester Langley observes, "though characterized by a disorderliness that often disgusted European visitors, was for a generation of Latin American intellectuals a model to be emulated." He also notes, "Latin Americans may have expressed admiration for the model republic and its Constitution, but in their governance they chose to preserve social order rather than fashion citizen republics."

Langley correctly observes that the Latin American political pattern after 1825 affected U.S.-Latin American relations. After the U.S. failure to attend the Panama Conference, the Adams administration tried to adjust to the rapidly changing structure in the newly independent nations. In most cases, disorder characterized the Latin American republics, and Washington found itself ill equipped to deal with the internal crises. The following period proved to be a challenging one for everyone.

Chasing John Bull in the Marketplace

After Latin American independence, U.S. policymakers primarily focused on economic issues. Washington dispatched agents to Latin American to negotiate bilateral treaties protecting American business interests from discriminatory duties and guaranteeing them access to Latin American markets. These efforts met with only limited success, as the British proved a formidable obstacle. London's historic relationship with many leaders of the region assured British nationals special privileges. In some places, the British concerns dumped their goods at low prices to squeeze out the competition. By the end of John Quincy Adams's term, the United States had no commercial treaties with the richest and most prosperous Latin American states.

The actions of U.S. diplomats often inadvertently aided British efforts. In this early period, one historian comments that "there was a stylistic distinction between the British and Americans that persisted into the twentieth century. Republican Americans professed to treat Latin American republicans as equals but regarded them as inferiors; the British generally regarded them as dogs but treated them with a modicum of respect."

A prime example of the stereotypical "ugly American" of the nineteenth century was Joel Poinsett. In the late 1820s, Adams sent him to Mexico as minister. Condescending, arrogant, and racist, the South Carolinian offended the Mexicans in many ways. Following Adams's instructions, he offered to buy Texas and part of California. His heavy-handed approach heightened Mexican fears of Yankee aggression. At the same time, he actively interfered in Mexico's domestic politics by helping establish a York rite Masons organization to offset a British dominated Scottish rite group. Both groups agitated against the Mexican government, angering its officials. Poinsett later claimed that his group had undermined the "machinations of the monarchical party. . . . Most unquestionably had it not been for my foresight and conduct, this gov[ernmen]t would have been overthrown and this country deluged in blood."

Poinsett's actions ensured failure. Despite his negotiation of two commercial treaties, neither the Mexican nor the U.S. government signed them. All of his intrigue and indiscretions ultimately led the Mexican government to ask for his recall. Unfortunately, Poinsett became to many Mexicans the prototype of the interventionist, condescending Yankee, a view many of his successors merely reinforced.

Despite the failure of Poinsett and others, there were a few diplomatic successes. In 1825, the United States signed an important treaty with the Central American Union. It contained the first complete reciprocity rule on trade and guaranteed rights of navigation and opening of ports. Clay called it "the most perfect freedom of navigation. . . . All the shackles which the selfishness or contracted policy of nations had contrived are broken and destroyed by this broad principle of universal liberality."

U.S. diplomats also achieved some successes with Brazil. In this case, the United States benefited from the ongoing war between Brazil and Buenos Aires over Uruguay. Rio and Washington signed a treaty similar to the Central American one, making trade with Brazil possible. The United States exported wheat and flour to Brazil, often exchanging those commodities for coffee, which replaced tea as the preferred American beverage.

Interests such as the House of Maxwell, Wright and Company (later Maxwell House), developed a prosperous coffee business, ensuring for much of the nineteenth century that Brazil remained an important U.S. trading partner.

Despite the inroads in Central America and Brazil, the Union Jack reigned supreme in most Latin American nations. By 1830, British investments in the region had grown to more than £40 million and loans exceeded $110 million. That year, Britain's annual trade topped $32 million. While a lucrative relationship continued, the overall U.S. trade with Latin America was $10 million in 1830, one-third of that with the British. Throughout the nineteenth century, this competition with the British continued as the United States sought to gain economic hegemony in the region.

Men on Horseback

While many factors explained the U.S. inability to compete economically with the British, the biggest difficulty in securing treaties revolved around the turmoil that engulfed Latin America after independence. Criollo elites controlled the new governments, but they divided over the best way to rule. On one side were the Liberals, people shaped by Enlightenment ideas of free trade, reduced privileges for the Catholic Church and the military, and limited democracy. Most supported decentralized federal systems to prevent tyrannical rule. On the other side, Conservatives wanted a strong Catholic Church and the military to maintain order and stability. Often members of the old economic elite, the Conservatives supported an insular economy reliant on native laborers. Finally, they believed in centralized, autocratic governments.

While divided on many issues, Liberals and the Conservatives shared a common fear of the lower classes. "The Creole liberators who guided their peoples to independence became, in triumph, leaders who turned inward to consolidate their power in societies where republican government took form but could not flourish," one historian observes. He adds: "Some . . . became dictators who despaired of the continent's future. Others fell before a rising generation of men on horseback who had little concern for hemispheric solidarity or representative government." The latter included José Antonio Páez in Venezuela, Juan Manuel de Rosas in Argentina, and Antonio López de Santa Anna in Mexico, all playing Conservatives and

Liberals off each other to gain power. These men instituted dictatorships that plagued Latin America for many years.

The failure of the republican experiments caused widespread disenchantment. Even Bolívar now despaired, writing a friend in 1829: "I am less inclined toward the federal form of government. Such a system is no more than organized anarchy, or, at best, a law that implicitly prescribes the obligation of dissolution and the eventual ruin of the state with all its members. I think it would be better for South America to adopt the Koran rather than the United States' form of government, although the latter is the best on earth." "Nothing more can be added; simply witness the unhappy countries of Buenos Aires, Chile, Mexico, and Guatemala. We, too, may recall our own earliest years. These examples alone tell us more than entire libraries," he lamented.

Meanwhile, people in the United States also had become disenchanted, apparently confirming the predictions of John Randolph and others that democracy could not flourish in Spanish lands. Most reports from private citizens and diplomats were negative. An American official in Bogotá, Colombia, in 1829 wrote: "No roads are repaired or made, no bridges built—no schools established—no vice discouraged—nor is there an improved administration of justice. The Treasury is empty, and no encouragement is extended to internal or external trade." Another American in Colombia wrote Vice President Martin Van Buren in 1830: "I have no confidence in the intellectual fitness of this people for free institutions, and still less in the private and public virtue of the majority of public men."

Other Americans noted similar conditions in the region. A person recently returned from Mexico and Colombia emphasized that the "same degree of ignorance, and an equal share of vanity prevail in both countries, but fanaticism deeper rooted in this [country], and republican liberty is trodden down by the expansive weight of military despotism." In 1832, an American diplomat in Buenos Aires reported: "the revolutions of these people are seditious—their knowledge chicanery and trick—their patriotism bluster, their liberty a farce—a well regulated tribe of Indians have better notions of national law, popular rights and domestic policy; . . . None of the South American governments have any idea of justice, but they may have some of national force when they see it."

Within a decade after independence, most Americans and many Latin American elites had become disenchanted with imposing democratic institutions in the region, although some hope existed. The failures created many problems in trade and diplomacy. For many years, the United States would try to find a way to expand economic opportunities (as well as territory) while dealing with dictatorships and monarchies. How to handle disorder, despotism, and other challenges perplexed U.S. diplomats.

The Age of Jackson

The turmoil in Latin America corresponded with the rise to power in the United States of Andrew Jackson in 1829. According to historian John Belohavek, "The Tennessean eagerly pursued a policy of promoting commercial expansion, demanding worldwide respect for the American flag, restoring American prestige and national honor, and fostering territorial growth." Jackson would tell Congress that his foreign policy "is daily producing its beneficial effect in the respect shown to our flag, the protection of our citizens and their property abroad, and in the increase of our navigation and the extension of our mercantile operations."

In regard to Latin America, Jackson wanted active relations. "But although drawn by the siren song of commerce, the President was repulsed by the constant political turmoil in Latin America that disrupted both trade and diplomatic ties, and his accompanying view of the Latin character bordered on disdain," Belohavek observes. Therefore, his administration devoted more time and energy to domestic affairs and other regions. This did not mean that he ignored Latin America. Jackson sent diplomats to negotiate commercial treaties and settle American claims for losses incurred during the wars of independence. There were, however, few successes, and relations with the Latin American republics grew tempestuous during Jackson's administration.

The First Malvinas Crisis

A representative example of U.S.-Latin American relations during Jackson's presidency occurred with Argentina. "Jacksonian diplomacy with Argentina was a tale of inept representatives, differing priorities, and lost opportunities," Belohavek comments. The stage was set for conflict in 1829, as Jackson took office. At the same time, the ruthless and dashing Juan Rosas unified the country under his control. Ruling with an iron fist, Rosas created alliances with the military and Catholic Church to validate his government, which lasted more than three decades.

A crisis developed in 1831, when the Rosas government gave control of the disputed Malvinas Islands to a Frenchman, Louis Vernet, who promised to make the deserted Atlantic islands productive. Disputes arose when Vernet banned American whalers and sealing ships from replenishing their supplies on the Malvinas. In the summer of 1831, Vernet seized an American schooner, the *Harriet,* for violating the edict and sent its crew to Buenos Aires to stand trial.

The incident ignited a firestorm. The Argentines, already angry over a perceived pro-Brazil bias among Americans, refused to release the ship and its crew. American Consul George Slacum inflamed passions. One scholar notes that Slacum "believed that the essential element in diplomacy was to assert, in the most intemperate language of his command, the self-evident and natural rights of the people of the United States to shoot and fish where they pleased."

The Argentine officials moved slowly in the courts to settle the issue, further infuriating Slacum. In short order, an eighteen-gun sloop, the *Lexington,* arrived in Buenos Aires. One contemporary described its commander, Silas Duncan, as "aggressive, fiery, and highspirited." Without official orders, Slacum and Duncan plotted to free the prisoners and punish Vernet. In late December, the *Lexington* sailed to the Malvinas, landed U.S. marines, and arrested several leaders of the colony as "pirates." They then helped the captain of the *Harriet* reclaim his possessions, and both ships returned to port in Uruguay a few weeks later.

The Argentines bitterly denounced the invasion and demanded reparations, as well as punishment of the perpetrators. The Jackson administration defended the action, claiming Americans had the right to fish off the Malvinas, to which the Argentines had only a dubious claim. Jackson now asked Congress for the right "to clothe the executive with such authority and means as they may deem necessary for providing a force adequate to the complete protection of American fishing and trading in the seas."

Despite the bellicose rhetoric, diplomacy prevailed. Jackson dispatched a political ally, Francis Baylies, to Buenos Aires. Once described by John Quincy Adams as "one of the most talented and worthless men in New England," Baylies was to ask Rosas to condemn Vernet's actions and recognize U.S. fishing rights. Upon arriving in Buenos Aires, Baylies stumbled when he insisted on an indemnity for Vernet's actions. The Argentines fired back, demanding reparations for the *Lexington's* actions and, again, that Slacum and Duncan be punished.

Neither side budged, and negotiations broke down. As Baylies prepared to return home, he wrote: "We have attempted to soothe, and conciliate and coax these wayward and petulant fools long enough. They must be taught a lesson, or the United States will be viewed with contempt throughout Latin America." Soon Baylies and Slacum departed, leaving no U.S. diplomat in Argentina. Talk of war echoed in the U.S. House of Representatives, although Jackson moved cautiously and stressed that Washington had suspended, not broken, diplomatic relations with Rosas. In addition, U.S. diplomats in Uruguay released the Malvinas prisoners. Yet, tensions remained high, as the Rosas government rebuilt fortifications and prepared for the defense of the islands.

The Monroe Doctrine on Trial

The Jackson administration never solved the problem on its own. The Argentines encountered difficulties reestablishing control over the islands when the British stepped in and solved the problem in their own way. In January 1833, the captain of the H.M.S. *Clio* landed troops. Basing the action on a claim dating to the eighteenth century, the British lowered the Argentine flag, replaced it with the Union Jack, and forced the Argentines to abandon the Malvinas. Soon thereafter, the British established a permanent military base.

The Argentines immediately protested. Buenos Aires asked Jackson to invoke the Monroe Doctrine. Already tired of the conflict over the islands, he refused. He did so for many reasons. Jackson would not endanger lucrative U.S. commercial relations with Britain over what he considered a minor issue. Furthermore, he recognized that he lacked the military resources as well as public support for any such action. Thus, Jackson informed the Argentines that the British claim predated Monroe's declaration, making it inapplicable. The Argentine claims against Great Britain over the Malvinas would remain unresolved for many years.

The possible implementation of the Monroe Doctrine also arose with the Brazilians around the same time. In 1826, King John VI of Portugal died. John's legitimate heir to the Crown of Portugal was King Dom Pedro of Brazil, who had ruled Brazil since 1822. Back in Portugal, Pedro's brother, Dom Miguel, claimed that Pedro's declaration of Brazilian independence prevented him from claiming Portugal's Crown. While Pedro chose to remain in Brazil and abdicated the Portuguese throne, he would not have

Miguel become king, naming him regent, instead. The arrangement disintegrated, however, when Miguel disavowed his brother's wishes and formally seized the Crown of Portugal, forming a rift between Brazil and its former mother country.

While the issue of whether the United States should recognize the new government of Dom Miguel—against the wishes of Pedro and the Brazilians—arose during the Adams administration, the retiring president gladly left the thorny problem to Jackson. After much debate, Jackson recognized Miguel's government, despite knowing doing so would anger Brazil. Fortunately, Jackson dispatched some good representatives to assuage momentarily the Brazilians' anger. Still, the problem festered. In 1831, Pedro again abdicated the throne in Brazil and traveled to Europe to take the Portuguese crown. Many people feared his action would provoke a Portuguese reprisal against Brazil. Concerned, the Brazilian officials asked for clarification about invoking the Monroe Doctrine. Much to their dismay, Washington responded that no operational feature existed and it would not interfere in the conflict between a mother country and its former colony. While the invasion never materialized, the Brazilians, like the Argentines and others, realized that despite having issued the Monroe Doctrine, the United States lacked any real power or interest to confront the European nations directly.

The Eternal Search for a Shortcut

One of the most important issues of Jackson's presidency was a Central American canal. Since the sixteenth century, people had dreamed of building a route across the isthmus to connect the Atlantic and Pacific Oceans and greatly facilitate trade and travel in the Pacific Basin. After the region achieved independence, the project received serious consideration. In 1829, Bolívar commissioned a study by a British engineer, John Lloyd, about building a canal across the Colombian province of Panama. With a positive report, the Colombians threw open bidding in 1834 to international construction companies, promising the winning bidder 100,000 acres of land and canal revenues for fifty years.

Three years earlier, in 1831, the competition had heated up to build a canal through Nicaragua. The Dutch won a contract to build a Nicaraguan canal, the route favored by most engineers. The Dutch company agreed to construct the canal and maintain and regulate it. In return, the Central

American republic would retain sovereignty over the canal and revenues once the Dutch company had recovered its investment.

Such actions sparked a flurry of activities in Washington. The United States feared the Dutch and British, who claimed British Honduras (modern-day Belize) were gaining influence on Nicaragua's Mosquito Coast. Washington responded by demanding equal treatment of Americans hoping to use any Dutch canal. It also instructed its agents to negotiate advantages for Americans, including buying stock in any foreign company building the canal.

Most American efforts failed miserably. Jackson sent to Nicaragua Charles Biddle, who instead traveled to Panama. There, some Panamanians convinced Biddle that "the opening of a canal for vessels of heavy tonnage is a chimera and that a canal for vessels of lighter draught [sic] cannot be accomplished north of Panama." Thus, Biddle negotiated with officials in Bogotá to build a road to the navigable Charges River and import two steamships to conduct trade across the isthmus. For Biddle's work, Bogotá promised a potential American canal-building company 140,000 acres, an additional 750,000 acres at fifty cents each, and a fifty-year lease. But Biddle's efforts were for naught, as Jackson lost interest when the Dutch plan failed. Biddle died soon afterward and an economic panic in 1837 cut off potential funding for the project. For the moment, the issue lay dormant.

Which Eagle over Texas?

The most contentious and complex foreign policy issue of Jackson's presidency concerned Texas. The Mexican government, called the "sick man of North America" by historian David Pletcher, inherited Spain's policy of encouraging foreign settlers to immigrate to Texas in order to create a buffer against more aggressive Americans by assimilating the new Mexican citizens into Catholicism and antislavery positions. Tens of thousands of Americans flooded into the eastern sections of the territory between San Antonio and the Sabine River. Led by agents such as Stephen F. Austin, who had contracted with the Mexican government to lead U.S. immigrants into Texas in exchange for large tracts of land, the new colonies thrived. But while most of the new colonists from the United States professed an allegiance to the Mexican government, the majority of them rejected any real assimilation.

Many of the Anglo settlers avoided politics, but by the early 1830s, a small and vocal group of agitators among them became active. One historian has characterized this group as filled "with schemes in their heads and guns in their hands—fleeing justice, fleecing Indians, gambling with lands and promoting shooting scrapes called revolutions." It included the slave smuggler William Travis and Sam Houston, a former Tennessee congressman and a close friend of Andrew Jackson. Calling for Texas's independence and its eventual annexation by the United States, this group helped set the stage for a serious conflict between Washington and Mexico City.

Even as tensions heightened in its northern province of Texas, the Mexican government faced many other problems. Constant struggles between Conservatives and Liberals, exacerbated by opportunistic individuals such as Antonio López de Santa Anna, plagued the country. Complicating things was Mexico's population, which comprised many different ethnic groups. In addition, foreign threats to the national sovereignty remained. In 1830, 3,000 Spanish troops temporarily occupied Tampico, and they threatened further operations. These conditions created instability. In the period 1829–44, Mexico saw fourteen presidents and twenty different governments.

Old Hickory and Texas

The Jackson administration sought to diffuse the problem by purchasing Texas. In 1829, the president dispatched Colonel Anthony Butler to Mexico City to offer the Mexicans $5 million for Texas. Jackson instructed Butler to emphasize that the United States needed an area to settle "free people of color," while the Mexicans would rid themselves of the troublesome Anglo immigrants as well as the fierce American Indian tribes that lorded over the Texas plains. But the Mexicans refused, so Butler concentrated on signing a trade agreement that granted the United States most-favored-nation status and no discriminatory duties.

As was Jackson's style, he persisted. He pressured Butler to renew talks with Lucas Alamán, chief of the Mexican foreign ministry, as well as with President Santa Anna, whom Butler called "a vile hypocrite and most unprincipled man." Butler informed Jackson he needed to use some of the $5 million to "facilitate negotiations." Jackson consented, arguing: "I scarcely ever knew a Spaniard who was not the slave of avarice, and it is not improbable that this weakness may be worth a great aid to us in this case."

The Butler mission ended abruptly in 1834. The general asked for several hundred thousand dollars with which to bribe Mexican officials. "Jackson drew a pragmatic line between knowing what certain governmental officials might do with the $5 million after it was delivered, and the prior act of paying bribes to Mexican officials to persuade them to cede the territory," one historian observes. Butler then urged Jackson to invade Texas and name him as governor. Furious, Jackson penned a letter to Butler in which he wrote: "A. Butler: What a scamp." After much debate, Butler departed Mexico, leaving historians to use terms such as "insolent, scurrilous, vain, ignorant, ill-tempered and corrupt" to describe him.

Creating the Lone Star Republic

All the diplomacy proved useless as internal events in Mexico facilitated conflict in Texas. In 1834, Santa Anna seized control in Mexico City and overturned the Constitution of 1824. Immediately, several Mexican states revolted, including Texas, the makeshift forces of which soon chased a Mexican army south. Santa Anna responded quickly, aiming to make an example out of the rebellious Texans. At the head of a superior force, Santa Anna advanced northward and surrounded the Alamo in San Antonio. Inside the mission compound, two hundred defenders, including James Bowie, former Tennessee congressman and American legend Davy Crockett, and a number of Tejanos, held out for nearly three weeks, fighting under the Mexican flag of the Constitution of 1824. In the end, Santa Anna's army slaughtered every one of the Alamo's defenders sparing only the lives of Susannah Dickinson, her small child, a black slave, and relatives of the nine Tejanos who had chosen to fight with the Texans. After his victory in San Antonio, Santa Anna moved his force north and east. Meanwhile, another Mexican column, this one under the command of General José Urrea, captured some 400 Texas defenders under the command of James Fannin near Goliad. Although Urrea made a plea for clemency, under direct orders from Santa Anna to do so, he treated the Texan force as traitors and executed more than 300 of them.

From the beginning of the rebellion, most Americans sympathized with the Anglo settlers. Texan agents scattered throughout the South and the Ohio River valley, collecting monies, arms, and munitions. Promising lands for service, many volunteers marched toward Texas. Mexican officials bitterly complained about the failure to stop recruiting efforts. In response, Washington announced its neutrality but turned a blind eye to those aiding General Sam Houston's ragged, fleeing army.

In the United States, headlines heralded news of the massacres at the Alamo and Goliad, fueling the flames in support of the rebels. One congressman emphasized that the Texans were "bone of our bone, and flesh of our flesh." The Chief Justice of the Supreme Court of Tennessee roared: "the savage barbarities of murdering Fanning [sic] and his core [at Goliad] after a Capitulation, has so enraged the people of this Country, that they were raising men to openly to fight St. Anna. . . . The men under 35, and all the women, are for having St. Anna shot, and the Texas Eagle planted on his capitol."

Fortunes changed for the Texans in April 1836. Supplied with arms, munitions, and new recruits from the United States, Houston caught unsuspecting advance columns of the Mexican army at the San Jacinto River. With the help of two cannons provided by the citizens of Cincinnati, Houston surprised Santa Anna's encampment and routed it. The Texans captured Santa Anna, who had tried to escape recognition by disguising himself as a private. They forced him to sign a treaty recognizing Texas independence and the southern border of the new republic at the Rio Grande and soon put him on a ship for Mexico, where he promised to enforce his mandate.

Caught between a Rock and Hard Place

In the United States, the Texans' victory created quite a stir. The normally decisive Jackson hesitated to recognize the new Republic of Texas. While privately delighted, he feared that recognizing a slave-holding territory so close to a presidential election might hurt the presidential aspirations of his vice president, Martin Van Buren. Divisions over recognizing Texas as a sovereign nation also existed in the House of Representatives, where abolitionist congressman now accused Jackson of conspiring to expand slavery. Furthermore, Mexico City repudiated Santa Anna's treaty and warned that Texas was still very much part of Mexico. Throughout the summer, Jackson and Congress vacillated on the recognition issue.

Jackson moved slowly. In the fall of 1836, he dispatched a special agent, Henry Morfit, to appraise the situation in Texas. After six weeks, Morfit reported that Texas could maintain its independence. It had a sufficient

army and a small navy for protection, and Mexico's internal divisions limited reprisals. The Texas government was well organized and had potential
financial security from lucrative land sales. By October, the first permanent
government of the Republic of Texas under President Sam Houston took
power.

Despite Morfit's report, Jackson waited. When the newly appointed
Texas minister to the United States met Jackson in December, he found
the president noncommittal. A Texan plebiscite in September overwhelmingly declared support for the republic's annexation by the United States,
embarrassing the president and further strengthening charges of conspiracy.
Jackson continued to fear inciting a confrontation with Mexico. When the
president gave his annual message to Congress soon thereafter, he threw
the decision to the legislative body.

The attitudes in Washington changed in early 1837, as the Texans made
overtures to the British, promising them exclusive commercial rights in the
republic in return for formal recognition. In early March, Congress passed
a measure giving Jackson the right to grant recognition and exchange representatives after he believed Texas had become "an independent power." On
March 3, a week before leaving office, Jackson appointed Alcee LaBranche
of Louisiana as American Chargé to Texas, and formal diplomatic relations
between the two nations began.

The affair in Texas significantly affected U.S.-Mexican relations. Obviously, it set the stage for future disputes with Mexico over westward
expansion, for Mexico never forgave the United States for wresting away
what it considered as part of it sovereign territory.

Furthermore, it fueled a long-standing arrogance in the United States,
validating a perceived superiority of the Anglo-Saxon culture. The ability
of a handful of determined whites to defeat the Mexican army strengthened this view. Other Mexican actions at Goliad and the Alamo enhanced
stereotypes of Mexican barbarism and decadence. The volatility of the matter was apparent.

Manifest Destiny or Manifest Design?

The westward expansion of the United States had been a constant feature
of American history. After the Louisiana Purchase, the impulse intensified.
In 1819, John Quincy Adams echoed a belief held by many when he argued
that "the United States and North America are identical." In the late 1830s,

the calls for expansion increased. The exploration of the Far West by John Fremont, and commercial expansion in the American Northwest led by John Jacob Astor fueled the fire. "In some ways American expansion was a natural, almost organic process. Americans always sought greater productivity through the cultivation of new lands. Problems generating from increased population, inadequate transportation, depressed agricultural prices, and general hard times also caused periodic migrations into new areas," observers note.

The institutionalization of the concepts in Adams's statement became known as "manifest destiny." One of its most famous promoters was newspaper editor and writer John L. O'Sullivan. In 1839, he wrote: "we may confidently assume that our country is destined to be the great nation of futurity." "We are the nation of human progress, and who will, what can, set limits to our onward march? Providence is with us," he argued. "In its magnificent domain of space and time, the nation of many nations is destined to manifest to mankind the excellence of divine principles; to establish on earth the noblest temple ever dedicated to the worship of the Most High—the Sacred and the True." Describing the ideal future world, O'Sullivan added: "Its floor shall be a hemispherepits roof the firmament of the star-studded heavens, and its congregation a Union of many Republics, comprising hundreds of happy millions, calling, owning no man master, but governed by God's natural and moral law of equality."

Six years later, O'Sullivan issued his most famous plea in the *Democratic Review*, which implanted manifest destiny into the American consciousness. For him, technology made the dream more realistic. Steamships and railroads enhanced the possibility of a nation extending sea to sea. O'Sullivan told his readers that the telegraph allowed "the editors of the 'San Francisco Union,' the 'Astoria Evening Post,' or the 'Nootka Morning News,' to set up in type the first half of the President's Inaugural before the echoes of the latter half shall have died away beneath the lofty porch of the Capitol, as spoken from his lips." To O'Sullivan, the United States had the "manifest destiny to overspread the continent allotted by Providence to the free development of our yearly multiplying millions." Manifest destiny meant "republicanism, religious freedom, states' rights, free trade, cheap land." A year later, an Indiana congressman told people "Go to the West" and predicted a United States occupying lands "from the Isthmus of Darien to Behring's straits."

A Stumbling Block

Despite the continued calls for new lands, the administrations of Martin Van Buren (1839–43), William Henry Harrison (1843), and John Tyler (1843–47) initially focused on domestic problems more than expansion. Antislavery forces played a significant role in curtailing the aspirations of land-hungry Americans. Their leaders characterized plans to assimilate Texas and beyond as a slave conspiracy. "Texas is the rendezvous of absconding villainy, desperate adventure, and lawless ruffianism—the ark of safety to swindlers, gamblers, robbers, and rogues of every size and degree," William Lloyd Garrison wrote in 1842 in his abolitionist vehicle *The Liberator*. He added: "Nothing homogenous is found among its population, except a disposition to extend and perpetuate the most frightful form of servitude the world has ever known."

Other opponents of slavery arose, creating international dynamics in the slave debate and affecting U.S.-Latin American relations. Again, the British played a significant part. Having abolished the slave trade in 1807 and freed all slaves in 1833, London wanted to destroy the institution. Soon thereafter, the British navy began stopping all ships suspected of carrying slaves, an action Washington condemned.

Problems intensified in 1841, when slaves seized an American ship, the *Creole,* while en route from Virginia to New Orleans. The rebels killed one sailor in the mutiny, and forced the captain to take its cargo of 135 slaves to Nassau in the British Bahamas. The British imprisoned the perpetrators of the crime, but immediately freed its human cargo. Washington protested this action, but, much to its consternation, London backed it. While London ultimately promised to discourage similar actions in the future, the freed slaves of the *Creole* never returned to the United States.

The British crusade against slavery was important in U.S.-Latin American relations for several reasons. First, it heightened tensions between the United States and Great Britain. Since many Latin American governments depended on the British for finance, investment, and economic concerns, the conflict further distanced some Latin Americans from the United States. Furthermore, most Latin American nations had abolished slavery and viewed the institution as an abomination. Nevertheless, the slavery issue did not alienate all Latin Americans, in particular the Brazilians and Cubans. Their nations remained the largest in the region to uphold slavery. The issue would remain divisive until the 1880s, when

Cuba and Brazil followed the lead of the United States (1865) and abolished slavery.

On another level, the British attacks on slavery reinforced the determination of southerners to expand slavery into the Southwest as the issue of Texas reemerged. While Washington moved cautiously toward annexation, the Texans asked Europe for financial and military support. The French attempted to secure lands with promises of military aid and recognition. London also reached out to the republic, recognizing it and establishing a legation in Austin. Some loans and economic pacts followed and the British tried to persuade the Mexican government to surrender its claims to its wayward province.

British actions in Texas heightened southern fears of a conspiracy by London to attack slavery. Many believed it would persuade the Texans to abolish the institution in return for support. American diplomats reported that a high British official had written: "by effecting the final abolition of Slavery in Texas, we at once extinguish that horrid traffic in a Country which, without our interference, might become one of the most extensive Slave Markets in America." Diplomatic intrigues followed, including the promise of Foreign Minister Lord Aberdeen to provide an Anglo-French guarantee of Texas's independence and pressure on the Mexicans to recognize it. In return, Aberdeen asked the Texans to promise not to join the United States. Word of this proposal set off a diplomatic firestorm in Washington, where Americans looked with renewed interest on Texas statehood. At the same time, Mexicans vacillated between plans to reconquer the territory and working with the British to stave off U.S. annexation.

The Last Acts of a Desperate Man

In the summer of 1844, the Tyler administration focused on Texas. Desperate for a political issue to promote his renomination, Tyler believed Texas's annexation would help. In April, he signed an annexation treaty and sought Senate ratification. Secretary of State John Calhoun argued that taking Texas would prevent the abolition of slavery, an institution "essential to the peace, safety, and prosperity" of the South. Abolitionists and "free soilers" countered that Tyler had no constitutional basis for the action. In addition, they warned of a bloody war with Mexico that would most certainly follow. The latter emerged victorious in June 1844, when the Senate voted 35–16 against the annexation treaty.

Despite the resounding defeat, the issue of Texas resurfaced in the presidential election of 1844. James Polk, Tennessee protege of Andrew Jackson, ran on a platform of "reoccupation of Oregon and re-annexation of Texas." Throughout the campaign, Democrats reminded voters that Whig candidate Henry Clay had helped negotiate Texas out of the 1819 Transcontinental Treaty, thus creating the problem. Clay responded that the United States should not take Texas if it meant war. Polk narrowly won the presidency, with some proponents of Texas's annexation heralding his victory as a mandate from the people.

Even before Polk took office, the issue came to a head. As one of his last acts in office, in January 1845 President Tyler proposed the passage of a congressional resolution that allowed the annexation of Texas: it passed the House by a vote of 120 to 98 and the Senate by 27 to 25. On March 1, three days before leaving the presidency, Tyler signed the bill and forwarded the invitation for statehood to Texas.

Mexico immediately denounced the action, its minister in Washington calling the resolution a direct usurpation of Mexican sovereignty. Soon thereafter he vacated the capital, effectively severing diplomatic relations. Two months later, London persuaded the Mexicans to try a different tactic. Mexico would recognize Texas in return for Texas rejecting annexation to the United States. This plan failed when a Texas convention voted unanimously to accept the U.S. offer, and Texas formally entered the Union on December 29, 1845.

Mr. Polk Marches to War

As several observers note, "Polk did not inherit an inevitable conflict with Mexico. Rather, the president made decisions and carried them out in ways that exacerbated already existing tensions and made war difficult to avoid." He recognized the potential for war with Mexico. Yet, he provoked Mexico even before Texas became part of the United States by telling the Texans to occupy the lands between the Nueces River and the Rio Grande in order to strengthen U.S. claims to that disputed region.

At the same time, Polk tried diplomacy to obtain Mexico's renunciation of claims north of the Rio Grande and allow the purchase of California and New Mexico. He found the Mexican government of José Joaquín Herrera open to discussions. Herrera had seized power in December 1844, driving Santa Anna into exile. But Herrera's position was tenuous. The Mexican treasury was empty and the nation firmly divided between Liberals and Conservatives. Now the Mexican government agreed to receive a U.S. commissioner with powers to address claims and the boundary disputes.

The Polk administration badly misjudged the situation and dispatched John Slidell to Mexico City as minister plenipotentiary. Polk ordered Slidell to offer the Mexicans $25 million for California and New Mexico, and to go as high as $40 million if necessary. At the same time, Commodore John D. Sloat and Lieutenant John C. Fremont made preparations for seizing California in the event of war.

When Slidell arrived in Mexico City in December 1845, he received a frosty reception. The Herrera government refused to meet with him because he held the title of minister rather than commissioner, implying Mexico's de facto acceptance of Texas's annexation. When the Mexican press uncovered Slidell's mission, it blasted Herrera. One report emphasized: "This vile government has been and is in correspondence with the usurpers. The Yankee . . . has departed for the North to say to his government to send a commissioner to make with our government an ignominious treaty on the basis of the surrender of Texas and we know not what other part of the republic."

The Straw that Broke the Camel's Back

Soon after the Herrera government rebuffed Slidell, a military coup occurred and a junta took power. It refused to negotiate with Slidell and denounced Herrera for "seeking to avoid a necessary and glorious war" and bringing on an "ignominious loss of dignity." When Slidell informed Polk of his failure, the president chose a policy of confrontation. In mid-January 1846, he ordered General Zachary Taylor to move his forces from Corpus Christi to the Rio Grande opposite Matamoros. Despite Mexican warnings that the action was an invasion, Taylor proceeded to the border with 4,000 troops. The Mexicans countered with a buildup of troops, and a clash appeared imminent.

Throughout March and April, Polk waited for Mexico City to capitulate to his demands. He sorely misjudged the Mexicans. Some in the United States and Europe believed that Mexico's army was a match for the American rabble, a point underscored by the British weekly *Britannia,* which called the United States "one of the weakest [powers] in the world . . . fit for nothing but to fight Indians."

Polk remained undeterred. On May 9, 1846, he held a meeting with his cabinet and proposed asking Congress for a declaration of war for unpaid claims and the rejection of Slidell's mission. It proved unnecessary. That evening, General Taylor reported a skirmish between U.S. and Mexican troops north of the Rio Grande, in which several Americans had been killed and wounded.

With the drawing of American blood, the president needed no other incentive. Two days later, Polk went to Congress and branded Mexico the aggressor. The president emphasized that "Mexico has passed the boundary of the United States, has invaded our territory and shed American blood upon the American soil. She has proclaimed that hostilities have commenced, and that the two nations are now at war." The House voted 174–14 for war and the Senate 40–2. Two days later, Congress appropriated $10 million for the conflict. Cries of "Mexico or Death!" and "Ho for the Halls of Montezuma!" echoed across the country. In Polk's home state of Tennessee, the government requested 2,800 volunteers, but 30,000 showed up, winning it the nickname the "Volunteer State."

Battle of Eagles

Many opponents derisively labeled the War with Mexico, "Mr. Polk's War." Despite its detractors, the conflict went well for the United States. U.S. troops and military leadership, especially in the technical areas of the navy and artillery, were superior to that of the Mexicans. Fremont and Stockton quickly took California. Taylor swept into northern Mexico and defeated Mexican generals including Santa Anna, who had persuaded Polk to allow him to return from exile in Cuba, promising to end the war and surrender California and New Mexico. By 1847, the forces of U.S. General Winfield Scott took Vera Cruz and followed the national highway all the way into Mexico City, without suffering a single defeat.

The victories only confirmed American views of their superiority. In 1846, the *Casket* (Cincinnati) published: "though the barbarians fall thick as hail, still as their disposition is warlike and as the slaughter of their armies by the superiority of scientific warfare and the unflinching bravery of men disposed to peace, would teach them helpful lessons. . . . The Mexicans will be led by this war to think of their weakness and inferiority." Future president Andrew Johnson called Mexico a "perfidious and half-civilized" nation and reminded his listeners that "the Anglo-Saxon race has been selected as the rod of her retribution." The *New York Evening Post* asked if the United States could "resign this beautiful country [Mexico] to the custody of the ignorant coward and profligate ruffians who have ruled it for the last twenty-five years? . . . Civilization and Christianity protests against this reflux of the tide of barbarism and anarchy." Many argued that the United States maintained the right to intervene and protect the Mexicans against their own weaknesses and anarchy.

Racism undergirded these views. Soldiers and journalists perpetuated images of Mexicans as a corrupt, indolent, morally bankrupt peoples dominated by the Catholic hierarchy. During the war, one soldier called the Mexicans "miserable inhabitants," adding that "the same fate await[s] them that happens to the Indian tribes of our own frontier. [T]hey will naturally vanish before civilization." The military governor of Mexico City, General John Quitman, called the Mexicans "beasts of burdens, with as little intellect as the asses whose burdens they share." The *Cincinnati Herald* voiced fears of annexing Mexicans "with their idol worship, heathen superstition, and degraded mongrel races." Not everyone agreed. Albert Gallatin wrote in 1848 that "all these allegations of superiority of race and destiny neither require nor deserve any answer; they are pretences [sic] . . . to disguise ambitions, cupidity, or silly vanity."

Lonely Voices in the Crowd

Despite the military victories, the War with Mexico proved unpopular with some Americans and demonstrated the inevitable differences of opinion regarding U.S. policy in Latin America. In Massachusetts, Henry David Thoreau went to jail for refusing to pay taxes to finance the war. Senator Thomas Corwin denounced southern aspirations for land and justified Mexican self-defense in February 1847, telling his colleagues: "If I were Mexican I would tell you, 'Have you not room in your own country to bury your dead? If you come into mine, we will greet you with bloody hands, and welcome you to hospitable graves." A young Illinois congressman, Abraham Lincoln, rose in December 1847 and questioned the exact location on which American blood had been spilled in April 1846, demanding that Polk respond. Some abolitionists even encouraged northern secession from the Union to protest the war. Ralph Waldo Emerson predicted that taking Mexican territory was like "the man [who] swallows arsenic, which brings him down in turn."

The opposition tried to undermine the war effort. Democrat David Wilmot, who had supported Texas's annexation but opposed expanding slavery, led the charge with the so-called Wilmot Proviso. He placed a rider to a military appropriations bill that allowed "neither slavery nor involuntary servitude" in any territory obtained from the War with Mexico. With Whig and northern Democrats' support, the bill passed the House but died during a Senate filibuster. Nevertheless, Wilmot continued attaching his proviso to subsequent bills, although the opposition defeated every attempt to pass it.

One of the most interesting sources of opposition to the war arose within the ranks of the U.S. military. Americans, many of them recent Irish immigrants, deserted and joined the Mexicans. Driven by pro-Catholicism within their ranks and Mexican promises of land, they fought with other foreigners in the San Patricio Battalion. The San Patricios marched into battle carrying a green flag with the Mexican eagle on one side and the image of Saint Patrick and "Erin Go Bragh" on the other. Battalion members distinguished themselves in battles at Monterrey, Buena Vista, and Churubusco. Most of them met death on the battlefield, but the American army executed others in the valley below Chapultepec after the U.S. flag rose over the castle. One observer called the hanging of thirty men simultaneously the "largest hanging affair on the North American continent."

While the San Patricios never numbered more than 200, the symbolic value of the group was important. Americans called them traitors, but the Mexicans revered the men as "Irish Catholic martyrs" and erected monuments to them. One Mexican historian notes "that the San Patricios are heroes in Mexico is beyond dispute, and deservedly so." Equally as significant, it foreshadowed a trend in American relations with Latin America, as American cultural homogeneity sometimes crumbled from within, first among Irish Americans and then among the Mexican Americans of the Southwest. Ultimately, this would help alter views of Latin Americans, and at least elevate the level of tolerance for Catholicism and other ethnic issues.

The Persistent Negotiator

Despite the fierce Mexican resistance, Scott's troops took Mexico City in September 1847. Afterward, Mexican resistance collapsed and peace negotiations began. Polk dispatched a State Department official, Nicholas Trist, with General Scott's army as chief negotiator. After U.S. forces entered Mexico City, Trist met with the Mexican government. Polk and others, filled with the euphoria of victory, contemplated annexing more of northern Mexico and possibly territory on which to build a proposed southern route for a trans-isthmian railroad. Polk tried to recall Trist, but the commissioner refused to return.

Trist ultimately negotiated the Treaty of Guadalupe Hidalgo, which ceded New Mexico and California and all the lands in between to the United States. In return, the United States paid Mexico $15 million and promised to assume any claims of U.S. citizens against Mexico. When the treaty arrived in January 1848, Polk grudgingly supported it. Meanwhile, the House had recently adopted a resolution declaring the war had been "unnecessarily and unconstitutionally begun by the President of the United States." Nevertheless, on March 10, 1848, the Senate approved the Treaty of Guadalupe Hidalgo 38–14. One disgruntled observer, Whig Philip Hone, noted that the peace was "negotiated by an unauthorized agent, with an unacknowledged government, submitted by an accidental President, to a dissatisfied Senate."

Consequences of War

The war significantly influenced the United States, Mexico, and U.S.-Latin American relations. As historian Otis A. Singletary notes, "what may appear to have been just another military exercise was instead a profoundly significant event, one that altered the face of the nation." The war left more than 12,000 Americans dead and many more wounded. Dirk Raat emphasizes "the forbidden fruit of Mexico, when consumed, proved fatal to the body politic, as slavery in the newly acquired territories became the major constitutional and political issue leading up to the Civil War." It also established a precedent for future presidents on how to wage a successful war "with all the vigor usually associated with 'more arbitrary forms of government.'" Future presidents would use Polk's model as a lesson for their own leadership, guaranteeing similar unilateral actions.

The war had a significant impact on U.S. economic development. The United States doubled in size, annexing the present-day states of Colorado, Arizona, New Mexico, and California. In the process, it obtained lands rich with minerals including gold, silver, and petroleum. The acquisition opened new farmlands and created markets for U.S. industries. In addition, the nation obtained excellent seaports to compete for lucrative trade in the Pacific Basin. The acquisition of the Southwest forever changed the United States and helped it grow from a regional power into a global one.

The conquest also started a significant demographic trend. The newly conquered areas were home to many Mexican families, some of whom had lived there for two centuries. Located primarily in New Mexico, Colorado, and sections of California and Texas, the Hispanic population, while often facing discrimination and loss of land, remained an important cultural and political force in the American Southwest, ultimately gaining strength and numbers with the arrival of new Latino immigrants.

On the Other Side

The war devastated Mexico. It resulted in more than 50,000 casualties and the immense loss of materials and foodstuffs destroyed and devoured by the invaders. More than 40 percent of Mexico's territory had been taken, along with immeasurable natural resources, severely limiting its economic development. While Mexico's economy was half the size of that of the United States in 1800, by 1867 it was only one-eighth as productive. The trend would continue throughout the nineteenth and twentieth centuries.

Yet some observers note positive aspects. The territorial losses could have been worse, as Mexico did retain the important states of Coahulia, Sonora, Chihuahua, and Baja California. Equally as important, the defeat helped spark Mexican unity. Writers such as Mexican Ramón Alcaraz wrote in *The Other Side* in 1850 in that "impartial history will some day illustrate forever the conduct observed by this Republic against all laws, divine and human, in an age that is called one of light, and which is, notwithstanding, the same as the former—one of force of violence." The war, when combined with the struggle against the French in the 1860s, gave Mexicans a point around which to rally disparate groups. The War of Northern Aggression, as some called it, helped create modern Mexico. It became part of its political culture, and many national heroes, such as the young military cadets who chose death over surrender at Chapultepec, became imbued in the national consciousness. What the Liberals and Conservatives had failed to do, the Americans had assisted.

The war had a significant, long-term, and negative impact on U.S.-Latin American relations. For many Latin Americans, it confirmed suspicions about their northern neighbors. The Monroe Doctrine, for all its emphasis on hemispheric solidarity, was a toothless document subordinated to U.S. territorial and economic desires. For many, the conflict confirmed the U.S., not Europe, as the greatest threat. This attitude was not easily overcome. More than a hundred years later, the Mexican novelist Carlos Fuentes wrote that in 1848, "the United States became the Jekyll and Hyde of our wildest continental dreams: a democracy inside, an empire outside."

Gold Fever

The War with Mexico helped shift American focus from Mexico to Central America. In 1849, prospectors discovered gold in northern California, sparking an exodus of Americans to the territory by 1850. Because traveling the overland route from the eastern and midwestern United States to California was a long and dangerous undertaking, the desired route was by ship to Central America, where passengers disembarked and crossed the isthmus by foot or mule. Ships waiting on the Pacific coast then took the gold seekers on to California. American entrepreneurs, including Cornelius Vanderbilt, grew wealthy managing this business and others facilitating trade with Asia. Consequently, the United States once again concentrated on building a trans-isthmus canal.

Many obstacles existed in constructing such a canal. The Central American federation had collapsed, and Washington found itself negotiating with independent nations. As in other parts of the former Spanish colonial system, turmoil characterized the internal affairs of the Central American nations. Liberals and Conservatives fought throughout the region, including in Nicaragua, where the two groups centered in two major cities, Leon and Granada. Periodic attempts to reunify the region only exacerbated the strife.

Clouding negotiation further was the ever-present specter of the British. They retained control of British Honduras, much to the consternation of the Guatemalans. Furthermore, they were prominent players along Nicaragua's Mosquito Coast. In 1848, they established a protectorate over the coastal town of San Juan del Norte (renamed Greytown by the British), a major component of the proposed canal route.

Policymakers in Washington responded quickly. American diplomats highlighted British aggression when negotiating for concessions from the fearful Central American nations. One of the earliest, Elijah Hise, secured treaties guaranteeing U.S. rights to build a canal and made promises to protect Nicaragua's sovereignty. His successor, Ephraim George Squier, successfully negotiated treaties with Nicaragua and Honduras, guaranteeing U.S. rights to construct a canal and strategic islands to protect it.

British officials recognized that the United States posed a potential threat to their own plans to construct a canal. They decided to address the Americans directly and found a willing U.S. Secretary of State in John Clayton, who had proposed "a great highway" across Central America "to be dedicated especially by Great Britain and the United States, to the equal benefit and advantage of all nations of the world." Sir Henry Bulwer traveled to Washington in December 1849 to open discussions. The two parties eventually signed the Clayton-Bulwer Treaty on April 19, 1850, in which both sides promised never to monopolize or fortify a canal and agreed that neither would "colonize, or assume, or exercise any dominion over . . . any part of Central America."

For the Central Americans, the treaty was bittersweet. As Lester Langley comments: "The Clayton-Bulwer settlement was symbolic of Central Americans' frustrations in trying to benefit by maneuvering one power against another only to discover that the diplomatic combatants could withdraw to their own domain and arrive at mutually beneficial arrangements." For them, the lesson of Clayton-Bulwer was that the core powers worked cooperatively to the detriment of the Central Americans.

Southern Dreams of Empire

While U.S. diplomats worked in Central America, the attention of many other Americans focused on the Caribbean islands. Southerners felt threatened by the Compromise of 1850, which incorporated California as a free state and allowed citizens in the Mexican cession to vote for or against slavery. The Compromise scared southerners who feared a coming imbalance in Congress and slavery's ultimate abolition. Historian Robert E. May emphasizes that the search for a "balance of power" had been "a cardinal principle of Southern political policy ever since the Missouri Compromise debates." To guarantee equal representation among the pro- and antislavery states, the most logical choice was to expand slave-holding areas in the Caribbean.

The clamor for new Caribbean territories was strong. Men such as publisher James D. E. B. DeBow called the Gulf of Mexico the "great Southern sea." Others believed that the creation of new states in the Caribbean Basin would permit the South to acquire "more power & influence than would a dozen wild deserts" of the American Southwest. Some predicted an easy process. One southern congressman argued that the peoples of the Caribbean republics waited "with swelling hearts and suppressed impatience" and would meet Americans "with joyous shouts of 'Welcome!' 'Welcome!'"

Filibusters Must Die!

Initially, southerners focused their energies on Cuba. That Spanish colony retained slavery and its racial composition and agro-export economy strongly resembled that of the American South. Discontented with Spanish rule, wealthy Cuban creole elites plotted against Madrid. Cuban exiles in New York, New Orleans, and other U.S. cities made speeches, published newspapers, and lobbied Congress in support of Cuban independence. Allied with sympathetic Americans, the movement gained strength throughout in the 1850s.

In response to the clamor, Washington tried to buy the island from the Spanish on several occasions. A representative voice among Americans was that of Mississippi Senator Albert Gallantin Brown. "I want Cuba, and I know sooner or later we must have it," he declared, "I want [all of the Caribbean islands] for the same reason—for the planting or spreading of slavery." In 1848, President Polk offered Madrid $100 million for the colony, but Madrid immediately rejected the offer. One Spaniard responded that his people "would prefer seeing [Cuba] sunk in the ocean" than surrendered to the United States.

When attempts to purchase the island failed, some Americans planned to seize it. Filibusters, many with the financial support of prominent Americans, began preparations. General Narciso López, a Venezuelan-born adventurer who adopted Cuba as his homeland, led the charge. With support from prominent southerners including Governor John Quitman of Mississippi, López organized his first filibustering expedition to Cuba in May 1850. He landed a group of 700 men on the Cuban coast, expecting a popular uprising to materialize. It never did, at which point he retreated to Key West just ahead of a Spanish warship. U.S. officials put him on trial for violating neutrality laws, but three separate New Orleans juries acquitted him.

Undeterred, López tried again in August 1851. He and a force of 500 men boarded ships, while sympathetic U.S. officials looked the other way. His company included William Crittenden, son of President James Buchanan's attorney general. "The star of Cuba . . . will rise beautiful and shining perchance to be admitted gloriously into the splendid North American constellation according to its inevitable destiny," López proclaimed. As before, he failed miserably. Shortly after he and his company landed, the Spanish killed or executed the filibusters, including Crittenden. They made a special example of López, whom they publicly strangled in Havana. Massive protests followed in New Orleans, leading to the sacking of the Spanish consulate in New Orleans and calls for "vengeance on the tyrant . . . blood for blood."

Even in the wake of the failures, Washington continued to try to purchase Cuba. It instructed U.S. Minister to Spain Pierre Soulé to offer Madrid

$130 million for the island. When rebuffed, Soulé met with U.S. minister to Great Britain, James Buchanan, and U.S. Minister to France, John Y. Mason, in Ostend, Belgium, to discuss the issue. Heartened by British and French preoccupation with the Crimean War, the U.S. representatives issued the Ostend Manifesto, in which they supported purchasing Cuba but emphasized that if Spain refused "then, by every law, human and divine, we shall be justified in wresting it from Spain if we possess the power." Although neither Washington nor Madrid officially recognized the manifesto, the statement sparked fierce debates. For the moment, however, tensions over Cuba subsided, as the Americans became embroiled in an internal crisis over slavery.

Grey-Eyed Man of Destiny

One of the most colorful filibusters with proslavery leanings was William Walker. The son of a Scottish immigrant and prosperous Nashville banker, Walker was small of stature with piercing gray eyes. As a young man, he received a medical degree from the University of Pennsylvania

General William Walker, circa 1857 (Webster Brothers). *Courtesy of the Smithsonian Institution, National Portrait Gallery, NPG.97.209*

and traveled in Europe, learning about socialism from the Hungarian revolutionary Lajos Kossuth. Afterward, he earned a law degree and moved to New Orleans, where he became a journalist. As such, he criticized the López expedition, promoted woman's suffrage, and supported the gradual abolition of slavery.

Ultimately, Walker's life changed dramatically after the death of his one true love, and he sought new challenges. He moved to San Francisco and worked on a newspaper. Once jailed for contempt for criticizing a judge's leniency, Walker was freed after a massive demonstration by several thousand San Franciscans on his behalf. Afterward, he fought a series of well-publicized duels with prominent citizens. Imbued with the ideas of "manifest destiny," he planned to seize Sonora and the lower Baja and annex it to the United States. In 1853, he led a ragtag group of mercenaries on his quest, which the Mexican army easily defeated.

But fate provided Walker yet another chance for power and glory. Invited by Nicaraguan Liberals to help fight the Conservatives, Walker traveled to Central America in 1855. Financed largely by southerners seeking a slave territory, and Cornelius Vanderbilt, who wanted more control over the Nicaraguan transit route, Walker organized and armed a band of fifty-eight men, later nicknamed "the Immortals." Within a year, Walker was president of Nicaragua. Ironically, he soon reimposed slavery, much to the delight of his allies. He declared that "with the negro-slave as his companion, the white man would become fixed to the soil; and they together would destroy the power of the mixed race which is the bane of the country."

The Walker government created a firestorm in Central America. The Costa Ricans and Hondurans declared war on Nicaragua and marched against him. Despite nearly universal condemnations of Walker, U.S. minister to Nicaragua John Hill Wheeler, a North Carolina slave owner, recognized Walker's government in 1856. He argued that in Nicaragua the "rich soil so well adapted to the culture of cotton, sugar, rice, corn, cocoa, indigo, etc. can never be developed without slave labor."

Walker's adventure was short-lived. He alienated Vanderbilt by giving control of the Transit Route to his competitors. The wealthy American responded by arming the Costa Ricans and providing them military advisors and technical support. Despite the odds, Walker and his men fought ferociously. During one battle, he demonstrated the mindset of many Americans. "We are engaged in no ordinary warfare. . . . We have come here as the advance guard of American civilization," he yelled to his troops, "Are we to be driven from the country merely because we were not born on its soil? Never! Never!" Ultimately, the Central Americans severed his logistical support and forced him from Managua. Only the assistance of sympathetic U.S. naval officers prevented his capture.

Amazingly, Walker remained undeterred and tried to return to Nicaragua and seize control in 1858 and 1860. The last time, the British intercepted his force and turned him over to Honduran officials, who placed him before a firing squad. Afterward, one Nicaraguan wrote: "God will condemn his arrogance and protect our cause."

Despite his death, Walker remained important. During the 1980s, one writer noted: "What matters at last is this: all over Central America, William Walker is remembered as the pattern and paradigm for American intentions. . . . He has become the core around which their national myths have been created . . . the heroic and successful struggle of the people of Central America against the arrogance and power of the North Americans. . . . Whoever their internal enemies are, they know for certain from which direction their external enemy had traditionally come."

Crisis Strikes the United States

The arsenic that the United States had ingested in 1848 ultimately extracted death in 1861 and ended the age of the filibuster. That year, the United States dissolved into two nations, a sectionalism related specifically to slavery. Thirteen southern states seceded from the United States to form the Confederate States of America and declared independence. They created a government and prepared to defend it. In the North, the newly elected president, the Republican free soiler Abraham Lincoln, urged that the Union must remain intact. By April, however, Confederate batteries fired on Fort Sumter, a federal outpost in South Carolina, igniting a full-scale conflict.

The American Civil War affected U.S.-Latin American relations in several ways. On the economic front, the northern blockade of Confederate ports severed most southern trade, especially in foodstuffs. Still, Northern merchants continued to trade in Latin America. In fact, the war aided the economic development of several Latin American countries, as the British and French mercantile industry searched for new sources to replace interrupted supplies of southern cotton. In Haiti and Brazil, cotton became more important. While the war weakened them, the economic bonds between the United States and Latin America were never severed.

On the diplomatic front, U.S. and Confederate officials were very active in Latin America. Most Latin Americans favored the Union because of its stand against slavery and their admiration for Lincoln's leadership. For Latin Americans, the conflict revolved directly around naval and commercial activities. Confederate blockade runners and privateers often used Latin American ports, even as U.S. officials worked to prevent their access to the harbors. Ultimately, the Union succeeded in pressuring Latin Americans to stop overt acts of hostility from originating in their ports, especially when the outcome of the war became apparent.

U.S. diplomats also worked with Latin Americans on another important front. With Lincoln's blessing, they sought to colonize newly freed slaves into countries in Central America and the Caribbean. As one historian underscores, the president "believed that slavery and the black presence lay at the root of the current U.S. crisis." "Removal of both these sources of discord could restore harmony to what was intended to be," she notes, "and what must remain, a white man's country." U.S. officials cooperated with private citizens to implement elaborate resettlement plans. The efforts, however, had very limited success, as most Latin Americans opposed importing the source of the conflict. Ultimately, only a few small-scale adventures progressed, and the colonization movement lost momentum by 1865.

Into the Fold

The American Civil War also affected U.S.-Haitian relations. During the period 1804–61, the United States withheld formal diplomatic recognition of the newly independent Haiti. Most opponents argued Haiti had limited economic potential and remained a volatile place. Yet, economic relations indeed flourished, as the United States became one of Haiti's chief sources of trade. While no U.S. diplomats resided in Haiti, commercial representatives operated there. By the early 1850s, prominent U.S. merchants began calling for the government to recognize Haiti. Still, a divided Congress and pro-southern presidents refused to do so.

As the historian Brenda Gayle Plummer remarks, "secession and the establishment of the Confederacy had created a unique opportunity for Washington to revise its Haitian policy." The move toward "abolition indirectly benefited Haiti by undercutting the rationale on which its universal ostracism had rested," she adds. Lincoln's desire to colonize freed slaves and the Spanish occupation of the Dominican Republic in 1861 forced a reevaluation. The president wanted Haiti's support in the resettlement enterprise. Furthermore, U.S. officials worried that Haiti and its ports might fall into Spanish hands. Many believed that these arguments were logical and recognition was long overdue.

Yet Lincoln faced many obstacles. Despite the Southern absence in Congress, the efforts to normalize relations created a firestorm. Supporters led by Senator Charles Sumner of Massachusetts argued that economic relations had flourished and that common sense called for the presence of U.S. officials to protect American citizens in Haiti. Others in Congress, including Massachusetts representative Daniel W. Gooch, pointed out that Haiti ranked twenty-first out of seventy-three in imports of U.S. goods. He also argued that Haiti would be a good ally in helping remove the Spanish from the Dominican Republic.

On the other side, the opponents based their arguments on the "racial implications of recognizing black states." Senator Garrett Davis of Kentucky warned that recognition of Haiti would undermine U.S. diplomacy because "negro wives and negro daughters" would attend Washington social events and offend proper sensibilities. Representative Samuel S. Cox of Ohio called recognition a radical abolitionist plot to break down racial barriers at home that would lead to the "welcome here at the White House [of] an African, full-blooded, all gilded and belaced, dressed in court style, with wigs and sword and tights and shoe-buckles and ribbons and spangles and many other adornments which African vanity will suggest." He asked what American would take such an ambassador seriously. "With what admiring awe will the contrabands [refugee freedmen] approach this ebony demigod!" he sounded off, "While all decent and sensible white people will laugh the silly and ridiculous ceremony to scorn." Despite this racially charged opposition, the United States extended recognition to the Haitian government on June 5, 1862.

While the economic relationship between the two nations grew, tensions remained, especially racism, as new forms of dealing with people perceived as inferior developed throughout the South and North. Haiti would remain a pariah among the Caribbean nations and only on a few occasions would the United States demonstrate more than passing interest in it throughout the remainder of the nineteenth century.

Europe Takes Advantage of America in Distress

The most serious issue in U.S.-Latin American relations in the 1860s was European intervention. Spain and France, with some initial British assistance, sought to regain their former colonial grandeur. In each case, Washington initially proved incapable of responding directly because of its preoccupation with internal strife. However, as the Civil War wound down, the U.S. began working in concert with the Latin Americans to challenge forcefully the French and Spanish. Ultimately, the crises in the Dominican Republic and Mexico ended with a return of Latin American sovereignty.

The first European intervention occurred in the Dominican Republic. At the invitation of President Pedro Santana, Queen Isabella II accepted the role of protector and made him governor. He justified the action on the grounds that his people needed Madrid's protection against the Haitians, from whom they had won independence in 1844. The Spaniards reestablished firm control over the country, alienating large sectors of the population, including Protestant Americans who suffered extreme persecution from a zealous Catholic bishop.

Initially, Washington responded carefully to the Spanish invasion. Secretary of State William H. Seward vainly protested Madrid's actions, but the Civil War prevented direct action. Yet the Americans aided in other ways. When the Dominicans began resistance in 1863, Washington officially maintained neutrality, fearful of provoking the European power. Still, most U.S. officials turned a blind eye to Dominican agents in the United States. Arms and supplies flowed southward, assisting the war against the Spanish. Soon the Spanish quit, fighting and disease having decimated their forces. In May 1865, the Spanish annulled the treaty of annexation and withdrew.

Napoleon's Folly in Mexico

The most serious European intervention of the 1860s occurred in Mexico. In 1857, the Liberals, under the leadership of Benito Juárez, took control. They promulgated the Constitution of 1857, which severely restricted the power of the Catholic Church, the army, and implemented land reform. The Conservatives rallied and momentarily defeated the Liberals, with Juárez retreating and organizing a guerrilla war. After two years of fierce fighting, the Liberals captured Mexico City and regained power.

The fighting precipitated European intervention. Once in power, Juárez declared a moratorium on debt payments, angering European and American investors. At the same time, Conservative agents spread throughout Europe recruiting support to overthrow the Liberal regime and replace it with a monarchy headed by a pro-Catholic European ruler. They found some supporters, despite Prince Klemens von Metternich of Austria warning "what a lot of cannon-shots it will take to set up an emperor in Mexico, and what a lot to maintain him there." In October 1861, diplomats from Spain, England, and France signed a convention establishing a military expedition to collect debts. Each party agreed that none would seek any "peculiar advantage." In December 1861, a multinational force of British, Spanish, and French seized Vera Cruz. Soon, the French and Napoleon III broke the agreement and sought to create a French-supported, European-style monarchy in Mexico.

After a year of fighting, the French took Mexico City. The Mexicans had resisted fiercely, winning a brilliant victory over a superior force at Puebla on May 5, 1862. Still, superior firepower combined with traitorous Conservative deeds ensured France's victory. In June 1863, an Assembly of Notables, composed exclusively of clerics and large landowners, invited Ferdinand Maximilian, younger brother of Emperor Francis Joseph of Austria, to take Mexico's Crown. Afterward, the assembly rigged a plebiscite to validate Maximilian's monarchy. By April 1864, the Austrian accepted and signed a treaty that committed France to his cause until 1867 in return for payment of debts and French military costs.

A Velvet and Then an Iron Glove

Washington apprehensively monitored the events in Mexico. Some Americans agreed that the Europeans had the right to demand repayment of debts, but as Napoleon III's imperial designs unfolded, the public wholeheartedly condemned the occupation. Fearful of alienating the French and driving them to recognize the Confederacy, Secretary of State Seward moved cautiously. In 1862, he warned the Europeans that "no monarchical government which could be founded in Mexico . . . would have any prospect of security or permanency." At the same time, Washington aided Mexico in other ways. The U.S. minister to Juárez's government supported its legitimacy and refused to recognize that of Maximilian. The U.S. government also encouraged private Americans to assist the Mexican forces with arms and munitions.

By 1864, the United States began to adopt a more belligerent stance, as the outcome of the Civil War appeared more secure. The *New York Herald* issued a bold proclamation that "as for Mexico, we will, at the close of the rebellion, if the French have not left there before, send fifty thousand Northern and fifty thousand Southern troops, forming together a grand army to drive the invaders into the Gulf. That is the way we shall tolerate a French monarchy in Mexico." In April 1864, the House of Representatives voted unanimously for a resolution that stated: "The Congress of the United States is unwilling by silence to leave the nations of the world under the impression that they are indifferent spectators of the deplorable events now transpiring in the republic of Mexico, and that they therefore think fit to declare that it does not accord with the policy of the United States to acknowledge any monarchical Government erected on the ruins of any republican Government in America under the auspices of any European power."

Once the Civil War ended, the United States increased its pressure on the French. Many Americans wanted to fight. Newly installed President Andrew Johnson had declared that "the day of reckoning is approaching. It will not be long before the Rebellion is put down. . . . And then we will attend to this Mexican affair, and say to Louis Napoleon, 'You cannot found a monarchy on this Continent.' An expedition into Mexico would be a sort of recreation to the brave soldiers who are now fighting the battles of the Union, and the French concern would be quickly wiped out." With Washington's approval, General Ulysses S. Grant sent 50,000 troops to the Texas border. In addition, he asked his commanders to recruit former Confederate and Union soldiers to fight for Juárez.

As bellicose talk arose, Seward focused on diplomacy. As one historian remarks, "his policy therefore was to push Napoleon gently with one hand, while courteously showing him the door with the other." In 1865, Seward dispatched a special minister to France, General J. M. Schofield, who believed Seward's instructions implied: "I want you to get your legs under Napoleon's mahogany and tell him he must get out of Mexico." In February 1866, Seward informed Paris that "we shall be gratified when the Emperor shall give to us . . . definitive information of the time when French military operations may be expected to cease in Mexico." The timing was important, as Napoleon already had decided to leave, his forces decimated by those of the Mexican resistance. Paris promised withdrawal in nineteen months.

Without French assistance, Maximilian's government collapsed, as Juárez's forces defeated the remaining Conservative loyalists, capturing the emperor in the spring of 1867. Juárez ignored pleas for leniency from Europe and some Americans. On June 19, a Mexican firing squad executed the Austrian and several Mexican traitors. The *Portland Transcript* (Maine) noted that "if anybody deserves to be shot it is Louis Napoleon. He is the chief criminal in this great national crime."

The U.S. response to the French intervention in Mexico was significant in that it helped to undermine some of the anti-Americanism that had developed from the War with Mexico. On the other side, it created a more positive image of Mexicans in the United States, translating into more economic and social exchanges after 1867. While mutual mistrust remained on both sides, relations improved dramatically for many years.

The period of the American Civil War also was significant in marking a change in U.S.-Latin American relations from that of the preceding thirty years. Disenchanted with U.S. expansionism and ethnocentrism, Latin Americans developed more favorable images of the United States from the struggle to maintain the union as represented in the leadership of Abraham Lincoln and the U.S. government's response to the European invasions. For them, according to one historian, "a powerful and reunited United States could brandish the Monroe Doctrine more fearsomely at the land-grabbers of Europe."

Continuities

The interdependence between Latin America and the United States intensified from 1825 to 1867. The economies of the respective nations became more intertwined as U.S. and Latin American merchants increased exchanges. As mentioned, coffee secured from Brazil replaced tea as the preferred drink in North America. The desire for American agricultural goods and some finished products increased and, while the British, Dutch, and French remained competitors, Americans increasingly gained a larger part of the growing Latin American market.

On the political and diplomatic fronts, interdependence became more apparent. The Spanish occupation of the Dominican Republic and the French occupation of Mexico had led to concerted diplomatic efforts to expel the Europeans. There were also many different levels of exchanges, as Latin America and the United States worked on issues of tariffs, the slave trade, settlement of the freed slaves after the American Civil War, and the negotiations of a canal route. While the northern nations became the most interdependent, the southern cone countries (Argentina, Chile, and Brazil) and the United States also became increasingly interdependent.

At the same time, the U.S. drive for hegemony surged ahead unabated. The United States made significant gains in the period, despite the British presence and Latin American resistance. The United States grew much more rapidly than did its southern neighbors, accelerating an asymmetry in natural resources, labor, and industrialization. The military occupation of northern Mexico further strengthened U.S. potential and contributed to renewed efforts at U.S. hegemony in Latin America, especially in the Caribbean and Central America. By 1867, despite having only recently concluded its horrific Civil War, the United States sat poised to move from a dominating power in the Northern Hemisphere to world-power status.

The Latin Americans, however, were not passive actors. Their economic growth was no longer as disproportionate, as both regions of the Western Hemisphere relied primarily on agriculture goods for export and the exchange of goods such as coffee and wheat remained comparatively similar. Leaders fought for favorable tariffs and trade with Washington and sought to protect native industries. They benefited from U.S. competition with Europe, and secured concessions, as Americans badly needed Latin American markets and goods during economic downturns.

On the political and diplomatic level, resistance to the U.S. hegemony took many forms. In one case, Mexico used military force to resist U.S. aggression, extracting a significant price in manpower and political prestige. Most Latin American nations benefited from alliances with Great Britain and internal divisions in the United States that prevented further territorial expansion, especially in Central America and Cuba. They established ties with individual Americans who favored their causes and opposed territorial expansion, especially abolitionists of the era. At almost every juncture, the Latin Americans watched U.S. actions warily and developed methods of resistance when necessary.

Finally, the period saw the beginning of the Latino population in the United States, most of whom were assimilated by the takeover of Texas and the Mexican cession of 1848. Still, other Latin Americans immigrated to the United States as business interests increased with Cuba, the Dominican

Republic, and Central America. Across the Southwestern United States, and increasingly in large U.S. cities, small but thriving Latino communities existed and would grow substantially over time, bringing new foods, work skills, languages, and other cultural forms into U.S. society.

SUGGESTIONS FOR ADDITIONAL READING

Good works on the foreign policy of Adams and Jackson include Samuel F. Bemis, *John Quincy Adams and the Foundations of American Foreign Policy* (1949), Mary Hargreaves, *The Presidency of John Quincy Adams* (1985); William E. Weeks, *Johns Quincy Adams and American Global Empire* (1992); Greg Russell, *John Quincy Adams and the Public Virtues of Diplomacy* (1995); John M. Belohlavek, *"Let the Eagle Soar!": The Foreign Policy of Andrew Jackson* (1985); H. W. Brands, *Andrew Jackson: His Life and Times* (2006); and Christian Maisch, "The Falkland/Malvinas Islands Clash of 1831–32: U.S. and British Diplomacy in the South Atlantic," *Diplomatic History* (Spring 2000).

The War with Mexico has spawned many good books, including David M. Pletcher, *The Diplomacy of Annexation: Texas, Oregon, and the Mexican War* (1973); Michael Hogan, *The Irish Soldiers of Mexico* (1997); Paul Bergeron, *The Presidency of James K. Polk* (1987), Gene Brack, *Mexico Views Manifest Destiny* (1975); John D. Eisenhower, *So Far from God: The U.S. War with Mexico* (1989); Richard Griswold del Castillo, *The Treaty of Guadalupe Hidalgo* (1990); Anna K. Nelson, *Secret Agents: President Polk and the Search for Peace with Mexico* (1988); and John H. Schroeder, *Mr. Polk's War: American Opposition and Dissent* (1973).

For more reading on the issue of "manifest destiny," see Reginald Horsman, *Race and Manifest Destiny: The Origins of Racial Anglo-Saxonism* (1981); Thomas R. Hietala, *Manifest Design: Anxious Aggrandizement in Late Jacksonian America* (1985); Anders Stephanson, *Manifest Destiny: American Expansionism and the Empire of Right* (1995); Frederick Merk, *The Monroe Doctrine and American Expansionism, 1843–1849* (1966); and T. Ray Shurbatt, ed., *United States-Latin American Relations, 1800–1850: The Formative Generations* (1991).

Good works on filibusters and southern views of empire include: Robert E. May, *The Southern Dream of a Caribbean Empire, 1854–1861* (1973) and *Manifest Destiny's Underworld: Filibustering in Antebellum America* (2002); Frederic Rosengarten, Jr., *Freebooters Must Die!: The Life and Death of William Walker, the Most Notorious Filibuster of the Nineteenth Century* (1976); Albert Z. Carr, *The World and William Walker* (1963); Charles H. Brown, *Agents of Manifest Destiny: The Lives and Times of the Filibusters* (1980); Tom Chaffin, *Fatal Glory: Narciso López and First Clandestine War Against Cuba* (1996); Brady Harrison, *Agents of Empire: William Walker and the Imperial Self in American Literature* (2004); Amy Greenberg, *Manifest Manhood and the Antebellum American Empire* (2005); Arnos A. Ettinger, *The Mission to Spain of Pierre Soulé, 1853–1855* (1932); and Joseph A. Fry, *John Tyler Morgan and the Search for Southern Autonomy* (1992).

For more on the American civil war and the U.S. role in helping expel the French, read Norman B. Ferris, *Desperate Diplomacy: William H. Seward's Foreign Policy, 1861* (1975); Alfred J. Hanna and Kathryn A. Hanna, *Napoleon III and Mexico: American Triumph over Monarchy* (1971); and Donathan C. Olliff, *Reforma Mexico and the United States* (1981).

CHAPTER THREE

From Naboth's Vineyard to the Big Stick

AFTER THE AMERICAN CIVIL WAR, the presidential administration of Ulysses S. Grant (1869–77) followed traditional patterns, focusing on regaining markets and raw materials in Latin America while also acquiring new territories to improve the U.S. position in the Caribbean Basin. At other points, it dealt with crises in European colonies. Amidst its stumbling and fumbling, the actions of the Grant administration reconfirmed to many Latin Americans that the U.S. Civil War had done little to change Washington's policies.

"Bloody Cuba"

Grant inherited a major crisis in Cuba. In 1867, the Spanish government levied higher taxes in Cuba, sparking an economic recession that caused a rebellion. In October 1868, the Cubans declared independence and asked Washington to annex the island. U.S. leaders hesitated. As historian Louis Pérez observes, the United States wanted to avoid dealing "with a successful Cuban separatist movement presided over by a Cuban provisional government, negotiating the terms of union as a more or less sovereign entity." The presence in Cuba of a large Afro-Cuban population, slavery, and Roman Catholicism also precluded U.S. support.

For ten years, the Cubans fought. Much to their consternation, Washington officially supported continued Spanish rule. Even when the Cubans simply requested that the United States recognize their country as a belligerent nation, Grant demurred, calling it "unwise and premature," and Secretary of State Hamilton Fish argued the Cubans possessed little capacity for self-rule. As a result, Washington still accepted Spanish rule, although it pressured Madrid to make reforms. Underlying this policy was a hope that the Spanish would eventually sell the island to the United States, leaving Washington to determine the path of Cuba's development.

While Grant and Fish did their best to avoid direct intervention in Cuba, Spanish actions nearly drew the United States into the conflict anyway. In October 1873, the Spanish seized a Cuban-owned vessel, the *Virginius,* which had transported guns and supplies to the rebels. The Spanish commander imprisoned the passengers and crew. After a hastily convened court martial, the Spanish shot fifty-three persons, including several Americans. The action outraged Americans, especially the Cuban American community, who called for revenge. Fish demanded an apology and compensation, although he recognized that the United States lacked resources to back any threat. Ultimately, he worked out a settlement that included indemnity for the executed Americans. Nonetheless, Madrid infuriated him when they promoted the officer who had been responsible.

Despite the *Virginius* incident, the United States remained a bystander in the war. By 1878, the insurrection ended, when the Spanish implemented reforms including the abolition of slavery, amnesty for the rebels, and the rescission of discriminatory taxes. Madrid also permitted a new political group, the Autonomist party. While opposing independence, it backed participation in the Spanish legislature and free trade. Nevertheless, a small minority of Cubans including José Martí refused to surrender. Working in the United States, the fierce nationalists would continue plotting to free their homeland.

The Santo Domingo Land Grab

While Grant avoided direct involvement in Cuba, he searched for other avenues of territorial expansion. He built on the actions of Johnson's secretary of state, William Seward, who tried but failed to buy the Virgin Islands from the Dutch in 1867. Seward also offered to buy a naval base at Samaná Bay in the Dominican Republic, but Congress refused to allot funds. A *Harper's Weekly* editor, whose views represented those of many Americans, wrote in February 1869: "It may be convenient to have a naval station in the West Indies, but is it wise to buy it by adding to our population nearly a million of creoles and West Indian negroes, and by the assumption of nobody knows what debts and liabilities."

The plans resurfaced when Grant took office. Despite opposition, he wanted to annex the Dominican Republic. He sent his personal secretary,

General Orville Babcock, to survey the "Gibraltar of the New World." A future member of the infamous "Whiskey Ring," Babcock allied with an equally nefarious group of Americans including William and Jane Cazneau and Joseph Fabens, who had significant interests in Dominican mines, banks, and port facilities and owned the frontage on Samaná Bay. They arranged a meeting between Babcock and the Dominican president, Buenaventura Báez, who one person described as "an active intriguer of sinister talents."

By November 1869, Babcock and Báez signed two treaties. The first committed the United States to annexing the Dominican Republic and paying off its $1.5 million debt. The second granted the United States the rights to buy Samaná Bay for $2 million if the Senate rejected the first proposal. Babcock returned home and presented the treaties to Grant. As one historian argues, "Grant was easily persuaded to fall in line, and he ardently embraced the annexation project. . . . It became an obsession."

Naboth's Vineyard

The battle over the annexation of the Dominican Republic became a nasty conflict between Grant and the chairman of the Senate Foreign Relations Committee (SFRC), Charles Sumner. The Massachusetts senator, a respected abolitionist, opposed the land grab. Many people believed Babcock and his allies were untrustworthy and leading Grant down the wrong path. War scares between the Dominican Republic and Haiti in early 1870 further exacerbated such fears. Other Americans condemned assimilating an "inferior" race, while many questioned whether the United States needed new territories. A *New York Nation* writer suggested: "If the national future be in peril at all, it is not for want of territory but from excess of it."

In early January 1870, Grant sent the annexation treaty to the Senate for approval. Sumner and his committee held hearings on the treaty and on March 15, 1870, rejected it by a vote of 5–2. Several days later, Sumner went to the Senate floor to promote a "free confederacy" in the West Indies, one in which the "black race should predominate" under U.S. protection.

After the initial setback, Grant rallied and began to lobby senators to support his program. In late May, he sent a special message to Congress. Calling the annexation of the Dominican Republic "a measure of national protection," he highlighted new commercial and strategic advantages. After

Annexation demonstration in Santo Domingo City, Dominican Republic, 1871. *Courtesy of the Library of Congress, LC-USZ62-92837*

shamelessly reporting that the Dominicans overwhelmingly supported annexation (the result of the rigged plebiscite was 15,169 to 11), he concluded the treaty was "a rapid stride toward the greatness which the intelligence, industry, and enterprise of the citizens of the United States entitle this country to assume among nations."

Despite Grant's strenuous efforts, the treaty failed. In late June, the Senate voted 28–28, far short of the two-thirds majority needed to secure its approval. Instead, the Senate voted 32–9 to create a commission to investigate the situation. When it met, Sumner went on the attack. In December 1870, he made his famous, "Naboth's Vineyard" speech, in which he compared Grant to King Ahab of the Old Testament, who had coveted his neighbor's vineyard and stolen it. Sumner denounced the pact in "the name of Humanity insulted, in the name of the weak trodden down, in the name of Peace imperilled, and in the name of the African race, whose first effort at Independence is rudely assailed." He urged Americans to respect their duty, which was as "plain [as] is the Ten Commandments. Kindness, beneficence, assistance, aid, help, protection, all that is implied in good neighborhood—these we must give, freely, bountifully, but their independence is as precious to them as is ours to us, and it is placed under the safeguard of natural laws which we cannot violate with impunity."

In early 1871, the commission supported annexation, but by this time many of its backers had lost steam. Renewed attempts to push the treaty failed, creating bitterness. President Grant even considered challenging Sumner to a duel. When he walked through Lafayette Park, the president shook his fist at Sumner's house and exclaimed, "that man who lives up there has abused me in a way which I never suffered from any other man living." The president had some measure of revenge, as Sumner lost his SFRC chair in March 1871.

But this failure derailed future annexation efforts. "Buried with the Dominican annexation treaty was the process of expansion through absorption," political scientist Lars Schoultz observes. "Since that moment in 1870, a consensus has existed in the United States that it is inadvisable to expand the nation's boundaries if it entails the addition of Latin Americans to the Union." "The single exception, Puerto Rico, was just that—an exception," he adds, "and one that virtually everyone in Washington still hopes will never be repeated."

The Industrial Revolution: Hits and Misses

President Grant's successors in the White House through Theodore Roosevelt were an unspectacular group of men who sought to accomplish little and, for the most part, succeeded. During this time, most Americans focused on domestic issues, including the final stages of westward expansion and the massive industrialization sweeping the United States during the 1870s and 1880s. The gold standard, tariffs, and veteran's benefits dominated politics, not foreign relations. At one point, Congress even considered dismantling the Foreign Service. The army, aside from a small Indian fighting force, fell into disrepair, while naval forces sat idle in shipyards. In this period, big business executives, bankers, and investors became the primary movers and shakers in American society.

This trend transferred to Latin America, where American businesspersons sought markets and investment opportunities. "After 1880, the United States would substitute for its earlier strategy of physical conquest one of economic domination through expanded trade and investment," one historian observes. Washington aided the process. Secretary of State James G. Blaine highlighted the change in attitudes when he stated the United States wanted "annexation of trade" rather than territory.

As Americans focused on economic growth, Latin American economies also expanded. Liberal economic ideology held sway, and its proponents advanced growth through foreign investment and free-market principles. Such policies prompted little industrialization. Leaders believed in Adam Smith's idea of "comparative advantage," which argued the producers of raw materials and finished goods benefited in a balanced manner. Therefore, most Latin Americans increased production of agro-export materials such as sugar, coffee, henequen (marijuana—at the time used in the manufacture of heavy-duty rope), and minerals and avoided investing in industrial development.

Unfortunately, Smith's theory was imprecise, and a trade imbalance rose, one in which those producing the finished goods raised costs while manipulating the prices of agricultural goods in commodity centers in New York, London, and Paris. The already asymmetrical economic relationship between the United States and Latin American nations would increase markedly in the second half of the nineteenth century.

"I've Been Working on the Railroad"

Several industries sparked the interest of American big business in Latin America, perhaps the most important of which was railroads. American capital, engineering, and experience in railroad building in the American West had prepared American developers for Latin American challenges. The relative lack of experience among Latin Americans caused their governments to turn to foreigners to build their infrastructures, so Americans and Europeans swept into the region throughout the late nineteenth century.

The place where Americans made the most significant inroads was Mexico. That country's shared border with the United States and the historical relationship between northern Mexicans and southwestern Americans made international ties stronger. The process accelerated when Porfirio Díaz took power in Mexico in the late 1870s. The Zapotec Indian had risen to fame during the war against the French, seized control of the government in 1876, and established a dictatorship that lasted more than three decades. He attracted foreign investors by expanding the power of the central government, thereby ensuring stability and order and guaranteeing optimal investment conditions.

The push-and-pull factors for America were strong. American travelers to Mexico reported rich opportunities there, and the U.S. government published pamphlets that called Mexico "a land upon which nature has lavished her bounty . . . with all that can minister to human want or luxury," and containing "everything requisite to make a rich country . . . [except] a good government and an intelligent and energetic people." Once Díaz ensured order, the pull increased. One newspaper editor wrote of Mexico in 1885 that "the feudal and spiritual lords have been shorn of their excessive powers . . . a stable and just government has been founded." By the turn of the century, many Americans agreed with Theodore Roosevelt's assessment that Díaz was "the greatest statesman now living."

Between 1867 and 1910, American investors poured more than $644 million into building railroads in Mexico. By the mid-1880s, U.S. entrepreneurs completed the Mexican Central Railroad, extending from Mexico City to El Paso, Texas, as well as the Mexican National, from the capital to Laredo, Texas. Along the way, branch lines of both railroads stretched into the rich mining and agricultural areas. Americans wanted the Mexican raw materials to flow northward and finished U.S. goods from the United States to flow south. By the onset of the Mexican revolution in 1910, more than 24,000 miles of railroads had been laid in Mexico, twenty-four times the railroad mileage in 1880.

The influx of Americans to construct railroads had a significant impact on land distribution in Mexico. The Díaz government followed Washington's model and financed railroad construction by awarding lands bordering the tracks to the backers of the ventures. Consequently, by 1910, Americans owned more than 22 percent of Mexico's lands. These included at least one hundred properties ranging between 100,000 and 500,000 acres. The publishing magnate William Randolph Hearst owned more than 7 million acres. When combined with rapid concentration of landholding among Mexican elites, the land available to most Mexicans shrank dramatically.

The results of land concentration significantly affected Mexican demographics. While villages communally held 40 percent of Mexico's lands in 1810, by 1910 that percentage had plummeted to 5 percent. In this time, 90 percent of Mexicans became landless, forced into debt peonage, the mines, or menial labor. Furthermore, Americans focused on agriculture and cattle for export. This meant a reduction in the production of basic Mexican foodstuffs, principally corn, and Mexico increasingly had to import more costly foreign goods, both finished goods and foodstuffs. In short, the Mexican poor lost more ground and fell further into debt.

Many Mexicans recognized the significance of the railroads and land concentration. In a commonly practiced ritual, Mexican peasants attached a Judas effigy to the headlights of locomotives. At some point, the people exploded it. According to historian Dirk Raat, the "Judas image, representing the people, was destroyed by the engine. This rite symbolized the rapacious technology of the railroad, a technology that consumed both the peasant and the corn." Ultimately, this discontent exploded into full-scale fighting in 1910, as peasants joined the first social revolution of the twentieth century.

Buried Treasures

Americans also focused heavily on mining enterprises in Latin America. Many went to Colombia and Chile, but most American capitalists concentrated on Mexico. In 1884, one observer wrote: "Mexico . . . is one magnificent but undeveloped mine—our India in commercial importance—our Cuba and Brazil in tropical products—our complement in general characteristics, resources, supply, and demand." Díaz facilitated growth by passing new laws in the 1880s that made production in Mexico less expensive. One American noted that "the mining laws of Mexico are far more advantageous to the operator than our own laws. The government protects you and requires nothing from you but the amount of your tax."

The Díaz government also ensured optimal labor conditions for mine owners. In the mines, Mexican laborers often worked fourteen hours a day in terrible conditions. They lacked proper housing and received low wages. Mexican officials, mostly from elite families, showed little concern for the miners' plight. Americans found the lack of restrictions and absence of pesky union organizers a definite draw. One callously remarked that it was cheaper to maintain a Mexican laborer than a good New England farm horse.

Americans poured into Mexico to exploit its rich deposits of silver, copper, and iron. Most settled in the northern states, closer to transportation centers and U.S. operations. One of the most successful mining magnates was William C. Greene. A New Yorker, he had moved west as a young man and became a rancher, winning the nickname "Colonel Greene" for his exploits in the Indian wars. One writer characterized him as a man with a "native talent for bluff" who built his empire "on glib promises, publicity, and devious bookkeeping." Greene arrived in the Arizona Territory in the 1880s and ultimately learned of potential wealth in northern Mexico near Cananea, only a short distance from the U.S. border.

Greene skillfully raised money for his endeavors. By the late 1890s, he established a prosperous mining enterprise at Cananea. He built smelters for copper and other minerals. Timing proved everything, as the expansion of electricity ensured a demand for copper for electrical wire. Money from investors and profits flowed into Greene's coffers. At its height, the Cananea mine produced 4,000 tons of ore a day and employed more than 5,500 persons. Greene's company built five office buildings, a clubhouse, a hospital, two sawmills, and a brickyard. Greene also began a ranching and lumber business and helped build branches from his enterprises to American rail lines to facilitate distribution of his products to U.S. markets.

By 1908, however, Greene's empire had dissolved. For many years, business competitors eyed his operation enviously. Mexican workers helped administer a coup de grâce to Greene. Union organizers arrived and questioned the pay disparity between American and Mexican workers and the lack of Mexican managers. In June 1906, Mexican workers walked off their jobs, demanding higher pay and an eight-hour workday. After Greene refused, a clash occurred when an American manager fired on a crowd, murdering several strikers. The mob retaliated, killing him. Now Greene requested assistance from American and Mexican officials. Díaz allowed Arizona Rangers to cross the border and help suppress the strike. Within a couple of weeks, the mine was fully operational. Nonetheless, the strike ruined Greene's reputation, allowing competitors to sweep in and take control. He died a few years later in an accident, an impoverished, broken man.

In addition to Greene, many other Americans established profitable enterprises in Mexico. Daniel Guggenheim developed a very successful mining company in Monterrey. His company, the American Smelting and Refining Company (ASRCO), became the largest privately owned business in the entire country by 1910. Others, including Edward L. Doheny, began exploiting vast deposits of petroleum. In 1907, Doheny founded the Huasteca Petroleum Company. By 1916, his wells earned $1 million per week. Ten years later, his company extracted 560 million barrels of oil, outstripping railroads as the largest U.S. investment in Mexico.

The activities of the mining and drilling interests were significant. Thriving industries controlled by Americans sprung up throughout Mexico. While ensuring new jobs and taxes, the complete dominance of the industries created hostility toward the foreign monopoly that enriched primarily a small group of indigenous capitalists such as Luis Terrazas, Enrique Creel, and Ramón Corral. The pay disparities and the inhumane treatment of the workers exacerbated tensions. Mexican nationalists began to call for the country's resources to benefit Mexicans rather than the wealthy foreign industrialists and stockholders. The problems exploded after 1910 with the Mexican Revolution, and the issue of subsoil rights and American control of Mexican lands would remain a volatile issue for many years.

Another significant result was the further extension of the fused society of northern Mexico and the Southwestern United States. Internal and foreign immigration to the sparsely populated area fueled growth. Higher wages, promises of land, and an end of the Indian "troubles" made the area especially attractive. While predominantly rural, significant development took place in Monterrey, El Paso, Laredo, Tampico, and numerous other border communities.

What resulted was a coalescing of the two countries. Extending three hundred miles on each side of the border, the border societies became even more interdependent. The people shared similarities in landscape, climate, economy, and culture. These changes accelerated existing conditions that had been in place for many years because of the long Hispanic presence in the southwestern United States. These peoples had more in common with one another than with their fellow U.S. citizens in far-off places such as Maine or Chiapas. Thus, the ongoing process of creating what some have referred to as "Mexamerica" hastened significantly in the period.

The Golden Fruit

Beyond Mexico, American entrepreneurs spread throughout Latin America in search of investment opportunities, markets, and raw materials. In Central America, great changes occurred between 1870 and 1900. While the search for a good canal site had initiated American interest in the area, Central America was emerging as a hot spot for economic opportunities. Perhaps the most significant long-term event was the signing of a contract between the Costa Ricans and Henry Meiggs to build a railroad from Puerto Limón to San José, the nation's capital. The government set aside land in the comparatively unpopulated Atlantic coastal lowlands and provided money to Meiggs, who had built railroads in Chile and Peru. Soon, he turned over the contract and operations to his nephew, Minor C. Keith.

Keith began his task in the early 1870s by importing thousands of Jamaican laborers to work in the tropical areas. Disease, difficult terrain, and a lack of funds hindered the operation. To offset his company's fiscal shortfall, he began planting bananas and organized the United Fruit Company (UFCO) to transport and market the fruit. By 1883, exports totaled 100,000 stems. Within seven years, that number reached 1 million. Suddenly, bananas had become a major crop in Costa Rica and competed with coffee as the major industry.

Keith became even more prominent in Costa Rican social, political, and economic affairs after he negotiated a contract with the Costa Rican government that committed UFCO to finishing the railroad and absorbing the existing debt. In return, he received 800,000 acres of land and a 99-year lease on the railroad. Additional negotiations placed a banana export tax of one cent per stem, a low rate that continued until the 1930s. From Costa Rica, UFCO extended its operations into other nations, including Guatemala and Honduras, creating what many critics called "the Octopus."

The banana industry brought more U.S. influence into Central America, the banana-growing region becoming an enclave where most natives rarely invested or traveled. U.S. managers dominated the area, buying and transporting goods and only occasionally interacting with the nation's central economy. U.S. companies paid limited taxes and nominally observed local labor laws, yet for the most part the enclave functioned without much interference. A new influx of U.S. businesspersons, missionaries, and adventurers followed. Cultural, political, and economic exchanges flourished, and U.S. citizens became some of the most influential foreigners in the Central America region.

A New Look?

As American capital flowed southward, Washington increasingly focused on promoting stability in Latin America rather than on territorial expansion. Saturation of domestic markets created gluts that caused depressions in the United States throughout the 1870s and 1880s. To offset this problem, Americans sought new outlets for their finished goods. Senator John

Miller of California told his colleagues, "new markets are necessary to be found in order to keep our factories running." To him, Latin America was a logical choice. "Here lies to the south of us our India," he added, "and if we have the nerve, and the foresight, and the sagacity to utilize it by proper methods we shall have new markets for our products and for our manufactures which will keep every loom, and every anvil, and every manfactory of this country in motion."

U.S. leaders began concentrating on how to assist private American investors and businesspersons in the region. The chief architect of early attempts to create optimal market conditions was Secretary of State James G. Blaine. The New York Republican worried about an imbalance of payments between the United States and Latin America and economic competition with the Europeans. According to historian Thomas Bailey, "Blaine's aim was to elbow aside foreign competitors by forming closer commercial ties south of the border. And since economic relationships could not flourish amid whistling bullets, Washington would use its good offices to terminate wars in Latin America."

Blaine carried cultural baggage into his efforts. He once remarked that the Latin Americans "are of hot temper, quick to take affront, ready to avenge a wrong whether real or fancied." About the stereotypical Latin American penchant for violence, he wrote that outbreaks "are not only frequent but are sanguinary and sometimes cruel," requiring "external pressure to keep them from war, when at war they require external pressure to bring them to peace." He believed Americans could present a positive "moral influence upon the Spanish-American people" to raise "the standard of their civilization."

Blaine stumbled during his first stint as secretary of state under President James Garfield. In November 1881, Blaine invited representatives from the Latin American republics (except Haiti) to Washington to discuss commercial relations and peace in the hemisphere. The impetus for the gathering was the ongoing War of the Pacific, which pitted Chile against Bolivia and Peru over the control of ore-rich lands. Blaine tried to intercede but met strong resistance from the Chileans, who held the upper hand in the conflict. Furthermore, U.S. representatives in each capital had sided with their respective governments, causing dissension. Blaine's efforts were for naught. When an assassin murdered Garfield in 1882, Blaine soon found himself temporarily out of a job in the new administration of Chester Arthur (1882–85).

The Pan-American Idea Matures

Despite Blaine's absence, his plans lived on. In 1888, Congress authorized President Grover Cleveland (1885–89, 1893–97) to call an Inter-American Conference. The invitation asked the conferees to consider "measures that shall tend to preserve and promote the prosperity of the several American states." It detailed seven other points, including the creation of a uniform system of customs regulations, plans for arbitration of differences, and "other subjects relating to the welfare of the several states represented."

Soon thereafter, the new president, Benjamin Harrison (1889–93), and his secretary of state, James Blaine, hosted the delegates of seventeen countries in October 1889. Blaine gave a rousing opening speech in which he outlined his hopes for the customs union and machinery for the arbitration of disputes. Then, the U.S. government packed the delegates onto trains for a whirlwind tour of forty-one American industrial centers. Presumably, the Americans wanted to impress the Latin Americans and persuade them to align with the United States rather than the Europeans. The gesture failed in some respects. Roque Sáenz Peña, future president of Argentina, complained that it appeared Blaine "wished to make Latin America a market, and the sovereign states tributaries."

The conference reconvened on November 18, 1889. Blaine presided over the meetings, which included discussion of reduced tariffs, the arbitration of disputes, and the construction of a Pan American railroad. Remembering past U.S. transgressions, the Latin Americans suspiciously questioned American motives. The customs union idea died for a fear of loss of sovereignty to the Americans. For similar reasons, the delegates killed the proposal to create a regional organization to arbitrate disputes.

The only major accomplishment of the conference was the establishment of the Commercial Bureau of the American Republic (forerunner of the Pan American Union) to collect and distribute economic and technical information. Other indirect results were the negotiation of several treaties of reciprocity. Interestingly enough, during debates on these treaties, Senator Eugene Hale of Maine proposed that Washington consider creating a common zone for the free trade of raw materials with the Latin Americans and the Canadians (which would have preceded NAFTA by more than a century), but it gained little support. Still, the Washington Conference established a precedent that eventually implemented many of the ideas of Blaine and others regarding the hemisphere.

The Rise of the Men in Gold Braids

Corresponding to Blaine's efforts was the rise of an aggressive new generation of U.S. military and political leaders. Many of these men were naval
officers who had languished in isolated posts with little opportunity for
career advancement in peacetime. One of the earliest to emerge was Commodore Robert Shufeldt, who wrote in 1878, "our merchant marine and
our Navy are joint apostles" in the struggle for markets and economic vitality. "At least one-third of our mechanical and agricultural products are now
in excess of our own wants," he added, "and we must export these products
or deport the people who are creating them." To win foreign markets, he
contended that "the man-of-war precedes the merchantman and impresses
rude people with the sense of the power of the flag." His ideas had some
effect. Two years later, Secretary of State William Evarts argued vigorously
that U.S. warships make frequent port calls in Latin America and Asia,
asserting that "the National flag must be carried to such coasts before the
merchant flag can be safely or profitably exhibited."

During the 1880s, an even more vocal group of officers espoused their
views, one of the most important of which was Captain Alfred Thayer
Mahan. An experienced naval officer and lecturer at the Naval War College, Mahan elucidated his ideas through his lectures, articles and essays,
ultimately complied into a book, *The Influence of Sea Power upon History*
(1890). His work helped shape a whole generation of American leaders.
Using historical examples, he stressed that a nation's greatness depended
on its ability to defend its access to raw materials and markets in peacetime
and the ability to take the battle to the enemy during war. The country needed a modern navy and strategic bases throughout the world to
provide commercial opportunities for American entrepreneurs along with
their protection. Finally, Mahan warned that the United States could not
continue to lag behind the Europeans, especially the rising states of Germany and Italy, in the race for prestige and power. His words found many
adherents, including Theodore Roosevelt.

Mahan and others succeeded in persuading a very stingy Congress of
the rightness of their view. In 1883, Congress funded the construction of
new ships, including modern steel-hulled, steam powered cruisers. By
the early 1890s, more than thirty new ships had been launched, including
armor-plated battleships. While still trailing the major sea powers, the
United States had dramatically closed the gap.

Not everyone agreed with Mahan and other proponents of expansion. Senator Carl Schurz warned his countrymen against the power of the "officers of the navy and others taking special pride in the development of our naval force, many of whom advocated a large increase in our war-fleet to support a vigorous foreign policy, and a vigorous foreign policy to give congenial occupation and to secure further increase to our war-fleet." He concluded, "these forces we find bent upon exciting the ambition of the American people whenever a chance for the acquisition of foreign territory heaves in sight." He correctly appraised that the U.S. Navy and its allies had laid the groundwork for justifying their existence in terms of war and conquest.

Flexing Newfound Muscles

As the Pan American conference ended, the United States encountered several challenges in South America. In the 1880s, Brazil, Argentina, Colombia, and Chile compared favorably to the United States in military power and political influence. As Washington concentrated on the Europeans, the larger Latin American nations began exerting their influence on issues of trade, territorial expansion, and inter-American leadership. Consequently, several confrontations in the early 1890s served as proving grounds on which the United States flexed its muscles to acquire regional hegemony.

One of the major competitors for the United States on the Pacific coast of South America was Chile. Its refusal to allow Washington to arbitrate the War of the Pacific, according to one observer, allowed the Chileans to administer "to the United States a snub as complete and successful as was ever given by one state to another." In 1882, Congressman Thomas Browne of Indiana told his colleagues that "any one of [Chile's] three ironclads can sink every wooden vessel in our wretched navy, and the contrast between her ability and our impotence is a daily source of shame to every citizen in our country who resides or travels between Panama and Cape Horn." The differences became more acute in the mid-1880s, when the Chileans purchased a modern battleship, the *Esmeralda,* which the U.S. *Army and Navy Journal* soon warned "could destroy our entire Navy, ship by ship, and never be touched."

With its newfound strength, Chile challenged the United States several times after the War of the Pacific. When the United States occupied

Colón, Colombia, on the Isthmus of Panama in 1885, Santiago ordered the *Esmeralda* to help restore order. Secretly, it ordered its captain to use whatever means necessary to prevent American attempts to annex the province. When the United States eventually withdrew, the Chileans publicly bragged that they had forced the Americans to turn tail and run.

Three years later, the Chileans added insult to injury when they formally annexed the Easter Islands, which many countries claimed and used. "Chile's newfound sense of self," historian William Sater observes, "galled those Americans who saw their nation's destiny inextricably linked to the economic penetration of the Pacific Basin." "Perhaps inspired by the Chilean example, the United States built a large fleet," Sater continues, "consequently, the next time Santiago and Washington clashed, it would be the Chileans, not the Americans, who retreated."

Brawling Sailors, Riotous Mobs

A major diplomatic incident nearly exploded into war in late 1891. On October 16 of that year, 117 sailors of the USS *Baltimore* received shore leave in Valparaiso, Chile. Several bar brawls erupted, leading to the death of two, the wounding of seventeen, and the imprisonment of thirty-six American seamen. The *Baltimore's* captain, Admiral Winfield Scott Schley, convened a board of inquiry and blamed the Chileans for the fights, highlighting that the police also beat the Americans. In response, Washington demanded a Chilean apology and reparations for the injured sailors.

The Chileans refused and conducted their own probe of the incident. Meanwhile, the U.S. minister to Chile, Patrick Egan, withheld vital information from the investigation. The Irish-born, naturalized U.S. citizen viewed the Chilean government as pro-British. As the inquiry continued, tensions heightened. During the interim, the injudicious Chilean foreign minister Manuel Matta called President Harrison's statement about the incident "erroneous or deliberately incorrect." Chilean ships practiced mock torpedo attacks on the USS *Yorktown* in Valparaiso harbor, adding to the insult.

Tensions remained high through January 1892, when the Chileans released their report and blamed drunken American sailors for having precipitated the fights and ensuing riots, and commended the police for their professional behavior. While it gave three Chileans brief jail sentences, Santiago demanded that several American sailors stand trial. Matta sent the report to Washington with a mild expression of regret and referred to the whole incident as a simple saloon brawl.

President Harrison was livid and demanded that Matta repudiate the report and apologize. The crisis appeared defused when Luís Pereira replaced Matta. The new minister agreed to submit the dispute to arbitration by a third party and disavowed Matta's statements. In return, Washington agreed to recall Egan. Problems arose, however, when Pereira failed to secure official support because most of the Chilean government had left the capital to escape the summer heat. Impatient, Harrison fumed. "We must protect those who, in foreign ports, display the flag or wear the colors of this Government against insult, brutality, and death, inflicted in resentment of the acts of their Government, and not for any fault of their own," he told congressmen. He then asked permission to prepare to take action against the Chileans.

The matter escalated almost immediately. The U.S. Navy began stockpiling weapons and readying for battle. One person stressed that the Chileans were "a foe worthy of any maritime people." In the meantime, the Americans found several allies in Latin America, including the Peruvians and Bolivians, who wanted revenge for their earlier defeat. Buenos Aires also offered the use of bases from which to launch an overland attack. The Europeans remained neutral.

Without friends, the Chileans capitulated. Now they offered to pay reparations, a sum of $75,000. They disavowed Matta's response and withdrew their request for Egan's recall. Harrison reported this to Congress, and prominent members of the foreign affairs committee encouraged the president to accept the terms. He took their advice, the matter passed into arbitration, and both sides stood down.

The significance of the *Baltimore* affair was multilayered. It highlighted many issues on both sides. On one hand, according to Sater, "racial mythology may have clouded the Chilean authorities' judgment." He argues the Chileans believed that the Anglo-Saxons lacked a sense of pride, and that "only Latins would endure sacrifice before betraying their principles." Conversely, many Americans viewed the Chileans contemptuously. One writer emphasized that even the "whitest Chilian [sic] resembles the sallow Spaniard. . . . The Chilian [sic] of today is a sad amalgamation of Spanish, Indian, and negro blood, and combines the bad qualities of those three races." He went on to say that the United States "would not be pushed around by racially inferior and immature nations."

While most Americans soon forgot the incident, the *Baltimore* affair caused much ill will toward them in Chile. One Chilean politician stressed that the Americans "are very dangerous and it is necessary to treat them with formality and care. . . . My cheeks still burn when I remember the unfortunate *Baltimore* incident. For that reason, I believe the best policy toward them is to have the best possible relations, but always, with the strictest formality and maintaining possible cordiality." The event even seeped into Chile's political mythology, including the story of Lieutenant Carlos Peña. When a U.S. warship stopped his ship and demanded it lower its flag as an apology for the *Baltimore* incident, Peña complied but promptly committed suicide to atone for his action. The story became very popular with anti-American Chilean nationalists. For many Chileans and others, the event foreshadowed a more potent U.S. political and military presence in Latin America.

Down Rio Way

Soon thereafter, the United States responded to a crisis in Brazil. Generally, U.S. relations with Brazil had been good since the latter had declared independence from Portugal in 1822. Emperor Pedro and his successors had opened Brazil's harbors to U.S. ships and many political, economic, and cultural exchanges followed. While some problems arose over claims for damages incurred by the Brazilians during the American Civil War, as well as at the hands of U.S. citizens during a regional conflict in the Rio Plata during the 1860s, trade in Brazilian coffee and sugar to the United States flourished.

In the 1880s, the political environment in Brazil changed dramatically. The ineptitude of the Crown's handling of a war with Paraguay significantly undermined the monarchy's credibility. Disillusioned Brazilians, strongly influenced by the positivist ideas of Auguste Comte, began plotting against Emperor Dom Pedro II. The movement received additional support from plantation elites after Dom Pedro abolished slavery in 1888. In November 1889, young military officers delivered an ultimatum to Dom Pedro, calling for his resignation and the creation of a republic. The emperor gathered his belongings in short order, marched to the docks of Rio, and boarded a steamer for Europe, never to return.

Most people in the United States were happy to see the last remnants of the European-style monarchy disappear from the hemisphere. The

U.S. minister Robert Adams called the action "the most remarkable ever recorded in history." Two days after the coup, Adams reported: "In my opinion the Republican form of government is securely established even though the present ministry may fall. Our constitution and flag have been copied and looking to future relations I desire our country to be the first to acknowledge the Republic." Washington complied, recognizing the new regime in early 1890. Within a year, the United States and Brazil signed a treaty of reciprocity and relations moved along well.

Protecting the American Flag

Anderson also correctly predicted a challenge to the government. In September 1893, disgruntled naval officers led by Admiral Custódio de Melo seized warships in Rio harbor and demanded the resignation of President Floriano Peixoto. Other groups soon joined the conflict. A stalemate followed, as Peixoto controlled the shore batteries, and the naval commanders blockaded the port.

The United States immediately declared neutrality and refused to recognize the rebels' belligerency, preventing their purchase of supplies in the United States. The Peixoto government tried to win sympathy by spreading rumors that the British, hoping to restore the monarchy and abrogate the treaty of reciprocity with the United States, supported the rebels. Tensions remained high on all sides.

Major problems ensued when the United States demanded the right to continue trade. The State Department ordered U.S. warships to the area to protect merchant ships going into Rio harbor but not to "otherwise interfere with Mello's line of fire." Historian Joseph Smith comments that "the policy was legally correct although its practicable enforcement would tend to restrict Custódio's operations and consequently favored the established government."

The standoff dragged on for several months. The State Department encouraged the U.S. minister to Brazil, Thomas L. Thompson, to negotiate an acceptable way for the U.S. merchants to load and unload their cargoes. Problems resulted, however, when the rebels imposed a full blockade. Their action corresponded with the arrival of U.S. reinforcements commanded by Admiral Andrew Benham. The aggressive American immediately informed the rebel commander that any interference with American shipping would prompt his swift retaliation. Soon thereafter, U.S. warships exchanged fire with the rebels, which effectively destroyed the rebels' last hope of cutting off the Peixoto government. In appreciation, the Brazilian president declared a national holiday on July 4, 1894.

The U.S. response to the Naval Revolt was important. Throughout the standoff and its conclusion, the United States had acted unilaterally, without European consultation or consent. Secretary of the Navy Hilary Herbert proclaimed that the "universal approach" adopted by Benham would "have far-reaching and wholesome influence in quite a number of countries where revolutions are so frequent as to almost constantly imperil the rights of American citizens." As Smith notes, "whatever his exact intention Benham had effectively demonstrated how the growing military power of the United States could be used to assert American rights in Latin America."

While Peixoto praised the U.S. intervention, American actions created ill will toward the United States. Many Brazilian nationalists, even those aligned with Peixoto, criticized the heavy-handed activities. The British minister in Rio reported that the American activities had created "a very bad impression on shore" and that the Brazilians "dread the ascendancy of the United States which they think that power wishes to exercise over all American states." Given American actions in Rio and Chile, many Latin Americans began looking northward with increasing apprehension.

A Matter of Honor

The United States responded proactively in Chile and Brazil, but the most important challenge occurred in Venezuela, where it faced off against Great Britain. For many years, the Venezuelans and the British contested the boundary between Venezuela and British Guiana. In the 1840s, a British subject, Robert Schomburgk, had surveyed the region and established a boundary. The Venezuelans refused to recognize his findings and claimed nearly half of British Guiana, while the British claimed parts of Venezuela, including the mouth of the Orinoco River. When prospectors uncovered gold in the disputed area, including one nugget weighing more than 500 ounces, the issue became critical.

Since the 1870s, the Venezuelans had sought U.S. support on the boundary dispute, arguing that the British had violated the Monroe Doctrine. In 1887, they increased the pressure on Washington after Caracas suspended diplomatic relations with London. The Venezuelan government hired a lobbyist, former U.S. minister to Venezuela William L. Scruggs, to

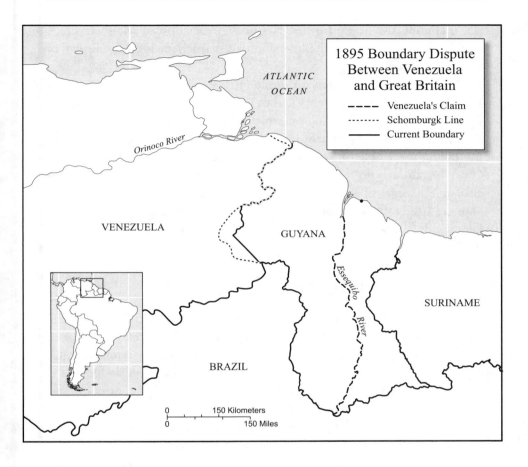

promote its claim. To raise consciousness, Scruggs published a pamphlet in 1895, "British Aggressions in Venezuela, or the Monroe Doctrine on Trial." The publication reached high-ranking U.S. officials, including the new secretary of state, Richard Olney. The Venezuelans also found a ready ally in President Grover Cleveland, well known for his sympathies toward underdogs.

Other reasons existed for the U.S. support of the Venezuelan claim. Washington feared that if the British succeeded in taking Venezuelan soil that it would set a precedent. U.S. policymakers had watched apprehensively as the Europeans carved up Asia and Africa, and London added fuel to the fire by temporarily seizing lands in Nicaragua. Finally, an economic depression of 1893 had reinforced the need to maintain access to foreign markets. U.S. merchants and businesspersons focused on Venezuela, including the newly formed National Association of Manufacturers, which selected Caracas as the first site for a permanent overseas display of U.S.-made products.

As the pressure mounted on President Cleveland, a young Massachusetts Republican senator, Henry Cabot Lodge, wrote in the *North American Review:* "If Great Britain is to be permitted to occupy the ports of Nicaragua and, still worse, take the territory of Venezuela, there is nothing to prevent her taking the whole of Venezuela or any other South American state. If Great Britain can do this with impunity, France and Germany will do it also. . . . The supremacy of the Monroe Doctrine should be established and at once—peaceably if we can, forcibly if we must." Another person advised Cleveland: "Turn this Venezuela question up or down, North, South, East or West, and it is a 'winner.'"

To the Brink with John Bull

In July 1895, Secretary of State Olney unleashed the opening salvo in the Venezuelan dispute, one called a "twenty-inch gun" salute by Cleveland. Without officially consulting Caracas beforehand, Olney issued a statement in which he accused the British of violating the Monroe Doctrine. "Today, the United States is practically sovereign on this continent, and its fiat is law upon the subjects to which it confines its interposition," he wrote. "Why?," he added, "because, in addition to all other grounds, its infinite resources combined with its isolated position render it master of the situation and practically invulnerable as against any or all other powers." He complained that London's refusal to negotiate deprived Venezuela "of her free agency and puts her under virtual duress." Finally, he warned that any British land grab was an "invasion and conquest of Venezuelan territory." Olney demanded that arbitration begin before the end of 1895.

The U.S. ambassador to Great Britain, Thomas Bayard, hand-delivered the message to Lord Salisbury, the British foreign minister and prime minister. Salisbury forwarded the document to the Foreign Office for study and recommendations. Finally, after months of delay, he refused to recognize the validity of the Monroe Doctrine and dismissed the call for arbitration. Some journalists characterized Salisbury's rebuff as having "civil indifference with just a touch of boredom" while others said it smacked of "the peremptory schoolmaster trying—with faded patience—to correct the dullards in Washington."

The British response demonstrated that they completely underestimated how seriously the Americans felt about the matter. Political scientist Lars Schoultz notes that "Britain in effect had flicked the chip off the Cleveland administration's shoulder, so now there could be no backing down." After reading the response President Cleveland was "mad clean through." To accept London's rebuff was tantamount to a loss of personal and national prestige, but to push toward war had its own dangers. After much haggling, the president and his advisors settled on a moderate course. On December 17, 1895, in a special message to Congress, Cleveland demanded that the British accept arbitration and asked Congress for money to create a commission to resurvey the boundary. With little debate, Congress approved the request.

American nationalists responded to Cleveland's actions with great fanfare. The Anglophobic Irish National Alliance pledged 100,000 volunteers in a potential war with England. In New York City, police commissioner Theodore Roosevelt declared: "Let the fight come if it must; I don't care whether our sea coast cities are bombarded or not. . . . Personally, I rather hope that the fight will come soon. The clamor of the peace faction has convinced me that this country needs a war." Some business executives lined up behind President Cleveland, hoping to spark the sputtering economy with massive defense expenditures. One senator from Nevada insisted the "war would be a good thing," even in defeat, because "it would rid the country of the English bank rule."

John Bull Blinks

With Americans clamoring for action, diplomats on both sides began to recognize the seriousness of the situation. London already faced grave difficulties with the Boers in South Africa and German intrigues in Asia and Africa. Ambassador Bayard also tried to temper Washington's messages. By mid-January, the British proposed a conference on the Monroe Doctrine and suggested submitting the boundary dispute to an international arbitral commission, although they attached significant conditions. The United States rejected it. Finally, Lord Salisbury acknowledged the U.S. right to intervene and establish the methods of arbitration. In addition, he recognized U.S. hegemony in the region, noting that two powers could not be "practically sovereign in this hemisphere."

With the British concession, the United States set down the ground rules for settling the dispute. It established an arbitration committee composed of two Americans, two British, and one other selected by a committee from the industrial powers, although eventually the Venezuelans had a say as long as their choice was not a Venezuelan. The treaty, which Washington forced upon Caracas, led Scruggs to complain that the U.S. sought to "bull-doze Venezuela." It exempted disputed areas that had been under the control of either party for more than fifty years, clearly aiding the British. In 1899, the arbitration committee handed down its findings, basically following the Schomburgk line, although the Venezuelans received some southern territory and control of the mouth of the Orinoco River.

The Orinoco dispute was important for several reasons. First, for the United States, it signaled a new confidence and willingness to challenge the Europeans in matters concerning the Western Hemisphere and declare that the "fiat of the United States was law." "It was an announcement that the United States intended to move upward on the hierarchy of nations, even if European powers thought the idea presumptuous," Schoultz observes. According to historian Thomas Paterson, the "Venezuelan crisis . . . marked a watershed in the history of American foreign relations." The United States had challenged the Europeans on the issue of the Monroe Doctrine and won. "It revealed a United States more sure of itself, more certain about the components of its 'policy' and willing to lecture others," he adds. It also ensured a new round of military spending as the United States built three new battleships in 1896 to serve in future crises.

The Latin American response was mixed. The United States had supported Venezuela's claims for arbitration. Yet it had acted arrogantly and unilaterally and failed to integrate effectively the Venezuelans into the process. For many Latin Americans, the Olney Doctrine, as represented in his message to the British, made it clear that the United States planned to expand its hegemony in the Western Hemisphere. "Venezuela was but the beginning, for the world was about to discover in Cuba and Panama what the Olney Doctrine meant," Schoultz underscores, "when it declared that the United States was practically sovereign on this continent."

"Cuba Libre"

During the Orinoco dispute, another storm brewed in Cuba. In 1895, José Martí and General Máximo Gómez rallied the Cubans. For many years, Martí and other Cubans in the United States promoted *"Cuba Libre"* (Free

Cuba). Through his writing and oratory, Martí pushed for an independence party to establish a democratic and egalitarian society. He called for racial justice and incorporated women into the movement. Criticizing privilege accumulated from birth, Martí clamored for an economy that distributed wealth and property more equally among all Cubans.

Martí had also developed very strong views about the United States while living there. While admiring many American ideals, he viewed negatively the racism and elitism of the American leaders of the period. As historian Louis Pérez observes, "Martí realized that North Americans represented the greatest threat to Cuban independence." To him, U.S. economic strength threatened Cuba's ability to reorient its economy after independence. Regarding North America, he noted, "here men do not learn to love one another, and neither do they love the soil where they were born, and where they toil tirelessly in brute struggle and exhausted by their efforts to exist. . . . Here the land has been badly distributed; and the unequal and monstrous production, and the inertia of monopolized land, leave the country without the safeguard of shared harvests, which feed a nation even if they do not make profit from it. The North is closing itself off and is full of hatred. We must start leaving the North."

Martí's views became rallying points for Cubans. The banner of independence and the creation of his ideal state won support among many Cubans. In 1895, they rose in armed rebellion, initiating a guerrilla war against the Spanish government. Still, many divisions existed within the rebel forces, most of whom focused on winning independence, not the complicated tasks of state building. While wary of the United States, most of the guerillas gladly accepted U.S. assistance in obtaining their primary goal of independence.

Slow to Act

For their part, most Americans enthusiastically supported the Cubans in their quest for independence. "Cuba Libre" groups sprouted throughout the United States, and material support began to flow to the Cuban rebels. U.S. attention heightened as the fighting escalated, catching American investors and businesspersons between the warring factions. Additional problems evolved when the Spanish commander, General Valeriano Weyler, started herding Cuban civilians into concentration camps. Tens of thousands of

Cubans died in the camps from disease, and Weyler's forces killed many more persons in the countryside.

The Cleveland administration watched the alarming events in Cuba but reacted to them only cautiously. Secretary of State Olney urged Madrid to accept mediation in the dispute, but it resisted. In the United States, public support for the Cubans mounted, sparked partly by sensationalist reports of Spanish atrocities on the island. William Randolph Hearst of the *New York Journal* and Joseph Pulitzer of the *New York World* practiced "yellow journalism," which one historian describes as a "lurid style, reckless liberties with the truth, imaginative illustrations, screeching headlines, and other devices" to try to outsell the other. One example from May 1896 highlights press coverage in which a correspondent in Cuba tells of "blood on the roadsides, blood in the fields, blood on the doorsteps, blood, blood, blood! The old, the young, the weak, the crippled—all butchered without mercy. . . . Is there no nation wise enough, brave enough, and strong enough to restore peace in this bloodsmitten land?"

If Cleveland moved slowly, Congress pushed hard. As the presidential election neared, Republicans blasted Cleveland's vacillation. Early in 1896, Congress formally recognized the Cubans' belligerence, ensuring several advantages. Congressional action, when combined with public pressure, prodded Cleveland to inform Madrid that U.S. intervention was inevitable if it failed to stop the "senseless slaughter." He called for "home rule," and warned that Washington had exercised restraint, but might soon abandon its "expectant attitude."

The Road to War

Within three months, Republican William McKinley (1897–1901) replaced Cleveland in the White House. The Civil War veteran moved slowly, his demeanor partly shaped by his experiences in the bloody conflict. McKinley's cabinet, however, comprised young men with no such memories. One of the most vocal of these "war hawks" was Assistant Secretary of the Navy Theodore Roosevelt, who once allegedly remarked that McKinley had "no more backbone than a chocolate éclair." Despite such a characterization, one historian believes the president was a "manager of diplomacy, who wanted expansion and empire without war and a settlement of the Cuban question without U.S. military intervention." McKinley told Congress in December 1897 that the United States must avoid intervention in Cuba if the Spanish followed "honorable paths" toward reform. He rejected a proposed annexation of Cuba as "criminal aggression," but stressed Washington would keep open its policy options.

The new president inherited a rapidly changing situation in Cuba, as Madrid initiated significant reforms. Tired of war in Cuba and the Philippines, the Spanish granted the Cubans some autonomy, recalled Weyler, dramatically altered the concentration-camp policy, and made concessions to American businesspersons on the island. Still, Cubans uniformly rejected these concessions and clamored for the Spanish to withdraw. General Gómez pledged that "it is the firm resolution of the army and people of Cuba who have shed so much blood in order to conquer their independence, not to falter in their just cause until triumph or death crowns their efforts." Loyalist Cubans likewise condemned the concessions. Riots erupted in Havana in January 1898, as Cubans crowded the streets to yell "Death to Autonomy" and "Viva Weyler!"

The Cuban rejection of Madrid's compromises marked a turning point. In January 1898, in the face of continuing loyalist riots, the McKinley administration sent the USS *Maine* to Havana to protect American citizens there. U.S. officials stressed their willingness to apply proactive policies to reach a satisfactory conclusion. Spanish officials protested, and some Americans recognized the potential powder keg. Mark Hanna, McKinley's chief political advisor, remarked it was like "waving a match in an oil well for fun."

With the *Maine* anchored in Havana harbor, tensions heightened in February. Enrique Dupuy de Lôme, the Spanish minister to Washington, injudiciously sent a letter to a friend touring Cuba. A rebel sympathizer intercepted the correspondence and turned it over to the *New York Journal.* Under a headline, "Worst Insult to the United States in Its History," Hearst published the letter, which called McKinley "weak . . . a bidder for the admiration of the crowd . . . a would-be politician." The letter inflamed American passions against the Spanish. Even those who personally agreed with the assessment denounced the Spaniard for insulting the American people. Soon thereafter, de Lôme resigned and left Washington. His departure, however, failed to assuage American anger.

Less than a week later, a much more serious incident occurred. On the night of February 15, an explosion rocked the *Maine.* The ship sank quickly, sealing the fate of the 260 American sailors aboard. McKinley immediately ordered a naval investigation, although most Americans pointed the finger at the Spanish. Many called for revenge, including Roosevelt, who wrote:

"personally I cannot understand how the bulk of our people can tolerate the hideous infamy that has attended the last two years of Spanish rule in Cuba; and still more how they can tolerate the treacherous destruction of the *Maine* and the murder of our men! I feel so deeply that it is with very great difficulty I can restrain myself." McKinley remained publicly silent, but he approached leaders of the House Committee on Appropriations and asked for legislation allocating $50 million for arms. Within a short time, Congress approved the request.

By mid-March, American war fever was running high. The naval commission blamed the explosion that had sunk the *Maine* on an external mine of unknown origins. U.S. officials largely ignored claims by Spanish investigators that an *internal* explosion had sunk the ship.[1] With the general public clamoring for retribution, McKinley sent Madrid an ultimatum. He demanded an armistice in Cuba by October 1, the immediate end of the concentration-camp policy, and U.S. arbitration of the dispute should the parties reach an impasse. Implicit was a demand for Cuban independence and U.S. supervision of the new nation. The Spanish made some further concessions, but refused to consider mediation and independence for Cuba.

By March 1898, the Cubans were near victory in the conflict. Madrid's concessions demonstrated it desperately wanted an exit strategy, leading General Gómez to observe in January that "the enemy is crushed and is in complete retreat from here, and the time which favored their operations passes without them doing anything." As the Americans debated intervention, he wrote from his base in central Cuba, "the enemy has departed, ceasing military operations and abandoning garrisons and forts which constituted his base of operations. Days, weeks and months pass without a column of troops appearing within our radius of action."

Many have argued that if this had indeed been the case, why did Washington directly intervene the following month? Pérez responds that "only the possibility of the transfer of Cuba to a potentially hostile foreign country seemed to trouble the United States more than the prospect of Cuban independence. Cuba was far too important to be turned over to the Cubans. Free Cuba raised the specter of political disorder, social upheaval, and racial conflict: Cuba as the source of regional instability and an inevitable source

---

1 In 1976, U.S. Admiral Hyman Rickover published a study that concluded that an internal boiler explosion had indeed caused the ship to sink.

of international tension." American's belief in their own racial and cultural superiority and their fear of disorder blinded them to their own rhetoric of self-determination and democracy. Some Americans believed that Washington needed to act before the Spanish surrendered.

A Splendid Little War

The Spanish refusal to meet McKinley's demands ended diplomatic efforts. Rebuffed, the president went before Congress on April 11, 1898, and delivered a message that outlined why the United States should intervene in Cuba. "In the name of humanity, in the name of civilization, in behalf of endangered American interests which give us the right and the duty to speak and to act, the war in Cuba must stop," he told the body. He then asked for powers to "secure a full and final termination of hostilities."

For eight days, Congress debated McKinley's request. Finally, on April 19, it passed a four-part resolution serving as a declaration of war. The points included Cuba's independence, Spain's complete withdrawal, and presidential power to achieve the goals. The fourth section, the Teller Amendment, was the most controversial. "The United States hereby disclaims any disposition or intention to exercise sovereignty, jurisdiction, or control over said island [Cuba] except for the pacification thereof, and asserts its determination when that is accomplished to leave the government and control of the island to its people," it emphasized. The debates over the Teller Amendment related strongly to why the United States fought the war. Many opposed it, including Olney, who feared Cuban self-rule. Others idealistically rejected charges that the war was an imperialist impulse. No matter, the many different sides finally agreed. By April 25, McKinley signed the declaration of war against Spain.

Dubbed "a splendid little war" by future Secretary of State John Hay, the Spanish-American-Cuban War went well for the United States. American volunteers including Theodore Roosevelt sailed to Cuba. As one observer commented a few years later, "for youth the Spanish-American War was a great adventure; for the nation it was a diversion sanctioned by a high purpose." While logistical problems slowed the American army momentarily, the Cubans kept the Spanish busy, and the U.S. Navy blockaded the island. Meantime, in the Far East, U.S. warships and marines helped capture the Philippines and Guam, cementing major bases for trade in Asia.

In Cuba, the war on land ended quickly. In late June, the Americans landed near Santiago. By mid-July, U.S. troops and Cuban irregulars had captured the city—this after Theodore Roosevelt and his "Rough Riders" had won fame for their combat bravado in their "charge up San Juan Hill." (Actually, it was Kettle Hill but, evidently, no one liked that ring of that.) At sea, the U.S. Navy destroyed the Spanish fleet as it tried to flee the area. U.S. troops also took Puerto Rico, losing only three men in that campaign. By August 12, the warring parties agreed to an armistice.

Problems immediately arose between Americans and Cubans. The U.S. Army commander in Santiago, William Shafter, prevented Cubans from entering the city. "The trouble with General Garcia was that he expected to be placed in command at this place; in other words, that we would turn the city over to him. I explained to him fully that we were at war with Spain and that the question of Cuban independence could not be considered by me," Shafter complained. In September, he finally allowed the Cuban army a victory march but immediately ushered them back to the countryside. Similar events took place all over the island, as American troops settled in to begin a military occupation.

In the meantime, Spanish and U.S. diplomats went to the bargaining table in Paris, although without Cuban or Filipino representatives. After six weeks, they signed a peace treaty. It called for the withdrawal of Spanish troops from Cuba and permitted U.S. occupation of the island. In addition, the treaty ceded Guam and Puerto Rico to the United States and Washington paid Spain $20 million for the Philippines. Immediately, the treaty set off a storm of debate, as some Americans criticized the attempts to assimilate foreign peoples forcibly. Despite such opposition, the treaty passed and the war officially ended.

Managing Empire

The fate of Cuba remained in limbo for several years. McKinley moved slowly toward self-rule for the nation, arguing against a "hasty experiment bearing within itself the elements of failure." At the same time, the president wanted to avoid a costly guerrilla war like the one currently raging against the U.S. occupation force in the Philippines, where more than 60,000 U.S. troops engaged the forces of the nationalist leader Emilio Aguinaldo. McKinley sought a middle ground in Cuba, a policy that respected the Teller Amendment but simultaneously ensured order in the new republic.

U.S. public opinion reflected the new ambivalence over Cuban independence. Some Americans continued to call for annexation as the best hope for a stable society in Cuba. Others called for immediate self-rule. Most Americans landed somewhere between the extremes; they believed that the Cubans needed lessons in self-rule before taking over, and they agreed with Senator Orville Platt's (chair of the Senate Committee on Relations with Cuba) characterization that "in many respects [the Cubans] are like children." Another observer, Andrew Draper wrote in *The Rescue of Cuba* in 1899: "We have taken the responsibility of freeing them from Spain; we are equal to the responsibility of deciding whether they are capable of governing themselves. If they can maintain government as we understand the term . . . our specific obligations to them are at an end; if not, then we shall have to continue to regard ourselves as their guardians." Adding to the complexity was the fact that many Cuban elites, fearful of the masses and potential reforms, supported American control and actively collaborated with U.S. officials.

While President McKinley and Congress debated the fate of Cuba, General Leonard Wood ruled the island as military governor and worked

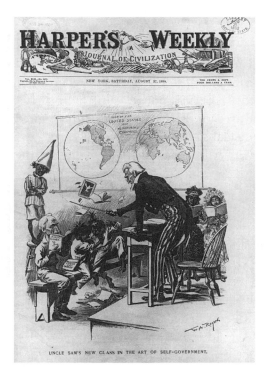

Cartoon showing schoolroom in which the teacher, Uncle Sam, hits two boys, "Cuban expatriot" and "guerrila," who are fighting. The caption reads "Uncle Sam's New Class in the Art of Self-Government." *Courtesy of Library of Congress, LC-USZ62-102382*

closely with Secretary of War Elihu Root to formulate policies. U.S. officials implemented some social reforms, primarily in education, health care, and public works. The U.S. Army formulated plans to create a new security force to maintain order after an American withdrawal. Finally, Wood prepared for the election of a constituent assembly to draft a constitution. In this area, certain American prejudices appeared. U.S. officials limited suffrage to males over the age of twenty-one who could read and write, had personal property valued at more than $250, or had served in the army before Santiago's fall. The restrictions prevented two-thirds of Cuba's males from voting, especially blacks and the poor. One U.S. official proudly boasted that "whites so greatly outnumber the blacks."

Many Cuban nationalists resented the U.S. intervention. "None of us thought that [the U.S. intervention] would be followed by a military occupation of the country by our allies," Máximo Gómez complained in 1899. He added that the Americans "treat us as a people incapable of acting for ourselves, and who have reduced us to obedience, to submission, and to a tutelage imposed by force of circumstances. This cannot be our ultimate fate."

Cuban nationalism and resistance left the United States searching for a satisfactory exit strategy. As Schoultz observes, "with continued occupation out of the question, the task facing Platt, Wood, Root, and like-minded U.S. officials was to devise a mechanism whereby the United States could grant formal independence but maintain control over people whom they considered unfit for self government." The U.S. officials ultimately settled on the Platt Amendment. Drafted in 1901, it effectively gave the United States control over an independent Cuba. It prohibited the Cuban government from entering treaties that "will impair or tend to impair the independence of Cuba," and denied the Cubans the right to accumulate public debt. Other articles provided for permanent U.S. military bases in Cuba and conceded Washington the right to intervene in Cuban affairs "for the preservation of Cuban independence, the maintenance of a government adequate for the protection of life, property, and individual liberty."

Wood had the task of forcing the Platt Amendment into the Cuban constitution, and widespread protests erupted when he announced his plan to do so. In 1900, in a pamphlet entitled "An Appeal to the American People on Behalf of Cuba," Salvador Cisneros Betancourt lamented that "[The Platt Amendment] if carried out, would inflict a grievous wrong on the people of Cuba, would rob them of that independence for which they have sacrificed so much blood and treasure." Nearly all Cubans denounced it, and the constituent assembly rejected it 24–2. Immediately, the Cubans sent a special delegation to Washington, but the Americans remained steadfast. The Cuban delegates returned home believing independence would never occur without the Platt Amendment. Reluctantly, the Cubans acquiesced on June 12, 1901. By May 1902, Wood sailed out of Havana harbor, ending the military occupation. Still, Senator Platt remarked: "The United States will always, under the so-called Platt Amendment, be in a position to straighten out things if they get seriously bad." For more than thirty years, the Platt Amendment would remain in force.

Calming the Savage Beast

The heavy-handedness of the United States in Cuba and other interventions in Latin American affairs caused a serious backlash against the United States, especially among Latin American intellectuals. Like Martí, many Latin Americans admired certain features of American culture, yet they increasingly viewed the United States more suspiciously and apprehensively. In a form of resistance, they began formulating and elucidating critiques of American ideas and popularizing the value of Latin American culture. The intellectuals would form a vanguard of nationalist resistance to U.S. imperialism in the twentieth century.

The writings of José Enrique Rodó shaped a generation of Latin American nationalists. A young Uruguayan, Rodó was well read and traveled. Strongly influenced by Comte, he believed positivism offered a model for Latin American development. He admired the United States for its emphasis on the "grandeur and power of work" that "placed in the hands of the mechanic in his shop and the farmer in his field the mythic club of Hercules." Other redeemable virtues included an emphasis on research, philanthropy, reverence for public education, and skills of improvisation. Yet despite such admiration, he believed that the United States was morally bankrupt in many areas.

In 1900, Rodó published *Ariel,* which underscored many of his views. In it, he borrowed characters from William Shakespeare's "The Tempest." For him, Caliban was the United States, a vulgar brute without polish or an understanding of beauty and morality. Rodó referred to the United States when he wrote: "I have disagreed with those who appointed themselves as watchdogs over the destiny of America and as custodians of its tranquility." The materialism and the inconsistency in the application of ideas by the United States toward its neighbors bothered Rodó. He warned that the "powerful federation is effecting a kind of moral conquest among us . . . and this is why the vision of an America de-Latinized of its will, without threat of conquest, and reconstituted in the image and likeness of the North, now looms in the nightmares of many who are genuinely concerned about our future."

Rodó urged Latin Americans to reject the materialism, elitism, and lack of spirituality of those in the United States. He addressed his work "to the youth of [Latin] America," and encouraged them to look to *Ariel* as symbolizing "the noble, soaring aspect of the human spirit. He represents the superiority of reason and feeling over the base impulses of irrationality." The Latin Americans should focus on the spiritual and issues of justice, morality, and Christian values, which he described as the "highest example of all." People should reject the paganism of the material world and stress "that sacred strength that you carry within you." Ultimately, by implication, Rodó empowered Latin Americans by arguing that the spiritual will calm the beast. "Can you envision it, this America we dream of?" he queried, "Hospitable to the world of the spirit, which is not limited to the throngs that flock to seek shelter in her. Pensive, without lessening her aptitude for action. Serene and firm, in spite of her generous enthusiasms. Resplendent, with the charm of incipient, calm purpose."

While few North Americans read Rodó's work until much later, many Latin American intellectuals knew of it and trumpeted its message. It became a model for Latin American nationalists to criticize the excess of the industrial revolution and the accompanying imperialism, while uplifting regional virtues and Latin America's own contributions to world culture. As others followed Rodó's example, anti-Americanism became an important feature in Latin American cultural circles, which in turn influenced whole generations of Latin American journalists, politicians, and educators.

Making the Dirt Fly

Soon after Rodó published *Ariel,* the United States underwent a significant change, when, in September 1901, an assassin's bullet struck down President McKinley. His successor was Theodore Roosevelt, who had joined the ticket in 1900, after his success charging Spanish fortifications in the Battle of Santiago. The outspoken Roosevelt came from a prominent New York family

Top: Steam shovels at the building of the Panama Canal. *Courtesy Library of Congress, LC-D4-73170*
Bottom: Teddy Roosevelt (center) and party visit the Panama Canal. *Courtesy National Archives, 188-G-22-2101*

and represented the new generation of Americans who believed in expanding the power of an industrialized United States to all corners of the world.

Roosevelt and his advisors focused quickly on finally building a trans-isthmian canal. The war with Spain had renewed interest in the project, as the U.S. Pacific Fleet was forced to travel all the way around South America's Cape Horn to reach Cuba. Roosevelt soon addressed a major obstacle to a canal, the Clayton-Bulwer Treaty. After tedious negotiations, Secretary of State John Hay and the British ambassador to Washington, Lord Pauncefote, signed an agreement in November 1901. It superseded the Clayton-Bulwer Treaty and permitted the United States to build and fortify a Central American canal, thus removing a major barrier to U.S. dominance of the route.

With the British out of the way, Roosevelt made construction of the canal a priority. Dubbed "The Accidency" by his critics, the president wanted to demonstrate that he was a man of action who would soon be "making the dirt fly" in Central America. Even as Roosevelt took office, a commission had recommended building the trans-isthmian canal across Nicaragua. Two principal reasons underlay this choice. First, the Nicaraguan site had the advantages of comprising the San Juan River and Lake Managua, both already navigable. Second, a French company headed by Ferdinand de Lesseps, builder of the Suez Canal, had won a concession from the Colombian government to construct a canal in Panama in the 1880s. While his New Panama Canal Company failed miserably, de Lesseps's successors had retained the concession and currently were asking the hefty sum of $109 million for it.

Working on the recommendation of the commission, in January 1902 the House of Representatives voted 308–2 to pursue the canal project in Nicaragua. Now, the French company in Panama, led by Philippe Bunau-Varilla, swung into action. It hired a high-powered American lobbyist, William Cromwell, who had personal access to Roosevelt and Hay. And it reduced the price of its concession to $40 million. Good luck also came the company's way. In May 1902, a major Nicaraguan volcano suddenly erupted. Thinking quickly, Bunau-Varilla found Nicaraguan stamps showing the volcano erupting and placed one of them on the desk of each senator. Cromwell and Bunau-Varilla succeeded, and in June 1902, Congress approved a measure that allowed Roosevelt to negotiate for the right of way in Panama. It also permitted him, "within a reasonable time and upon reasonable terms," to conclude an agreement with Nicaragua.

Secretary of State Hay immediately set about the task of dealing with Colombia, of which Panama was a territory. By January 1903, he and a Colombian diplomat, Tomás Herrán, signed an accord. The treaty granted the United States the right to build a canal zone six miles wide. In return, the United States promised Colombia a payment of $10 million and annual payments of $250,000 after nine years, with the lease on the zone renewable in perpetuity. Immediately, Bogotá expressed reservations and told Herrán to wait for new instructions. The U.S. Senate refused to delay and approved the treaty in March 1903.

Problems resulted when the Colombians balked at the original agreement. Desperate for funds, the Colombians asked the New Panama Canal Company for $10 million to facilitate the transfer of rights, and raised the original price to $15 million. The action angered Roosevelt who fumed, "those contemptible little creatures in Bogotá ought to understand how much they are jeopardizing things and imperiling their own future." "You could no more make an agreement with the Colombian rulers than you could nail currant jelly to the wall," he complained. The American press also branded the Colombians as "thieves" and "brigand Senators." The *New York Commercial Advertiser* asked: "What other world power has ever hesitated to use force under similar circumstances."

The Roosevelt administration reacted to the Colombians' delay by arguing they were honor bound to sign the treaty negotiated by their representative. As is often the case, bullying tactics ensured negative results. The Colombian Congress unanimously rejected the Hay-Herrán Treaty in August 1903.

"I Took the Isthmus"

With the 1904 election approaching, Roosevelt needed a diplomatic victory. Even before Colombia rejected the treaty, Cromwell and Bunau-Varilla began formulating plans for Panama's secession from Colombia and American ownership of the canal. Plotting from the New York Waldorf-Astoria Hotel during the summer 1903, the group planted newspaper stories of Panama's plan to rebel and grant the United States "the equivalent of absolute sovereignty over the Canal Zone." They also gathered money for bribes of Colombian officials and organized a small army.

Roosevelt and Hay carefully monitored the plans. During a meeting between the president and Bunau-Varilla on October 10, the Frenchman asked Roosevelt where he stood regarding a Panamanian revolt. While officially noncommittal, Roosevelt responded: "All I can say is that Colombia by her action has forfeited any claim upon the U.S. and I have no use for a government that would do what that government has done." Less than a week later, Hay informed Bunau-Varilla that an American flotilla had steamed for the isthmus. The Frenchman alerted his colleagues in Panama that the ships would reach Panama on November 2. That day, the USS *Nashville* anchored in Colón.

Heartened by the appearance of U.S. ships, the Panamanians launched their rebellion on November 3. By the end of the day, the rebels had formed a provisional government and unveiled a constitution, one written in New York. Some problems had developed earlier in the day, when 400 Colombian troops disembarked in Colón. The commander of the *Nashville* received a message ordering him to provide reinforcements, although miscommunication prevented any landing of troops. Still, the Panamanians reacted quickly. They separated the Colombian commander from his troops and offered him an $8,000 bribe. Soon thereafter, he ordered his troops to board a steamer and left the country. In one day, and with only one death, the new Republic of Panama was born.

Roosevelt and Hay immediately extended diplomatic recognition to an independent Panama. Within several days, Bunau-Varilla, (who received permission from the provisional government to represent Panama), began negotiations. By November 18, the two parties had signed the Hay–Bunau-Varilla Treaty, despite the fact that a new Panamanian group was on the way. It gave the United States a ten-mile strip of land and "the United States all the rights, power and authority within the zone . . . which the United States would possess and exercise as if it were the sovereign of the territory within which said lands and waters are located the entire exclusion of the exercise by the Republic of Panama of any such sovereign rights, power or authority." It also granted the United States the right "at all times and its discretion" to protect the canal. In return, the Panamanians received $10 million and an annual rent of $250,000, as well as a promise from Washington to maintain Panama's independence.

Rough Riding a Treaty

Controversy swirled around the treaty. The new Panamanian delegation opposed the liberal terms, but not too loudly. Several Americans reminded them that without U.S. assistance, Colombia would reconquer their fledgling republic. There was also significant dissent in the Senate among those still backing a Nicaraguan canal. Others believed the treaty established a quasi-colony in Latin America. Senator Edward Carmack of Tennessee voiced dissatisfaction, stating "there never was any real insurrection in Panama. To all intents and purposes there was but one man in that insurrection, and that man was the president of the United States."

Undeterred by the criticism, Roosevelt moved forward and sent the treaty to the Senate for ratification in early December. In a message to Congress, he denied any role in the rebellion. "No one connected with this Government had any part in preparing, inciting, or encouraging the late revolution on the Isthmus of Panama," he bellowed, "and that save from the report of our military and naval officers . . . no one connected with this Government had any previous knowledge of the revolution except such as was accessible to any person of ordinary intelligence who read the newspapers and kept up a current acquaintance with public affairs." He argued Colombian threats to Americans had sparked U.S. military actions. According to Roosevelt, "it was only the coolness and gallantry" of the small band of American sailors and marines that "prevented a murderous catastrophe."

Roosevelt's explanation clearly failed to correspond with the facts, a point noted by many people, including his advisors. In a cabinet meeting, Roosevelt asked: "Have I defended myself?" Elihu Root, who soon replaced Hay as secretary of state, responded: "You certainly have Mr. President. You have shown that you were accused of seduction and you have conclusively proved that you were guilty of rape." Others outside the administration expressed unbridled skepticism. Hearst emphasized that the "Panama foray is nefarious. Besides being a rough-riding assault upon another republic over the shattered wreckage of international law and diplomatic usage, it is a quite unexampled instance of foul play in American politics."

Despite the criticisms, Roosevelt pressed the Senate for ratification, urging it to follow the Panamanian Congress's example. After spirited debate, on February 23, 1904, the Senate voted 66–14 to accept it. Immediately, Washington purchased the assets of the New Panama Canal Company for $40 million, a significant share of which went to Bunau-Varilla. The Panamanians received their money and almost immediately American engineers began work. Within ten years, the canal opened; it was undeniably one of the greatest technical achievements of the century. The United States now had a major new cog in its economic and military machine, as its ingenuity, not to mention its bravado, had shrunk the trip from New York City to San Francisco from 13,165 miles to 5,300 miles.

Even after the signing of the treaty, many problems remained, including issues such as tariffs and postal deliveries. Many Americans approached them apprehensively. One wrote that "it must be remembered that the masses of [the Panamanian] people are schooled and experienced in all kinds of uprisings, agitations, and popular excitements, and great harm might be done on some occasion if there were not a force, like a company of marines . . . the effect of whose moral presence, even if they did not participate in preserving order, would maintain quiet or protect property." Over time, through coercion and diplomacy, the United States worked out results favorable to it, including the dissolution of the small Panamanian army.

Placing Salve on the Wounds

While the Panamanians seemed pesky, the major problem now facing the United States was the Colombians. In 1906, the U.S. minister in Bogotá reported that "you could not realize how strong still was the feeling, amounting almost to intense hatred, among the people of Colombia against the United States." Secretary of State Elihu Root, who had taken over the post in mid-1905, tried to heal the wounds. He pushed for a straightforward U.S. apology to Colombia, but Roosevelt refused. Now Root tried other tactics, including the arrangement of payment to Colombia by Panama for its percentage of the national debt owed in 1903. Despite these actions, the Colombians proved unwilling to forgive and forget.

The controversy persisted for many years. Roosevelt fueled the dispute in 1911, when he bragged at a speaking engagement that "I took the Isthmus." Elsewhere, he boasted: "I took the Canal Zone and let Congress debate; and while the debate goes on the Canal does also." A firestorm followed. The House of Representatives formally investigated the president's actions. Nine days of sworn testimony followed, including that of William Cromwell. Aided by a massive report from Hearst's *New York World*, which had fought a libel battle against Roosevelt in 1909, the committee produced a 700-page chronicle that outlined U.S. abuses. While no formal charges or indictments arose, the report clearly embarrassed Roosevelt and his colleagues.

Subsequent administrations made efforts to settle the problem. In 1914, the administration of Woodrow Wilson, the first Democratic one since that of Grover Cleveland, took the initiative. Secretary of State William Jennings Bryan, with the president's approval, signed a treaty that expressed "sincere regret that anything should have occurred to interrupt or mar the relations of cordial friendship that had so long subsisted between the two governments" of the United States and Colombia. The treaty called for a $25 million indemnity paid directly to Bogotá. Roosevelt called the treaty "an attack upon the honor of the United States," and partisan bickering later killed it. Finally, in 1922, the Senate ratified a similar treaty that expressed "sincere regrets" and paid the Colombians $25 million for its lost territory.

The U.S. actions in Panama were important. "Convinced that Colombians and Panamanians could not be relied upon to act responsibly," Lars Schoultz observes, "the United States had seized control over the single most valuable piece of Latin America's territory." "For the next seven decades, the Panama Canal Zone would stand as the most obvious legacy of the age of imperialism in United States policy toward Latin America," Schoultz concludes.

"Speak Softly and Carry a Big Stick"

The Panama Canal consumed much of Roosevelt's early energy, but other problems in Latin America developed regarding debts and forced payment. His response would place his mark on the Monroe Doctrine. As early as 1901, he explained his position: "There is a homely adage that runs 'speak softly and carry a big stick; you will go far'. . . . If the American nation will speak softly and yet build and keep at a pitch of the highest training a thoroughly efficient navy," he stressed, "the Monroe Doctrine will go far."

It would not be long before Roosevelt put his words into action in Venezuela. Since 1899, the dictator Cipriano Castro had ruled that nation. On several occasions, he deferred payment on government debts, mainly held by British and German citizens. He also insisted that all claims be processed through the Venezuelan judicial system, infuriating many Europeans and Americans. In December 1902, the Europeans, with U.S. acquiescence, bombarded fortifications, and blockaded the country.

The usually decisive Roosevelt responded cautiously. A year earlier, he had told Congress that while the United States wanted fair and open trade in Latin America, it "would not guarantee any state against punishment if it misconducts itself, provided that punishment does not take the form of the acquisition of territory by any non-American power." He wrote a German diplomat, "if any South American misbehaves toward any European country, let the European country spank it." This apparently included Venezuela, as Roosevelt characterized Castro as an "unspeakable villainous monkey." Momentarily, U.S. officials closely monitored the situation and warned the Europeans not to seize any territories.

While the British retreated, the Germans pushed forward in 1903. In January, German ships destroyed Fort San Carlos. Afterwards, the International Court at The Hague validated the blockade and extended preferential treatment to the Europeans in securing claims against foreign governments. The actions and court ruling alarmed Washington. Many Americans feared the Germans would react similarly in other areas of turmoil, ultimately seizing customs houses, properties, and territory.

In response, Roosevelt delivered a message to Congress in December 1904. Recently victorious at the polls and now able to ignore Democratic charges of imperialism, Roosevelt outlined what became known as the Roosevelt Corollary to the Monroe Doctrine. He opened: "it is not true that the United States feels any land hunger or entertains any project as regards the other nations of the Western Hemisphere save such as are for their welfare. All that this country desires is to see the neighboring countries stable, orderly, and prosperous." The main thrust of the statement was that the "chronic wrongdoing, or an impotence which results in a general loosening of the ties of civilized nation, and in the Western Hemisphere the adherence of the United States to the Monroe Doctrine may force the United States, however reluctantly, in flagrant cases of such wrongdoing or impotence, to exercise as an international police force." "We would interfere with them only in the last resort," he stressed, "and then only if it became evident that their inability or unwillingness to do justice at home and abroad had violated the rights of the Untied States or had invited foreign aggression to the detriment of the entire body of American nations."

Generally, most Americans endorsed the president's statements. Racism, elitism, and paternalism dripped from the ink on the document. With the Panama Canal and Puerto Rico, the United States had ended its territorial ambitions, and now Washington focused on creating stability and order. The U.S. economy demanded more markets and raw materials, and, as Cuba had demonstrated, revolutions hurt American business interests. In strategic terms, the Roosevelt Corollary also responded to the looming German threat in Latin America. Roosevelt would protect American concerns and the Latin Americans from themselves and the Europeans, by bayonet point if necessary.

"To Roosevelt"

The Roosevelt Corollary, when combined with U.S. actions in Panama, provoked condemnations of Roosevelt by many Latin Americans. In 1905, the well-known Nicaraguan poet Rubén Darío wrote a poem titled, "To Roosevelt." In it, he told the president: "You are primitive and modern, simple and complex; you are one part George Washington and one part Nimrod." "You think that life is a fire," he added and "that progress is an irruption that the future is wherever your bullet strikes. No." He concluded that "and though you have everything, you are lacking one thing: God!"

Outside of the cultural realm, the Latin Americans resisted U.S. hegemony by addressing the issue of forced collection of debts. In 1902, Argentine Foreign Minister Luis Drago forwarded to Washington a formal diplomatic note in which he argued the ideas of Argentine jurist Carlos Calvo. In what became known as the Drago Doctrine, Drago underscored the point that sovereign immunity entitled foreign investors and creditors with no special privileges in other nations. Drago quoted Alexander Hamilton: "contracts between a nation and private individuals are obligatory according to the conscience of the sovereign, and may not be the object of compelling force. They confer no right of action contrary to the sovereign will." While acknowledging that "the fact that collection cannot be accomplished by means of violence does not, . . . render valueless the acknowledgment of the public debt, the definite obligation of paying it," but Drago noted that "the collection of loans by military means implies territorial occupation to make them effective, and territorial occupation signifies the suppression or subordination of the governments of the countries on which it is imposed."

Drago clearly aimed his statements at Washington by stressing that European actions contradicted the Monroe Doctrine. He emphasized that "there can be no territorial expansion in America on the part of Europe, nor any oppression of the peoples of this continent, because an unfortunate financial situation may compel some one of them to postpone the fulfillment of its promises. In a word, the principle which she would like to see recognized is: that the public debt cannot occasion armed intervention nor even the actual occupation of the territory of American nations by a European power."

Washington feared the implication of the Drago Doctrine. The fact that its arrival coincided with American inactivity in Venezuela in 1902 made Hay and Roosevelt uncomfortable. The secretary of state submitted the Drago Doctrine to the State Department for study. The department's solicitor warned against accepting Drago's argument because it might preclude U.S. intervention in cases of mismanagement and debt collection. Therefore, Washington officially rejected Drago's argument. Nevertheless, its reasoning had impressed Roosevelt, who wrote in 1914: "I am inclined to think we shall ultimately come to the doctrine of the distinguished Argentine international jurist, Senor Drago." Over time, it would become more accepted into inter-American relations and international law.

Talking the Talk, Walking the Walk

For the moment, Washington rejected Drago's views and implemented the Roosevelt Corollary, the first test of which took place in 1905 in the Dominican Republic. For many years, mismanagement there had compiled huge national debts. The precipitating crisis that sparked Washington's interference occurred when an arbitrator gave the U.S. Domingo Improvement Company the right to the revenues of the Puerto Plata Customs House in order to try to erase a $4.5 million debt. Immediately, the Dominicans defaulted. In response, the company seized the customs house, sparking an uproar among Dominican nationalists and European creditors.

Fearing European intervention to protect their citizens' claims, Washington pressured the Dominicans to accept U.S. control of all customs houses. After several weeks of negotiations, under the watchful eye of U.S. warships patrolling nearby, the two nations signed a treaty. The United States took over the customs houses, retaining 45 percent to pay Dominican expenses and 55 percent to compensate debtors. After a great deal of wrangling, the Senate ultimately ratified the treaty, although opponents characterized the action as reflecting the mindset; "you mind your business and we'll mind yours." Poet Wallace Irwin also poked fun at the intervention. "Here's a bumper to the doctrine of Monroe, roe, roe, and thee neighbors whom we cannot let alone; through the thirst for diagnosis we're inserting our proboscis, into everybody's business but our own."

A New Charge Up San Juan Hill

Soon after the United States intervened in the Dominican Republic, Washington returned its attention to Cuba. In 1906, Cuba's first president, Tomás Estrada Palma, rigged an election to retain power. Believing that the United States would protect his government, no matter how fraudulent the election results, Estrada and his Moderate Party ruthlessly pushed forward. They believed Root's pronouncement in 1904 that "no such revolutions as have afflicted Central and South America are possible there [in Cuba], because it is known to all men that an attempt to overturn the foundations of that government will be confronted from the overwhelming power of the United States." On the other hand, the opposition Liberal Party thought Washington would surely intervene to defend democratic practices. Their protests to the U.S. government, however, received no sympathy. At the time, Roosevelt was focusing on hot spots in Asia and Africa and wanted to avoid overseeing Cuba's election process.

Now the Cuban Liberals adopted another tactic. They rationalized that the Platt Amendment would ensure intervention to protect American lives and properties, thereby helping unseat Estrada. In the summer of 1906, they attacked Estrada's forces and destroyed American-owned properties. By September, Estrada did indeed request U.S. assistance, and soon thereafter, the USS *Denver* arrived in Havana. Acting without official orders, the U.S. captain landed a battalion of sailors to help restore order. Though Roosevelt soon rescinded the captain's order, the damage had been done. The president fumed: "I am so angry with that infernal little Cuban republic that I would like to wipe its people off the face of the earth. All we have wanted from them was that they would behave themselves and be prosperous and happy so that we would not have to interfere." An important congressional Republican, Henry Cabot Lodge, echoed Roosevelt's feelings. "Disgust with the Cubans is very general. Nobody wants to annex them, but the general feeling is that they ought to be taken by the neck and shaken until they behave themselves."

To handle the problem, Roosevelt sent Secretary of War William Howard Taft to Cuba to investigate the problem. Taft cabled Washington that the "situation is most serious," and asked for reinforcements. Within a short period, nine American warships anchored in Havana. When Estrada and his allies tried manipulating him, Taft established a provisional government. Soon thereafter, he returned to Washington, leaving behind Charles Magoon as provisional governor. Supported by 5,000 U.S. troops, Magoon controlled the island for twenty-eight months while Roosevelt publicly scolded the Cubans for their "insurrectionary habits, and informed them that if they continued to act up it was "absolutely out of the question that the Island should continue independent." Finally, in 1909, U.S. troops withdrew, turning control over to the elected government of Liberal president José Miguel Gómez.

The intervention was important for several reasons. According to historian Louis Pérez, "Power contenders derived one important lesson from 1906: when all else failed, or did not succeed quickly enough, the destruction of North American property could serve as the continuation of Cuban politics by other means." He also asserted that "the United States intervened in 1906 to displace a government held in disfavor by the opposition served to vindicate Liberal policy." The fact that the Liberal Party won power "suggested that there was more than one way to redress grievances and obtain political ascendancy." This specter of the Platt Amendment and the subsequent interventions in 1912 and 1917 weakened Cuban attempts at self-rule.

When Roosevelt stepped down in 1909, he left a significant legacy of U.S.-Latin American relations. He established dangerous precedents for future U.S. leaders and engendered a great deal of hostility toward the United States. Root recognized this in a speech in 1909, in which he told an audience that "two-thirds of the suspicion, the dislike, the distrust with which our country was regarded by the people of South America, was the result of the arrogant and contemptuous bearing of Americans." The United States had assumed a position as paternalistic protector of the hemisphere. A major difference in 1909 was that the United States had the military and economic power to enforce many of its policies in Latin America. This new position of power would carry with it a great deal of personal and diplomatic costs when future presidents found the task of policing the region extremely difficult.

Continuities

From 1868 to 1909, the United States and Latin America became more interdependent than at any preceding time. On the economic level, American businesspersons and investors became a powerful force as the United States industrialized and became a leading world power. More Latin American goods fueled the development of the large factories and fed the workforce. At the same time, U.S. engineers flowed into the region to build railroads, mines, and the Panama Canal, and helped create new industries such as the banana plantations.

The economic climate fostered political and diplomatic interdependence. Unprecedented efforts at cooperation (and some would say domination) occurred with economic negotiations at such meetings as the Washington Conference in 1889. The Venezuelans pushed Washington to side with it during the Orinoco dispute. Efforts to form trading blocs and build infrastructure projects such as the Inter-American railway intensified this interdependence.

With increased U.S. interdependence came an increased drive at establishing U.S. hegemony over Latin America. American businesspersons began to replace Europeans in many areas as the dominant foreign interest. Americans continued to expand in the northern zones, but increasingly played a substantial role in the mines and railroads in Chile, Colombia, and Venezuela. U.S. goods and accompanying cultural symbols and ideals gradually became preponderant in the region.

With economic penetration proceeding, Washington's political and diplomatic drive for hegemony became more heavy-handed. As the United States grew in military power, it became more activist in expanding its control over the region, particularly the Caribbean Basin. Military interventions and diplomatic brinkmanship became more commonplace as the U.S. Navy grew larger and U.S. desires to supplant the British and protect against German encroachments swelled. The results were intervention and confrontation in Chile, Brazil, Venezuela, Colombia, Mexico, Cuba, Puerto Rico, the Dominican Republic, and Nicaragua. And these were only signs of things to come.

Nevertheless, one should not infer that the Latin Americans were passive actors in any of these processes. The Cubans, Panamanians, and Venezuelans consistently sought to protect their national interests, and they attempted to manipulate the United States often. They played an active role in winning their independence and called on Washington for assistance, although without always understanding the full consequences of those requests. On the cultural level, the Latin American intellectuals became more vocal in their criticisms of the United States, and their work often highlighted the hypocrisy of the North Americans. They often found willing American allies, who prevented the United States from seizing even more Latin American lands and staying longer than they were welcome, thereby weakening the unity of the drive for hegemony.

Finally, the period of the late nineteenth century saw the rise of new Latino forces in the United States. The Southwest continued to meld into a more unified culture, economically and culturally. The United States welcomed more immigrants from Cuba and the new colony of Puerto Rico. The demographic changes the newcomers effected would only continue as the United States tied closer to those areas and others such as the Dominican Republic and Panama. The Latino population grew substantially in cities such as New York, Miami, Tampa, Mobile, and New Orleans. In each case, the Latinos brought their cultural traditions, which they imposed with increasing frequency on the mainstream U.S. society.

SUGGESTIONS FOR ADDITIONAL READING

For the story of Grant and Charles Sumner's battle, see Sumner Welles, *Naboth's Vineyard: The Dominican Republic, 1844–1924* (1925).

For business interests and their impact on the region during the period, see David M. Pletcher, *Rails, Mines, and Progress: Seven American Promoters in Mexico, 1867–1911* (1958) and *The Diplomacy of Trade: American Economic Expansion in the Hemisphere, 1865–1900* (1998); Stewart Watt, *Keith and Costa Rica: A Biographical Study of Minor Cooper Keith* (1964), J. Peter Grace, *W. R. Grace, 1832–1904, and the Enterprises He Created* (1953), Jimmy Skaggs, *The Great Guano Rush: Entrepreneurs and American Overseas Expansion* (1994); Thomas P. McCann, *On the Inside: A Story of Intrigue and Adventure, on Wall Street, in Washington, and in the Jungles of Central America* (1976); Stacy May and Galo Plaza, *The United Fruit Company in Latin America* (1958); Ramón Ruiz, *The People of Sonora and the Yankee Capitalists* (1988); Thomas Schoonover, *Dollars over Dominion: The Triumph of Liberalism in Mexican-United States Relations, 1861–1867* (1978) and *The United States in Central America, 1860–1911: Episodes in Social Imperialism and Imperial Rivalry in the World System* (1991); Thomas Schoonover and Lester Langley, *The Banana Men: American Mercenaries and Entrepreneurs in Central America, 1880–1930* (1995); Dan La Botz, *Edward L. Doheny: Petroleum, Power, and Politics in the United States and Mexico* (1991); Michael Monteón, *Chile in the Nitrate Era: The Evolution of Economic Dependence, 1880–1930* (1982); and Carlos Marichal, *A Century of Debt Crises in Latin America: From Independence to the Great Depression, 1820–1930* (1989).

For the rise of the United States as a power in the region, reference Richard H. Bradford, *The Virginius Affair* (1980); Joyce S. Goldberg, *The Baltimore Affair: United States Relations with Chile, 1891–1892* (1986); and Joseph Smith, *Unequal Giants: Diplomatic Relations between the United States and Brazil, 1889–1930* (1991).

For an overall appreciation of the changes in U.S. foreign policy during the late 19th century, there are many good works including Robert L. Beisner, *From the Old Diplomacy to the New, 1865–1900* (1975), Walter LaFeber, *The New Empire: An Interpretation of American Expansionism, 1860–1898* (1963), H. Wayne Morgan's, *From Hayes to McKinley, National Party Politics, 1877–1896* (1969), Charles S. Campbell Jr., *The Transformation of American Foreign Relations* (1976), Henry E. Mattox, *Twilight of Amateur Diplomacy: The American Foreign Service and Its Senior Officers in the 1890s* (1989); Julius Pratt, *Expansionists of 1898: The Acquisition of Hawaii and the Spanish Islands* (1931); Ernest May, *American Imperialism: A Speculative Essay* (1968); Goran Rystad, *Ambiguous Imperialism: American Foreign Policy and Domestic Politics at the Turn of the Century* (1975); David Healy, *U.S. Expansionism: The Imperialist Urge in the 1890s* (1970), Richard D. Challener, *Admirals, Generals, and American Foreign Policy, 1898–1914* (1973), Michael H. Hunt, *Ideology and U.S. Foreign Policy (1987);* William Livezey, *Mahan on Sea Power* (1947); and Robert Seager II, *Alfred Thayer Mahan: The Man and His Letters* (1975).

Sections on the Orinoco dispute include Joseph Smith, *Illusions of Conflict: Anglo–American Diplomacy Toward Latin America, 1865–1896* (1979), Stuart Anderson, *Race and Rapprochement: Anglo-Saxonism and Anglo-American Relations, 1895–1904* (1981); and Bradford Perkins, *The Great Rapprochement, 1895–1914* (1968).

For more on the Spanish-American-Cuban War, see Louis A. Pérez, *The War of 1898: The United States & Cuba in History and Historiography* (1998), *Cuba Between Empires, 1878–1902* (1983); James H. Hitchman, *Leonard Wood and Cuban Independence, 1898–1902* (19); John L. Offner, *An Unwanted War: The Diplomacy of the United States and Spain over Cuba, 1895–1898* (1992); David Trask, *The War with Spain in 1898* (1981); Lewis L. Gould, *The Spanish-American War and President McKinley* (1982); Philip S. Foner, *The Spanish-Cuban-American War and the Birth of American Imperialism, 1895–1902* (1972); Hyman G. Rickover, *How the Battleship "Maine" Was Destroyed* (1976); Irving Werstein, *1898: The Spanish-American War* (1966); Frank Freidel, *The Splendid Little War* (1958); G. J. A. O'Toole, *The Spanish War: An American Epic–1898* (1984); Edward J. Berbusse, *The United States in Puerto Rico, 1898–1900* (1966); David Healy, *The United States and Cuba: Generals, Politics, and the Search for Policy* (1963); and José A. Cabranes, *Citizenship and the American Empire* (1979).

Cuban sources on the war include: Miguel Varona Guerrero, *La guerra de independencia de Cuba, 1895–1898* (1946); Herminio Portell Vilá, *Historia de la guerra de Cuba y los Estados Unidos contra España* (1949); Emilio Roig de Leuchsenring, *Cuba no debe su independencia a los Estados Unidos* (1950); Aníbal Escalante Beatón, *Calixto García, Su campaña en el 95* (1978); and Cosme de la Torriente, *Calixto García cooperó con las fuerzas armadas de los EE. UU. En 1898, cumpliendo óddenes del gobierno cubano* (1952).

For more on those who opposed the expansion, good works include: Robert Beisner, *Twelve Against Empire: The Anti-Imperialists, 1898–1900* (1968); and E. Berkeley Tompkins, *Anti-Imperialism in the United States: The Great Debate, 1890–1920* (1970).

For books on Roosevelt and his foreign policies, see Howard K. Beale, *Theodore Roosevelt and the Rise of America to World Power* (1956); Frederick Marks, *Velvet on Iron:*

The Diplomacy of Theodore Roosevelt (1979); Nathan Miller, *Theodore Roosevelt: A Life* (1992); Richard Collin, *Theodore Roosevelt's Caribbean: The Panama Canal, the Monroe Doctrine, and the Latin American Context* (1990); *Theodore Roosevelt, Culture, Diplomacy, and Expansion: A New View of American Imperialism* (1985); H. W. Brands, *TR: The Last Romantic* (1997); Lewis Gould, *The Presidency of Theodore Roosevelt* (1991); and Raymond A. Esthus, *Theodore Roosevelt and the International Rivalries* (1970).

Good works on the Panama rebellion and the building of the Panama Canal include Gerstle Mack, *The Land Divided: A History of the Panama Canal and Other Isthmian Canal Projects* (1944); Marry W. Williams, *Anglo-American Isthmian Diplomacy, 1815–1915* (1916); and David McCullough, *The Path Between the Seas: The Creation of the Panama Canal, 1870–1914* (1977); and Ovidio Diaz Espino, *How Wall Street Created a Nation: J. P. Morgan, Teddy Roosevelt, and the Panama Canal* (2001); and John Lindsay-Poland, *Emperors of the Jungle: The Hidden History of the United States in Panama* (2003).

CHAPTER FOUR

The Era of Bad Feelings

In 1906, Secretary of State Root declared the United States needed new foreign markets, especially those in Latin America that possessed "surplus of capital beyond the requirements of internal development." He contended that Latin America had raw materials, while the United States provided the technology and business acumen to use them. To him, Latin Americans were "polite, refined, cultivated," while Americans were "strenuous, intense, utilitarian." Ultimately, he stressed: "Where we accumulate, they spend."

"Dollar Diplomacy"

In 1909, the new Republican president, William Howard Taft, agreed with Root's assessment in stressing the primacy of economics over military intervention and diplomatic bullying. Taft wrote regarding the Roosevelt Corollary that "the reason why I find a doctrine so hard to subscribe to is not that I would not be willing to have the United States sacrifice much to secure the elevation and benefit of the people of South America, but the character of the Governments of that continent is so miserable and the absolute hopelessness of any improvement under present conditions so appalling that it would seem as if we were protecting nothing but chaos, anarchy, and chronic revolution." Once president, Taft complained that he should have the "right to knock their heads together until they should maintain peace."

The people who surrounded Taft shared his views on Latin America. Secretary of State Philander Knox, a corporate lawyer firmly tied by marriage and profession to the captains of industry, believed in a "measure of benevolent supervision over Latin American countries." He argued for a U.S. guidance that "will reflect credit upon the hegemony of our race and

131

further advance the influence of Anglo-Saxon civilization." From all of this would emerge "prosperity [which] means contentment and contentment means repose. The most effective way to escape the logical consequences of the Monroe doctrine is to help them to help themselves. . . . We diminish our responsibilities in proportion as we bring about improved conditions."

The fundamental responsibility of the Foreign Service in Taft's presidency was to promote American businesses, leading one observer to note that "Dollar Diplomacy meant diplomacy helping dollars." In turn, foreigners doing business with Americans would prosper, allowing stability and order and diplomatic relations to flourish. Knox emphasized that he supported a "spirited foreign commercial policy." As one historian writes, his slogan should have been "every diplomat is a salesman," and that "the Almighty Dollar came to supplant the Big Stick."

In the grand scheme, Secretary Knox and Taft devoted little energy to Latin America, leaving most details to Assistant Secretary Francis Mairs Huntington Wilson. Root called him "suspicious" and "egotistical," and "a fellow of the most dangerous character for diplomatic service." Yet Wilson was popular in Taft's administration because he shared its vision. He would espouse "a diplomacy seeking the political and economic advantage of the American taxpayer, the American nation." To him, money helped diplomacy because it used "the capital of the country in the foreign field in a manner calculated to enhance fixed national policies. It means the substitution of dollars for bullets."

Social Darwinism also shaped the views of Wilson, who argued that "the march of civilization brooks no violation of the law of the survival of the fittest." He stressed that "nature, in its rough method of uplift, gives sick nations strong neighbors and takes its inexorable course with private enterprise and diplomacy as its instruments. And this course is the best in the long run, for all concerned and for the world."

The paternalism inherent in Roosevelt's Big Stick thrived in Taft's "Dollar Diplomacy." Government officials would work with private citizens, principally bankers and entrepreneurs, in Latin America and elsewhere. U.S. economic power would protect American interests by guaranteeing markets, raw materials, and access to strategic bases. In turn, U.S. dollars and technology (as well as cultural exchanges) would uplift inferior peoples.

The growth of U.S. commerce in Latin America under Taft was impressive. Imports from the region, primarily foodstuffs and raw materials, increased by 86 percent in four years. U.S. exports to Latin America also increased, by 39 percent. U.S. businesses invested heavily in the region's railroads, government work projects, and agricultural enterprises, and loans for development from American banks flowed southward. By 1912, the United States received 34.4 percent of all Latin American imports, while the British received 19.7 percent, the Germans, 11.88 percent, and the French 7.8 percent. By a small margin, the British dispatched the largest percentage of materials to Latin America at 24.84 percent, while the United State sent 24.5 percent, the Germans 16.6 percent, and the French 8.3 percent. These numbers would only grow in favor of the U.S. once World War I began in 1914.

The Original "Banana Republic"

One of the best examples of "Dollar Diplomacy" in Latin America developed in Honduras. In 1905, an American entrepreneur named Samuel Zemurray arrived in the country. Within a few years, he bought 20,000 acres of land and established a thriving banana company rivaling UFCO. Zemurray and his competitors, according to historian Walter LaFeber, "bought up lands, built railroads, established their own banking systems, and bribed government officials at a dizzying pace." Honduran politicians encouraged the development, happy to receive occasional customs receipts.

By the end of the Taft administration, U.S. banana companies dominated the economy of Honduras. In 1913, they accounted for two-thirds of Honduras's exports, and the country imported 80 percent of its goods from the United States. American builders constructed railroads through the banana-producing zones, linking them to ports. However, few rail lines reached into other parts of the country, including the capital of Tegucigalpa, which had no major rail service for many years.

Washington's interest in Honduras accompanied that of U.S. investors and businesspersons. In 1907, a civil war and potentially widespread regional war threatened Zemurray's efforts. That year, rebels led by Miguel Dávila overthrew President Manuel Bonilla. Dávila proved very friendly with anti-American elements in Honduras, and the British threatened to collect huge debts. As a result, Knox tried to negotiate a deal with American banker J. P. Morgan to buy Tegucigalpa's debts. When diplomatic efforts failed, Zemurray financed an insurrection by Bonilla, one led by

American adventurer Lee Christmas. In 1911, the U.S. Navy helped settle the problem by allowing Bonilla's forces to land in northern Honduras. When Dávila's forces counterattacked, U.S. marines protected the insurgents. U.S. Consul Thomas G. Dawson forcefully interfered, leading to Dávila's resignation and Bonilla's return to power.

The new government granted favorable concessions to Zemurray (who eventually sold his holdings to UFCO in 1929 for $32 million) and American bankers. As LaFeber underscores, "if Honduras was dependent on the fruit companies before 1912, it was virtually indistinguishable from them after 1912." Dollar diplomacy combined with a little "gunboat diplomacy" had won the day and firmly established the United States as the dominant power in Honduras. From this point forward, Honduras became the model of what later became known pejoratively as a "banana republic."

Hell Hath No Fury Like a Suitor Spurned

The U.S. intervention in Honduras had been inextricably tied to the events unfolding in neighboring Nicaragua, where since 1893, Liberal leader José Santos Zelaya had ruled and encouraged foreign investment, promulgated a liberal constitution, and stirred controversy by trying to reestablish the Central America Union. Until the early 1900s, Washington had maintained good relations with Zelaya, hoping to secure a canal concession. After 1903, however, relations soured when the United States turned its attentions toward Panama. Zelaya, like a suitor spurned, became increasingly anti-American in his rhetoric and actions.

For many Americans, Zelaya posed a significant obstacle to stability in the region. In particular, his plans for a unified Central America had sparked conflict with Guatemalan dictator Estrada Cabrera, leading to the U.S. and Mexican arbitration in 1906. A year later, the Roosevelt administration hosted the Central American leaders. The meetings produced a treaty of peace and amity, plans for an integrated road network, and a Central American Court of Justice. The latter was an attempt by progressive American reformers to maintain peace. Billionaire Andrew Carnegie happily provided $100,000 for the purchase of a building to house the court.

Despite the conference, the relationship between the United States and Zelaya deteriorated as Taft assumed the presidency. Washington had tired of Zelaya's willingness to negotiate with foreign entrepreneurs to build a competing canal. German curiosity particularly worried U.S. policymakers.

Since its unification in the 1870s, Germany had made significant inroads in Latin America. Many German immigrants had become prominent citizens in Central American nations, particularly Costa Rica and Guatemala. In Nicaragua, a German representative reported in 1905 that his country should support Zelaya's rule since he had been "generally friendly toward German interests, and . . . a strong government like his offered the best guarantee against U.S. intervention."

Our Way or the Highway

In 1909, an opportunity presented itself for the United States to dislodge Zelaya. Conservative forces led by Juan Estrada revolted in the Bluefields area of the Mosquito Coast. U.S. investors in the area provided substantial material assistance to the rebels, and the U.S. consul in the Bluefields, Thomas Moffat, openly backed Estrada. The tensions escalated when Zelaya's forces seized two U.S. citizens for helping plant mines in the San Juan River. After a hastily convened trial, the Nicaraguans executed them. In retaliation, the United States broke relations with Zelaya. Soon thereafter, he resigned and fled into exile, trying to forestall a U.S. intervention. In his place, the Nicaraguan Congress selected José Madriz.

Washington refused to recognize the new Madriz government, arguing that it was too anti-American. During the ensuing fighting, Washington played an important role. When Madriz's forces appeared near victory in May 1910, U.S. marines landed to protect American lives. One of the marines was Smedley Butler, who called the Nicaraguans "the most worthless, useless lot of vermine [sic] I have struck yet, even worse than our 'Little brown brothers' the Filipinos." The marines told Madriz's troops that they could attack, but without guns because bullets might hit Americans. This effectively stopped the advance and by August, Estrada captured the capital of Managua.

As was often the case, the hard part of victory was establishing a viable government. Estrada's attempts collapsed under charges of his sellout to the Americans. His replacement, Adolfo Díaz, negotiated loans that gave large American financiers control of Nicaragua's national bank, 51 percent of the railroads, and receipts of the customs houses. Díaz even proposed that the two countries sign an agreement "permitting the United States to intervene in our internal affairs to maintain peace and the existence of a lawful Government."

The thorny problem of how to respond perplexed U.S. officials. Knox told a Managua audience in the summer of 1911 that "I beg to assure you . . . that my Government does not covet an inch of territory south of the Rio Grande." Still, later that year, Knox emphasized: "We are in the eyes of the world, and because of the Monroe Doctrine, held responsible for the order of Central America, and its proximity to the Canal makes the preservation of peace in that neighborhood particularly necessary."

That July, Nicaraguan nationalists moved against Díaz. Minister of War Luis Mena joined with dissident groups to oust the president. By September, the rebels appeared near victory. On Taft's orders, 2,700 American troops invaded. After brutal fighting, including the U.S. Marine occupation of the Liberal stronghold of León, the rebels surrendered. In November, U.S. forces supervised a presidential election, which Díaz won. While the bulk of troops withdrew, 130 remained in place as a "legation guard" to serve as a warning of Washington's closeness to Managua. Díaz would remain in office until 1916, although more as an American puppet than a Nicaraguan leader.

The first U.S. intervention in Nicaragua of the twentieth century was important for several reasons. It demonstrated that a "Big Stick" did indeed accompany "Dollar Diplomacy." This led Butler to later write that "it is terrible that we should be losing so many men fighting . . . all because Brown Bros. [the New York City banking house] have some money down here." The intervention also bound the United States to Nicaragua. This relationship would have significant benefits in preventing competing interests for the Panama Canal, as the Nicaraguans signed the Bryan-Chamorro Treaty in 1916 that gave the United States exclusive rights to build a Nicaraguan canal. It also ensured U.S. interference in Nicaragua's affairs, a process that would prove costly in both lives and monies.

Sitting on the Lid of a Pressure Cooker

The most pressing problem in U.S.-Latin American relations during Taft's term developed in 1910. The aging Mexican dictator Porfirio Díaz had promised to step down but proceeded to fix his own reelection that year. Led by a wealthy northern landowner, Francisco Madero, a broad-based group of laborers, peasants, intellectuals, and businesspersons revolted. While different people enlisted in the rebel cause for various reasons, a unifying factor was nationalism. The dominance of foreign interests in the Mexican economy and the uneven development had inflamed regional passions. As Dirk Raat notes, "when Madero and his hacendado peasant, and labor supporters challenged the porfirian government in 1910–1911, they were questioning the role of U.S. imperialism in Mexico and the regime's relationship to the United States."

During the fighting, Washington maintained a wait-and-see attitude. President Taft emphasized that he wanted to "sit tight on the lid and it will take a good deal to pry me off." He had supported Díaz, stressing that the Mexican president "has done more for the people of Mexico than any other Latin-American had done for any of his people . . . the truth is they need a firm hand in Mexico and everybody realizes it." In 1909, Taft traveled to Ciudad Juárez and met Díaz, becoming the first sitting U.S. president to visit Mexico. He worried that the $2 billion in American investment would be "greatly endangered if Díaz were to die and his government go to pieces." Recognizing the frailty of the Mexican, Taft concluded, "I can only hope and pray that his demise does not come until I am out of office."

Powers beyond his control denied Taft his wish. The fighting in the revolution was extremely brutal, and Díaz's army could not contain the rebels. Over time, Madero's forces gained strength as supplies flowed into Mexico from the United States, despite the latter's official policy of neutrality. After defeating government forces at Ciudad Juárez, the insurgents marched south. By May 1911, the aging dictator fled into exile. A year later, Madero won the presidency in the first open national elections in Mexico in many years.

The Ugly American

The election of Madero did not settle Mexico's problems. He proved unpopular with many people. He was cautious and moved slowly on reforms. In the state of Morelos, rebel leader Emilio Zapata denounced the new president for failing to redistribute land. Dissidents still aligned with Díaz also attacked the new president, and scattered anti-Madero movements gained momentum through 1912 and 1913.

One of the most vociferous critics of Madero was U.S. Ambassador Henry Lane Wilson. He had arrived in Mexico in 1909 and developed a good relationship with Díaz. Like many Americans, he carried cultural baggage, claiming that "practically all of the material development of Mexico is due to American enterprise, initiative, and capital." He blamed Mexico's backwardness on its Indian population and race mixing. "Wher-

Franklin Delano Roosevelt (right) with Woodrow Wilson (third from the left), Joseph Daniels (second from left) and William Jennings Bryan (left) at a Flag Day Celebration in Washington, 1913. *Courtesy of the Franklin D. Roosevelt Library*

ever the Indian element predominates, . . . the tendency to anarchy and revolution is very marked," he noted. When Madero took over, the two men immediately clashed, as the ambassador characterized the president as weak and suffering from mental illness. To Wilson, Madero "believed that the Mexican people should be governed by kindness and love, which, in my judgment, showed a deficient mental grasp of the situation." He thought only a strong hand, such as that administered by Díaz, could provide sufficient order to protect American entrepreneurs and guarantee Mexico's progress.

Throughout his tenure, Wilson flooded the State Department with stories of anarchy in Mexico. His reports pushed U.S. intervention to reestablish order. Taft and Knox refused direct intervention, believing that they could not effectively affect the outcome. In 1913, Wilson responded to the inaction and overstepped his bounds. He began actively plotting with reactionary elements in the Mexican military led by General Victoriano Huerta to overthrow Madero. The insurrectionists sought Wilson's approval before launching a coup in February, in which they arrested, then murdered Madero. Soon thereafter, Huerta pressured Congress to make him provisional president.

Despite Ambassador Wilson's efforts, his days in Mexico were numbered, as a new administration had taken power in Washington. The newly inaugurated Woodrow Wilson (no direct relation) dispatched a special agent to investigate the ambassador's actions. He concluded that the ambassador was guilty of "treason, perfidy and assassination in an assault on constitutional government." The action left a dark stain on U.S.-Mexican relations just as the true Mexican revolution was beginning.

The Priest Takes Over

In 1912, Woodrow Wilson won the presidency, defeating Taft and former president Theodore Roosevelt, who had run on the "Bull Moose" party ticket. The first Democrat in office since 1896, Wilson was the son of a southern Presbyterian minister. Well-educated, he had a Ph.D. in international affairs from Johns Hopkins University, and he had been president of Princeton University before becoming governor of New Jersey. Strongly imbued with a progressive spirit and Christian idealism, Wilson believed such principles could uplift American society. He promoted a doctrine "which gives wide freedom to the individual for self-development and yet guards that freedom against the competition that kills, and reduces antagonism between self-development and social development to a minimum." He wanted to limit the "power of unscrupulous and heartless men to outdo the scrupulous and merciful in trade or industry."

Wilson's ideas for domestic development corresponded with his international visions. Idealistically, he believed that the United States should serve as a model of democratic-capitalist development to other nations. He denounced "Dollar Diplomacy" as "mere commercial exploitation and the selfish interests of a narrow circle of financiers extending their enterprises to the ends of the earth." Wilson's first secretary of state, William Jennings Bryan, shared his ideals. The outspoken, anti-imperialist Bryan called "Dollar Diplomacy" "a phrase coined to describe a policy of government under which the state department has been used to coerce smaller nations into recognizing claims of American citizens which did not rest upon a legitimate basis."

During his presidency, Wilson devoted much attention to foreign affairs, including Latin America. He elucidated his Pan-American vision in October 1913 in Mobile, Alabama. "One of the chief objectives of my Administration will be to cultivate the friendship and deserve the confidence of our sister republics of Central and South America," he declared, then added, "I want to take this occasion to say that the United States will never again seek one additional foot of territory by conquest." To implement his viewpoint, he argued that "we dare not turn from the principle of morality, and expediency is not the thing that must guide us and we will never condone iniquity because it is most convenient to do so." He addressed "Dollar Diplomacy" when he emphasized "it is a very perilous thing to determine the foreign policy of a nation in the terms of material interest. It not only is unfair to those with whom you are dealing, but it is degrading as regards your own actions."

Teaching Them to Elect Good Men

The most pressing problem that Wilson inherited was the issue of recognizing the Huerta government. In most preceding cases, the United States had ultimately extended diplomatic recognition to all governments, no matter how they had obtained power. Wilson was anxious to spread the gospel of democracy. In addition, he was influenced by the legal reasoning of Carlos Tobar of Ecuador, who argued that only governments that acquired power by free elections deserved recognition (later known as the Tobar Doctrine). Therefore, Wilson steadfastly refused to recognize Huerta.

From the start, Wilson denounced the new Mexican leadership as "a government of butchers." He told a reporter: "My ideal is an orderly and righteous government in Mexico; but my passion is for the submerged eighty-five per cent of the people of the Republic who are now struggling toward liberty." Earlier in the Mobile address, he had aimed several sections of the speech at Huerta. "We can have no sympathy with those who seek to seize the powers of government to advance their own personal ambitions. . . . As friends . . . we shall prefer those who protect private rights and respect the restraints of constitutional provision."

Despite pressure from American business interests and the Europeans, Wilson tenaciously resisted extending recognition. He even told a British visitor, "I am going to teach the South American republics to elect good men!" To ensure this goal, Wilson sent a special emissary to Mexico, John Lind, in August 1913. Once there, Lind promised recognition if Huerta signed an armistice with rebel factions and allowed free elections in which he would not participate. The general refused. Mexican Foreign Minister Federico Gamboa complained that if Huerta accepted, "all the future elections for president would be submitted to the veto of any President of the

United States." The tensions escalated as Wilson ordered an arms embargo and advised Americans to leave Mexico.

An Affair of Honor

American and Mexican intransigence led to confrontation. In April 1914, Mexican officials arrested U.S. sailors unloading supplies in Tampico for violating a restricted zone. The Mexican commander immediately released the Americans and expressed his regrets for the overzealous action. Unsatisfied, Rear Admiral Henry T. Mayo demanded a formal apology and twenty-one gun salute for the "hostile act." Wilson backed the officer fully, calling the crisis an "affair of honor."

The relatively minor affair resulted in a major confrontation. Wilson formulated plans to seize the customs houses at Tampico and Vera Cruz to deprive Huerta of revenues. The efforts accelerated when U.S. agents learned that the German merchantman *Ypiranga* approached Vera Cruz with arms intended for Huerta. On April 20, Wilson asked Congress for authority to use troops "to obtain from General Huerta and his adherents the fullest recognition of the rights and dignity of the United States." With congressional approval, U.S. troops occupied Vera Cruz despite dogged Mexican resistance.

As Thomas Bailey underscores, "Wilson was now out on the end of a limb. He could not risk the humiliation of withdrawal without atonement from Huerta. Yet a full-fledged Mexican war, which seemed to be the only other alternative, was unthinkable." Wilson found himself in a more precarious position when rebel leader Venustiano Carranza rejected U.S. assistance; some insurgents even talked of uniting with Huerta's forces to expel the Americans. In the meantime, the ABC Powers (Argentina, Brazil, Chile) offered to mediate the crisis, presenting a plan for creating a provisional government through direct negotiations and American withdrawal. All sides rejected it. Finally, the matter ended when Carranza's forces drove Huerta into exile in July. Carranza soon established a government. By November, American troops had left Vera Cruz.

The New Dimension

A complex variable in U.S.-Latin American relations entered the equation in August 1914. That month, Europe exploded into war after a Serb nationalist in Sarajevo assassinated the visiting heir to the Austrian throne,

Archduke Ferdinand. Great Britain, France, and Russia squared off against Germany and the Austro-Hungarian Empire. A century of comparative continental peace ended abruptly and violently, as new weapons of mass destruction caused heavy casualties during the first year of the conflict.

There were several consequences of World War I for the United States and Latin America. First, the economic penetration of Latin America by American entrepreneurs increased, as European competitors became preoccupied with the fighting. European imports to Latin America declined as the belligerents stepped up their war production. German merchants and bankers in particular faced a much more difficult task in penetrating the British blockade to reach Latin America. American businessmen jumped into the void, as did Latin Americans, who developed their own native industries to replace the European imports on which they had grown dependent.

On a strategic level, the United States watched closely the moves of the Europeans to shore up their access to raw materials and potential military bases. While the Wilson administration declared neutrality, its policies clearly aided the British and the French. American military supplies, foodstuffs, and loans flowed to the nations of both sides, but the bulk of all such exports went to the Allied Powers. Subsequent German actions including the use of unrestricted submarine warfare and sabotage of U.S. industries by German agents, drove the Americans more squarely into the camp of an "unneutral" neutrality favoring the Allies, a point recognized by many Americans including Secretary of State Bryan, who resigned in 1915 to protest the policy.

"To Help Them in the Most Feasible Way Possible"

During the period preceding official U.S. entry into the war in April 1917, the Wilson administration carefully monitored German activities in the Caribbean. U.S. officials focused initially on weakening German economic interests. Linked to these actions were fears that German bankers and businesspersons might try to destabilize governments, creating pressure for concessions that might include military bases for the Axis. The onset of submarine warfare and the potential establishment of German operations near U.S. ports and the Panama Canal deeply worried U.S. officials.

Less than a year after the war began, the United States intervened in Haiti to guard against European interference there. For many years, turmoil had plagued Haiti, as numerous strongmen used political patronage and money to seize power. In mid-1915, anarchy appeared imminent under the rule of President Vilbrun Guilaume Sam, whose brutality sparked an uprising. An incensed crowd, angry at the brutal murder of political prisoners, stormed the French legation, into which the president had fled. Once they got their hands on him, they literally tore Sam apart and proceeded to parade his severed body parts through the capital of Port-au-Prince. Soon thereafter, the unified diplomatic corps requested U.S. occupation of the city in late July 1915.

U.S. troops, under the command of Rear Admiral William Caperton, quickly established control of the major cities. Immediately, Wilson and the new secretary of state, Robert Lansing, denied any desire for territory. Wilson wrote, "our object . . . is not to subordinate them, but to help them in the most practical and most feasible way possible." To Wilson, the United States would reform Haiti.

Yet, as political scientist Hans Schmidt observes, "the belief that Haitians were inherently inferior . . . led to the grotesque perversion of the declared missionary ideal of spreading liberal democracy." Caperton planned elections, cabling Washington: "Next Thursday . . . unless otherwise directed, I will permit Congress to elect a president." He also forced the Haitian legislature to accept a treaty that permitted the United States to intervene to protect lives and guarantee efficient government. It compelled the new president to appoint two Americans, selected by the U.S. president, to act as general receiver of revenues and financial advisor. Finally, it created a constabulary "organized and officered by Americans." As military commander, Smedley Butler effectively took control of the country. He worked with Assistant Secretary of State Franklin Delano Roosevelt to write a new constitution. When the legislative assembly balked at Roosevelt's inclusion of a provision guaranteeing protections for foreign landowners, Butler dissolved the body and conducted a plebiscite, in which the Haitians accepted the new constitution by a vote of 98,225–768.

Within a year, the Marines effectively destroyed most opposition, although bursts of violent resistance occurred periodically. Racism dominated the new administration. Arriving U.S. personnel demanded segregated quarters and facilities, including restaurants and hotels. When the Tuskegee Institute offered the services of their experts to help rebuild the country, the U.S. Navy refused to transport them. In particular,

Butler was a notorious racist. He wrote home: "I am reduced to a very humiliating position, am simply the very subservient chief of a nigger police force." Later, when newly elected president Sudre Dartiguenave tried to enter a limousine ahead of Roosevelt, Butler seized the Haitian by the coat collar and pulled him back. Roosevelt stepped aside, but the damage had been done. Later, Butler would tell a Senate investigating committee that "we were imbued with the fact that we were trustees of a huge estate that belonged to minors."

The U.S. occupation of Haiti lasted until 1934, when then President Franklin Roosevelt officially ended it. In that time, U.S. businesspersons, principally bankers and sugar producers, nearly eliminated foreign interests, including Germans and French, who had held important positions before the occupation. American attempts to improve the lives of the Haitians with better infrastructure, education, and health-care projects proved limited and ineffective. Typically, Americans focused on urban areas and regions dominated by American businesses. When the United States arrived in 1915, Haiti was one of the poorest nations in Latin America; it remained so when U.S. troops left in 1934.

Another Verse, Same Song

Within a year of landing in Haiti, the U.S. Marines also occupied the Dominican Republic. Since the United States had implemented its customs receivership there, U.S. officials played a significant role in the nation. Constant political instability characterized by coups and assassinations plagued the country. German intrigues in the area heightened fears in Washington. When wholesale fighting erupted in May 1916, Caperton seized Santo Domingo and sought to establish order.

Within two months, most resistance had ended. At that point, the Dominican Congress elected Francisco Henríquez y Carvajal as interim president. Problems persisted, however, when Carvajal refused to accept a treaty granting the United States control of government expenditures and the establishment of a Dominican constabulary under U.S. command. In November 1916, Captain Harry S. Knapp established U.S. military control. As political scientists G. Pope Atkins and Larman Wilson note, "U.S. rule was not carried out through puppet presidents as was being done in Haiti. . . . The military government suspended the Dominican Congress, prohibited political party activity, and took away Dominican civil and political liberties." While preaching democracy and self-determination, Wilson failed to match words with actions.

The eight-year intervention of the Dominican Republic was very costly to the American treasury and prestige. Most Dominicans opposed it and refused to cooperate. At several junctures, major uprisings occurred, resulting in many deaths and atrocities. Other Dominicans adopted non-violent means, using the anti-imperialist American press to highlight U.S. abuses, including the torture of suspected insurrectionists. Latin American intellectuals and newspaper editors joined the chorus in condemning the United States for its inconsistency and hypocrisy, most of all Wilson, who suppressed civil liberties in the Dominican Republic. While American businesses gained more footholds through it, the intervention caused subsequent U.S. presidents to find ways to withdraw from the quagmire, which President Calvin Coolidge finally accomplished in 1924.

Diplomacy amid Revolution

Mexico remained the most serious problem facing the Wilson administration. The victorious revolutionaries there convened in Aguacalientes in October 1914 to address significant political, social, and economic questions. Personal agendas doomed the conference, however, and the country drifted back into civil war, with Carranza representing the moderates and Francisco "Pancho" Villa and Emilio Zapata taking more radical courses. Villa marched north and resumed fighting, while Zapata returned home to Morelos to marshal his forces. Meanwhile, Carranza's troops led by Alvaro Obregón fought to reunite the country.

The continued fighting threatened to draw the United States into the conflict. Wilson maintained neutrality until the Mexicans finally provided a clear winner. For many Americans, Carranza was the best choice because he was a moderate reformer. Most opposed Zapata and his plans to redistribute lands, but many looked to Villa as a romantic figure and potentially a good selection. Well-versed in self-promotion, Villa had tried currying the favor of Americans through the press and even films. Wilson went so far as to characterize Villa as a Robin Hood who had spent "a not uneventful life in robbing the rich in order to give to the poor." Still, historian John Womack called the Villastas "restless and hard to please, utterly free, unconscious, overwhelming, . . . [more] a force of nature than of politics . . . [who] had no definite class interests or attachments."

Throughout 1915, fighting consumed Mexico. In the north, Mexican border towns became major battlegrounds between Carranza and Villa. Each sought to control the flow of American materials and finance their war efforts. Before long, Carranza's forces gained the upper hand following the battle of Celaya in April 1915. Over the summer, American officials considered de facto recognition of Carranza's government, but withheld formal recognition. They feared supporting him too early, and U.S. diplomats wanted some leverage in order to weaken some of Carranza's proposed reforms, principally the restrictions on the petroleum industry and prohibitions against foreign ownership of Mexican land. Finally, in October 1915, after reports that German agents were conspiring with Huerta and Villa, the United States agreed to recognize Carranza's government, although Washington emphasized it expected the nation to follow up by holding general elections that included the Zapatistas and Villastas.

Bring Me the Head of Pancho Villa

For nearly two years, Wilson had avoided direct intervention in the revolution. The angry nationalist response to the U.S. invasion of Vera Cruz had made him leery. Furthermore, both Wilson and Lansing believed that the Germans wanted the United States embroiled in Mexico to prevent Washington from focusing on Europe. In early 1915, Lansing wrote: "German desires to keep up the turmoil in Mexico until the US is forced to intervene; therefore, we must not intervene. . . . It comes down to this: Our possible relations with Germany must be our first consideration; and all our intercourse with Mexico must be regulated accordingly."

Events in Mexico prevented Lansing from fulfilling his priorities. Villa, angry over the U.S. recognition of Carranza's government, began to attack Americans on both sides of the border. He stopped a train and summarily executed several American engineers. On March 9, 1916, his forces looted the town of Columbus, New Mexico, killing seventeen Americans. Wilson responded by sending General John J. "Black Jack" Pershing and 7,000 men and several aircraft after Villa. For nearly a year, Pershing's forces vainly chased Villa across northern Mexico, sparking a dangerous clash with Carranza's forces when the Mexican president demanded that the U.S. Army withdraw from Mexico. Ultimately, Pershing retreated in February 1917, as Europe now dominated U.S. attention.

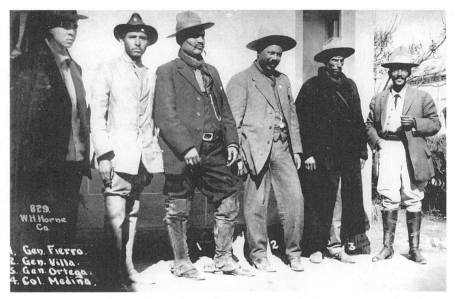

Pancho Villa (third from right) and several Mexican generals. *Courtesy National Archives, ARC Identifier 533444*

The German Indiscretion

Three days after Washington announced the withdrawal of U.S. troops from Mexico, the Germans resumed unrestricted submarine warfare against all ships going to or from its enemy nations. Wilson responded by beginning active preparations for war. In late February, Mexico returned to the spotlight. British intelligence agents turned over to Washington an intercepted telegram from the German foreign secretary Arthur Zimmerman to Carranza that proposed a military alliance between Mexico and Germany. It stipulated that if war broke out between Germany and the United States, Mexico would attack the United States. Following victory, Germany would help the Mexicans recover lands lost in the Mexican-American War. The publication of the telegram pushed the United States closer toward war.

The German actions provoked Wilson into asking Congress for and receiving a declaration of war against Germany in April 1917. The U.S. commitment to the conflict in Europe dramatically altered U.S. relations with Carranza. During early 1917, more problems had surfaced in addition to Pershing's expedition, principally the promulgation of a new Mexican constitution. The document contained several sections that particularly distressed Americans, including articles severely limiting the Catholic Church and the liberal protection of labor. The most volatile was Article 27, which allowed the expropriation of private property for the public interest. It provided that "only Mexicans by birth or naturalization" could gain the right "to acquire ownership in lands, waters and their appurtenances." The United States protested vigorously, fearing the retroactive expropriation of American-owned property and businesses.

Despite the tumultuous relationship between Wilson and Carranza, the former moved cautiously, preferring negotiation to confrontation. At first, the Americans promised official recognition (de jure) if Carranza would sign a treaty repudiating retroactivity in Article 27. He refused but promised conservative application of the measure, assuaging some fears. When Carranza won an election in March 1917, Washington extended formal diplomatic recognition. For a while, tensions eased: the Americans turned their attentions to Europe, and the Mexicans focused on creating stability under their new constitution. Ultimately, an assassin's bullet would stop Carranza, and a stroke severely limited Wilson's ability to settle the problem. Their successors inherited the unresolved issues.

Wilson's Legacy

From the end of the fighting in Europe in late 1918 to his retirement in early 1921, Wilson focused on negotiating a lasting peace, building on the principles of his "Fourteen Points," which, ironically, promoted self-determination for all sovereign nations. At Versailles, his calls for formation of a League of Nations and collective action to ensure order and stability won acceptance by the major powers. Many Latin Americans applauded Wilson's version of a new world order and joined the League. Still, Wilson's own intransigence and partisanship led to failure to secure U.S. participation in the League. As in many realms, Wilson's legacy was one of frustration and failure, as idealism clashed with the realpolitik that dominated foreign policy.

Much like his grand world vision, Wilson had comparable goals for a Pan-American community based on democratic and capitalist development. However, his legacy in this regard lay more in his actions than his rhetoric. More than any preceding U.S. president, Wilson employed military force in Latin America. In his presidency, the U.S. directly intervened in the affairs of more than six nations. As Schoultz stresses, "the Wilson administration supervised the most active period of military intervention in the history of U.S.-Latin American relations." Lester Langley adds that "his Mexican policy alone would earn him the badge of infamy among hemispheric critics of the United States."

Republican Ascendancy

In the 1920 presidential race, Republicans made Wilson's Latin American policy an issue, as they condemned the costly interventions and promised changes. They received further ammunition when Democratic vice-presidential nominee Franklin D. Roosevelt injudiciously bragged that in the League of Nations, the United States automatically had the votes of Cuba, Panama, Nicaragua, the Dominican Republic, and Haiti. He added, "I have had something to do with the running of a couple of little republics. The facts are that I wrote Haiti's constitution myself, and if I do say it I think it is a very good constitution."

The Republican presidential nominee, Warren G. Harding, jumped on the issue. "If I should be . . . elected President of this just and honorable Republic, I will not empower an Assistant Secretary of the Navy to draft a constitution for helpless neighbors in the West Indies and jam it down their throats at the point of bayonets borne by United States Marines. . . . Nor will I misuse the power of the Executive to cover with a veil of secrecy repeated acts of unwarranted interference in domestic affairs of the little Republics of the Western Hemisphere." Later, however, Harding reflected American ambivalence when he bragged he was one of the "Americans who believe in the good old Monroe Doctrine of America dominating the affairs of the New World."

Harding won and took office in 1921. He and his secretary of state Charles Evans Hughes began formulating plans to reduce the U.S. military presence in the Caribbean. Despite campaign promises to withdraw from Haiti, the administration maintained troops there. A congressional committee supported the decision, arguing that a withdrawal would ensure "the abandonment of the Haitian people to chronic revolution, anarchy, barbarism, and ruin." Not everyone agreed. Senator William Borah of Idaho emphasized that "we ought to get out of Haiti and out of every place where we have no right. It may be true that they are not capable of self-government as we understand it, but it is their government." Anti-imperialists tried but failed to cut funding for the U.S. occupation.

The anti-imperialists had more success in ending the U.S. occupation of the Dominican Republic. Dominican nationalists had waged a very skillful propaganda campaign in the United States, highlighting abuses by U.S. Marines and the hypocrisy of the U.S. intervention. Racial issues also played a role, as Americans differentiated between the Dominicans, especially the lighter-skinned elites, and the darker-skinned Haitians. In mid-1921, Harding sent Sumner Welles to the Dominican Republic to negotiate an American withdrawal. Within a year, the parties signed a treaty that allowed for the establishment of a provisional government, renegotiated the debt, and planned national elections. By September 1924, the U.S. Marines withdrew, and Horacio Vásquez took control. While the United States remained a potent force because it maintained control of customs receipts, blatant vestiges of U.S. imperialism dissipated.

Before the U.S. withdrawal from the Dominican Republic, Washington created a future source of conflict. Determined to reduce the military's influence, U.S. officials created a national constabulary. They wanted an apolitical force that maintained order, and they instructed the U.S. Marines to establish a military academy to train Dominicans. One of the first graduates of this school was Rafael Leonidas Trujillo y Molina. He steadily moved up the hierarchy, properly ingratiating himself with important American officers and members of the Dominican elite, including President Vásquez. By 1927, Trujillo was a brigadier general. Within three years, he took power, which he never relinquished until his assassination in 1961. During that time, he established a virtual fiefdom in the country, relying on the U.S.-supplied National Guard and patronage to sustain his dictatorship.

Over time, a controversy developed regarding U.S. responsibility for Trujillo's authoritarianism. As Atkins and Wilson acknowledge, the "United States was at least indirectly responsible for Trujillo through its training of him and establishing the constabulary that became his source of power." At the same time, they note that the United States "did not intend for the Dominican armed forces to be used as an instrument for overthrowing constituted government or for maintaining a military dictatorship." The intentions of the U.S. government notwithstanding, the establishment of the Trujillo regime demonstrated a lack of understanding of Latin American cultures. U.S. leaders had hoped to transplant U.S. values and institutions

into an alien society in which the military had historically played a significant political role. Believing they could ensure change, the Americans had
helped create a monster. U.S. policy-makers would repeat the mistake in
Cuba, Nicaragua, and Haiti.

The Ghost of Taft

In the larger scheme of foreign affairs, Harding and his Republican successor
Calvin Coolidge (1923–29) focused more on economic issues than had their
predecessors. Returning to Taft's "Dollar Diplomacy," they hoped American
capital and technology would ensure U.S. dominance of foreign markets.
The economic downturn immediately following World War I further fueled
the push for new opportunities. Throughout the 1920s, economic development would remain a cornerstone of Republican foreign policy.

World War I had accelerated the process of U.S. economic dominance
in Latin America. Before the conflict, the United States was the hegemonic
power in Central America and the Caribbean, while the British remained
the dominant force in South America, albeit with strong competition from
the Germans and French. As historian Michael Krenn observes, World
War I caused a change: "While the tangled alliances on the Continent
proceeded along the path to slaughter, the United States found itself in a
pleasantly surprising situation vis-à-vis South America. Almost overnight
the war had accomplished what a century of U.S. doctrines and economic
policies had failed to effect: the nearly complete removal of the European
grip on that region."

For the most part, the Harding and Coolidge administrations allowed
private interests to lead, supporting their efforts mainly through the Commerce Department headed by Herbert Hoover. What resulted was an ad
hoc pattern of investment and development formulated primarily by individual businesspersons, located mainly in the Northeast and the West Coast.
Groups such as the American International Corporation (AIC) invested
millions of dollars in Latin America. Its board of directors included members of the most important American companies in the region including
W. R. Grace and Company, American Telephone and Telegraph, and General Electric. Throughout the 1920s, these groups bought Latin American
companies, plantations, and mines.

American bankers also played a substantial role in this new phase of
dollar diplomacy. Loans to foreign governments increased dramatically.

After World War I, the United States had emerged as a creditor nation for the first time in its history, and American bankers looked all over the world for new opportunities to increase their holdings and maximize their profits. From 1920 to 1924, $529 million flowed into Latin America, 18.6 percent of all U.S. loans, surpassed only by those going to Western Europe. The numbers increased during the period 1925 to 1929 to more than $1.158 billion, or 32.2 percent of all U.S. loans. The gross profits on the loans in the decade exceeded $81 million. While British bankers remained competitive in South America, the United States truly made substantial headway.

The efforts of the American entrepreneurs led to significant gains in Latin American trade, especially in areas where they had trailed European competitors before 1914. In 1913, U.S. exports to South America were $178 million. By 1927, they reached $465 million, an increase of 160 percent. Imports from Latin America also grew substantially. By 1927, total trade had risen to more than $1 billion, and the United States had passed Great Britain as the region's leading trading partner. The European nations, meanwhile, would need many years in which to rebuild their war-damaged industrial bases.

The Petroleum War

The Harding and Coolidge administrations' relationship with Mexico highlights a significant trend in U.S.-Latin American relations in the 1920s, specifically efforts to respond to nationalist challenges. Washington's pro-business position directly clashed with Latin American economic nationalism. While not limited to Mexico, the nationalists of that nation, led by President Alvaro Obregón (1920–23) and President Plutarco Elías Calles (1924–28), would play hardball with Washington.

The Harding administration had inherited significant problems in the U.S. relationship with Mexico. Wilson's interventions had only fueled further ill will toward the United States, while Carranza's assassination in 1919 sparked a new round of infighting and removed the leader who had implemented the provisions of the Constitution of 1917 only tenuously. The new president, Obregón, was quick to challenge American interests in Mexico after taking office in 1920. Tensions remained high when Washington refused to extend diplomatic recognition to the new government, arguing that the Mexicans needed to pay American claims resulting from the destruction of the revolution. In particular, U.S. policymakers hoped to hold out recognition to force Obregón to compromise on Article 27 of the Mexican Constitution.

The issue of Article 27 was important because American petroleum interests had a substantial place in the Harding administration. Oil men immediately attacked Obregón when he chose to retroactively apply Article 27. Businessmen Harry F. Sinclair and Edward L. Doheny helped organize several organizations to demonize the Mexican position. They found a receptive audience in the Harding administration, primarily Secretary of the Interior Albert Bacon Fall (later jailed for his role in the Teapot Dome Scandal), who declared, "So long as I have anything to do with the Mexican question, no government of Mexico will be recognized, with my consent, which does not first enter into a written agreement promising to protect American citizens and their property rights in Mexico."

Many other Americans of the day agreed that how the government settled the Mexican issue was important. The Bolshevik assault on capitalism heightened American fears of restricted markets and raw materials. It was imperative, many felt, to settle the issue with Mexico favorably and forcefully, especially since other Latin Americans viewed Mexico as a leader. As a result, Harding continued to withhold recognition of Obregón's government. Secretary of State Charles Evans Hughes warned: "no State is entitled to a place within the family of nations if it destroys the foundations of honorable intercourse by resorting to confiscation and repudiation."

But the Obregón government refused to buckle. Fortunately for the new president, the Mexican Supreme Court intervened. In September 1921, it ruled that the Mexican government could not seize the rights of the Texas Company since it had conducted "positive acts" as outlined by the constitution. These included actions such as oil exploration or drilling prior to May 1, 1917. Therefore, the court declared Article 27 invalid in that case. Some problems remained, because Mexican law required five consecutive concurring decisions before a ruling became a binding precedent. This occurred within a year, and it freed Obregón to enter negotiations on the issue without any charges of having sold out.

By the spring of 1923, both countries had named commissioners, who conducted their first meetings on Bucareli Street in Mexico City. The final accord, known as the Bucareli Agreement, had the Mexican government supporting the concept of "positive acts" in future negotiations with American companies. In addition, both countries agreed to establish a commission to adjudicate the claims of U.S. citizens. In return, Washington extended diplomatic recognition, and a U.S. ambassador arrived in Mexico City in early 1924, the first in five years. That summer the Republicans proudly boasted in their platform that "our difficulties with Mexico have happily yielded to a most friendly adjustment."

New Presidents, New Tensions

In 1924, Obregón turned over power to a fellow Sonoran, Plutarco Calles. The former governor held a fervent commitment to the revolution. He immediately alienated Mexicans and Americans alike when he implemented constitutional limitations on the Catholic Church, deporting foreign priests and closing parochial schools. In response, conservative Catholics rose in arms in the Cristero Revolt, leading to savage fighting. American Catholics, led by the Knights of Columbus, denounced Calles and compared him to the Bolsheviks in Russia. Over time, the propaganda had some success.

His anti-Catholic policy was incendiary, but Calles created a more divisive issue when he announced plans to expropriate 2.5 million hectares of land for redistribution to peasants. Simultaneously, his administration drafted legislation to apply Article 27 retroactively. He stated that foreign investors had come to Mexico with plans to "take everything and leave nothing," and he stressed that he would "safeguard what belongs to Mexico." The new legislation severely tightened the definition of "positive acts" and placed a fifty-year limit on subsoil rights. The law appeared ready for implementation in 1926.

The new petroleum law created new pressures. Secretary of State Frank Kellogg sent a letter of protest even before the Mexican Congress had voted on the matter. He released a statement that the Coolidge administration "will continue to support the Government in Mexico only so long as it protects American lives and American rights and complies with its international engagements and obligations. The Government of Mexico is now on trial before the world." U.S. Ambassador to Mexico James R. Sheffield was intemperate in his support of American businesspersons. He wrote a friend that Calles and his advisors were motivated by "greed, a wholly Mexican view of nationalism and an Indian, not Latin, hatred of all peoples not on the reservation." These stereotypical views, combined with the rising belief in the Coolidge administration that the Mexicans had come under Moscow's influence, led some Americans to call for direct military intervention.

Political Pilgrims as Diplomats

Tensions remained high as Calles refused to compromise. By 1920, the negative stereotypes of Mexicans held by many Americans were reinforced in books and films. A *New York Times* editorial argued that "to the average American the Mexican of today is an insurgent or a bandit or, at any rate, a conspirator against his own Government." One of the most popular villains in the burgeoning American cinema was the "cowardly and underhanded 'greaser.'"

Nevertheless, some people challenged these views, both during and after the revolution. One influential group was the "political pilgrims," a term employed by historian Helen Delpar. These men and women, often tired of the gross materialism of the United States, searched elsewhere for models of development and ways of life. Their ranks included Ernest Gruening, editor of *The Nation* and future U.S. senator. He used his magazine and books to praise the revolution and its accomplishments. Other important proponents of Mexico included Frank Tannenbaum, Carleton Beals, and Alma Reed. They worked hard to offset the negative propaganda pushed by the oil companies and the Catholic Church, often succeeding in shaping the opinion of important American legislators. Their works also encouraged more cultural exchanges between the countries, especially in the arts and education, and heightened the interests of tourists and others traveling to Mexico, where they formed their own opinions.

In other areas, Mexicans themselves did yeoman work in creating favorable impressions of their country. Muralists José Clemente Orozco and Diego Rivera garnered rave reviews for their work, which glorified the pre-conquest era and the Mexican Revolution. Mexican playwrights, composers, and musicians such as Julián Carillo, Miguel Covarrubias, and José Mojica established ties with the American artistic community and won admiration for their abilities. Equally as important, actors in the film industry such as Dolores del Río and Ramón Navarro helped break down stereotypes of Mexicans in Hollywood. These contacts combined with efforts by Mexican government officials, including Secretary of Education José Vasconcelos, helped lay the groundwork for better understanding and cooperation.

Changing Demographics

Another factor working toward a rapprochement between the United States and Mexico was the increased Mexican presence in the United States. Mexican Americans already had a strong influence in the Southwest, as their labor sustained ranches, farms, mines, and industrial centers. In 1900, there were approximately 500,000 Mexican Americans in the United States. During the period 1900–09, thousands of Mexicans legally immigrated to the United States, and the numbers increased dramatically during the revolution, as 162,595 Mexicans fled northward. The need for affordable labor ensured that Americans welcomed the hard-working newcomers. By 1920, there were more than 1 million Mexican Americans living in the United States.

The 1920s, however, saw a significant backlash against foreign immigration to the United States. In 1921 and 1924, Congress passed the first broad-based immigration restriction acts. As one historian notes, "a contradiction existed between those who sought to maximize profits by bringing in Mexican labor and those who saw Mexicans as a threat to the homogeneity of Anglo society." Congressional representatives from the Southwest urged the Department of Agriculture (which argued Mexican labor assisted reclamation projects) and Department of State (which contended that restrictions hurt Pan-Americanism) to prevent the new quotas from applying to Mexicans. From 1920 to 1929, 427,000 Mexicans became legal immigrants. Some might note that the U.S. government created the Border Patrol in 1924, but, interestingly enough, it focused not on Mexicans but on Chinese laborers disembarking in Mexico and entering the United States. The new force also concentrated on preventing drugs and alcohol not Mexicans, from crossing the border.

Significant restrictions on all immigration led to forced deportations of Mexican aliens and even some Mexican Americans during the Great Depression, but in the first three decades of the twentieth century, the Mexican American population in the United States increased dramatically. While Mexican Americans and Mexican immigrants faced terrible discrimination, their presence in the United States helped create an important minority voice. In some states, especially New Mexico, people of Mexican heritage began to win political positions. The voting bloc, while often disenfranchised, was still a potentially important voice that some whites respected and courted. This established at least some basis of understanding, albeit a limited one, that helped improve U.S.-Mexican relations over time.

The Peace Progressives

Another significant factor pushing conciliation and compromise was the presence in Congress of anti-imperialist legislators tired of viewing U.S. foreign policy as an extension of business interests. They included Senators Borah, George Norris of Nebraska, and Robert M. LaFollette of Wisconsin. As historian Lorenzo Meyer notes: "In the view of Borah and other members of Congress, the time had come to stop supporting the activities of the Knights of Columbus and the oil and banana companies abroad; such a policy, which was forever creating a climate for intervention, was prejudicial to U.S. interests in the hemisphere." Strongly shaped by the progressive beliefs in self-determination and self-rule, the anti-imperialist senators challenged the Coolidge administration's policies in Mexico and later Nicaragua.

The senators employed several methods to undermine the influence of the bankers and oil companies. In early 1926, Norris demanded that the State Department publish diplomatic correspondence with Mexico. He and others hoped to demonstrate the undue influence of the oil companies in shaping U.S. policy. They attacked the administration's characterization that Calles had fallen under Moscow's direction. Senator Burton Wheeler of Montana scoffed at Kellogg's testimony in early 1927, telling people that "ever since the Swedes up in Minnesota threw him out of the Senate, Kellogg has been seeing a red behind every bush." Finally, Senator Borah chaired sessions of the Senate Foreign Relations Committee in 1927 that reviewed the administration's Mexican policy. Working with information provided by Mexico City, he dragged numerous State Department officials in front of the committee to justify their actions. According to historian Samuel Flagg Bemis, Borah and others successfully "spiked the guns of the interventionists."

The Good American

Responding to congressional criticism, the Coolidge administration changed its policies. One of its first moves was to replace Ambassador Sheffield with Dwight W. Morrow. An Amherst classmate of Coolidge, he was a banker in the House of Morgan with progressive impulses. In response to

Ambassador Dwight Morrow (center) with J. Reuben Clark and President Rubio Ortiz
of Mexico, circa 1925. *Courtesy Library of Congress, LC-USZ62-113166*

U.S. intervention in Cuba, Morrow wrote that he recognized the United
States might run Cuba better. But "as I get older," he wrote, "I think I
become more and more convinced that good government is not a substitute for self-government. The kind of mistakes that America would make
in running Cuba would be different from those that the Cubans make,
but they would probably cause a new kind of trouble and a new kind of
suffering." With these ideas firmly entrenched, he left for Mexico City,
remarking that "I know what I can do for the Mexicans. I can like them."

Immediately, the new ambassador was remarkably successful. He met
personally with Calles, negotiating in good faith and recognizing the
Mexican positions. As one historian points out, "Morrow accomplished
in exactly three weeks what his predecessors had been unable to do in
two years—convince President Calles that it [the United States] would
not violate any basic principle of the Mexican Revolution to void the most
offensive sections of the 1925 petroleum law."

Throughout his tenure, Morrow relied heavily on personal diplomacy.
He met regularly with Calles to discuss the issues, going out of his way to
promote good relations. At Morrow's invitation, the American celebrities
Charles Lindbergh and Will Rogers toured Mexico, winning wide public

acclaim. By 1927, Morrow had persuaded Calles to compromise on Article 27. Under pressure from Calles, the Mexican Supreme Court ruled that companies that had worked on their properties before 1917 could retain ownership. Morrow also acted as an intermediary in the Cristero Revolt, inviting Father John J. Burke to help negotiate an end to the conflict. By his last annual message to Congress, Coolidge proudly, and correctly, stated that "our relations with Mexico are on a more satisfactory basis than at any time since the revolution."

The Morass in Nicaragua

While the Coolidge administration avoided a military confrontation in Mexico, it failed elsewhere. Early in the 1920s, the United States hosted a Central American Conference to try to stabilize the region. The meeting resulted in several agreements, including the nonrecognition of governments having assumed power by force, establishment of international commissions to settle disputes, limitations on the size of armies, and promises not to interfere in the domestic affairs of neighboring nations. While only a few countries ever ratified the entire agreement, Washington believed progress had been made. Nevertheless, Secretary of State Hughes warned that the United States would not "tolerate much disturbance in the Caribbean region because of the vital importance of our self-defense of the Panama Canal."

Despite these efforts, a civil war in Nicaragua led to direct U.S. intervention. After a contested presidential election there in 1924, the Coolidge administration, hoping that the Nicaraguans would solve the problems peacefully, withdrew the marine legation in 1925. Fighting erupted, however, when Conservative forces led by Emiliano Chamorro overthrew the government. Washington withheld recognition of the Chamorro government and avoided direct interference until Liberals under the command of Juan B. Sacasa counterattacked. Their having signed a pact with the Calles government in 1926 led the State Department to conclude that Calles had "the unquestionable aim of ultimately achieving a Mexican primacy over the Central American countries." Secretary of State Kellogg even believed that the Mexicans wanted to help the Communists seize a foothold in the region. The State Department produced a report, *Bolshevik Aims and Policies in Mexico and Latin America,* which highlighted Communist activities in Nicaragua.

The United States faced a dilemma. As historian Walter LaFeber stresses, "Coolidge and Kellogg solved the problem in the time-honored fashion," by sending in the U.S. Marines along with negotiators, who secured Chamorro's resignation by giving him $20,000 and safe passage to Europe. In his place, Adolfo Díaz became interim president. When political instability continued, Coolidge ordered 2,000 marines into Nicaragua. He then dispatched a special emissary, Henry Stimson, to negotiate with Sacasa and the Liberals. They relented in the face of U.S. pressure, with the exception of one Augusto César Sandino. Stimson arranged the Peace of Tipitapa, which called for a cease-fire and the holding of fair elections, which Liberal José Maria Moncada won in 1928. The terms of the agreement also mandated supervision by the marines of congressional elections in 1930 and the training of a national constabulary. For the moment, Stimson's mission appeared successful.

Bandit or Revolutionary?

Nevertheless, tensions in Nicaragua remained. The major problem was Sandino. The bastard son of a wealthy landowner, he had received a good education. During his twenties he had worked in Mexican oil fields, where he became imbued with the revolutionary ideas sweeping the country. He returned to Nicaragua in 1926 and began organizing workers in the gold mines. When the fighting broke out, he used his own money and outfitted a small force to fight the Conservatives. When the Liberals signed the agreement with Stimson and the Conservatives, Sandino bitterly complained that Moncada would "at the very first opportunity sell out to the Americans." Believing himself to be "the one called to protest the betrayal of the Fatherland," Sandino and his small band retreated to the hills and began waging a guerrilla war against the government.

For five years, U.S. Marines fought Sandino's forces. Rarely numbering more than 1,000, the Sandinistas lived off the land and relied on the goodwill of peasants to survive. At its peak, the U.S. occupation numbered 5,000 marines. Throughout the conflict, Nicaraguan and U.S. officials characterized the Sandinistas as bandits. Working with the fledgling Nicaraguan National Guard, the marines chased Sandino's forces all over the northern provinces. Atrocities occurred as marine aviators and ground troops destroyed villages and crops in attempts to weaken Sandino's sup-

General Sandino (center) and staff. *Courtesy National Archives, 999-WNC-371*

port. The occupation proved very costly to the United States in manpower, monies, and international prestige.

Opposition to the U.S. intervention developed quickly in the United States and throughout the rest of Latin America. The All-America Anti-Imperialist League held meetings in major American cities denouncing the intervention. Guest speakers included Sandino's half-brother Socrates who compared his brother's struggle to those of Simón Bolívar and George Washington. Journalists led by Carleton Beals, who personally interviewed Sandino, began publishing stories in magazines such as *The Nation* that glorified Sandino's efforts to end Nicaragua's domination by U.S. business interests.

Opposition to the Coolidge administration's policy found other forums. Senator Wheeler suggested that if the United States wanted to "stamp out banditry, let's send them to Chicago to stamp it out there. . . . I wouldn't sacrifice . . . one American boy for all the damn Nicaraguans." Senator Norris chastised Coolidge for employing the marines to "destroy human life, to burn villages, to bomb innocent women and children from the air." Others focused on economic factors. Alabama senator Thomas Heflin complained that "our army is now being used to collect the debts of Wall Street financiers." Many legislators called for the immediate withdrawal of the U.S. military, and they proposed cutting the occupation's funding.

The small but vocal groups had an impact. Kellogg cabled General Frank McCoy, in charge of U.S. military occupation in Nicaragua, and complained to him that "there is a great deal of criticism in this country about the way in which these operations are being dragged out with constant sacrifice without any concrete results. . . . People cannot understand why the job cannot be done, and frankly I do not understand myself." Others in Washington shared the feeling but found themselves unable to develop an acceptable exit strategy.

Pan Americanism on Trial in Havana

While the Coolidge administration floundered in Nicaragua, the Sixth International Conference of American States convened in Havana in January 1928. Anticipating trouble over the intervention in Nicaragua and the occupation of Haiti, the United States dispatched former Secretary of State Hughes to lead the American delegation. Even President Coolidge attended the opening ceremonies, arriving conspicuously on a U.S. battleship. In the opening session, Cuban President Gerardo Machado praised the United States: "Intense is our joy and complete our faith in the future destinies of our hemisphere when, gazing over this hall, adding brilliancy to this transcendental occasion, we behold the illustrious person of His Excellency Calvin Coolidge, Chief Executive of the greatest of all democracies." Coolidge followed with an inoffensive speech and immediately boarded the ship for the trip home.

Despite the comparatively innocuous opening of the conference, a series of clashes followed between what one person calls "the United States and its toadies versus independent Latin America." The most important issue was a report by the Rio Commission of Jurists, which stated that "no state may intervene in the internal affairs of another." El Salvadoran Gustavo Guerrero led the charge to adopt a nonintervention clause. For some time it appeared that the U.S. delegation, with the assistance of its allies, would completely bury the nonintervention proposal. On the last day, however, Guerrero made a stand. Speeches condemning intervention followed and an exasperated Hughes defended the right of action, especially "interposition of a temporary nature," to protect lives and property. Hughes won the day, and the conference ended without any adoption of a nonintervention clause. It would be another five years before the Latin Americans raised the issue again, in Santiago, and, as with many issues, Calvin Coolidge would leave it for his successor, Herbert Hoover, to address.

Continuities

In the early part of the twentieth century, interdependence between the United States and Latin America increased dramatically. On the economic level, for the first time, the United States became the preponderant power, as World War I greatly reduced competition. American investments in and imports and exports from the region increased dramatically in the period, as Latin Americans increasingly provided goods that American consumers liked and raw materials that fueled American factories.

With this commerce came cultural trappings that included films, novels, and other forms of American popular culture that extolled the values of U.S. society. At the same time, Latino cultural influence in the United States increased, as Latino actors became more prominent in Hollywood and other artists, led by Diego Rivera, became widely acclaimed. In the Southwest, the Latino styles of architecture remained popular, and new forms of Latin American cuisine and holidays became incorporated into American society.

On the political front, Washington became more intertwined with Latin America through its constant meddling and intervention, especially in the northern areas nearer the United States. The drive for political hegemony was strong, first as the United States battled the perceived European threats and then as the revolutionary spirit swept the region in the aftermath of the revolutions in Mexico and the Soviet Union. The bayonet of the marines when accompanied by the entrepreneur strengthened the U.S. position in Latin America.

Despite the gains, the Latin American response to U.S. hegemony was increasingly one of resistance. Violent resistance to U.S. intervention occurred in Mexico, Nicaragua, the Dominican Republic, and Haiti. Nationalists throughout the region condemned U.S. imperialism and worked with progressive Americans to undermine the rationales and funding for the U.S. military invasions.

Economic nationalists also became stronger, as Mexico set a standard for the use of expropriation of major industries and fought mightily to control its own natural resources. Through negotiation, the use of threats, and other tactics, the nationalists increasingly fought back to try to regain control of native industries and more equally share the benefits of the extraction of raw materials. These efforts extended to cultural realms, wherein nationalists extolled the benefits of the ideals and traditions of their respective countries and questioned the value of the gross materialism and hedonism of the U.S. society.

The turmoil of the Mexican Revolution and the fighting in the Caribbean continued the process of pushing immigrants into the United States to seek jobs and escape the chaos. In Florida, New York, and the Southwest, the Latino population grew to become economically and politically powerful. These trends continued to gain momentum, at least until the Great Depression temporarily slammed on the brakes.

SUGGESTIONS FOR ADDITIONAL READING

For general works on the period, see Dana G. Munro, *Intervention and Dollar Diplomacy in the Caribbean, 1900–1921* (1964); David Healy, *Drive to Hegemony: The United States in the Caribbean, 1898–1917* (1988); Whitney T. Perkins, *Constraint of Empire: The United States and Caribbean Interventions* (1981); and Lester Langley, *The Banana Wars: An Inner History of American Empire, 1900–1934* (1983).

Books on Cuba during the early twentieth century include Allan R. Millet, *The Politics of Intervention: The Military Occupation of Cuba, 1906–1909* (1968); Louis A. Perez, Jr., *Cuba Under the Platt Amendment, 1902–1934* (1986); Jules R. Benjamin, *The United States and Cuba, 1880–1934: Hegemony and Dependent Development* (1977); and José M. Hernández, *Cuba and the United States: Intervention and Militarism, 1868–1933* (1993).

Good general works on Wilson include John Milton Cooper, Jr., *The Warrior and the Priest: Woodrow Wilson and Theodore Roosevelt* (1983); David D. Anderson, *Woodrow Wilson (1978);* Burton Kaufman, *Expansion and Efficiency: Foreign Trade Organization in the Wilson Administration* (1974); and Arthur Link, *Woodrow Wilson: Revolution, War, and Peace* (1979).

The historiography of the U.S. response to the Mexican Revolution and other interventions has been well developed. Good works include Mark T. Gilderhus, *Pan American Visions: Woodrow Wilson in the Western Hemisphere, 1913–1921* (1986) and *Diplomacy and Revolution: U.S.-Mexican Relations under Wilson and Carranza* (1977); N. Gordon Levin, *Woodrow Wilson and World Politics: America's Response to War and Revolution* (1968); Frederick S. Calhoun, *Power and Principle: Armed Intervention in Wilsonian Foreign Policy* (1986); Linda B. Hall and Don M. Coerver, *Revolution on the Border: The United States and Mexico, 1910–1920* (1988); Friedrich Katz, *The Secret War in Mexico: Europe, the United States, and the Mexican Revolution* (1981); John Hart, *Revolutionary Mexico: The Coming and the Process of the Mexican Revolution* (1987);

Kenneth J. Grieb, *The United States and Huerta* (1969); and Robert E. Quirk, *An Affair of Honor: Woodrow Wilson and the Occupation of Vera Cruz* (1962).

For more on interventions in the period, see Bruce J. Calder, *The Impact of Intervention: The Dominican Republic during the U.S. Occupation, 1916–1924* (1984); David Healy, *Gunboat Diplomacy in the Wilson Era: The U.S. Navy in Haiti, 1915–1916* (1976); Hans Schmidt, *The United States Occupation of Haiti, 1915–1934* (1971); Robert D. Johnson, *The Peace Progressives and American Foreign Relations* (1995); Brenda Gayle Plummer, *Haiti and the Great Powers, 1902–1915* (1988); and Truman P. Clark, *Puerto Rico and the United States, 1917–1933* (1975).

Good works on the interwar years include Joseph Tulchin, *The Aftermath of War: World War I and U.S. Policy toward Latin America* (1971); Michael Krenn, *U.S. Policy toward Economic Nationalism in Latin America, 1917–1929* (1990); Richard Lael, *Arrogant Diplomacy: U.S. Policy toward Colombia, 1903–1922* (1987); Paul W. Drake, *The Money Doctor in the Andes: The Kemmerer Missions, 1923–1933* (1989); Kenneth J. Grieb, *The Latin American Policy of Warren G. Harding* (1976); and Stephen J. Randall, *The Diplomacy of Modernization: Colombian-American Relations, 1920–1940* (1977).

For more on the issues of petroleum and other concerns with Mexico during the 1920s, see Helen Delpar, *The Enormous Vogue of Things Mexican: Cultural Relations between the United States and Mexico, 1920–1935* (1992); Lorenzo Meyer, *Mexico and the United States in the Oil Controversy, 1917–1942* (1972); Linda B. Hall, *Oil, Banks, and Politics: The United States and Postrevolutionary Mexico, 1917–1924* (1995); Robert Freeman Smith, *The United States and Revolutionary Nationalism in Mexico, 1916–1932* (1972); and Merrill Rippy, *Oil and the Mexican Revolution* (1972).

Good works on U.S. intervention in Nicaragua and Central America include Henry Stimson, *American Policy in Nicaragua* (1927); Godfrey Hodgson, *The Colonel: The Life and Wars of Henry Stimson, 1867–1950* (1990); Neill Macaulay, *The Sandino Affair* (1967); William Kamman, *A Search for Stability: United States Policy toward Nicaragua, 1925–1933* (1968); Thomas J. Dodd, *Managing Democracy in Central America: A Case Study, United States Election Supervision in Nicaragua, 1927–1933* (1992); Marvin Goldwert, *The Constabulary in the Dominican Republic and Nicaragua: Progeny and Legacy of United States Intervention* (1962); Richard Salisbury, *Anti-Imperialism and International Competition in Central America* (1989); and Jürgen Buchenau, *In the Shadow of the Giant: The Making of Mexico's Central American Policy, 1876–1930* (1996).

CHAPTER FIVE

The Era of the Good Neighbor

FROM 1929 TO 1945, THERE WAS A SIGNIFICANT CHANGE in U.S. policy toward Latin America. During this period, the Great Depression decimated almost every nation, and war clouds began to form over Europe and Asia. President Herbert Hoover tried to improve U.S. and Latin American ties by rejecting intervention and developing more positive relationships. While events overwhelmed Hoover, his successor, Franklin D. Roosevelt, promised a New Deal for all Americans, and this idealism extended into foreign policy. In the case of Latin America, Roosevelt and his advisors built on Hoover's actions to implement the "Good Neighbor" Policy that ushered in a new era in U.S.-Latin American relations. Despite its flaws, it brought a closer spirit of cooperation and conciliation than ever before.

A New Day?

Like the delay on the issue of nonintervention, Coolidge turned over many of his Latin American problems to his successor, Herbert Hoover. A well-known humanitarian, Hoover wanted to overhaul U.S. policy in Latin America. Immediately following his election, he made a seven-week goodwill trip to the region, visiting over half of the countries. As secretary of commerce, he had written that he had "developed an increasing dissatisfaction with our policies toward Latin America. I was convinced that unless we displayed an entirely different attitude we should never dispel the suspicions and fears of the 'Colossus of the North' nor win the respect of those Nations." During his inaugural address, Hoover emphasized that "we have no desire for territorial expansion, for economic or other domination of other peoples." In regard to the U.S. military in Nicaragua and Haiti, he declared that "we do not wish to be represented abroad in such a manner."

As Hoover arrived in the White House, members of the State Department and others began to agree with domestic opposition to the use of force in Latin America. In 1928 in his Memorandum on the Monroe Doctrine, Undersecretary of State J. Reuben Clark argued that the 1823 declaration "states a case of United States vs. Europe, and not the United States vs. Latin-America." He repudiated the current intervention in Nicaragua as rationalized by the Roosevelt Corollary, emphasizing that "it is not believed that this corollary is justified by the terms of the Monroe Doctrine, however much it may be justified by the application of the doctrine of self-preservation." While allowing for some forms of intervention, Clark reassured Latin Americans that the Monroe Doctrine was not "an instrument of violence and oppression" but "a wholly effective guaranty of their freedom, independence, and territorial integrity against the imperialistic designs of Europe." Coolidge had refused to release Clark's document, but in 1930, Hoover did so. Historian Alexander DeConde concludes that the Clark Memorandum was responsible for "stripping Monroe's original message of its various excrescences and corollaries."

Escape from Nicaragua

To affect his policies of nonintervention and become a "good neighbor" in Latin America, President Hoover first had to extricate U.S. forces from Nicaragua. For several years, the United States had organized a National Guard there to serve as an apolitical internal security force patterned after the Dominican model. Marines trained and supplied the new corps with arms and equipment. When Hoover took over, however, he worked with Secretary of State Stimson to implement troop withdrawals.

Despite such actions, Sandino refused to lay down his arms until the Americans left. Several factors aided him in his nationalist cause. In 1929, a devastating depression hit the United States, drying up government revenues for costly occupations. The Senate grew impatient and increased its pressure to end the occupation. By early 1931, the Senate passed a resolution declaring that it was "the sense of the Senate that the President should immediately withdraw" U.S. troops from Nicaragua. That same year, the Japanese invaded Manchuria. The United States protested vigorously, but Stimson lamented that the U.S. presence in Nicaragua weakened his ability to criticize the imperialistic actions of other nations. Consequently, the pace of troop withdrawals increased significantly and combat patrols ended in June 1931. By the election of 1932, only 400 marines remained. Finally, on January 2, 1933, the last marine left Nicaragua, and Juan Sacasa took the presidency.

The Bitter Aftertaste

Unlike its predecessor, the Hoover administration successfully extricated itself from Nicaragua. In 1932, it also negotiated the complete withdrawal of U.S. forces from Haiti. By October 1934, all U.S. forces had indeed withdrawn from Haiti, leaving power in the hands of Sténio Vincent. Supported largely by the Garde d'Haiti, he maintained law and order. As Brenda Gayle Plummer notes, however, "the United States had neither changed nor reformed Haitian politics but inadvertently strengthened and assured the survival of many of its worst features."

In both Nicaragua and Haiti, U.S. policies had laid the groundwork for dictatorship by establishing a *Guardia Nacional*. In Nicaragua, it became apparent that the plan for an apolitical military had backfired. During the occupation, the ambitious Anastasio Somoza García, whom Walter LaFeber calls the "United States' most important and lasting gift to Nicaraguans," rose through the ranks. Having studied in the United States, where he learned English, he used his cultural ties such as his love of baseball to ingratiate himself with Americans. He married the daughter of a wealthy Nicaraguan and became a successful businessman. As LaFeber adds, "shrewd, brutal, and unequivocally pro-North American, Somoza became a natural candidate to lead the new National Guard, despite his lack of military training." By the time the marines withdrew, Somoza controlled the National Guard.

Before long, Somoza set his sights on higher prizes. First, he eliminated potential competition, the most troublesome of which was Sandino, who, as promised, had laid down his arms and retired to establish a cooperative farm. In 1934, Sandino traveled to Managua to discuss issues with President Sacasa concerning the National Guard. As he left, a squad of guardsmen, under orders from Somoza, commandeered his car and drove Sandino and several lieutenants to the airport, where they were shot to death with machine guns.

Over the next two years, Somoza gained strength through murder, intimidation, and fraud. U.S. officials looked on but did little about the situation. When Somoza announced his presidential candidacy in 1936,

President Sacasa and others forwarded a letter to the U.S. State Department requesting assistance in restraining Somoza and complaining that the U.S.-created National Guard "would eventually constitute a threat to peace and order." Roosevelt's secretary of state, Cordell Hull, replied that the United States could not interfere, since the "special relationship" had ended in 1933. After fraudulent elections, Somoza took control and established a family dictatorship that lasted until 1979.

By the late 1920s, the Great Depression and anti-imperialist frustration over the interventionism of the preceding three decades forced Herbert Hoover to formulate new ways of interacting with Latin America. Despite his enlightened attitude and good intentions, the economic devastation in the United States overwhelmed his administration. His tenure was too short-lived, as the American people selected someone else to address the calamity of the Great Depression. It was his successor, Franklin D. Roosevelt, who institutionalized the "Good Neighbor" policy and healed many of the wounds opened in the first third of the century.

The "Good Neighbor" Policy

As historian Alexander DeConde notes, Hoover pursued "his ideal of the 'good neighbor,' and produced dividends during his administration and later." Yet Roosevelt became identified with the policy. As assistant secretary of the navy, Roosevelt had played a significant role in President Wilson's interventionist policies. But by the time he assumed the presidency in 1933, Roosevelt was a politician matured by his battle with polio and other challenges. He supported the Democratic platform that called for "no interference in the internal affairs of other nations" and for "cooperation with nations of the Western Hemisphere to maintain the spirit of the Monroe Doctrine." A friend of the Roosevelt family, Sumner Welles, had a special influence on FDR's views of the region. The future undersecretary of state wrote Roosevelt a special memorandum saying that "the creation and maintenance of the most cordial and intimate friendship between the United States and the other republics of the American Continent must be regarded as a keystone of our foreign policy." Roosevelt took the message to heart.

Early in his presidency, Roosevelt set a positive tone. In his inaugural address, he called for a Latin American policy based on the "good neighbor—the neighbor who resolutely respects himself and, because he does so, respects the rights of others—the neighbor who respects his agreements in and with a world of neighbors." Several months later, the president stated that the "definite policy of the United States from now on is one opposed to armed intervention."

Almost immediately Roosevelt matched his words with deeds. At the Seventh International Conference of American States meeting in Montevideo, Uruguay, in December 1933, Secretary of State Cordell Hull backed a resolution stating that "no state has the right to intervene in the internal or external affairs of another." Underlying all of this, however, was a belief in reciprocity. The Latin Americans would maintain order for promises of nonintervention. Clearly, the Roosevelt administration preferred a carrot rather than a stick, but it would protect American interests.

The declaration of the Good Neighbor policy evoked positive responses from most Latin Americans, many of whom also liked FDR's New Deal. *La Nación* in Buenos Aires praised it, emphasizing that the "policy of the 'Big Stick' and later 'policy of the Dollar' have passed into history." *El Mecurio* in Santiago, Chile, wrote that "confidence and trust in the United States" has replaced "the profound animosity which existed when Mr. Roosevelt became President." Even Mexico's delegate to the Montevideo Conference, José Manuel Puig Casauranc, stated: "there is in the White House an admirable noble, and good man—a courageous man who knows the errors of the past but who feels that the errors belong to the past." Critics remained, but Roosevelt had won over many people.

The Good Neighbor Tested

Shortly after taking office, the Roosevelt administration faced a major challenge in Cuba, as the Cubans revolted against authoritarian president Gerardo Machado, who had ruled since 1924. The upheaval threatened American interests there, so Roosevelt dispatched Welles to help negotiate a settlement. As historian Louis Pérez points out, Washington hoped that through its efforts U.S.-backed groups would "secure access to power and subsequently be linked to the United States by ties of gratitude and indebtedness." In the meantime, protecting U.S. strategic and business interests in Cuba remained the primary goal.

Throughout the summer the talks continued, as Cuban groups familiar with the American role desperately tried to exploit it for their own gain. Machado tried to appease the Americans with several compromises, including electoral reform and the release of political prisoners. Unimpressed, Welles pressured Machado to retire. He even subtly threatened armed intervention should he refuse to step down, but Machado boldly told Welles that he would welcome such a move, as it would solidify his support under the banner of nationalism. Nevertheless, army officers overthrew Machado in August 1933.

The crisis could have ended there, but it did not. Welles supported the interim presidency of his long-time friend Carlos Manuel de Céspedes, but it lasted less than a month. Noncommissioned officers led by Sergeant Fulgencio Batista overthrew Céspedes. The Provisional Revolutionary Government selected nationalist Ramón Grau San Martín as its leader. The junta immediately implemented reforms under the banner of "Cuba for Cubans." It abrogated the Platt Amendment, began land reform, and established a Ministry of Labor to protect Cuban workers.

These reforms set the stage for conflict, as they alienated the old elites, the military, and the United States. Welles complained that "American properties and interests are being gravely prejudiced and the material damage to such properties will in all probability be very great." When the Cubans requested Mexican assistance to train its military, Welles responded by appealing for direct U.S. military intervention. Although the State Department refused, the request emboldened the opposition, especially army dissenters led by Batista.

Although Welles left Cuba in December 1933, the groundwork for Grau's demise had been laid. Batista's forces mobilized in January 1934, removing Grau and replacing him with Carlos Mendieta, although Batista held the real power. Four days later, the United States recognized the Mendieta government. That same year, Washington and Havana agreed to abrogate the Platt Amendment, passed favorable tariff concessions, and provided loans to the Cuban government. As one Cuban noted, "American diplomacy has many resources; when the steel of her warships is not convenient, she uses the docile backbone of her native lackeys." Equally as important, the defeat of Grau and his reforms laid the basis for challenges to American dominance almost twenty years later.

The Cuban case exposed one of the most significant flaws in the Good Neighbor policy. For most Americans the policy meant rejecting military intervention. The official abrogation of the Platt Amendment demonstrated one thing, but Welles's interference and having turned a blind eye to the actions of the military illustrated another. Many Latin Americans wanted the Good Neighbor policy to exclude economic and diplomatic coercion. Because of continuous Latin American pressure and foreign threats, the policy would continue to evolve.

Dollar Diplomacy Meets the Good Neighbor Policy

A driving force in the Good Neighbor era was Secretary of State Hull, who desperately wanted economic revitalization in Latin America. The Great Depression and Hoover's tariff policies had strangled international commerce. In 1929, U.S. imports from Latin America reached more than $1 billion and exports topped $911 million. By 1932, however, Latin American imports had fallen to $323 million and exports to $195 million. Hull believed the United States needed to stimulate trade to escape the Great Depression. "International commerce is not only calculated to aid materially in the restoration of prosperity everywhere, but it is the greatest civilizer and peacemaker in the experience of the human race," Hull emphasized. Like Wilson, he believed that economic competition and exclusion caused war. If interdependent economies existed, then nations would move to eliminate conflict.

The cornerstone of Hull's foreign economic policy was reciprocal trade. As historian Dick Steward notes, "the major diplomatic concern of the New Deal was the search for foreign markets; Latin America and the reciprocity negotiations played an early and vital role in this search." In March 1934, the Roosevelt administration asked Congress to grant the president power to raise or lower tariffs with individual countries by 50 percent. With such a bargaining tool, Roosevelt could limit trade restrictions and open new markets. Some Republicans attacked its constitutionality, but the Democratic majority passed the recommendation.

Within another year, the United States negotiated a reciprocal trade treaty with Cuba. Washington followed by concluding similar agreements with Colombia, Brazil, and Haiti. The negotiations were often tedious, and Latin American nationalists fought to protect their industries and interests. Despite such challenges, by 1941 the United States had reciprocal trade treaties with Venezuela, the Central American nations, and Ecuador. In 1942, it signed agreements with the Andean republics and Mexico.

To supplement the treaties, Hull also helped mastermind the creation of the Export-Import Bank in 1934. It extended credit to Latin American governments to purchase American goods, and Cuba became the first country to receive funds from the institution in 1934. In the initial stages, the Bank played a minor role because of its expense, but by 1939, the heightened fear of the fascists in Latin America increased Bank efforts. It would emerge as a major player in U.S.-Latin American relations during World War II.

The trade agreements and loans helped reignite commerce in the region. Exports of American goods to Latin America increased from $215 million in 1933 to $363 million in 1936 and $548 million by 1939. Imports from Latin America rebounded from $316 million in 1933 to $493 in 1936 and $517 million by 1939. The outbreak of World War II and the retraction of European competitors further strengthened the economic relationship between the United States and Latin America.

Brewing Storm Clouds

Events in Europe increasingly shaped U.S. policy in Latin America from the mid-1930s forward. Many Americans and Latin Americans watched the ominously increasing power of the fascist dictatorships in Italy, Germany, and Japan. In the early 1930s, fascist aggression became more commonplace. The Japanese conquered Manchuria in 1931 and the Italians took Ethiopia in 1935. Then Hitler oversaw Germany's annexation of Austria in 1935 and began rebuilding Germany's might from the ashes of World War I and the Great Depression. These totalitarian dictatorships suppressed all dissent and dissolved civil liberties. Added to this was an ongoing U.S. preoccupation with the Soviet Union, over which Joseph Stalin now ruled with an iron hand. A dark cloud seemed to be hovering over democracy everywhere.

Many Americans believed that the rise of fascism threatened U.S. interests. Most, however, wanted to avoid another costly intervention in Europe, hoping the British and French could contain the Germans and Italians. Nevertheless, they kept an eye on German and Italian immigrants who flowed into Latin America in the early twentieth century. Brazil alone was already home to more than 800,000 Brazilians of German heritage and another 100,000 German nationals. In Argentina, Chile, Peru, Costa Rica, and Guatemala, Germans and Italians were prominent citizens and many of them actively worked with their native governments to create cultural, political, and economic ties to their homelands.

In response to the perceived fascist threat in Latin America, the United States called for a special conference. In November 1936, the conference opened in Buenos Aires, one of the hotbeds of Latin American fascism.

Earlier in the month, a crowd stood in a downtown theater and shouted: "Death to the Jews! Death to the Protestants!" Hull warned beforehand that the "Axis penetration had made rapid, alarming headway" in Argentina. Sufficiently concerned, President Roosevelt went to Buenos Aires as a "traveling salesman for peace." In his opening speech, he cautioned non-American states seeking to "commit acts of aggression against us," and promised them they would "find a Hemisphere wholly prepared to consult together for our mutual safety and our mutual good."

After heated debates, the participants signed several major agreements. They accepted a resolution committing each nation to settle peacefully all disputes between countries, building on the precedents established in negotiations between Paraguay and Bolivia during the Chaco War. Each signatory supported a much stronger statement denouncing intervention in the internal affairs of other states. In the process, Washington achieved some of its primary goals. The delegates agreed to consultation among American states in the event of an external power threatening regional security, although no plan of action evolved. Nonetheless, this was an important step in preparing the hemisphere for resisting the fascist threat. The cooperation and conciliation of the Good Neighbor had paid some dividends.

The Mature Good Neighbor

A true test of the Good Neighbor policy arose in Mexico. There, Nationalist Lázaro Cárdenas won the presidency in 1934 and proceeded to implement major provisions of the Constitution of 1917. The government seized millions of acres of land and redistributed it to peasants. Native and foreign landowners denounced the action. Tensions with Washington heightened in early 1938 when Mexican oil workers protested low wages and the lack of white-collar jobs in the foreign-dominated oil industry. When the companies refused to consider these demands, Cárdenas expropriated the oil industry, giving promises of compensation but also guaranteeing to "burn the oilfields to the ground rather than sacrifice our honour."

Problems arose when the American companies valued their properties at $260 million. The Mexicans balked at such claims, citing earlier records when companies had assessed the value of their lands for much less. The American companies responded by attacking the Mexican government in the U.S. press and on Capitol Hill. They accused Cárdenas of harbor-

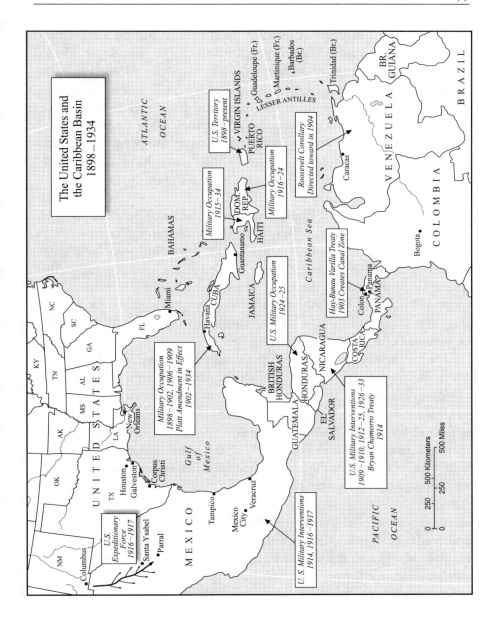

The United States and
the Caribbean Basin
1898–1934

U.S. Territory
1898–present

Military Occupation
1915–34

Military Occupation
1916–24

Roosevelt Corollary
Directed toward in 1904

U.S. Military Occupation
1924–25

Hay-Bunau Varilla Treaty
1903 Creates Canal Zone

Military Occupation
1898–1902, 1906–1909
Platt Amendment in Effect
1902–1934

U.S. Military Interventions
1909–1910, 1912–25, 1926–33
Bryan Chamorro Treaty
1914

U.S.
Expeditionary
Force
1916–1917

U.S. Military Interventions
1914, 1916–1917

ing fascist and Communist sympathies and portrayed the Mexicans as
thieves and outlaws. Soon after the expropriation decree, oil company
representatives visited Secretary of State Hull and important congressional representatives to demand personally an immediate return of their
properties.

While the oil companies assailed the Cárdenas government, several defenders of Mexican rights emerged, led by U.S. Ambassador to Mexico Josephus Daniels. He complained to Hull that "the oil and other big interests here have no sympathy with the Good Neighbor policy. They go to bed every night wishing that [Porfirio] Díaz were back in power and we carried the Big Stick and had Marines ready to land at their beck and call." When Washington tried coercing compromise by reducing U.S. purchases of Mexican silver, Daniels wrote Roosevelt that "We are strong. Mexico is weak. It is always noble in the strong to be generous and generous and generous."

As was often the case, Roosevelt chose a middle-of-the-road path. He feared driving the Mexicans into the arms of the fascists and creating a hostile neighbor. Therefore, he recognized the Mexican government's right to seize the subsoil rights but steadfastly called for fair compensation. After several years of haggling, the two countries submitted the dispute to arbitrators. Ultimately, U.S. oil companies received $42 million. At the same time, Cárdenas established a state-controlled oil company (PEMEX) that became one of the world's major exporters of oil.

This battle over the expropriation was significant for many reasons. For Mexicans, the struggle became symbolic of national pride. The date of the expropriation decree, March 18, became a national holiday. Lorenzo Meyer emphasizes that it was "the historic moment in which the Nation's sense of self-worth was reborn." Many Mexicans, according to Meyer, believed that they had shaken "off once and for all . . . the imperialist shackles that had held Mexico back for so long and prevented the nation from developing and relying on its own strength and ability." Historian Dirk Raat adds that "the oil barons, chiefs of a once domineering foreign enclave, were finally slain. They would join the corpses of ambitious army officers, rash priests, and feudal landlords. Mexico was to become a modern state." Mexico's example would become a model for postwar nationalists seeking to end foreign economic hegemony.

The actions of the Roosevelt administration proved to many Latin Americans that the United States truly subscribed to the Good Neighbor policy and that Washington no longer served as an instrument of big business. On the eve of World War II, a harsher response could have ensured a backlash. As one historian notes, when Mexico entered World War II, it was as "a co-operative ally of the United States, rather than the snarling neighbor she had been in World War I."

Challenging the Nazis

By the late 1930s, the United States began to respond more forcefully to the growing fascist threat in Latin America. In 1937, the Japanese invaded China. A year later, Hitler annexed the Sudetenland and ultimately all of Czechoslovakia. Germany and Italy supported the victorious forces of General Francisco Franco, who established a fascist dictatorship in Spain in 1939. Everywhere, the fascists appeared on the move.

American fears of fascist expansionism were not unfounded. Berlin began establishing networks of spies, saboteurs, and intelligence-gathering operations. Joseph Goebbels, Hitler's propaganda chief, spread messages praising Germany's emphasis on racial purity, anti-Semitism, and anticommunism. The Germans hoped to mobilize Latin American support by building on these ideas and highlighting American and British imperialism.

Creating a Hemispheric Safety Belt

U.S. officials responded by becoming more vigilant in the Western Hemisphere. Throughout 1937 and 1938, the State Department and the White House received numerous reports on Nazi activity in Latin America. German efforts to buy Mexican oil in return for military equipment especially alarmed Washington. Hull wrote that the fascist danger was no longer "limited to the possibility of a military invasion. It was more acute in its indirect form of propaganda, penetration, organizing political parties, buying some adherents, and blackmailing others. We had seen the method employed with great success in Austria and in the Sudetenland. The same technique was obvious in Latin America." American policymakers feared that Latin American elites, especially those in the military, would ally with Germany and Italy.

In late 1938, U.S. diplomats traveled to the Eighth International Conference of American States in Lima. Unlike earlier meetings that stressed nonintervention and mediation, this conference focused on regional security. Many Latin Americans, especially those from the left and intelligentsia, joined Washington in its efforts to contain fascism.

For more than two weeks, Hull and his team labored to secure a declaration of hemispheric solidarity amid challenges, especially from pro-Nazi Argentines. Finally, on Christmas Eve 1938, the delegates voted unanimously for the Declaration of Lima. It committed the American republics to convene a meeting of ministers should a foreign power threaten any American nation. It added that "it is understood that the Governments of the American Republics will act independently in their individual capacity recognizing fully their judicial equality as sovereign states." Hull and Roosevelt called the declaration a great victory, despite criticism that it lacked specific obligations. Nevertheless, the German minister in Peru reported to Berlin that "important resolutions adopted by the conference are directed against us."

Within a year of the Lima conference, the first meeting of the foreign ministers consultative body took place in Panama. Shortly after the outbreak of the war in Europe, they signed the Declaration of Panama, which erected a "security belt" extending an average of 300–700 miles from the coastlines of the Americas. It stated that the countries had an "inherent right" to keep "free from the commission of any hostile act by any non-American belligerent nation." Like many international decrees, it lacked powers of enforcement, as demonstrated by the *Graf Spee*[1] incident in the Rio de la Plata in December 1939. Despite this failure, the Declaration of Panama moved the United States and the Latin American republics toward a full-scale alliance.

Doing Business with Dictators

A direct consequence of U.S. emphasis on nonintervention and unified opposition to the fascists was U.S. acceptance of Latin American dictators as allies. Washington was prevented from removing authoritarian regimes, which in some cases it had helped create. As fear of the fascists increased, U.S. officials moved from tolerance of dictatorships to openly courting them. While such policy was hopelessly hypocritical, Washington believed it had to use any means necessary to prevent European and Asian fascists from gaining a foothold in the Americas.

The United States relied on economic and military assistance to promote closer relations. In September 1940, Congress approved President Roosevelt's request for an additional $500 million for the Export-Import Bank to promote trade. Loans to twelve governments including those of Brazil, Argentina, and Haiti flowed southward. Furthermore, the Panama

---

1 A German battleship that had taken refuge in Montevideo. Ultimately, the *Graf Spee* was forced out to sea to meet waiting British warships. Its captain scuttled the ship to prevent its capture.

Conference had created the Inter-American Development Commission to help fund public works and infrastructure. Clearly, the fascist threat had loosened American purse strings and increased the speed of interdependence on many economic levels.

Regional dictatorships grew in strength. Perhaps the best example was that of Nicaraguan dictator Anastasio Somoza, of whom an American diplomat once said "he's a son-of-bitch, but he's our son-of-bitch." In 1939, Somoza traveled to Washington. As was often the case, the Nicaraguan had impeccable timing, as the administration used his visit as a dress rehearsal for the arrival of the king and queen of England. Roosevelt, Hull, and the full cabinet met Somoza at the train. Then they traveled by motorcade down streets lined by a crowd complemented by 5,000 troops as fifty planes flew overhead. Somoza spoke to a joint session of Congress, and the United States gave him more than $2 million to help finish the Nicaraguan section of the Inter-American highway. As Paul Coe Clark notes, Somoza turned the trip "into political and personal gain at home." The Nicaraguan newspapers and radio stations popularized his special relationship with Roosevelt.

The whole fanfare disheartened some liberal democrats, as *Time* called him "Dictator Somoza." Several congresspersons denounced the special privileges he had received during his visit, especially as Washington condemned totalitarian regimes elsewhere. Many Latin Americans expressed similar disgust. A Mexico City newspaper complained that the Good Neighbor was "transforming itself into a league of 'mestizo' dictators, with the United States destined to guarantee the slavery of Latin American peoples."

Around the same time, General Rafael Trujillo of the Dominican Republic visited the United States, over the objections of several State Department officials, including Sumner Welles. In Washington, Trujillo's supporters held formal dinners and the dictator toured Arlington Cemetery and marine headquarters at Quantico. He held public meetings with Roosevelt and Hull and visited many prominent congressmen. He then traveled to West Point, where he received a twenty-one-gun salute. Afterwards, he moved onto New York City, where Representative Hamilton Fish saluted him as "a builder greater than all the Spanish Conquistadores together." At all events, flash bulbs popped and photographs subsequently appeared in his country to demonstrate the friendship of the United States and the foolishness of Trujillo's domestic opponents.

Soon thereafter, other dictators, including Batista, traveled to Washington, where each one received a warm welcome. Their promises of providing bases and military assistance won them reciprocal promises of U.S. aid. Historian Eric Roorda notes that by the end of the 1930s, the "Good Neighbor policy demonstrated to a generation of Caribbean dictators that they were free to run their countries however they pleased, so long as they maintained common enemies with the United States: first the fascists, then the communists." Clearly, the Good Neighbor and the emphasis on defense had unfortunate long-term effects on U.S.-Latin American relations.

A Crisis Brewing

With the economic assistance and programs such as the Inter-American Highway linking markets and providing means of transferring troops and supplies, the Latin Americans and the Americans prepared for a potential fascist onslaught. Their fears heightened in the spring of 1940, when Hitler's troops consolidated Germany's domination of continental Europe.

Urgent calls for a meeting of American republics followed. Many feared the Germans would occupy the regional territories of France, Denmark, and Holland. Despite German threats of retaliation, the foreign ministers issued the Act of Havana in July 1940. It called for occupation by the American republics to prevent the transfer of conquered European territories to hostile powers. In reality, the act reinforced the no-transfer idea of the Monroe Doctrine. The delegates also reaffirmed that an attack on any nation in the hemisphere was an attack on all and would be met with a common defense.

The Roosevelt administration enthusiastically praised the Havana resolutions. Fortunately for Washington and the Latin American republics, the Germans never forced any confrontation over the colonies. Some potential problems arose in 1940 in Martinique, where a Vichy officer had a small naval force including an aircraft carrier. Negotiations and the appearance of Free French forces to seize the island removed the danger. Washington soon negotiated the "destroyers for bases" agreement with London that granted the United States ninety-nine-year leases on bases in the British Caribbean, including the Bahamas and Jamaica, in exchange for fifty World War I vintage destroyers. By late 1940, Washington aggressively worked in conjunction with the Latin Americans to protect its interests.

Culture Wars

On a nonmilitary front, Roosevelt approved the creation of the Office for the Coordination of Commercial and Cultural Relations between the American Republics (later renamed the Office of Coordinator of Inter-American Affairs [OCIAA]) in late July 1940. Headed by Nelson Rockefeller, who for several years had urged Roosevelt to establish a propaganda machine to counter that of the Nazis, the OCIAA had a mandate to "strengthen the bonds between the nations of the Western Hemisphere" and help coordinate hemispheric defense. Rockefeller bragged that the "United States came in with a program of truth in answer to enemy lies." The OCIAA started with a budget of $3.5 million and a few hundred employees but grew to oversee more than $45 million and employ 1,500 people by 1945.

The OCIAA had many responsibilities and worked in conjunction with the Division of Cultural Relations of the State Department. Emphasizing public works and economic development projects drained a lot of energy from the OCIAA. But it also focused on creating cultural ties to undermine fascist efforts to win sympathy, a sort of struggle for the "hearts and minds" of the Latin Americans. As one official stated, "friends must be won and held, the enemy frustrated, divided, and conquered."

The OCIAA dramatically expanded efforts to promote U.S. ideas and institutions in Latin America. It recorded radio programs in Spanish and Portuguese, bought advertising space to promote U.S. positions in pro-American newspapers and magazines, and distributed more than 40,000 copies of its monthly magazine, *En Guardia,* to prominent Latin Americans. The OCIAA also helped build libraries and cultural institutes and sponsored exchanges in the arts and sports. Thousands of educational exchanges also occurred throughout the war and continued into the postwar era.

The OCIAA also worked with the film industry to achieve its goals. The director of the film department of the OCIAA, John Whitney, wrote that it was important to "share in the task of imparting the full force of the meaning of freedom and sovereignty to a quarter of a billion people in the Americas. The menace of the Nazis and its allied doctrines, their techniques and tactics, must be understood from Hudson Bay to Punto Arenas. Whatever the motion picture can do as a basic job of spreading the gospel of the Americas' common stake in this struggle, there that job must and shall be done." As a result, one historian believes that "Hollywood's attitude toward the Latin American countries suddenly bordered on reverence." The U.S. film industry began producing documentaries praising Latin Americans, and an abundance of commercial movies appeared that featured Latin America, including *The Road to Rio, They Met in Argentina, Simon Bolivar,* and *That Night in Rio.*

The OCIAA effectively influenced Hollywood. It paid the producers of Twentieth Century Fox $40,000 to cut scenes in *Down Argentine Way* (1940) of an Argentine gigolo and crooked horseplayer for fear of alienating Argentines. In the case of the film *Juarez,* a very favorable portrayal of the Mexican president that compared him to Lincoln, it asked the producers to cut a scene of an American diplomat threatening the French with the Monroe Doctrine, not wanting to detract from the Mexican role in expelling the Europeans. The OCIAA also pressured Hollywood not to release in Latin America any negative portrayals of the U.S. government, including the 1939 classic, *Mr. Smith Goes to Washington.* Throughout the war, the OCIAA promoted the American way of life and the evils of the enemy.

Several observers recognized the significance of the efforts of Rockefeller and many other Americans in increasing awareness of Latin America. Historian Hubert Herring believed that the attempts to win Latin American affection broke out "like a speckled rash on the skin of the North American body politic." A leading public opinion journal reported that "the wooing of Latin America had developed . . . into what is substantially a shotgun wedding" as the United States scrambled for the affections of the Latin Americans. Not everyone thought the effort would succeed. Yale professor Nicholas Spykman believed failure was imminent because "it was based on nothing other than an unexamined notion that if the peoples of the hemisphere could only get to know each other they would come to like each other." In turn, he stressed that "sympathy does not determine policy; policy tends to determine sympathy."

Despite such criticisms, Washington's aggressive actions in the region in 1940 helped reduce Nazi influence by making fascism less appealing. As historian Alton Frye acknowledges, "there would still be ominous eddies, but by the summer of 1940 the Nazi cause was in retreat in the New World and the American republics faced with growing confidence the ordeal which was to come."

Dangerous Times

By mid-1941, the United States was an unofficial belligerent in World War II. In the North Atlantic, its naval forces escorted British ships through waters infested with "wolfpacks" of German subs. U.S. troops occupied Allied bases in Iceland and Greenland to free those countries' troops for service. Most important, the United States provided billions of dollars of military assistance to the Allies through the program known as Lend-Lease, approved by Congress in March 1941. Despite strong opposition from iso-lationist legislators and others in the United States who believed in arming America first, the Act went forward and materials were sent to the Allies from America's rapidly multiplying munitions plants.

Lend-Lease materials also poured southward starting in late 1941. Each of the major Latin American countries, with the exception of Argentina, received U.S.-made military equipment. Typically, U.S. military advisors followed to train Latin American troops in the use of the weapons. More than $475 million in Lend-Lease aid went to Latin America from 1941 to 1945. Brazil ($347 million), Mexico ($38 million), and Chile ($22 mil-lion) received the most aid, although smaller countries such as Nicaragua ($885,000), the Dominican Republic ($1.45 million), and Guatemala ($1.73 million) also secured substantial assistance. The aid packages included coastal guns, rifles, machine guns, and fighter planes. While most American strategists believed that no Latin American army could resist an invasion by a well-trained foreign army, they hoped the materials boosted coopera-tion and helped suppress internal fascist threats.

The Americans and British also began working on methods to remove Nazis from the region. In the summer of 1941, agents of the two gov-ernments created a Proclaimed List that identified 1,800 Latin American individuals and businesses with suspected Axis sympathies. Washington declared its intentions to treat these persons as potential subversives. This meant a prohibition on trade with their businesses and the freezing of their assets in the United States. Initially, many Latin Americans condemned the Proclaimed List as unilateral action on the part of the United States. Still, most accepted it, especially after the United States and many Latin American nations formally entered the war in December 1941.

Throughout the conflict, the FBI and British Intelligence added names to the Proclaimed List. In most cases, Latin Americans cooperated with U.S. and British agents to ferret out suspected Nazi sympathizers as well as spies and saboteurs. In sixteen Latin American countries, officials confiscated properties and arrested people. By 1945, more than 8,500 Latin Americans were interned, 3,000 of them sent to special camps in the United States.

War!

By the end of 1941, Americans and Germans had fired on each other in the North Atlantic. However, Hitler wanted to avoid direct U.S. intervention, and Roosevelt believed he lacked what was a necessary provocation for war. Unexpectedly, provocation came from the Far East. Throughout 1940, Washington and Tokyo had bickered over Japanese actions in China and French Indochina. The United States embargoed oil and other vital materials from the Japanese to force concessions. Undeterred, the Japanese chose war over compromise. On December 7, 1941, they launched a surprise attack on Pearl Harbor, in Hawaii, killing more than 2,500 Americans and sinking much of the U.S. Pacific Fleet.

The Japanese attack provoked widespread condemnations. Several hours before the U.S. Congress declared war on Japan, the Costa Rican Legislative Assembly adopted a similar measure. Many Latin American republics followed Costa Rica's example. Several days later, Hitler declared war on the United States. In turn, most Latin American republics declared war on Germany and Italy. Still, several countries waited because, especially in South America, they still had strong economic ties with Europe and housed influential immigrant groups. The fact that the Axis appeared likely to win also posed a dilemma for leaders in Brazil, Chile, and Argentina.

Down Rio Way

In response to war, a special meeting of foreign ministers occurred in January 1942 in Rio de Janeiro. Hull dispatched Welles as the U.S. representative with instructions to convince "all the Republics to sign a joint declaration to break off relations with the Axis powers." Hull emphasized that "this was a life-and-death struggle, the result of which could only mean freedom and advancement for Latin America or domination and probably occupation by the Axis."

As before, Argentina and others challenged the United States at the Rio Conference. Latin Americans of German and Italian descent wanted no part in breaking relations with the homeland and supporting the Allies. Furthermore, the Axis victory appeared possible in early 1942, as Germany controlled the continent and its submarines strangled Great Britain. In the Far East, the Japanese pushed forward. With the outcome of World War II unclear, some Latin American countries wanted to keep economic and diplomatic doors open.

Still, the United States called for a clear severing of diplomatic relations between the Latin Americans and the Axis powers. What the ministers put forth fell a bit short: "The American Republics, in accordance with the procedures established by their own laws and in conformity with the position and circumstances obtaining in each country in the existing continental conflict, recommend the breaking of their diplomatic relations with Japan, Germany and Italy," the resolution read. When Hull learned that Welles had signed the agreement, he personally gave him a tongue lashing on the telephone while Roosevelt listened. After much debate, the U.S. accepted the watered-down version of its original document. Nevertheless, by the end of the year, only Chile and Argentina maintained relations with the Axis powers, although Chile soon reversed its position.

The Latin American Contribution

In military terms, the Latin Americans provided only limited assistance to the Allies. The Brazilians sent to Europe an expeditionary force comprising one division of 25,000 men and supporting air units. Despite initial failures attributable to lack of training and poor equipment, the Brazilians distinguished themselves in the Italian campaign and helped capture the German stronghold of Monte Casino. The Mexican government also sent an air force squadron to fight in the Pacific. The 201st Squadron, trained in the United States, fought in the Philippines in 1944. In addition, the Mexican government allowed Mexican citizens to join the U.S. Army; more than 250,000 Mexicans served under the American flag: more than 1,000 of whom died in combat.

Latin America's most important contribution to the Allied war effort was raw materials. Petroleum, copper, tin, zinc, quinine, and agricultural goods flowed to the United States and Great Britain. In the process, the United States, and Latin America's economic interdependence increased

reliance

dramatically. Whereby, 55 percent of Latin American exports went to Europe in 1938, the number declined to 20 percent by 1945. Imports from Europe were 44 percent in 1938 but only 7 percent at war's end.

Although regional economies grew during the war, many Latin Americans complained that the United States benefited unfairly. U.S. agencies placed price controls on Latin American goods. Instead of allowing the open market to set prices, which undoubtedly would have kept prices higher, the United States imposed restraints. Some Latin Americans also accused U.S. leaders of undermining their attempts to industrialize and failing to compensate for the comparative disadvantage that Latin Americans faced in the exchange of raw for finished goods. Chilean poet Gabriela Mistral urged Latin America manufacturers: "Help us conquer or at least to restrain the deadly invasion . . . from blond America, which wishes to monopolize our markets and to overwhelm our farms and cities with its machinery and textiles."

Other Latin Americans complained that the aid provided to them amounted to only a small percentage of what Washington sent elsewhere. They correctly pointed out that by 1945, Latin America received less than 1 percent of all the U.S. foreign assistance. What they accepted, one Panamanian noted, was not given "as a means of building Latin American goodwill. We are pretty sure that every dollar spent was in response to some strategic need and the need of developing areas the use of which was necessary for the protection of the United States." These valid criticisms continued for many years.

While some Latin Americans voiced discontent with economic policies, wartime cooperation continued. Another significant contribution was the donating of air and naval bases to combat German submarines and surface raiders in the Atlantic and Pacific Oceans. Cuba, Mexico, Nicaragua, Brazil, the Dominican Republic, and others provided the Allies naval and air bases or signed treaties for reciprocal use of airfields and ports. Others permitted the United States to build radar stations, especially in the Caribbean.

Latin Americans cooperated with Washington in other ways, such as counterintelligence. In Mexico, FBI agents worked with future president and Secretary of the Interior Miguel Alemán, Minister of Communications General Maximino Ávila Camacho, and Postmaster General Fernando Ramírez to help uncover Nazi activities. Employing mobile radio detectors, mail checks, and surveillance, the joint operation succeeded in liquidating most Nazi activities and led to the arrest of Gestapo officers Werner Georg Nicolaus and Karl Hellerman. Other countries followed similar patterns and generally thwarted Nazi efforts.

Los Braceros

Mexico made another significant contribution to the U.S. war effort. It sent large numbers of workers to the United States to fill vacancies on farms and in factories caused by the massive induction of Americans into the military. Since the onset of the Great Depression, the U.S. immigration policy had kept Mexican immigration in check, even leading to forced deportations in the early 1930s. The United States' entry into the war changed priorities and undid resistance to Mexican immigration.

Various groups successfully banded together to change U.S. policy in 1942, principally southwestern farmers and politicians. In August 1942, the United States and Mexico signed an intergovernmental agreement known as the *bracero* program, which allowed the U.S. government, working in conjunction with Mexico's Departments of Interior and Labor, to negotiate contracts with Mexican laborers. Workers in the bracero program received protection under Mexican labor laws that guaranteed transportation, living expenses, and wages. Other provisions provided for safeguards under existing U.S. labor laws regarding occupational diseases and accidents.

While the United States negotiated similar treaties with the Bahamas, Barbados, and Jamaica, the majority of the workers who came to the United States were Mexican, who composed more than 70 percent of the 309,538 wartime laborers. The number peaked in 1944, when 62,000 braceros entered the United States. They found their numbers supplemented by undocumented workers, whom many American farmers and business owners continued to employ. In a four-year period, the braceros sent an estimated $205 million back to their families, and many of them acquired new skills and returned home better trained. In addition, they gained a knowledge of American culture (although a negative perception in too many cases) and carried the stories of the riches of the United States back home, sparking new efforts to immigrate, legally and illegally, in the postwar era. This helped accelerate the demographic revolution of the United States, especially the Southwest.

The bracero program continued until 1964, when the United States, under pressure from labor unions and other interest groups, did not renew it. But it had been important for many reasons. As one observer commented in 1943, it was "an unprecedented experiment in inter-American labor migration." The agreement was also significant to U.S.-Mexican relations because of the equality of the negotiation. A Mexican scholar notes, "it afforded the Mexican government the opportunity to put forth the conditions which it considered pertinent in attempting to . . . secure protection for its workers." This program and other cooperative efforts helped continue the rapprochement between the United States and Mexico, although problems remained.

El Pato Donald Va a la Guerra Mundial Segunda

Throughout the war, Rockefeller and the OCIAA pushed what the State Department called "the greatest outpouring of propagandistic material by a state ever." From the start, Hollywood films carried the message of hemispheric solidarity against the fascists. An interesting partnership developed between Walt Disney and the OCIAA. In 1941, Rockefeller approached the cartoonist about producing several films promoting inter-American friendship. The OCIAA provided Disney $70,000 for a trip to the region, and promised an additional $50,000 for four films. Disney, eager to open new markets, gathered seventeen people for a three-month tour, stopping in Argentina, Brazil, Chile, Peru, and Mexico.

From his trip, Disney produced a series of feature-length films. Each promoted very positive images of Latin Americans. In late 1942, he released *Saludos Amigos,* a series of four short films, linked together in a travelogue. In it, Donald Duck visited Lake Titicaca and Goofy was a gaucho. Disney interspersed live action 16mm film with the cartoon characters. The film opened to great acclaim in Latin America in December 1942. One observer called it "a potent piece of propaganda." A reviewer, John T. McManus, wrote "as a whole is not the fable-minded Disney child of before, . . . it is a fairly sophisticated young man of the Western world, exchanging bright and pointed pleasantries with our Latin American friends, bringing our viewpoints into accord like a witty ambassador, and generally doing a job in hemisphere relations that no one before has managed to achieve."

Three years later, Disney produced another feature film on Latin America. In *The Three Caballeros,* Donald Duck joined José Carioca and Panchito to visit several countries including Brazil and Mexico. Disney employed Latin American composers and actors including Dora Luz, Carmen Molina, and Aurora Miranda to act and sing in the film. During their travels, the characters shared stories about the cultural and historical traditions of the countries they visited. Even the colors Disney and his technicians chose reflected the Latin American use of pastels and other vibrant colors. Large audiences in Latin America and the United States flocked to see the movie.

Disney's efforts produced a financial success for him in Latin America. As his empire grew in the 1950s to include Disneyland and related products, Latin Americans remained loyal customers. Latin American and U.S. critics would later denounce Disney for trivializing Latin American traditions and as representing American cultural imperialism that glorified capitalism (Uncle Scrooge for example). Nevertheless, Disney did for a time extol Latin American traditions and present positive portrayals. His efforts also linked several generations of Latin Americans and Americans with common cultural symbols, a process that accelerated after 1945 when television, films, and sports enhanced ties.

Organizing the Hemisphere for the New World Order

As early as 1942, during the Rio Conference, Sumner Welles had declared that "When peace is restored, it is to the interest of the whole world that the American Republics present a united front and be able to speak and act with the moral authority to which, by reason of their own enlightened standards as much as by reason of their number and their power, they are entitled." A few weeks later, he added that "I cannot believe the peoples of the United States and the Western Hemisphere will ever relinquish the inter-American system they have built up. Based as it is on sovereign equality, on liberty, on peace, and on joint resistance to aggression, it constitutes the only example in the world today of a regional federation of free and independent peoples. It lightens the darkness of our anarchic world. It should constitute a cornerstone in the world structure of the future."

Once the tide had turned and Allied victory looked probable, U.S. policymakers began formulating plans for organizing the postwar economic and political world along lines suggested by Woodrow Wilson. The first step was the Moscow Conference in October 1943, in which the major participants (the United States, the Soviet Union, and Great Britain) declared they would build an organization to promote "international peace and security." Latin Americans, many already veterans of the League of

Nations, backed the idea, which also allowed for regional organizations to work within the larger whole.

Once the basic principles evolved, the United States and Latin America began cooperative efforts on several fronts. All the Latin American states except Argentina participated in the Conference on Food and Agriculture and Relief and Rehabilitation Administration. In July 1944, the Latin Americans attended a conference at Bretton Wood, New Hampshire, helping create the International Monetary Fund (IMF). Latin Americans obtained two of the twelve directorships and a seat on the executive board of that body. In August, the major powers met at Dumbarton Oaks (on the outskirts of Washington, D.C.), where they laid the groundwork for the United Nations that called for a General Assembly, a Security Council, and a Court of Justice. Disagreements arose as Washington pushed for the inclusion of Brazil on the important UN Security Council in spite of the protests by Soviets and jealous Latin Americans. Other Latin Americans complained about other structures and the weakening of regional organizations such as the Pan American Union. Still, scores of Latin Americans supported many of the concepts of Dumbarton Oaks.

A Different March to Chapultepec

The wartime cooperation carried over into the final year of the war, with the nations of the Western Hemisphere jockeying for position. In February 1945, they gathered in Mexico City at the Chapultepec palace to discuss postwar issues. The United States wanted to focus on stamping out fascism, while most delegates preferred to debate economic development and political issues, including the diplomatic isolation of the Argentine government.

The new U.S. secretary of state, Edward R. Stettinius, headed the U.S. delegation, ironically entering Chapultepec nearly one hundred years after U.S. forces had stormed it. As he prepared for the trip, Stettinius demonstrated his own bias. "The United States looks upon Mexico as a good neighbor, a strong upholder of democratic traditions in this hemisphere, and a country we are proud to call our own."

Despite a condescending attitude by some U.S. representatives, the delegates reached several resolutions immediately. They quickly founded a permanent military agency to coordinate the standardization and trade in armaments. They also agreed to try to eradicate any fascist threat and passed a resolution that "no Axis leader, official, or agent who is guilty of crimes against law and civilization in this war will be able to escape punishment by finding refuge in this hemisphere."

While consensus existed on military planning and eradicating the Nazis, some disagreements arose. The Latin Americans pushed proposals strengthening their participation in the United Nations, reorganizing the Pan American Union, and assuring economic vitality. Another major issue revolved around how to strengthen the inter-American security system. Delegates presented several competing proposals, including renunciation of force except in self-defense and obligating all the nations to use whatever means necessary to protect the territorial integrity of any American state. Ultimately, delegates tabled most resolutions until the next official meeting scheduled for 1947.

After much debate, the diplomats issued the Act of Chapultepec, which continued the sanctions on Axis nations. Part III of the Act recommended a "regional arrangement for dealing with such matters relating to the maintenance of international peace and security." While creating no machinery to administer it, the Act emphasized that the activities must be "consistent with the purposes and principles of the general international organization when established." The nations had committed themselves to continuing wartime cooperation, although Argentine dissent never received formal debate.

Most Americans and Latin Americans looked on the Chapultepec Conference as establishing the framework for postwar cooperation, although methods and goals among the various parties diverged. Rockefeller concluded that the conference was the "culmination of the Good Neighbor Policy and as an attitude pursued by President Roosevelt and his Government consistently over the last twelve years." It would be a high-water mark in U.S.-Latin American relations. Several weeks after the conference ended, President Roosevelt died and changes began to occur.

Present at the Creation

Shortly following Chapultepec, Latin American delegations traveled to San Francisco to create the United Nations. Nineteen Latin American nations attended, making the region a potentially powerful force among the forty-six member nations. An example involved the push to include Argentina. At first, Washington opposed seating the Argentines, but under pressure from the Latin Americans, it relented.

The United States and the Latin American republics agreed on issues such as support for allowing regional organizations within the larger body. Yet many differences surfaced regarding the distribution of power within the general assembly, voting procedures, and the Security Council veto power. The challenges often became contentious, leading one senator to complain to Rockefeller: "Your God-damned peanut nations aren't voting right. Go line them up." Despite the differences, the United States and Latin America accepted the final charter and joined the United Nations.

Defending the Faith

By mid-1945, some Latin Americans expressed reservations about a limited role in the postwar era. Others chafed at U.S. intransigence in dealing with the Argentines. Still, others believed that their wartime economic sacrifices had gone unnoticed in Washington. One Colombian writer stressed that "if we are relegated to the position of colonial countries, our industries ruined, our economies mere markets for foreign products, our sovereignty reduced to hopeless mediocrity—then that revulsion, that wave of savage hatred of the United States will explode in an uncontrolled protest." While the voices of dissent remained comparatively muted, they were gathering momentum.

In addition to the Latin Americans, there were U.S. citizens who began questioning Roosevelt's policies in Latin America. In 1943, in a visible break with Roosevelt's Good Neighbor policy, Senator Hugh Butler (R-NE) traveled southward. Motivated partly by partisan politics in a presidential campaign cycle, he soon published an article in Reader's Digest. In it, Butler reported that he was "astonished and appalled that our Good Neighbor policy—backed by six thousand million U.S. dollars—has widely become a hemispheric handout that is neither good nor neighborly." Denouncing "boondoggles" and Latin American corruption, he proposed that "we should insist that, according to their ability to pay, what we do for the nations of Latin America is matched, dollar for dollar, by what Latin America does for itself."

The official reactions to Senator Butler's opinions in the United States and Latin America were unfavorable. Most Latin Americans called the charges "unjust and outrageous," particularly the emphasis on corruption, and as Bryce Wood notes, they resented "the Senator's implication that they were begging for favors from the United States." Americans also lined up to criticize Butler, including members of his own party led by Herbert Hoover, Wendell Willkie, and Thomas A. Dewey. Butler's article, however, represented the views of some Americans and gained more of an audience as deep-seated mistrust and negative stereotypes of Latin Americans resurfaced.

As the war ended in September 1945, the Good Neighbor remained in place but changes already were underway. The experienced diplomat and historian Donald Dozer emphasizes that "gratitude for the high example and costly sacrifices of the United States in the defense of the Western Hemisphere against totalitarianism in the war would clearly not be enough to sustain Latin America's continued loyalty after the war. Coolness replaced cordiality. Old jealousies, suspicions, and even hatreds were revived. Latin Americans detected a deterioration in the United States['] interest in their culture and their ideas." "The feeling became more prevalent that the United States had taken more from Latin America than it had given in return during the war, that it had taken advantage of Latin America's security dependence upon it to acquire war materials at its own prices, and that as the war ended it was returning to its traditional attitude of neglect, even contempt, toward the Latin American peoples," he concluded. While on the surface, relations remained comparatively cordial, significant differences existed.

The death of Roosevelt marked the beginning of the end of the Good Neighbor policy. His successor, Harry Truman, lacked the commitment to Latin America and the policy. Furthermore, some of Roosevelt's advisors who supported the policy, such as Welles and Hull, left the State Department and other agencies and were replaced by more Eurocentric people who believed that Latin America remained a stable ally without the stroking provided by FDR. A new era had begun to evolve, and a return to old ways appeared imminent.

Continuities

The interdependence between the United States and Latin America increased dramatically during the 1930s and World War II. For the most part, the European and Asian economic and political power diminished dramatically by 1945, although not completely. The United States became very reliant on the Latin Americans to provide more raw materials for rebuilding Europe's devastated industrial sector, while the United States reciprocated with more loans and trade agreements.

On the political and diplomatic level, the United States and Latin America became even closer, as the nonintervention of the Good Neighbor paid dividends in goodwill and the countries closed ranks against the external fascist threat. This enhanced efforts such as building infrastructure and offering military aid throughout the region, which included training with U.S.-provided arms and equipment. The strengthening of ties extended to the efforts at creating a hemispheric defense zone and culminated with United Nations participation.

While relations improved, the period of the Great Depression and World War II strengthened the U.S. hegemony in the region, although without the heavy-handed interventions and pronouncements of the preceding thirty years. The European competitors lost substantial ground during the war, and the United States filled the void, economically and politically. U.S. music, films, magazines, and lifestyles became more acceptable throughout the region. Although Latin American nationalists fought back and denounced the cultural imperialism, American ideas and products still managed to infiltrate the region.

Despite the U.S. drive to hegemony, the Latin Americans, as always, were not passive players. First, they won the removal of the U.S. military occupations by force and diplomatic maneuvering, as well as an end to the Platt Amendment. They also secured significant victories during the period regarding international law, principally the U.S. acceptance of non-intervention. They won other victories such as more respect in international organizations like the UN, where the United States advocated the Brazilians for leadership roles. The war and the need for hemispheric unity, and the contributions by the Latin Americans to the war effort, clearly had paid dividends.

In business relations, the Good Neighbor economic components such as loans and grants ensured more development and in some areas industrial bases that went on to compete successfully with U.S. products in internal markets. Economic nationalists also won several battles. The Cárdenas administration won a significant victory in the petroleum and land-reform battle that the United States accepted without resorting to the dirty tactics previously employed against other nationalists. The war clouds in Europe clearly had played a role, but many could argue that the Mexicans merely fulfilled through sheer determination the plans that they had begun during the revolution.

Finally, the period saw significant growth in the Latino population in the United States. While the era started with deportations, it culminated with the bracero program and the recruiting of Latin American workers, principally Mexicans, for service on farms and in factories of the United States during the war. The Latin American population increased in the United States as Mexicans, Puerto Ricans, Dominicans, Jamaicans, and Cubans continued to enter the country and create new communities and traditions. The war helped accelerate the process and helped ensure a new consciousness regarding U.S. citizenship, as many Latinos served abroad in the U.S. military and returned home demanding more respect and equality.

SUGGESTIONS FOR ADDITIONAL READING

For more on Hoover and his presidency and foreign policies, reference Alexander DeConde, *Herbert Hoover's Latin American Policy* (1951); Lewis E. Ellis, *Republican Foreign Policy, 1921–1933* (1968); Vaughn D. Bornet and Edgar E. Robinson, *Herbert Hoover: President of the United States* (1975); Joan Hoff, *Herbert Hoover: Forgotten Progressive* (1975); and David Burner, *Herbert Hoover: A Public Life* (1979).

For good books on the Good Neighbor, reference Irwin Gellman, *Good Neighbor Diplomacy: United States Policies Toward Latin America and Secret Affairs; Franklin Roosevelt, Cordell Hull, and Sumner Welles* (1995); Bryce Wood, *The Making of the Good Neighbor Policy* (1961) and *The United States and the Latin American War, 1932–1942* (1966), David Green, *The Containment of Latin America: A History of the Myths and Realities of the Good Neighbor Policy* (1971); Frederick B. Pike, *FDR's Good Neighbor Policy* (1994); Dick Steward, *Trade and Hemisphere: The Good Neighbor Policy and Reciprocal Trade* (1975); Frederick C. Adams, *Economic Diplomacy: The Export-Import Bank and American Foreign Relations, 1934–1939* (1976); J. Manuel Espinoza, *Inter-American Beginnings of U.S. Cultural Diplomacy, 1936–1948* (1976); Edward O. Guerrant, *Roosevelt's Good Neighbor Policy* (1950); and James Schwoch, *The American Radio Industry and Its Latin American Activities, 1900–1939* (1990).

For U.S. relations with the dictators and nationalists during the 1930s and 1940s, see Paul Coe Clark, Jr., *The United States and Somoza, 1933–1956: A Revisionist Look* (1992); Knut Walter, *The Regime of Anastasio Somoza, 1936–1956* (1993); Eric Paul Roorda, *The Dictator Next Door: The Good Neighbor Policy and the Trujillo Regime in the Dominican Republic, 1930–1945* (1998); Michael Grow, *The Good Neighbor Policy and Authoritarianism in Paraguay: United States Economic Expansion and Great-Power Rivalry in Latin America during World War II* (1981); Paul J. Dosal, *Doing Business with the Dictators: A Political History of United Fruit in Guatemala, 1899–1944* (1993); David E. Schmitz, *Thank God They're on Our Side: The United States and the Right Wing Dictatorships, 1921–1965* (1999) Friedrich E. Schuler, *Mexico between Hitler and Roosevelt: Mexican Foreign Relations in the Age of Lázaro Cárdenas, 1934–1940* (1998);

Stanley Hilton, *Brazil and the Great Powers, 1930–1939: The Politics of Trade Rivalry* (1975); and Irwin Gellman, *Roosevelt and Batista: Good Neighbor Diplomacy in Cuba, 1933–1945* (1973).

For prewar and wartime relations, see Alton Freye, *Nazi Germany and the American Hemisphere, 1933–1941* (1967); David Haglund, *Latin America and the Transformation of U.S. Strategic Thought, 1936–1941* (1984); Leslie B. Rout and John F. Bratzel, *The Shadow War: German Espionage and United States Counterespionage in Latin American during World War II* (1986); R. A. Humphreys, *Latin America and the Second World War* (1982); Stanley Hilton, *Hitler's Secret War in South America, 1939–1945: German Military Espionage and Allied Counterespionage in Brazil* (1981); Randall B. Woods, *The Roosevelt Foreign-Policy Establishment and the "Good Neighbor": The United States and Argentina, 1941–1945* (1979); Frank D. McCann, *The Brazilian-American Alliance, 1937–1945* (1973); Ronald C. Newton, *The "Nazi Menace" in Argentina, 1931–1947* (1992); and Stephen Niblo, *War, Diplomacy, and Development: The United States and Mexico, 1938–1954* (1995).

For more on the bracero program, reference Richard B. Craig, *The Bracero Program: Interest Groups and Foreign Policy* (1971); Ernesto Galarza, *Merchants of Labor: The Mexican Bracero Story: An Account of the Managed Migration of Mexican Farm Workers in California, 1942–1960* (1964); and Barbara A. Driscoll, *The Tracks North: The Railroad Bracero Program of World War II* (1999).

CHAPTER SIX

The Death of the Good Neighbor

The postwar world changed dramatically as the United States became the preponderant economic and political force in the world. The Good Neighbor policy declined as Truman took office and U.S. leaders became distracted by other regions and obsessed with preventing the spread of communism in Latin America. Truman and his successor would pursue a policy characterized by a general malaise with occasional outbursts of energy to attack perceived threats.

Cracks in the Good Neighbor's Foundation

One of the most glaring examples of the deteriorating commitment to the Good Neighbor policy was Washington's wartime relations with Buenos Aires. From the Rio Conference forward, the United States pressured Buenos Aires to sever relations with the Axis powers and crackdown on Nazi spies. Nationalistic and pro-fascist Argentines resisted. U.S. diplomats led by Hull complained that hemispheric unity demanded unanimous opposition. In response to dissent, the United States implemented an embargo on Argentina and distributed no additional assistance to that nation after the Rio Conference. The British, who were dependent on Argentine beef and other goods, urged negotiation and conciliation, but Washington kept up the pressure.

This confrontation escalated in late 1943. A military coup in Bolivia sparked concern in Washington. The United States believed the pro-fascist Argentine military, working in conjunction with Nazis, planned to disrupt trade and hemispheric defense. Assistant Secretary of State Adolf Berle wrote that the Argentines wanted "to set up an Argentine-controlled Fascist bloc running as far North as Peru." He emphasized that they "are working hand in glove with the Germans."

Problems continued in 1944, despite the fact that the government of General Pedro Ramírez severed relations with the Axis powers. Within two weeks, however, General Edelmiro Farrell led a military coup. Believing that fascists had sparked the coup, Washington refused to recognize the new government, stressing that Argentina "has openly and notoriously been giving affirmative assistance to the declared enemies of the United Nations." Roosevelt ordered acting Secretary of State Stettinius to "make a face to the Argentineans once a week. You have to treat them like children."

The United States withheld recognition of the Farrell government until March 1945, after negotiations at Chapultepec made Argentine membership in the United Nations contingent on "complete solidarity and a common policy among the American states." The Argentines finally declared war on Germany and Japan and promised vigorous actions against fascism. Yet once the Farrell government took its place in the United Nations, it reneged on the bargain. The dictatorship strengthened the military, where many Argentine officers harbored pro-Nazi sympathies, including Vice-President Juan Domingo Perón. It also suppressed opposition, leading to vocal denunciations throughout the hemisphere.

Perón versus Braden

The standoff with the Farrell government corresponded with a changing attitude in Washington regarding U.S. cooperation with dictators. Since its inception, the Good Neighbor policy was derided by critics for strengthening totalitarian rulers. During the war, *Hoy*, a Mexico City newspaper, acknowledged that "the majority of our presidents [in Latin America], are assassins, thieves, and infamous men" whom Washington had assisted with Lend-Lease and Export-Import credits. Liberal Americans and Latin Americans who hated fascist dictatorships in Europe and Asia decried Washington's hypocrisy and urged U.S. officials to promote democracy to enhance hemispheric solidarity. Idealistically, they addressed one of the major critiques of the Good Neighbor policy.

The shift in attitudes became more apparent in November 1945. At that time, Washington supported the proposal of Uruguayan Foreign Minister Eduardo Rodríguez Larreta, which recommended "multilateral collective action" against American states that violated the basic rights of its citizens and failed to honor its international obligations. Initially, the proposal found little backing among other states because of its apparent intention

CANADA

UNITED STATES
Washington D.C.

NORTH
ATLANTIC
OCEAN

CUBA
Castro seizes power, 1959
Bay of Pigs, 1961
Missile crisis, 1962
U.S. embargo, 1960–present
Mariel boatlift, 1980

MEXICO
Migrant, debt and immigration issues, 1945–present
NAFTA 1994

Gulf of Mexico

Miami

Havana

MEXICO

HAITI
U.S. military intervention, 1994

GUATEMALA
U.S. supported coup against Arbenz government, 1954
Bloody Civil War, 1954–1992

Mexico City

JAMAICA

VIRGIN ISLANDS

PUERTO RICO

DOMINICAN REPUBLIC
U.S. military intervention, 1965

EL SALVADOR
Civil War, 1970's–1991

Caribbean Sea

GRENADA
U.S. military intervention, 1983

HONDURAS
Base of contras, 1980–1990

Caracas

TRINIDAD & TOBAGO

VENEZUELA

GUIANA

SURINAME

FRENCH GUIANA

NICARAGUA
U.S. sponsored Somoza regime overthrow, 1979
Contra War, 1980–1990

Bogota

COLOMBIA

COSTA RICA
President Oscar Arias organizes peace plan, 1988–1991
Environmental issues

Quito

ECUADOR

VENEZUELA
Anti-Nixon riots, 1958
Founding member of OPEC, 1960
Nationalization of petroleum industry, 1974

PANAMA
Canal riots, 1959, 1964
Panama canal treaties, 1978
U.S. military intervention, 1989–1990

PERU

COLUMBIA
Drug War, 1989–present

BRAZIL

Lima

BRAZIL
U.S. supported coup, 1964
Issues of rain forest, 1980's–present

PERU
U.S. trained army overthrows government, 1962
Drug War, 1989–present

La Paz

BOLIVIA

Brasilia

PACIFIC

OCEAN

CHILE
U.S. Supported coup overthrows Salvador Allende in 1973

CHILE

PARAGUAY

Asuncion

Rio De Janeiro

ARGENTINA

Santiago

Buenos Aires

Montevideo

URUGUAY

The United States and Latin America 1945–present

★ U.S. Military Sites
o Soviet Missile Sites, 1962

ARGENTINA
Malvinas War, 1982

SOUTH
ATLANTIC
OCEAN

0 500 1000 Kilometers
0   500   1000 Miles

FALKLAND ISLANDS

to single out Argentina and the collateral attacks on Somoza, Trujillo, and other dictators. Some U.S. support of the idea, however, signaled opposition within the State Department against not only the Argentines, but also other dictatorial regimes.

To demonstrate the shift, the Truman administration dispatched veteran diplomat Spruille Braden to Argentina in May 1945. With elections approaching in February 1946, and the heavy-handed Perón the apparent choice of the ruling regime, Braden began an effort to uproot fascists in Argentina. He emphasized that "if we appease now and allow the situation to drift, we will either be faced for a long time to come with a Fascist anti-U.S.A. Government under German tutelage and or eventually revolution." Braden's vocal opposition made him a celebrity. He appeared on the cover of *Time* with an insect sprayer pointed at a map of Argentina containing swastikas. Although Braden left Argentina to become assistant secretary of state in September 1945, active opposition to Perón continued.

Throughout the six months preceding the Argentine election, U.S. officials opposed Perón. They received some unlikely assistance when Argentine military rivals seized Perón and imprisoned him. Perón's supporters, mostly blue-collar workers, flowed into the streets to demand his release. Their demands were met, but the whole incident confirmed the suspicions of U.S. diplomats, who concluded that the mass demonstrations "indicate that Perón plans a proletarian, totalitarian dictatorship with army and police support."

Washington went to great lengths to prevent Perón's election. Two weeks before the voting, the State Department delivered Braden's *Blue Book* to the press and Latin American governments. In an extended memorandum on Argentina, he argued that "the totalitarian machine in Argentina is a partnership of German Nazi interests with a powerful coalition of active Argentine totalitarian elements, both military and civilian." One historian calls the publication "so wildly inaccurate as to be irresponsible." The memorandum ignored domestic realities and greatly exaggerated Nazi influence, and received little support among Latin Americans, who resented U.S. interference. The efforts to sway the electorate failed miserably, as Perón's supporters developed the slogan, "Braden or Perón." Even some former opponents joined his side and helped swing a very close election to Perón. One U.S. journalist observed that the victory was "the most single defeat that U.S. diplomacy has undergone for many years."

Perón's victory angered Braden, but President Truman had tired of the failed policy to combat fascism. A growing preoccupation with communism prompted the United States to remove Argentine companies from the Proclaimed List, unfreeze gold reserves, and in early 1947 establish full relations with the Perón government. State Department official John Moors Cabot concluded that there are "two essential reasons why we can not interfere in the internal affairs of other nations. First, our treaty obligations bind us. However, behind these obligations is our feeling that it is unwise to attempt such interference. When we have attempted it the results have been counter-effective, having harmed the democratic groups we wished to help." In addition, it made the process of taking steps toward interfering much easier, even when justified in terms of doing the right thing. The Good Neighbor foundation had more visible cracks following this episode.

Seeing Red Everywhere

The confrontation with Perón and its ultimate resolution demonstrated several trends in U.S. foreign policy during the postwar era. The compromise with the Argentine government in 1947 reflected a change in attitude among many U.S. policymakers at the onset of the Cold War. While some were dedicated to the basic principles of the Good Neighbor, modifications were under way. Truman and his foreign policy establishment would face many new challenges in dealing with Latin American nations.

The deterioration of U.S.-Soviet relations was a growing concern to Washington during the postwar period. During the war, Washington had actively cooperated with Moscow to defeat the Nazis. It also encouraged Latin Americans to work with Communist groups, with the goal of creating a united front. U.S. officials even encouraged Soviet commercial and political officials to travel the region and build relationships with Latin Americans.

By early 1946 however, historical fears of the spread of communism dating back to 1917 began to rekindle as the Soviets occupied Eastern Europe and Communist parties competed for power in Asia and the Middle East. To sound the alarm, in March 1946, former British prime minister Winston Churchill visited Fulton, Missouri. As Truman watched, Churchill gave his famous "Iron Curtain" speech, in which he warned against Soviet expansionism and appeasement of aggression. Soon thereafter, a young

U.S. diplomat in Moscow, George F. Kennan, cabled Washington with his evaluation of the Soviets and their dictator, Joseph Stalin. Kennan characterized the Soviets as naturally aggressive and willing to employ any means to undermine the Western democracies. Kennan argued that the Soviets had to "be contained by the adroit and vigilant application of counterforce at a series of constantly shifting geographical and political points." His containment argument became the cornerstone of U.S. foreign policy for the next forty years.

Anticommunism would not immediately dominate U.S.-Latin American relations, but it gradually became an issue. As Walter LaFeber notes about Latin America "after the struggle [World War II], and despite promises to the contrary, Washington neglected its neighbors while sending goods and money to rebuild Europe." Despite the snub, some U.S. diplomats and persons such as Nelson Rockefeller contended that unless the United States "operated with a solid group in this hemisphere" that it "could not do what we wanted to do on the world front." However, most U.S. policymakers focused on Europe, where famine and poverty threatened to sweep the Communists into power in several countries. Consequently, regional experts and U.S. diplomats in the Latin American capitals became the primary functionaries of U.S. policy, one that increasingly lacked coherence and consistency.

The Good Guys Win a Few

While the Cold War escalated, some prominent U.S. diplomats and Latin Americans attacked the authoritarian rulers of the region. Some successes had already occurred. In Guatemala in 1944, middle-class groups led by university students and young army officers overthrew the long-time dictator Jorge Ubico. Guatemalans held open elections won by Juan José Arévalo. He soon implemented policies comparable to those having resulted from the Mexican Revolution. In Venezuela in 1945, Rómulo Betancourt won power at the head of the *Partido Acción Democrática* (Democratic Action Party). Betancourt had lived in exile for many years, plotting against the Venezuelan dictators. Originally a founding member of the Costa Rican Communist Party, he had rejected communism and focused more on nationalist programs, including the sharing of the income of the petroleum industry and developing democratic institutions.

The victories of democratic and nationalist leaders in Guatemala and Venezuela heartened others who opposed dictatorships in the Caribbean Basin. State Department officials helped by extending diplomatic recognition to the new governments and praising their accomplishments, as well as providing them some economic and military assistance. Flush with success, Assistant Secretary of State Braden and others continued attacking regional dictators. When the U.S. military asked for increased military sales to the region in late 1946, Braden successfully opposed most attempts. He complained that they would "perpetuate the grip of reactionary groups" and "impose a heavy burden for unproductive purposes on the weak economies of Latin America, thus retarding social progress."

"Get Our S.O.B."

In the aftermath of World War II, many Latin American democratic liberals and State Department officials focused on Somoza. Through intimidation and fraud, he had been able to hold power in Nicaragua since the mid-1930s. Throughout the Great Depression and World War II, Washington had supported Somoza as a loyal ally. Yet the State Department under Braden changed course and began to pressure Somoza to hold free elections. When he did so in March 1947, Somoza's handpicked successor, Leonardo Argüello, won the contest. Conflict soon followed, as Argüello replaced some of Somoza's cronies and tried to limit Somoza's power. Within several weeks, Somoza overthrew Argüello and replaced him with his uncle, Victor Román y Reyes. Disgusted, the State Department withdrew the U.S. ambassador to Nicaragua.

For more than a year, Washington withheld recognition of Román y Reyes's puppet government. Various compromises surfaced, including open elections after Somoza was exiled. Despite the pressure, Somoza held steady. He counterattacked by accusing his enemies of harboring Communist sympathies. His efforts ultimately succeeded. By May 1948, a new group of State Department officials, strongly influenced by the escalating Cold War, finally reestablished full formal relations. With this action, they killed the last gasp effort to promote democracy over security needs for many years.

As historian Judith Ewell correctly notes, by 1948 "those in the State Department who argued for the encouragement of democratic institutions resigned, retired, or lost out to those who believed that continental unity and a pledge of nonintervention better secured U.S. interests." She adds, the "United States government viewed Latin America through a European lens, and many of the New Deal experts on Latin America drifted out of the circles of influence. Old suspicions about the volatility and immaturity of the Latin American masses again cast doubt on politicians who courted their own citizens."

The Times Are a Changin'

As the State Department challenged Somoza, Communist paranoia in the United States increased significantly, as the nation plunged into its second "Red scare." In March 1947, the president asked for and received $400 million to provide economic and military assistance to the governments of Greece and Turkey, promising "to support free peoples who are resisting attempted subjugation by armed minorities or by outside pressures." His statement became known as the "Truman Doctrine." At the same time, the Truman administration implemented a loyalty oath program to ferret out suspected Communists in the U.S. government, with special attention paid to the State Department.

Some U.S. diplomats already had sounded the alarm about Soviet intentions in Latin America. U.S. Ambassador to Argentina George Messersmith wrote in late 1946 that "there is no doubt that the inter-American system will remain under constant attack from Moscow in the countries of the Americas . . . Argentina and Colombia are really the only two countries in the Americas today which [we] can depend upon completely to combat Soviet influence and penetration." The newly created Central Intelligence Agency (CIA) echoed his concerns. During 1947, the CIA scrambled for information as it replaced the FBI as the intelligence-gathering agency in Latin America. In November 1947, the CIA released a document called "Soviet Objectives in Latin America." In a very pessimistic tone, it predicted that Latin American Communists would provide Moscow only limited direct support during a conflict. Instead, the Soviets planned espionage and sabotage operations to deny the United States access to strategic materials. The Soviets, the CIA observed, planned to achieve their goal by working with labor unions and other leftist groups to coordinate underground activities. It judged that few countries, with the exception of Mexico, Argentina, Paraguay, and the Dominican Republic, could prevent the Soviets from achieving their goals.

Creating Fortress America

One of the first steps that the United States took in preparing for hemispheric defense against the perceived Soviet threat occurred at the (second) Rio Conference in August 1947. Hoping to build on established patterns of wartime cooperation, American and Latin American delegates focused on the creation of a regional security organization. After much debate and haggling, the delegates adopted the Rio Pact. This treaty provided that an attack on any nation in the Western Hemisphere by another state, including other regional states, would prompt action by all signatories. One U.S. diplomat called the Rio Pact a preservation of the "unilateral character of the Monroe Doctrine," while Latin Americans looked at it as a guarantee of protection against aggressive neighbors.

One major disappointment for the Latin Americans at Rio was the failure to discuss economic development. They saw the United States investing huge quantities of funds in Europe, with the new secretary of state, George C. Marshall, announcing the "Marshall Plan," a massive, billion-dollar aid package to help war-torn European nations, including the former Axis Powers, rebuild. The Latin Americans, hoping for financial compensation for their wartime adherence to price controls, met roadblocks everywhere. President Truman traveled to Rio to tell the delegates that they would not receive substantial funds because "the problems of countries in this hemisphere are different in nature and cannot be relieved by the same means and the same approaches which are in contemplation for Europe." Like many of his predecessors, he added that in Latin America "a much greater role falls to private citizens and groups."

Some Americans and Latin Americans argued that the region desperately needed a massive aid policy to raise the overall standard of living for all Latin Americans and to undermine growing labor and peasant unrest. As one political scientist observes, "Far from the Soviet Union's borders, Latin America was not yet threatened, and so it did not require much attention." Therefore, Washington focused on long-term models of private investment for Latin America, with a few programs such as Truman's Point 4 program designed to provide limited technical assistance projects. Throughout the era, U.S. policies promoted free enterprise and foreign investment that maintained Latin America as a producer of raw materials and a market for U.S. and European finished products. As Lester Langley highlights "this meant, inevitably, Latin America's acquiescence in the American developmental model, which did not meet the hemisphere's needs because it conformed to American and not Latin American priorities."

A Test in the Switzerland of the Americas

In 1948, as the Truman administration focused on Europe and the civil war in China, a test of U.S. policies regarding communism arose in an unlikely place, the normally peaceful Costa Rica. For several years, problems had been brewing there. During World War II, the Costa Rican Communist Party (renamed the Vanguard Popular in 1942), composed primarily of banana workers and small craftsmen, had allied with the government of President Rafael Calderón Guardia (1940–44) to advance reforms including Social Security and Labor Codes. Led by Manuel Mora, the Vanguard Popular remained a small but influential political force in Costa Rica into the postwar period and the presidency of Calderón's hand-picked successor, Teodoro Picado.

The Cold War interjected itself into Costa Rica's internal strife that arose in 1948. Initially, U.S. diplomats had emphasized that the Costa Rican Communists had few ties with Moscow and that Picado and Calderón had no Communist sympathies. However, by 1947 the embassy in San José reported a growing uneasiness with Communist activities. After the announcement of the Truman Doctrine, Vanguard members marched and carried placards reading, "Down with the Truman Plan: We do not wish to be cannon fodder for Yankee imperialism." U.S. officials concluded that the Vanguard appeared "at least open to Moscow penetration" and held to a "way of thinking far from ours." By November 1947, the CIA concluded that "with the possible exception of Costa Rica, no Latin American Government is today publicly cooperating with the Communists."

Even as these warnings went out, a confrontation arose. In February 1948, the opposition candidate Otílio Ulate defeated Calderón. Calderón's allies, including Vanguard deputies, annulled the election and prepared to name Calderón as president. In the meantime, opposition forces rallied around José Figueres. The fiery Figueres had been exiled in 1942 for criticizing Calderón, and he had returned to his homeland to plan an armed revolt. Virulently anti-Communist, Figueres had joined with other Caribbean Basin exiles under the leadership of President Arévalo to establish liberal democracies. When the fighting began in March 1948, Arévalo dispatched arms, supplies, and aircraft to aid Figueres against Picado, Calderón, and Mora.

During the early stages of the fighting, U.S. officials maintained a wait-and-see policy. They knew little about Figueres, although the U.S. military attaché J. R. Hughes visited the rebel camp and received a briefing about rebel plans immediately preceding the outbreak of intense fighting. High officials in the State Department remained preoccupied with preparing for the upcoming Bogotá Conference and believed that the normally peaceful Costa Ricans quickly would settle the issue. They left most decisions to the Central American desk officer, William Tapley Bennett (a virulent anti-Communist), and the U.S. ambassador to Costa Rica, Nathaniel Davis. But as the fighting escalated and the Communists took prominent positions, U.S. officials grew more apprehensive. They feared that the Communists would use the chaos to seize power, following the example recently employed in Czechoslovakia. At this point, they adopted policies that aided the rebels, including Davis directly negotiating with Figueres, an action that served as informal recognition of the rebels by the most powerful force in the region. In addition, the State Department pressured Somoza not to aid his business partner Calderón. At the same time, it only issued muted protests to the Guatemalans about their interference in the contest. Ultimately, the rebels emerged victorious and outlawed the Communist Party, driving its leaders into exile.

The U.S. response to the Costa Rican Civil War of 1948 demonstrated the ambivalence and the mercurial nature of U.S. policy. Most State Department and White House officials focused elsewhere, ignoring for the most part the two months of brutal fighting that claimed 2,000 lives. Lower-level diplomats directed U.S. policy designed to remove the Communists and recreate stability. While not premeditated and often not overt, these actions resulted in the removal of a perceived Communist threat. Clearly, Davis and others failed to observe the spirit of nonintervention, although they had not returned the United States to the heavy-handed military interventions of the 1920s. Nevertheless, in this middle ground, the pendulum appeared to swing back toward the old days.

Out with the Old, In with the New

During the Costa Rican Civil War, Latin American delegates convened in Bogotá, Columbia, to create a regional organization to administer the Rio Pact. Many Latin Americans hoped to revisit the issue of a Marshall Plan for the Western Hemisphere, but Marshall disappointed them. "We must face reality," he told the delegates, "my people find themselves faced with

the urgent necessity of meeting staggering and inescapable responsibilities—humanitarian, political, and financial—all over the world, in western
Europe, in Germany and Austria, in Greece and Turkey, in the Middle
East, in China, Japan and Korea." Marshall again emphasized a reliance on
private enterprise and foreign investment for development.

Despite the lack of grand concessions, the Latin Americans won some
victories at Bogotá. The United States agreed to work to ease problems of
dislocations of the boom-and-bust trade in raw materials. Washington also
promised to push U.S. companies to provide "paid annual vacations" and
"permanence of tenure to all wage earners," whom companies could not
discharge "without just cause." U.S. officials generally accepted the labor
provisions, but warned it might not necessarily enforce all of them.

During the conference, the United States concentrated primarily on
hemispheric defense. As the conference convened, the U.S. National
Security Council reported to Truman that "the ultimate objective of Soviet-
directed world communism is the domination of the world." Events during
the conference fueled suspicions of Soviet influence. On April 9, an assassin killed Colombia's powerful Liberal Party leader, Jorge Eliecer Gaitán.
Angry crowds thronged the streets, blaming the murder on the leader of
the Colombian Conservative Party, Laureano Gómez. The mobs attacked
government buildings and ransacked conference meeting areas. U.S. officials fled to the suburbs and formulated plans for evacuation. They never
had to implement them, however, because Colombian troops regained
control after several days, but only after 300 persons had died.

The rioting in Bogotá fueled Marshall's fears of Communist subversion.
He blamed international communism for trying to disrupt the formation
of a regional body. He emphasized that the Colombian Communist party
chief, Montaña Cuellar, had called on rioters to burn the presidential palace.
Marshall also linked Communist activities in Costa Rica with Communist
actions in Colombia. For those who feared Communists were everywhere,
the rioting appeared to justify the efforts to strengthen the Rio Treaty.

The final major product of the Bogotá conference was the creation of
the Organization of American States (OAS) to replace the Pan American
Union. The OAS established administration for hemispheric consultation
and the Advisory Defense Committee to coordinate military development and activities. To the delight of the U.S. diplomats, most delegates
denounced communism and some even called for "a multilateral inter-
American anti-Communist agreement." U.S. delegates hesitated to go

so far. They justified their action on the wording of the recently penned
National Security Council Report No. 16 (NSC 16), which argued "that
there would be many cases in which such anti-Communist agreements
would be directed against all political opposition, Communist or otherwise, by dictatorial governments, with the inevitable result of driving leftist
elements into the hands of the Communist organization." The Americans
succeeded in tabling the proposal.

U.S. policymakers, however, lost several battles over the structure and
wording of the OAS Charter. Over U.S. objections, the Latin Americans voted for several articles that reflected a fear of a return to old ways.
Article 15 of the Charter stated that "no state or group of States has the
right to intervene, directly or indirectly, for any reason whatever, in the
internal affairs of any other State." Article 16 strengthened the concept of
non-intervention. It stated that "no state may use or encourage coercive
measures of an economic or political character in order to force the sovereign will of another State and obtain from it advantages of any kind."
With the chartering of the OAS in 1948, Bolívar's dream of a united hemisphere appeared at least superficially attained.

During the second half of the Truman administration, Washington
paid less attention to Latin America. The region appeared stable and
Communist influence there contained, so U.S. policymakers focused
their attention elsewhere, especially Europe and Asia. The preoccupation
with communism affected policymaking within the State Department,
the White House, and Congress. From 1948 forward, most policymakers
viewed everything through the European lens of battling Soviet expansionism. Consequently, the wartime cooperation between the United States
and Latin America deteriorated as nationalism intensified. The U.S. cozi-
ness with dictators redeveloped, for on the surface, everything appeared
tranquil. Nevertheless, the potential for civil unrest was mounting.

A Policy of Neglect and Protecting the Status Quo

With the Bogotá conference, U.S.-Latin American cooperation in establishing a regional community peaked. Now, for the first time in its history,
the United States found itself as the world's primary leader. The year 1949
proved especially important. The Soviets exploded an atomic bomb, ending the perceived U.S. monopoly in nuclear weapons technology and
ensuring massive new expenditures for conventional weapons. The United

States saw its Chinese allies defeated by Communists led by Mao Zedong, adding more than 500 million people to the Communist camp. In Eastern Europe, the Middle East, and Southeast Asia, nationalists often aligned with Communists to fight U.S.-supported reactionary regimes. Only Latin America appeared firmly in the U.S. corner.

Many people acknowledged that maintenance of the status quo had become the cornerstone of U.S. policy in Latin America. Adolf A. Berle, an experienced State Department official, complained as early as 1945: "Men [in high office] who know the hemisphere and love it are few and those who are known by [the] hemisphere and loved by it are fewer still." In 1949, he had grown more pessimistic, denouncing the "sheer neglect and ignorance." "We have simply forgotten about Latin America," he added.

Other factors played into the United States' lapsing Latin American policy. The charges of communism within the State Department by Wisconsin senator Joseph McCarthy had a chilling effect. By 1950, Security Division investigations of the Foreign Service decimated several divisions. In the Latin American section, Red-baiting smear tactics wiped out the career of a rising star, Laurence Duggan, who committed suicide in 1948 after people accused him of Communist sympathies. Into the void created by McCarthyism flooded people with little or no understanding of Latin America and who viewed the region through the lens of Soviet efforts at world domination. As Lars Schoultz notes, "For Duggan's surviving colleagues, extreme caution and militant anticommunism became the twin lodestones of the Cold War Foreign Service."

The Search for Stability

With few proactive ideas evolving, one of the cornerstones of U.S. policy in the late 1940s was maintaining stability. Several factors were an influence. First, U.S. diplomats wanted to concentrate on Asia and Europe. Second, most believed U.S. investment would ensure economic development, aware that companies and banks would not pour money into unstable areas. Finally, some feared that the Communists might take advantage of turmoil anywhere to gain power or undermine U.S. influence. As historian Charles Ameringer notes, "the main concern of the United States was the Soviet Union, and it did not want anybody making waves in the Caribbean that might expand the Cold War there."

A major problem for U.S. policymakers remained that the democratic liberals in the region had continued their efforts against dictators. Unfortunately for them, Braden and others who supported their cause had left. Instead, most U.S. diplomats accepted conditions of the OAS charter that prevented intervention in the domestic affairs of other countries. These included the military junta in Venezuela headed by Carlos Delgado Chalbaud, who overthrew President Rómulo Gallegos in late 1948. Soon thereafter, another military man, Marcos Pérez Jiménez, took power and ruled Venezuela dictatorially for the next ten years.

In response to criticisms of U.S. inaction, Secretary of State Dean Acheson accepted the "occasional disappointments" with the demise of democratic governments but ironically argued that engaging dictators served "our long-range objectives in the promotion of democracy." In addition, some U.S. policymakers believed that military strongmen in charge in Latin America provided the best barrier to Communist expansion.

Consequently, Washington worked to thwart the efforts of a group of democratic liberals that became known as the "Caribbean Legion." This group of Dominican, Nicaraguan, and Honduran exiles planned operations to overthrow their dictators. Guatemala provided assistance to the Legion, and Costa Rica served as a base for the Legion in their primary efforts against Somoza and Trujillo.

Costa Rica's assistance to the exiles immediately provoked a regional crisis in which the United States played a significant role. In December 1948, Somoza supported an attack by Calderón and several hundred followers against a junta headed by Figueres. Some conservative Americans greeted the invasion of Costa Rica favorably, since Figueres had nationalized the banking industry and forced a renegotiation of the existing UFCO contract. Still, Figueres maintained the support of many Americans who viewed Costa Rica's democracy as an important model for democratic development, despite its recent upheaval.

Washington desperately sought to prevent the fighting from spreading. When the conflict began, the Costa Ricans asked the OAS to denounce Nicaragua's violation of the Rio Pact. The OAS responded quickly by creating a special commission to investigate the charges. A U.S. representative joined the group that traveled aboard U.S. airplanes to tour the area. Simultaneously, Washington pressured Somoza to withdraw his support and pushed Figueres to remove Nicaraguan exiles from his country. The efforts of the United States and OAS succeeded. Nicaragua backed off, forcing Calderón's army to retreat. In return, Figueres promised to stop revolutionary activity in his country. For the moment, tensions subsided.

The activities of the Caribbean Legion remained potentially volatile for another year. In the summer of 1949, the exiles tried again to overthrow Trujillo after an aborted attempt in 1947. From bases in Cuba, Haiti, and Guatemala, they planned an air assault with reinforcements arriving by sea. The plan failed miserably. Trujillo uncovered it and denounced Communist elements in the Legion. In addition, Mexican officials interned the bulk of the forces when they stopped there en route from Guatemala to the Dominican Republic. Only one plane reached its destination at Luperón. Government forces soon dispersed the attackers, executing several Americans, pilots and others. They transported the other prisoners to Cuidad Trujillo, tortured them, and forced confessions implicating Arévalo and Figueres. Trujillo concluded that he had been "the victim of international communism personified by the rulers of Cuba, Guatemala, and Costa Rica."

In response to the Luperón incident, the United States pushed the Inter-American Peace Committee (IAPC), an arm of the OAS, to make recommendations to end the fighting. The United States sought, according to Ameringer, "a no-fault solution" that ensured the region would "get rid of the Caribbean Legion without appearing to defend Trujillo." The IAPC ultimately issued a document called "Fourteen Conclusions." It included provisions for preventing revolutionary activity in countries while encouraging the "exercise of democracy" as a "common denominator of American political life." The U.S. Ambassador to the OAS, Paul Daniels, declared it reaffirmed the policy of non-intervention and argued that "only careful and scrupulous adherence to the rule of law in our inter-American relations . . . will achieve that high measure of solidarity and mutual confidence on which our future economic, social, and cultural progress depends." Within a few years, this statement would appear hopelessly hypocritical.

Tío Sam Arms His Friends

During the period 1945–52, the twenty major nations of Latin America received less economic assistance from the United States than did the two tiny European nations of Belgium and Luxembourg. Washington, however, dispatched comparatively large quantities of military equipment as well as military advisors to Latin America. As early as 1946, the U.S. Joint Chiefs of Staff (JCS) emphasized that "the Western Hemisphere is a distinct military entity, the integrity of which is a fundamental postulate of our own security in the event of another war."

In this early phase of the Cold War, the military and the foreign service often differed over military policy. The soldiers wanted continued cooperation under Lend-Lease, despite believing that Latin American militaries would provide little direct support in a major conflict. They wanted, according to historian Chester Pach, "to secure goodwill and maintain the orientation of the other American nations toward the United States." The diplomats, on the other hand, worried that the military arms policy would further entrench the dictators and fuel a regional arms race. By late 1947, the perceived Soviet menace negated the State Department's objections.

By 1950, Truman approved NSC 56/2, titled "United States Policy Toward Inter-American Military Collaboration." It called for U.S. cooperation with Latin Americans to design a coherent and comprehensive hemispheric defense plan. Further, it supported military assistance "to assure adequate implementation of the Hemisphere Defense Scheme." With the outbreak of the Korean War, the Truman administration found a Congress willing to appropriate massive amounts of money for defense aid. In 1951, Congress approved $38.1 million for Latin American military development, an amount that quickly rose to $51.7 million by 1952. Throughout the Cold War, U.S. military assistance continued to flow southward in increasing amounts.

A New Interpretation of the Monroe Doctrine

Shifting attitudes regarding the Communist menace affected State Department policy in the early 1950s. One of the primary persons formulating U.S. policy toward Latin America was Assistant Secretary of State for Inter-American Affairs Edward Miller. He had more experience in Latin America than did many of his counterparts, as his father owned sugar plantations in Cuba. Privately, he believed that Latin Americans wanted to ignore the Cold War and return to a time when the "Good Neighbor was virtually our sole foreign policy." To him, the 1930s and World War II "had fostered an exaggerated and extreme sense of self-importance on the part of individuals connected with Latin American governments." In an executive session of the House Foreign Relations Committee, he told the representatives that during the early Good Neighbor era "we went too far in the direction of not protecting American interests."

In mid-1950, Miller outlined what became known as the Miller Doctrine. In it, he acknowledged that interventions in the early twentieth century were regrettable, albeit justified by the Monroe Doctrine and "necessary evils" and "protective interventions." He warned that "if the circumstances that led to the protective interventions by the United States should arise again today, the organized community of American states would be faced with the responsibility that the United States had once to assume alone." Miller rationalized intervention thusly: "The fact is that the doctrine of non-intervention never did proscribe the assumption by the organized community of a legitimate concern with any circumstances that threatened the common welfare. On the contrary, it made the possibility of such action imperative. Such a collective undertaking, far from representing intervention, is the alternative to intervention. It is the corollary of nonintervention." Miller concluded: "Communist political aggression . . . bears directly on the purpose of the Monroe Doctrine, which is as much our national policy today as it ever was." The Rio Pact was now "a Monroe Doctrine of our inter-American community."

The Miller Doctrine marked a dramatic public shift. It moved away from promises of nonintervention in the domestic affairs of other American states that had evolved slowly during the 1930s. Miller also said nothing about any desire to promote democracy as many Latin Americans focused on it. The growing differences between Americans and the Latin Americans became wider with the Miller Doctrine. "What Miller left unanalyzed was the policy the United States would adopt," historian Stephen Rabe stresses, "if it could not convince the Latin American nations to sanction an intervention against another American republic." Washington had moved one step closer toward returning to old patterns.

To undergird his arguments, Miller approved the publication of an article, "On a Certain Impatience with Latin America," by Louis Halle of the State Department Policy Planning Staff. Appearing in the July 1950 issue of *Foreign Affairs* (written under the pseudonym "Y"), the article emphasized Washington's impatience with spreading democracy at the cost of security issues. Halle paternalistically underscored that in the 1820s Latin Americans "were quite unready to assume the responsibility for self-government. The result was a sordid chaos out of which Latin America has still not finally emerged." "A tradition of political behavior marked by intemperance, intransigeance [sic], flamboyance and a worship of strong men," remained a Latin American tradition. He added, "worship of the 'man on horseback' is another manifestation of immaturity. It is a characteristic of adolescence, this admiration for the ruthless hero who tramples down all opposition, makes himself superior to law, and is irresistible to passionate women who serve his pleasure in droves."

Halle's article contained all the paternalism, racism, and elitism often present in American viewpoints. The absence in the State Department of experts on Latin America, people genuinely concerned with promoting hemispheric unity through equalized relationships, clearly shaped Miller's and Halle's statements. The United States no longer had time to waste on the region. It wanted stability, a point underscored by George Kennan when he visited Latin America in the spring of 1950. To U.S. policymakers, if dictatorships provided order, that was a reflection on their people. Washington had no time to tutor them in democracy at this important juncture of the Cold War.[1]

A Cool Wind Blows North

Many Latin Americans recognized the shift in U.S. attitudes and policies underway since 1947. Latin American politicians, newspaper editors, intellectuals, and labor leaders denounced Washington in growing numbers for allowing the growth of the imbalance of trade and reliance on private capital. Anti-American novels and books began to appear. Literary works included Joaquín Gutiérrez's *Puerto Limón* [Lemon Port] (1950), Ramón Amaya Amador's *Prisión verde* [Green Prison] (1950), Paca Navas Miralda's *Barro* [Mud] (1951), and Miguel Angel Asturias's *Viento fuerte* [Strong Wind] (1951). More scholarly books included Ramón Oliveres', *El imperialismo yanqui en América; la dominacion política y económica del Continente* [Yankee Imperialism in America: The Political and Economic Domination of the Continent] (1952) and Genaro Carnero Checo's, *El aguila rampante; el imperialismo yanqui sobre América Latina* [The Rampant Eagle: Yankee Imperialism in Latin America] (1956). Recurring themes were exploitation of labor by American businesses, and Washington's role in maintaining poor conditions in the region.

One of the most violent manifestations of anti-Americanism was an assassination attempt of President Truman in 1950. For many years,

[1] Kennan wrote after his visit, "It seems to me unlikely that there could be any other region of the earth in which nature and human behavior could have combined to produce a more unhappy and hopeless background for the conduct of human life."

Puerto Ricans had condemned the U.S. occupation of the island and its domination by American businespersons and wealthy Puerto Ricans. Poverty and unemployment were rampant, and the American governors had done little to address economic and political disparities. A strong independence movement evolved, one demanding immediate nationhood. The fact that the United States granted the Philippines their independence in 1946 strengthened these calls.

On November 1, 1950, two Puerto Rican nationalists, Grieselio Torresola and Oscar Collazo, appeared in Washington and tried to force their way into the temporary presidential residence at the Blair House, where Truman was staying. A gunfight ensued as Collazo died from a shot to the head, but the Puerto Ricans had managed to kill one guard and wound two others. Agents captured Torresola, who received a death sentence, which Truman later commuted to life imprisonment. President Jimmy Carter ultimately pardoned him. When asked why he had wanted to kill Truman, who supported Puerto Rican self-determination and had appointed the first Puerto Rican as governor, Torresola responded he was "just a symbol of the system" and added, "You don't attack the man, you attack the system."

Another point of contention between the Latin Americans and the United States was the Korean conflict, which began in June 1950. Walter LaFeber calls the Latin America reaction to U.S. action in Korea "tepid at best, hostile at worst." Secretary of State Acheson called an emergency meeting of foreign ministers in Washington. While most member nations had supported UN action against North Korean aggression, only a half dozen Latin American countries, including El Salvador, Costa Rica, and Colombia, responded to calls for troops—most of whom the U.S. military rejected with the exception of the Colombians. The Latin American dignitaries present promised "rhetorical" support and signed an agreement increasing their nation's production of strategic materials, but they tied their support to a statement highlighting Latin America's lack of economic development.

The Latin American response disappointed the White House. Secretary Miller ascribed to it "apathy and sullenness resulting from the feeling that the United States had abandoned Latin America in the postwar era and is giving priority to new friends in other parts of the world." During a trip to Latin America, Miller met with the Brazilian Foreign Minister, João Neves da Fortura, who agreed with his assessment. He told Miller that "Brazil's present situation would be different and our cooperation in the present emergency could probably be greater" had Washington developed "a recovery plan for Latin America similar to the Marshall Plan for Europe." Miller returned to Washington and proposed additional assistance, but his pleas fell on deaf ears. Preoccupied with the Asian war, the Truman administration maintained the policy of neglect vis-à-vis Latin America for the remainder of his term.

Resurgent Latin Nationalism?

Despite the region's lack of support for the Korean War, the Truman administration concluded that the Latin Americans remained pro-American and that the Communists in the region posed no significant threat. In fact, the State Department concluded the Communists had "lost ground." In late 1951, Miller assured a congressional committee that the Soviet presence in Latin America "at this time will not be great." By 1952, only Mexico, Argentina, and Uruguay had formal diplomatic relations with the Soviets.

Yet, significant challenges loomed on the horizon, as Latin American nationalism grew out of pent-up frustration with economic underdevelopment, stratified societies, foreign domination of native industries, and political authoritarianism. Despite optimism over the few inroads communism had made in the region in 1952, some U.S. officials feared nationalism might pave the way for its spread. As historian David Green notes, even as early as 1946, "the long jump between anti-Americanism and communism was becoming shorter and shorter." In the early 1950s, it narrowed even further.

The Tin Revolution

One of the first major nationalist challenges for the Truman administration's Latin American policy originated in 1951, in Bolivia where the Nationalist Revolutionary Movement (MNR), led by Víctor Paz Estenssoro, easily won the presidential election. When the army and the ruling leaders denied the MNR power, its supporters, led by a large contingent of tin miners, took to the streets. After some bloody confrontations, the army and elites surrendered, and the MNR took power in April 1952.

The nationalist MNR would walk a tightrope in dealing with the United States. Within a short period, the MNR expropriated Bolivia's three largest tin-mining companies, the most important industry in the country. In addition, they implemented land reforms, imposed universal suffrage, and stripped the army of its power. While the expropriation affected only a small group of Americans, anti-Communists in the United States sounded the alarm about MNR radicalism. One U.S. diplomat reported that "the MNR has accepted Communist support and might collaborate with the Communists or even fall under their domination if it came to power." The archbishop of Acre, José Clement Maurer, cautioned that "there is a danger of the advent of a Communist regime in the country." Bolivian leaders, however, emphasized the anti-Communist and pro-American orientation of the revolution.

Washington exercised caution in responding to the Bolivian revolution. "At the end of the 1952 revolution, there was no alternative to the MNR government: there was no army, nor was there another party capable of governing. The only alternative appeared to be chaos with advantage, if any, to the Communists," historian Bryce Woods explains. The administration extended recognition to the new government since no Communists had participated in the revolution or maintained prominent positions in the regime.

After extending recognition, U.S. officials focused on issues of compensation and keeping leftists from power. The United States found a comparatively compliant Bolivian government. Its leaders recognized that the U.S. government was the largest customer of tin. Furthermore, Bolivia needed emergency loans and food supplies and requested such assistance. When Washington asked for fair monetary compensation, the Bolivians worked hard to accomplish it. At other junctures, U.S. officials expressed concern over the appointment of a suspected Communist to teach at the military academy. Soon, Vice President Hernán Siles Zuazo cancelled the position. Even leftists such as Bolivian labor leader Juan Lechín told his followers that "in contrast to United States hostility to the Communist-influenced regime of Arbenz, the United States had helped the indigenous regime in Bolivia." This process of cooperation continued when Dwight David Eisenhower assumed the U.S. presidency in 1953.

The Bolivian episode underscored that the United States and Latin American nationalists could coexist. But the situation in Bolivia was unique in several ways. Americans had only a small investment in the tin industry, and a smaller comparative interest in the country. As such, U.S. interest-group pressure on the Truman and Eisenhower administrations

THE DEATH OF THE GOOD NEIGHBOR

proved minimal. For their part, the Bolivians proved willing to cooperate with the United States, recognizing U.S. strength. Compromises occurred on both sides, limiting conflict. Despite relatively cordial U.S.-Bolivian relations, challenges that appeared in the not-so-distant future rendered dramatically different results.

Ike Takes Over

As American policymakers dealt with the revolutionary junta in Bolivia, a heated presidential contest between the Republican nominee Dwight D. Eisenhower and Democrat Adlai Stevenson developed in 1952. Eisenhower, the former U.S. Army general and Supreme Allied Commander in Europe in World War II, was an attractive candidate, running on his war record and promises to battle corruption and end the quagmire in Korea. On the other side, the Democrat Stevenson stood in the shadow of Truman, an unpopular president.

Latin America received some attention during the campaign. In October 1952, Eisenhower made a speech in which he criticized Truman's Latin American policy. He emphasized that during World War II "we frantically wooed Latin America," but that after the war the United States "proceeded to forget these countries just as fast," and "terrible disillusionment set in throughout Latin America." He believed that the Truman administration had reneged on its promises of economic development, leading to downturns "followed by popular unrest, skillfully exploited by Communist agents there." "Through drift and neglect," Eisenhower stated, the Good Neighbor had become "a poor neighbor policy." The Republican platform reiterated these points, complaining that the "people of other American Republics are resentful of our neglect." It promised that "our ties with the sister republics of the Americas will be strengthened."

When Eisenhower won in November 1952, he selected John Foster Dulles, the son of a Presbyterian minister, as secretary of state. As a young man, Dulles worked for the New York City law firm of Sullivan and Cromwell, whose clients included UFCO. During his early career, he had traveled in Latin America on company business. Toward the Latin Americans, Dulles maintained a paternalistic attitude, telling someone in 1953 that "you have to pat them a little bit and make them think you are fond of them." Virulently anti-Communist, Dulles took seriously the threat of communism in the region, stating in 1953 that "conditions in Latin America are somewhat comparable to conditions as they were in the mid-thirties when the communist movement was getting started. . . . Well, if we don't look out, we will wake up some morning and read in the newspapers that there happened in South America the same kind of thing that happened in China."

Although Dulles certainly wanted to prevent Communist infiltration in Latin America, he focused on Indochina and Iran when Eisenhower took over. The president sent his brother Milton, president of Pennsylvania State University, on a fact-finding tour of Latin America in 1953, but little developed from his report. Dulles told the new assistant secretary of state for Inter-American affairs, John Moors Cabot: "I want you to devise an imaginative policy for Latin America—but don't spend any money." Cabot complained that Washington gave India more money to purchase trains than it provided to all of Latin America.

Despite his campaign promises, Eisenhower's economic policy during his first term differed little from that of his predecessor. A good example of the mindset was NSC 144/1, which appeared in March 1953. It called on the United States to encourage "Latin American governments to recognize that the bulk of the capital required for their economic development can best be supplied by private enterprise and that their own self-interest requires the creation of a climate which will attract private investment." In response, Cabot warned that "we cannot indefinitely continue the present discrimination against our sister republics in this hemisphere without gravely prejudicing our relations with them." He emphasized that the upper classes were "exercising an almost feudal control" and that the reliance on "trickle-down" economics would not destroy the Communists' appeal. Despite his analysis, the administration stayed the course.

Latin Americans recognized early on that things had not changed under Eisenhower. In 1954, Alberto Zum Felde, a respected Uruguayan literary critic, expressed his opinion that "the imperialist phenomenon persists in deeds although in a much less aggressive form than before, smoothed down, hidden under gloves and the speeches of Good Neighbor policy." He incorrectly appraised the situation as a change toward an iron-fist approach neared.

David vs. Goliath

Despite virtually ignoring the region during its first term, the Eisenhower administration focused on a particular Latin American nation. In Guatemala, U.S. policymakers became alarmed with the growing radicalism of the government led by Jacobo Arbenz. Arbenz's primary goal, one shared by his predecessor, Arévalo (1944–50), was the creation of a democratic and more egalitarian society and an end to U.S. economic hegemony. Both men sought to end the abuses of the peasants and Mayan Indians (which included forced labor) and fully incorporate everyone into society. Their reforms included increased education, labor protections, and more health care programs for Guatemalans, most of whom had languished in an authoritarian system for centuries.

The most controversial reform was land expropriation and redistribution, a program designed to integrate the dispossessed into the economy and weaken the elites who had dominated the country for many years. It started a major dispute. In the first year of the land-reform implementation, the government distributed 740,000 acres (most taken from Germans during World War II) to more than 8,000 farmers. Within two years, 87,569 farmers received an additional 917,659 acres, including some of Arbenz's own land. The government backed the land grants with credits for agricultural materials and technical assistance. As historian Richard Immerman observes, by 1954, "Guatemala remained underdeveloped, but there was discernible progress."

From the start, the Arbenz government encountered opposition from Guatemalan elites and UFCO. In the early 1950s, UFCO owned more than 550,000 acres (over 40 percent of the country's arable land) of which only 15 percent was in cultivation. The government wanted to expropriate the idle lands and offered the company $1.185 million in a bond at 3 percent interest, the amount at which UFCO had valued its property for tax purposes in 1952. UFCO ignored its own figures and claimed the property was worth $15.8 million, for which it presented a bill to the Arbenz government. Naturally, Arbenz scoffed at the invoice.

A standoff ensued, as the Eisenhower administration took power in 1953. UFCO lobbied the State Department and the White House for assistance and found allies in Dulles and his brother, Director of the CIA Allen Dulles. UFCO representatives and others drew parallels between the expropriation of lands and Communist activities. They also noted that the Guatemalan Communist party openly participated in the country's politics and even worked in the government agencies administering the land-reform program. UFCO added to the charges by waging a media campaign, headed by its public relations officer Ed Whitman (the husband of President Eisenhower's personal secretary). It included full-page spreads in the *New York Times* highlighting the alarming events ongoing in Guatemala and production of films including, *"Why the Kremlin Hates Bananas."*

The lobbying efforts succeeded. The Eisenhower administration increasingly concentrated on Guatemala. Undersecretary of State Walter Bedell Smith reported that "the most important question facing the Cabinet was to make up its mind that Latin America is important to the United States" and that "timely action was extremely desirable to prevent Communism from spreading beyond Guatemala." President Eisenhower added soon thereafter that "one American nation has succumbed to Communist infiltration," a reference to Guatemala.

Project PBSUCCESS

Once convinced of a Communist threat, the Eisenhower administration formulated plans to remove it, turning preparations over to the CIA. In late 1953, Eisenhower approved Project PBSUCCESS, a plan to overthrow Arbenz. The CIA found a willing local leader in Colonel Carlos Castillo Armas, who had led an unsuccessful coup in 1950, during which he had been wounded and imprisoned. He later escaped. Now, with the material assistance of the United States and Somoza, a small band of anti-Arbenz Guatemalans, complemented by mercenaries including U.S. pilots flying World War II–vintage airplanes, began training in Nicaragua.

On the diplomatic level, the Eisenhower administration increased the pressure. Washington appointed a new ambassador to Guatemala, John E. Peurifoy, who arrived in November 1953. A veteran of the prosecution of alleged Communist Alger Hiss (of the U.S. State Department) and anti-Communist actions in Greece, Peurifoy immediately complained to the Guatemalan foreign minister that "agrarian reform had been instituted in China and . . . China was today a Communist country." Soon afterward, he told Arbenz that "in view of inadequacy of normal diplomatic procedures in dealing with a situation, there appears no alternative to our taking steps which would tend to make more difficult continuation of regime in Guatemala." He added "if the President is not a Communist he will certainly do until one comes along."

Dulles also went on the offensive. In March 1954, the Tenth Inter-American Conference convened in Caracas, Venezuela, where Dulles made an impassioned speech to denounce international communism as "alien intrigue and treachery." He pushed a resolution that allowed "appropriate action in accordance with existing treaties" if Communist control of a nation existed or appeared imminent. He never mentioned Guatemala, but his intent was clear. The Guatemalan foreign minister, Guillermo Toriello Garrido, called the secretary of state's proposal "merely a pretext for intervening in our internal affairs." He characterized it as an example of the "internationalism of McCarthyism." Despite Toriello's efforts, a watered-down resolution passed easily, although others pushed through a parallel pronouncement that sought to attack communism by promoting human rights, democracy, and economic development.

One of the most pressing problems for the United States remained convincing people that Moscow controlled Arbenz. Dulles admitted that he could not "produce any evidence clearly tying the Guatemalan government to Moscow." Some people argued that conservative institutions in Guatemala, especially the military and Catholic Church, would counter Communist influence. Furthermore, the State Department concluded that in UN votes, Guatemala's position differed little from that of other Latin American nations. Finally, many observers pointed out that only four of Guatemala's fifty-six congressmen were Communists.

Despite the lack of evidence and repeated assurances to Latin America that his administration backed a policy of nonintervention, Eisenhower moved forward with PBSUCCESS. He received a boost when the Arbenz government purchased 2,000 tons of military equipment from Czechoslovakia after Washington refused to grant it a license to purchase U.S.-made arms. The weapons made their way from Europe to Guatemala aboard the Swedish freighter *Alfhem,* the progress of which the CIA carefully monitored. Some agents debated whether to dispatch the navy to intercept the ship, but it eluded U.S. authorities and landed in Puerto Barrios. Among the people waiting to meet the vessel was Ambassador Peurifoy. Washington exploded, arguing that the purchase proved Soviet complicity in arming the Guatemalans for subversive activities in Central America.

By June, the U.S.-backed rebels were ready to move. The CIA believed: "Arbenz would not be backed by his army in the event of an anticommunist revolution." Many knew about the planned attack, as Peurifoy bragged in April that "we are making out our Fourth of July reception invitations, and we are not including any of the present administration." On June

17, 1954, the day before the invasion, Danny Peurifoy, son of the ambassador, ran home and told his mother that "there's no school this afternoon because there is going to be a revolution at 5:00."

The following day, Armas moved his ragtag band of 150 Guatemalans and mercenaries six miles into Guatemala to Esquipulas. There, they held their position and waited. The CIA-sponsored radio broadcasts told of the thousands of rebels marching on the capital, possessing flamethrowers, artillery, and an air force. Over Guatemala City, three mercenaries flew sorties, bombing and strafing the presidential palace and other government facilities. The CIA knew that Arbenz's government could crush the invasion at any moment, but it relied on the belief that "the entire effort is thus more dependent upon psychological impact rather than actual military strength" and that Armas had only to create the "impression of substantial military strength" and the correct impression of U.S. backing. They also had provided substantial military assistance to Nicaragua and Honduras in case they needed their help.

The actions succeeded. Terror gripped the capital, and Arbenz grounded his air force for fear of defections. He waffled, and the army stayed in its barracks. The Guatemalans tried diplomacy, taking their case to the United Nations to seek an injunction against foreign aggression, in which Washington denied playing any role. In a heated debate in the Security Council, U.S. Ambassador to the UN Henry Cabot Lodge defended his bosses, telling the Soviet ambassador to "stay out of this hemisphere and do not try to start your plans and conspiracies over here." The UN Security Council ultimately decided to submit the matter to the OAS. The Soviets vetoed the plan, arguing that the U.S.-dominated OAS would do nothing.

As the UN debated, the rebel movement floundered for a week. It neither moved nor sparked an internal uprising. Further problems arose after the Guatemalans shot down the little rebel air force. Eisenhower, over the protests of several advisors who feared reinforcements would demonstrate U.S. complicity, approved the requisition of new aircraft. As the planes continued to bomb and strafe his palace, Arbenz continued to waver. Those around him, including a young Argentine named Ernesto "Che" Guevara, encouraged him to rally the people. But when Arbenz finally ordered the distribution of arms to the workers and peasants, the army officers refused to obey his command. On June 27, he fled into exile. Armas and company blithely stepped in. Two subsequent attempts by moderates to form a government without Armas failed. By July 7, Armas became provisional president. In October, he held nationwide elections to sanction officially his rule; he won by more than 486,000 votes, with only 400 opposing.

Bitter Fruit

The Eisenhower administration immediately extended diplomatic recognition to the Armas government. It denied any role in the coup, arguing Armas had defeated the Communist menace alone. At the Illinois State Fair, the president proudly proclaimed that "in Guatemala, the people of that region rose up and rejected the Communist doctrine, and said in the terms of the spirit of the agreement of Caracas, 'You shall not come here and establish yourselves.'" Dulles was even more direct. "The people of Guatemala have now been heard," and they had removed "an alien despotism which sought to use Guatemala for its own evil ends." For Dulles, the "loyal citizens of Guatemala . . . in the face of terrorism and violence against what seemed insuperable odds, had the courage and the will to eliminate the traitorous tools of foreign despots." In none of the speeches and reports that followed was any mention of U.S. involvement made. It would take two more decades to uncover the extent of that involvement.

Armas was a dutiful ally. In one of his first acts, he returned nearly all of UFCO's lands and displaced the peasants occupying them. He abolished the taxes on profits of foreigners. In other areas, he abrogated the labor laws and declared most labor unions illegal. He also created the National Committee for Defense against Communism. Its broad-ranging powers included arresting suspected Communists, including some on lists provided by U.S. officials. Subsequently, the police and military detained thousands of persons, torturing and murdering many of the prisoners. Armas also promulgated a new constitution that granted dictatorial powers to the executive branch. He packed courts and local municipalities with his cronies and returned Guatemala to authoritarian rule similar to that of Ubico.

The legacies of the CIA-sponsored coup were many. As Richard Immerman underscores, "the intervention in Guatemala produced lasting effects on United States relations with the underdeveloped nations of the world in general and with Latin America in particular." For Washington, it damaged relations with its Latin American neighbors. Most Latin Americans knew about its role in Arbenz's overthrow. Mistrust and suspicion of Washington gained an even stronger foothold among its neighbors.

For the Guatemalans, the coup replaced a reformist government with an authoritarian one. Bloodshed and violence followed, first with the mass roundup of alleged Communists and then with the assassination of Armas in 1957. For nearly five decades, leftist guerrillas have fought the successive governments of Guatemala, with peasants and Mayan Indians often caught in the middle. Since the CIA-sponsored rebellion, observers estimate that more than 200,000 Guatemalans have died in the conflict. Today, the country remains terribly stratified with poverty rampant, as the revolutionary aims of the 1940s remain unfulfilled.

Dictators Are Our Friends

As demonstrated in Guatemala, high-ranking U.S. policymakers, including Secretary of State Dulles, believed that pro-U.S. authoritarian regimes served American interests more than did nationally minded democracies that lacked enthusiasm for anti-communism. Dulles made this point clear to U.S. diplomats. Robert Woodward, who worked in the Latin American division and later as U.S. ambassador to Costa Rica, reported that Dulles instructed him to "do nothing to offend the dictators; they are the only people we can depend on." For Dulles, the dictators provided stability, suppressed communism, opened the doors to foreign investment, and protected U.S. companies against pesky labor unions.

Sadly, there are many more examples of the United States aiding dictators throughout Latin America. After Armas took power, U.S. aid to Guatemala increased from $463,000 in 1954 to $10.7 million. When he toured the United States in late 1954, he received a ticker-tape parade in New York City, a twenty-one-gun salute in Washington, D.C., honorary degrees from Columbia and Fordham Universities, and a place of honor at a White House dinner during which Vice President Richard Nixon toasted him as a "courageous hero." Later, he received a special trip to Colorado to visit with President Eisenhower.

During the mid-1950s, this closeness with known dictators increased. Eisenhower bestowed the Merit of Honor upon Peruvian dictator Manuel Odría and Venezuelan strongman Marcos Pérez Jiménez. After a meeting with all of the heads of Latin America, Eisenhower wrote that General Alfredo Stroessner of Paraguay and Somoza "stood out." After a visit to Latin America in 1955, Vice President Nixon compared Cuba's Batista to Abraham Lincoln and called him "a very remarkable man." In addition, most State Department officials reflected the administration's policy. U.S. Ambassador to the Dominican Republic William Pheiffer called Trujillo "an authentic genius who thinks and labors, primarily, in terms of the best interests of his people." All of this translated into military and economic assistance for the dictatorial regimes, ultimately creating more animosity among the peoples of Latin America toward the United States.

Duel at the Border

Not everyone in the United States agreed with supporting dictators. In the postwar period, a small but vocal group of anti-Communist liberals began calling for change. They argued that U.S. cooperation with dictators actually allowed communism to mature in the repressed and impoverished totalitarian states. Individuals from groups such as the Americans for Democratic Action (ADA) and Inter-American Association for Democracy and Freedom (IADF) were at the vanguard. Prominent members included labor activists Robert Alexander and Serafino Romualdi, celebrities such as Pearl Buck and Eleanor Roosevelt, and academicians like Arthur Schlesinger, Jr. Individuals such as New Dealer Adolf A. Berle, Jr., who acted as advisor to the White House from the 1930s forward, and members of Congress such as Senators Paul Douglas of Illinois and Wayne Morse of Oregon shared such convictions. They believed that the Venezuelan Betancourt, Víctor Raúl Haya de la Torre in Peru, and Figueres were positive role models for Latin American leaders. They went to great lengths to persuade the administration to rethink their policies.

The tensions among the different positions surfaced in 1955 in Costa Rica and demonstrated an ambivalence in U.S. policy. In 1953, Figueres had won the presidency and his party, the National Liberation Party, had swept into power. They implemented a series of reforms that included renegotiating a contract with UFCO after Figueres threatened expropriation. Ultimately, UFCO compromised, but not before bad feelings developed. In addition, Figueres also angered Dulles when he refused to attend the Caracas Conference to protest the choice of the site as validating the dictatorship of Pérez-Jiménez. From that point forward, Dulles, along with conservatives in Congress, aligned with the Caribbean dictators and accused Figueres of having Communist sympathies.

Most likely with the encouragement of some CIA operatives, Nicaraguan iron man Somoza began making plans to overthrow Figueres with the assistance of his old friend, former Costa Rica president Rafael Calderón. For years, Figueres had supported Caribbean exiles, including Betancourt, and Nicaraguan liberal democrats, one of whom Somoza captured in April 1954 during an assassination attempt. Tensions heightened along the border as the regional dictators lined up behind Somoza, especially the Venezuelans, who were angry with Figueres for harboring Betancourt.

Tensions remained high for six months, bursting forth into open conflict in early 1955. Now, Calderón's forces, led by Picado's West Point–educated son, followed the exact plan employed by Armas in Guatemala. They traveled a few miles into Costa Rica, well within the protection of Somoza's well-armed National Guard. Meanwhile, a small number of World War II–era fighter planes flown by mercenaries that had served Armas strafed San José. At the same time, a rebel radio station identified as the "Voice of the Authentic Anti-Communist Revolutionary Army" compared Figueres to Arbenz and called on Costa Ricans to expel him. Because of the way the plan unfolded—not to mention Dulles's antipathy toward the events—Figueres later accused the CIA of having helped the rebels; evidence supports his thesis. Even if the CIA had played no active role in the takeover, it certainly possessed advance knowledge of it.

In response, Figueres and his allies sprang into action. He benefited from the State Department having replaced a conservative anti-Communist Republican ambassador, Robert Hill, with a much more liberal U.S. ambassador, Robert Woodward. A critic of Dulles's policy of supporting authoritarian regimes, Woodward quickly moved to assist the Costa Ricans through various channels. In addition, Schlesinger, Jr., Berle, and Senator Douglas petitioned Eisenhower to protect Central America's only true democracy.

The lobbying efforts succeeded. The Eisenhower administration supported OAS efforts to negotiate a peace and flew an OAS committee to the area to investigate the charges of Nicaraguan complicity. U.S. diplomats warned Somoza about his treaty obligations and emphasized that "public opinion and Congress here [are] aroused by [the] possibility that revolutionary forces [are] receiving air and ground facilities sources outside Costa Rica." Equally as important, the United States sold weapons and military supplies to the Costa Ricans, including four P-51 Mustang fighter aircraft. The arms proved the difference, despite continued verbal sparring that included Somoza (the Nicaraguan pistol champion) challenging Figueres to a duel at the border. Figueres replied to Somoza that he should "grow up," going on to describe him as "crazy as a goat in the summer sun." Still, he accepted the challenge, but only if they held said duel on the deck of the Soviet submarine that Somoza claimed he had recently captured. Needless to say, the battle of honor never occurred.

The real fighting ended in late January 1955, as the rebels retreated into Nicaragua. *Time* noted that Figueres's "blue-jean militia armed with their own rifles" had "beat Picado, the West Pointer, and a well-armed and trained rebel force." Universal support for the U.S. decision to aid the Costa Ricans developed as an editorial in America observed "it cannot be said that the United States intervened on this occasion in support of a corrupt and dictatorial regime whose only claim for help is that it maintains order while suppressing communism."

Clearly, this episode demonstrates that in a few instances U.S. leaders could support democratic movements in the region. The Dulles brothers enjoyed watching Figueres squirm, but most Americans believed that the Costa Rican government was a model for Latin America and that Figueres had impeccable anti-Communist credentials. Still, U.S. leaders went only so far in promoting and protecting democracy. For much of the Eisenhower administration, the White House tended to side with dictators over reformist democrats. It reinforced this stance in 1956, after an assassin's bullet struck down Somoza. Eisenhower dispatched a military transport to take the dictator to an American hospital in the Canal Zone, in which he died despite the best efforts of U.S. Army doctors. Clearly, the United States liked order more than it did reform and change.

An Alternative Vision to Underdevelopment

As Stephen Rabe observes, "because it was winning the cold war in Latin America, the Eisenhower administration saw little need to refashion its foreign economic policies." The lack of direct U.S. assistance and reliance on private investment remained a cornerstone of U.S. economic policy until the end of the administration, when the rise of Fidel Castro and other events pushed U.S. policymakers to rethink their stance. Throughout the decade, Latin Americans blamed capitalist development models for the chronic underdevelopment in the region. In some ways, this threatened U.S. hegemony more than nationalization ever did.

The center of this realignment of thought was the Economic Commission for Latin America (ECLA), a United Nations organization created in 1948. Designed as a think-tank, the ECLA employed economists and technicians to analyze Latin America's economic underdevelopment and make recommendations for change. The founders, led by the respected Argentine economist Raúl Prebisch, purposely chose Santiago, Chile, over OAS headquarters in Washington for their offices. Soon participants began meeting and studying Latin America's economic weaknesses and strengths and espousing policy alternatives.

As historian Thomas Skidmore and political scientist Peter Smith note, "ECLA helped to produce a Latin American mentality in economic analysis." While far from uniform, the basic idea of ECLA was that a divided world existed, with the industrialized nations composing the "core" and the unindustrialized producers of raw materials composing the "periphery." Challenging leading Western economists, ECLA thinkers argued that the trade relationship between the United States and the other core nations had adversely affected Latin America's development. According to their analysis, the process had started in the nineteenth century, as core nations industrialized and Latin American continued producing raw materials. According to historians Peter Klarén and Thomas Bossert, "ECLA argued that instead of benefiting both trading partners equally, according to the laws of comparative advantage of neoclassical economics, the terms of trade had turned against Latin America." An uneven exchange arose as the prices for raw materials (set typically in the core) fell while the price of finished goods increased. ECLA argued that only when the periphery severed or reduced its relationship with the core, such as during the world wars or major depressions, did more-balanced growth occur. Once periphery-core relations resumed, a cycle of disadvantage returned.

Many members of ECLA began proposing changes for the relationship and reducing the imbalance in trade. One of the most important proposals was import-substitution industrialization (ISI). Economists believed that if a country developed its own industrial base in consumer goods, such as automobiles and household goods, as part of a diversified economy, then the uneven distribution of wealth would diminish. To accomplish these goals, governments needed to provide tax incentives, some state monies, and high import tariffs to protect fledgling industries. Other necessary changes included tax reform, more equal distribution of income, and land redistribution. To finance these programs, the core should provide capital to peripheral nations through the IMF and World Bank. ECLA estimated Latin America required more than $1 billion annually for ten years to achieve the desired growth. While viewed by some as radical, at no point did the proposals of ECLA challenge the basic concepts of the influx of foreign capital, free and open international trade, and the rights of private property.

ECLA proposals found favor among many centrist politicians throughout Latin America during the 1950s, including Getúlio Vargas and Juscelino Kubitschek in Brazil, Eduardo Frei in Chile, and Arturo Frondizi in Argentina. They implemented various ISI policies and accompanying reforms, much to the consternation of the Eisenhower administration, which saw the programs as attacks on free enterprise and open trade. Indeed, for several years U.S. diplomats tried to abolish ECLA. As Stephen Rabe notes, the Eisenhower administration believed ECLA proposals would create "state enterprises with the potential to become bloated with bureaucracy and responsive to political whims rather than sound economic analyses." One administration official stressed that governments were "to create conditions favorable to the investment and growth of private capital and enterprise." Others complained that if the United States provided economic assistance to Latin America at this time, it might give "impetus to a basic trend toward socialist economies." Washington pushed for private investors to contribute to the proper "attitudes of mind" and at "a minimum cost to our Government."

The efforts at ISI reform had some early successes in Brazil and several other countries, but it was never a panacea. Washington consistently attacked state-run industries, including those that already existed, such as PEMEX. Using promises of economic and military assistance, it successfully beat back the perceived socialist onslaught. Other problems plagued the ISI model, for many of the industries it stimulated and protected proved inefficient. Most countries lacked a sustainable internal market, and their domestic products could not compete with long-established U.S. and European brands. Furthermore, foreign companies learned to use the multinational corporation (MNC) to circumvent efforts to protect native industries. By the early 1960s, most ECLA-inspired efforts had failed and some people had begun to look to decidedly more radical development models.

Eisenhower's Diplomatic Pearl Harbor

Washington's apathy and continued support for military dictators created a powder keg. In May 1958, it exploded. The State Department worked in conjunction with the White House to arrange for Vice President Nixon to make a "goodwill mission" trip to Latin America. He requested that the State Department arrange visits with "local citizens in reasonably large numbers" and especially the "man in [the] street." Nixon expressed a willingness to "meet controversial figures and discuss controversial subjects." On the latter, historians Michael Weis and Marvin Zahniser emphasize that the growing leftist threat made Nixon want "to demonstrate that spokespersons for democracy and capitalism had valid viewpoints that were reasonable and defensible in the marketplace of ideas." By doing this, he would "encourage like-minded politicians in Latin America to speak up on behalf of such concepts."

With the exception of scattered protests and negative editorials, the trip started uneventfully in Uruguay, Argentina, Paraguay, and Bolivia. Next, Nixon traveled to Peru, where relations were strained, mainly over issues of protectionism. Many Peruvians also resented Eisenhower's awarding the Legion of Merit to the deposed dictator Manuel Odría. The animosity was especially high among the Alianza Popular Revolucionaria Americana (APRA). During Odría's dictatorship (1948–56), he imprisoned and killed APRA members.

As early as a year before Nixon's trip, some U.S. officials underscored growing nationalist and anti-American sentiment in Peru. Despite warnings of potential problems at the University of San Marcos, Nixon trekked off to the institution, where angry protestors greeted him at the gates by hurling insults, rocks, and spoiled fruit at him. At one point, Nixon jumped onto the trunk of his limousine and assumed a prize-fighter's stance, yelling: "You are cowards, you are afraid of the truth!" Unfazed, he traveled to the nearby Catholic University and disrupted student elections to challenge hecklers. Finally, he returned toward his hotel, where he had an encounter with a "weird-looking character . . . [with] bulging eyes" who spat in his face. Nixon responded by kicking the man in the shins, and a Secret Service agent accosted the assailant. Once in the safety of his quarters, Nixon labeled the protests as Communist inspired.

Despite the events in Peru, Nixon moved to his next stops of Ecuador and Colombia, where he managed to avoid any unsavory incidents. Then it was off to Venezuela, which proved a terrible mistake. That country, despite massive oil revenues and huge foreign investment, had many problems. The average per capita income was $500 a year, and all but the elites faced a short life expectancy and limited educational and healthcare opportunities.

Only months before, the U.S.-backed dictator Pérez-Jiménez had fled to Miami along with his hated police chief Pedro Estrada following a coup. Meanwhile, a ruling junta composed of many different groups had taken control and scheduled presidential elections. In this environment, many Venezuelans remembered the massive U.S. military and economic assistance that Pérez-Jiménez received, as well as Eisenhower having awarded the dictator the Legion of Merit.

Nevertheless, Nixon visited Caracas. As the vice president and his wife stepped off the plane, a Venezuelan band began playing the national anthem. Nixon stood at attention, as required by protocol, which gave a crowd of angry demonstrators a good opportunity to pelt the couple with garbage and spit on them from an overhang. Before long, Mrs. Nixon's red dress had been stained brown from tobacco juice. After the music stopped, Secret Service agents rushed the Nixons off to waiting limousines. As the motorcade sped down the highway, with Nixon cursing the Venezuelan foreign minister for having allowed the Communists to embarrass him, the traffic stalled. A mob appeared armed with rocks, pipes, and clubs. For twelve minutes, it terrorized the vice president and his entourage. Nixon persuaded one secret service agent with a drawn gun who declared himself ready to "get some of these sons-of-bitches" to restrain himself. Finally, a resourceful driver found an escape path for the group that ultimately reached the U.S. embassy.

The whole event had a dramatic flair. On hearing of the riots, President Eisenhower and his advisors organized a rescue force of several hundred marines and paratroopers, in "Operation Poor Richard." News of the plan leaked out, further embarrassing Nixon and leading Caracas to warn that "under no circumstances could the Government and people of Venezuela request or permit the intervention of foreign military forces on national territory." The crisis slowly defused, and the junta took no chances for a repeat performance, as Nixon shortened his visit and returned to the airport under heavy security.

On the last leg of his "goodwill mission," Nixon visited Puerto Rico, where he received a warm welcome. Then he finally returned to Washington, where Eisenhower, FBI Director J. Edgar Hoover, and others met him at the airplane to congratulate him for his exemplary service and courage. Signs in the crowd read "Don't let those Commies get you down, Dick," and "Communist cowardice loses—Nixon courage wins." Nixon would parlay the whole event into political advantage by portraying himself as a tough leader while under fire.

Lessons Learned

The "goodwill mission" spurred on an already existing reevaluation of U.S. policy in Latin America. A respected journalist called Nixon's trip a "diplomatic Pearl Harbor" and called for heads to roll at the State Department. Senator Wayne Morse (I-OR), already a strong critic of the administration's Latin American policy, began conducting hearings in the Foreign Relations Subcommittee on Inter-American Affairs. The Senate Foreign Relations Committee (SFRC) announced a two-year policy review. Soon thereafter, prominent members of the SFRC and others, led by Senators John F. Kennedy and Hubert Humphrey, called for a reappraisal of U.S. military aid to the nonindustrialized world.

The Eisenhower administration initially ignored requests for changes, focusing on Nixon's accusation that the protestors "without any doubt were Communists." Nixon acknowledged, however, that "Communists spearheaded the attack, [but] they had a lot of willing spear carriers with them." CIA director Dulles characterized the mission as a "shock" that had "brought South American problems to our attention as nothing else could have." Optimistically, he said the trip "may have long range benefits for the South American countries." In addition, the president again sent his brother Milton on a fact-finding trip to Latin America. He returned, warning that "a surging, swelling revolutionary demand, not just for aid, but for rapid social revolution in country after country" threatened to engulf the region.

Slowly, changes began to occur. While resisting calls for reduced military assistance to the dictators, the administration altered economic policies. Within a few days of Nixon's return, the administration reversed earlier opposition to negotiations on international price-support agreements for commodities, including coffee. It also asked for $2 billion more for the Export-Import Bank. Soon thereafter, the State Department announced U.S. support for the creation of the Inter-American Development Bank (IADB). By April 1959, the IADB received capitalization of $1 billion, with Washington providing 45 percent of the monies. Within two years, it began making loans to fund economic development projects.

There were also diplomatic changes following the "goodwill mission," as the Eisenhower administration reevaluated its policy on dictatorships and moved toward U.S. support for democracy. In August 1958, Eisenhower greeted the new Venezuelan ambassador, telling a crowd that "authoritarianism and autocracy of whatever form are incompatible with the ideals of our great leaders of the past." To make a point, he granted a request from the new Betancourt regime and began deportation proceedings against Pérez-Jiménez. Still cautious however, the administration opposed the Betancourt Doctrine that called for the OAS to recognize only "regimes born of free elections and respecting human rights." This was going too far, too fast for many U.S. policymakers.

Eisenhower and his advisors also laid the groundwork for future changes. In February 1959, he approved NSC 5902/1, which recognized Latin America as an underdeveloped region whose aspirations for change were "rising more rapidly than they are being satisfied." It argued that Washington had failed to make "efforts in all fields commensurate with the magnitude of the problems" and that a "consistent and continuing major effort will be required." The report noted the strengths of the existing policies, but argued that under "exceptional circumstances" the United States needed to consider grants rather than loans. Still, as Stephen Rabe underscores, "the Eisenhower administration altered its Latin American policy without substantially refashioning it."

The Shot Heard Round the World

While the events during Nixon's trip shocked Americans, a bigger threat to U.S. hegemony arose in Cuba. Since the early 1950s, Batista had faced a determined enemy in Fidel Castro. As a young man in 1953, Castro led a disastrous attack on the Moncada barracks in Santiago. Jailed for two years, he wrote a manifesto that outlined his desire to restore constitutional government and guarantee more equitable economic and social opportunities for all Cubans. He emphasized the legacy of José Martí, never mentioning Marx. After the publication of his tract, he tried again to overthrow Batista, in 1956 at the head of the 26th of July Movement (timed to commemorate the Moncada attack). Accompanied by his brother Raúl and Che Guevara, Castro began a three-year guerrilla war in the mountains of the Sierra Maestra. Over time, he gained a strong following among those tired of the corrupt Batista government and foreign control of the economy as well as liberal democrats, such as Figueres and Betancourt, throughout the hemisphere.

The Eisenhower administration had apprehensively watched the revolution unfold, fearful of losing a strong anti-Communist ally on an island only 90 miles off the coast of Florida. As early as 1955, FBI Director Hoover had reported that Castro and his followers "may pose a threat to the internal security of the United States." In response, at a rally in Union City, New Jersey, in October 1955, FBI agents arrested and interrogated Castro. Other activities highlighted U.S. preferences. When Nixon attended Batista's inauguration in 1955, he had called him "remarkable . . . strong, vigorous." Another U.S. diplomat characterized Batista as "an expert administrator" whose country "has had a rebirth and a genuine resurgence." U.S. business executives also liked Batista, one emphasizing: "We have made peace with Batista. We know what our taxes and hidden taxes are going to be."

Yet some, even Batista supporters, saw the weakness of the Cuban society. Outgoing ambassador to Cuba Arthur Gardner wrote that "it is hard for a person who comes to Cuba and sees so many signs of building and prosperity to realize that only a few miles back from the city hundreds of thousands of people have only the bare necessities of life. Until this sore has been healed by the opportunity to work, Cuba will remain in a restless stage." In response, the new ambassador to Cuba, Earl E. T. Smith, received instructions to "alter the prevailing notion in Cuba that the American Ambassador was intervening on behalf of the government of Cuba to perpetuate the Batista dictatorship." Soon after arriving, Smith criticized the regime for its "excessive police action" in dispersing a group of mothers protesting its policies.

The problem for the Eisenhower administration was the search for an acceptable alternative to Batista other than Castro. As Stephen Rabe notes, "Smith was convinced that Castro would not honor international obligations or U.S. investments and that only Communists would benefit from Batista's collapse." In 1958, Washington pressured Batista to hold elections, hoping that someone more acceptable than Castro might prevail. The plan backfired, as Batista rigged the contest in favor of his choice, Dr. Andrés Rivero Aguero. When Cubans protested, Batista unleashed his army and air force, which indiscriminately destroyed civilian targets. Now Washington suspended arms shipments to Cuba and pressured Batista to resign. By mid-December, State Department officials informed him that "the United States will no longer support the present government of Cuba." On New Year's Eve, Batista fled and Castro moved in to fill the leadership vacuum.

Communist or Nationalist?

In 1959, the major question in Washington was whether the Cuban revolutionaries were nationalists or Communists and what, if any, was the relationship between these two groups. In the early stages, most U.S. officials characterized Castro as a nationalist. In December 1959, Undersecretary of State Christian Herter reported that Communists had participated in the 26th of July movement to "some extent," but "there is insufficient evidence on which to base a charge that the rebels are Communist-dominated." The CIA added that the Communists would probably participate in the new government, but Allen Dulles told a congressional committee that Castro was not a Communist, and that Communists were not likely to "force Castro to adopt policies to which he is opposed." Yet he also told the NSC that the new Cuban leaders "had to be treated more or less like children. . . . They had to be led rather than rebuffed. If not they were capable of almost anything."

The Eisenhower administration immediately recognized Castro's government. The Cuban leader won great acclaim in the United States, even

Fidel Castro addressing the crowd in Havana on the second anniversary of the revolution. *Courtesy Library of Congress, LC-USZ62-118203*

appearing on the *Ed Sullivan Show* and the *Jack Paar Show*. U.S. diplomats believed that the two nations would remain close. "Cuba is accustomed to U.S.-type goods and U.S. operations," one embassy official wrote. Many characterized Castro as a driven opportunist with an "undeviating urge for fame and political power," yet showing no affinity for communism.

To deal with the new regime, Washington dispatched to Havana professional diplomat Philip Bonsal, a well-known proponent of economic and social reform in Latin America. The State Department wanted an experienced hand to deal with Castro in case he took a hard turn to the left. The fact that Castro had maintained only limited relations with the Cuban Communist party before the revolution did not ease fears among hard-line anti-Communists. Some embassy officials warned that "some danger flags are already up and need to be closely watched." These included the legalization of the Communist party. Castro also made several anti-U.S. speeches to emphasize "the Platt Amendment is finished" and that Cubans would "neither sell themselves, nor falter nor become intimidated by any threat."

Despite such warnings, many U.S. officials remained optimistic. Under-secretary of State Roy Rubottom predicted that after a tumultuous year or so Cuba would settle down and fulfill the "potential greatness in the Cuban Revolution." In April 1959, the National Press Club in Washington invited Castro to speak. Eisenhower took a golf trip to Georgia during Castro's visit to the capital, leaving Secretary of State Christian Herter and Vice President Nixon to handle the informal meetings with the new Cuban leader. Herter concluded that Castro failed to share "the same idea of law and legality we have in the United States" and "confused the roar of mass audiences with the rule of the majority in his concept of democracy." In short, Herter characterized Castro as an "enigma" and urged watchful waiting. The vice president agreed with the appraisal. Nixon argued that Castro appeared bent on pursuing socialism, but not communism, and predicted that Castro would become "a great factor in the development of Cuba and very possibly in Latin American affairs." All that was necessary was for Washington "to orient him in the right direction."

After Castro returned home, a confrontation on the island nation immediately developed. The Cuban government slashed the price of electricity charged by the U.S.-dominated Cuban Electric Company. In March, it nationalized the U.S.-owned subsidiary of the International Telephone and Telegraph Corporation (ITT). Finally, Castro asked Caracas for a $300 million loan to help end his country's dependence on the United States, contending that "relying on private investment in the building of the economic future for Cuba is like curing cancer with Mercurochrome."

The major policy that alarmed U.S. diplomats was the promulgation of the Agrarian Reform Law in May 1959. Following the example of the Mexican Revolution, the Cuban government expropriated all estates larger than 1,000 acres. It agreed to pay Cuban currency bonds for the declared value of the lands from the 1958 tax rolls and created a National Institute of Agrarian Reform (NIAR) to redistribute the lands to small private owners and cooperatives. Finally, the law prohibited foreigners from owning land. Adding fuel to the growing charges that Communists had inspired the acts, was the fact that Castro appointed a Cuban Communist, Antonio Núñez Jiménez, to head the NIAR.

Washington reacted quickly, as American landholders lost millions of acres. Some U.S. officials called for "prompt, adequate, and effective compensation." Others talked about cutting Cuba's sugar quota in retaliation, especially after more Communists took positions in Castro's government. People such as former ambassador Smith and Cuban military defectors led by Pedro Díaz Lanz, labeled Castro a Communist. Still, many U.S. diplomats, including Bonsal, urged caution and continued engagement.

High Drama in the Caribbean

By early 1960, the relations between Havana and Washington had deteriorated further. Castro stepped up his anti-U.S. sentiment, denouncing the use of Florida's airfields by Cuban exiles to drop propaganda and, allegedly, a number of bombs on Cuba. Eisenhower, on the other hand, deduced that "the Communists like to fish in troubled waters, and there are certainly troubled waters there." The gulf widened as Castro welcomed Soviet First Deputy Premier Antanas Mikoyan to open a trade exhibition in Havana. Soon afterward, the Cubans signed a trade agreement with Moscow, which promised to buy 100 million tons of Cuban sugar over the following five years and extend Castro $100 million credit for industrial purchases. Clearly, the Soviets had seen a real opportunity to interject themselves into the Western Hemisphere.

The Eisenhower administration counterattacked in the summer of 1960. It cut Cuba's sugar quota, effectively embargoing the staple for the year. Next, it pressured U.S. oil refineries in Cuba not to process recently purchased Soviet oil. In response, Castro nationalized the refineries owned by Texaco, Esso, and Shell. As historian Richard Welch observes, "U.S. efforts at economic coercion . . . strengthened rather than weakened Castro's political authority; they made it easier for the Russians to accept the application of the Cuban suitor; they enhanced the importance of supplies and markets for the Cuban revolutionary regime."

The final break began in July 1960. Soviet Premier Nikita Khrushchev made a public speech condemning U.S. policy toward Cuba and pledged his support for Castro's "struggle for freedom and national independence." "Figuratively speaking, in case of need, Soviet artillerymen can support the Cuban people with their rocket fire if the aggressive forces in the Pentagon dare to launch an intervention against Cuba," he roared. Eisenhower responded: "I affirm in emphatic terms that the United States will not be deterred from its responsibilities by the threats of Mr. Khrushchev. Nor will the United States, in conformity with its treaty obligations, permit the establishment of a regime dominated by international communism in the Western Hemisphere."

Efforts at negotiation and accommodation ended. In the United Nations, U.S. Ambassador Henry Cabot Lodge pronounced the Monroe Doctrine "fully alive," adding and that it "will be vigorously defended by the United States." At the OAS meeting in San José, Costa Rica, in August, the United States pushed forward a proposal denouncing extra-continental intervention in the region. More important, in March 1960, Eisenhower approved a plan, eventually code-named "Project Zapata," that allowed the CIA to recruit and train Cuban exiles to overthrow Castro. The CIA also formulated plans to assassinate Castro. They recruited Mafia figures to arrange a "gangland-style killing." One operative proposed placing an explosive seashell in Castro's favorite diving area. Another outlandish plot involved trying to destroy Castro's masculinity by placing thallium salts, a depilatory, on his shoes to cause his beard to fall out.

Castro's intelligence knew about the U.S. efforts. Che Guevara emphasized that "what happened in Guatemala will not happen here." In response, Castro strengthened his military forces and began purchasing arms from the Soviet bloc. Washington intensified its pressure, embargoing all materials to Cuba except food and medicine. In protest, Castro traveled to the United Nations, in which he made a four-hour speech blasting U.S. imperialism. Several months later, he signed a statement supporting the Soviet foreign policy. As the Eisenhower administration prepared to leave office, it terminated diplomatic relations with Cuba on January 2, 1961. President

Eisenhower had left a festering problem and many others for his successor, John F. Kennedy.

Continuities

The immediate postwar period saw an apex of interdependence between the United States and Latin America. Foreign competition in the markets disappeared for the first decade almost completely, as devastated European and Asian economies could offer few challenges. In the political realm, most Latin Americans, especially those wanting to maintain the status quo, looked to the United States for leadership. The treaties at Rio and Bogotá further cemented military and political ties. Those nations that promoted policies perceived as radical, such as Guatemala and Cuba, found themselves isolated. At no preceding point had U.S. hegemony found itself with so few challenges.

Yet there were rumblings of discontent. Nationalists in Bolivia, Brazil, Argentina, and elsewhere actively challenged the United States on many issues. In particular, the use of or threat of nationalization of foreign-owned businesses remained a potent tool. Furthermore, they increasingly relied on new models of development, such as ISI, that threatened U.S. business interests by focusing on domestic industrial growth.

On the political front, they employed several strategies. They used their positions in the OAS and the UN to leverage for U.S. economic and military aid. The nationalists also increasingly condemned the United States for its support of dictators and found many American and international allies in the struggle to end the grip of the militaries and elites in Latin America. In one case, the nationalists resorted to violence to try to assassinate the U.S. president and draw attention to the problems in place. Finally, some nationalists such as Castro openly defied Washington and utilized various methods of dissent, including nationalization and alliance with the Soviet Union to break his country's dependence on its pushy northern neighbor. His model would embolden other leaders throughout the region.

SUGGESTIONS FOR ADDITIONAL READING

For good works on the immediate postwar era, see Chester J. Pach, Jr., *Arming the Free World: The Origins of the United States Military Assistance Program* (1991); John Children, *Unequal Alliance: The Inter-American Military System, 1938–1978* (1980);

Bryce Wood, *The Dismantling of the Good Neighbor Policy (1985); Donald Dozer, Are We Good Neighbors? Three Decades of Inter-American Relations, 1930–1960* (1961); Thomas Leonard, *The United States and Central America, 1944–1949* (1984); Michael Krenn, *The Chains of Interdependence: U.S. Policy toward Central America, 1945–1954* (1996); Gerald K. Haines, *The Americanization of Brazil: A Study of U.S. Cold War Diplomacy in the Third World, 1945–1954* (1989); Elizabeth A. Cobbs, *The Rich Neighbor: Rockefeller and Kaiser in Brazil* (1992); Charles Ameringer, *The Democratic Left in Exile: The Anti-Dictatorial Struggle in the Caribbean, 1945–1955* (1974) and *The Caribbean Legion: Patriots, Politicians, Soldiers of Fortune, 1946–1950* (1996); Jim Siekmeier, *Aid, Nationalism and Inter-American Relations: Guatemala, Bolivia, and the United States* (1999); Stephen Streeter, *Managing the Counterrevolution: The United States and Guatemala, 1954–1961* (2000); Kyle Longley, *The Sparrow and the Hawk: Costa Rica and the United States during the Rise of José Figueres* (1997); and Steve Schwartzberg, *Democracy and U.S. Policy in Latin America during the Truman Years* (2003).

General works on the Eisenhower administration include Stephen Ambrose, *Eisenhower (1983–84);* Jeff Broadwater, *Eisenhower and the Anti-Communist Crusade* (1992); Blanche W. Cook, *The Declassified Eisenhower: A Divided Legacy* (1981); Robert Divine, *Eisenhower and the Cold War* (1981); Fred I Greenstein, *The Hidden Hand Presidency: Eisenhower as Leader* (1982); Chester J. Pach, Jr., and Elmo Richardson, *The Presidency of Dwight D. Eisenhower* (1991); and Herbert S. Parmet, *Eisenhower and the American Crusades* (1972).

Specific books on U.S.-Latin American relations during the Eisenhower administration include Stephen G. Rabe, *Eisenhower and Latin America: The Foreign Policy of Anticommunism* (1988); Burton Kaufman, *Trade and Aid: Eisenhower's Foreign Economic Policy, 1953–1961* (1982); Michael Gambone, *Eisenhower, Somoza, and the Cold War in Nicaragua, 1953–1961* (1997); G. Atkins Pope and Larman C. Wilson, *The United States and the Trujillo Regime* (1972); Cole Blasier, *The Hovering Giant: U.S. Responses to Revolutionary Change in Latin America* (1976); and Brad Coleman, *Colombia and the United States: The Making of an Inter-American Alliance, 1939-1960* (2008).

For more on the 1954 Guatemalan intervention, see Richard Immerman, *The CIA in Guatemala: The Foreign Policy of Intervention* (1982); Stephen Schlesinger and Stephen Kinzer, *Bitter Fruit: The Untold Story of the American Coup in Guatemala* (1982); Piero Gleijeses, *Shattered Hope: The Guatemalan Revolution and the United States, 1944–1954* (1991); Nick Cullather, *Secret History: The CIA's Classified Account of Its Operations in Guatemala, 1952–1954* (1999); and Juan José Arévalo, *The Shark and the Sardines* (1961).

For more on the relationship between Castro and the United States, reference Richard E. Welch, Jr., *Response to Revolution: The United States and the Cuban Revolution* (1985); and Thomas G. Paterson, *Contesting Castro: The United States and the Triumph of the Cuban Revolution* (1994).

CHAPTER SEVEN

Years of Hope, Years of Frustration

THE COLD WAR DOMINATED U.S. POLICIES during the Truman and Eisenhower presidencies. Despite repeated promises of modifications in U.S. exchanges by various groups, Washington had focused on Europe and Asia during the postwar period. The disastrous trip of Richard Nixon and the rise of Fidel Castro had brought U.S. attention back to the demands by Latin Americans for economic and political development. These events occurred late in his term, but Eisenhower began the process. Yet, it would be his successor, John F. Kennedy, who would gain the notoriety for the major reorientation in emphasis on Latin America.

Camelot and Latin America

The young former senator from Massachusetts inherited many problems in Latin America. Although JFK was an ardent anti-Communist, during his service on the SFRC he supported nationalist causes, called for public economic assistance, and condemned U.S. aid to military dictators. In 1959, he stressed that Castro might "have taken a more rational course after his victory had the United States Government not backed [Batista] so long and so uncritically."

During his 1960 campaign against Nixon, Kennedy intensified his attacks on Eisenhower's policies, directly linking Nixon to them. Eisenhower's handling of Cuba provided ammunition. During one campaign speech, Kennedy emphasized that Eisenhower and Nixon had "permitted a Communist satellite ninety miles off the coast of Florida, eight minutes by jet." He told another crowd that Cuba could become "a base from which to carry Communist infiltration and subversion through the Americas." During the campaign, liberal democratic advisers, including Arthur Schlesinger, Jr., and Adolf Berle, urged Kennedy to increase attacks on the dictators. Despite the fact that the Eisenhower administration had made changes, including economic programs such as the Social Progress Trust Fund and severing diplomatic relations with Trujillo of the Dominican Republic, the Massachusetts senator promised changes. These included economic development and support of democracies, broadly defined in a program that became known as "The Alliance for Progress."

The Grand Promise

In the general election, Kennedy defeated Nixon by a very narrow margin. Soon thereafter, Kennedy fulfilled his campaign promise to alter U.S. policy in Latin America. On March 13, 1961, he invited 250 dignitaries, including most of the Latin American diplomats in Washington, to a White House dinner, during which he gave a speech promising a Marshall Plan for the Americas that would make the 1960s a "decade of development." The new president guaranteed economic grants and loans to increase educational and technical opportunities. In the course of the speech, broadcast later throughout the hemisphere, Kennedy called on the United States to unite in a "vast cooperative effort, unparalleled in magnitude and nobility of purpose, to satisfy the basic needs of Latin American people for homes, work and land, health and schools—*techo, trabajo y tierra, salud y escuela.*"

The Kennedy administration moved quickly to implement the President's plans. He requested and received from Congress an appropriation of $500 million for aid to Latin America. Emergency food shipments flowed to the region, and the administration helped establish a Seasonal Marketing Fund to provide price stabilization for regional commodities. He helped Bolivia and several other countries secure emergency loans to help stabilize their economies.

Throughout the summer, Kennedy prepared for a meeting of the Latin American states at Punta del Este, Uruguay, where he planned to unveil his entire plan. A new sense of urgency gripped the administration in January 1961, when Khrushchev praised national revolutions sweeping the world. The Soviet premier claimed that the Soviet system, not that of the United States, would ride this tidal wave of revolutions. In relation to the Western Hemisphere, he praised Castro's "war of national liberation" for stopping the "onslaught of [the] imperialist." Such statements helped unite Americans in support of Kennedy's Alliance for Progress. Humanitarian considerations drove many liberals, but conservatives also joined the choir

John F. Kennedy in Costa Rica in 1963 with the Alliance for Progress banner in the background. *Courtesy of the John F. Kennedy Library, no. KN.C27376*

to sing the praises of its potential to prevent the rise of more "Cubas" by raising living standards throughout Latin America.

In August, Kennedy and his entourage traveled to Uruguay. During the opening session of the Inter-American meeting, he proudly promised U.S. aid to Latin America in the amount of $1 billion for the first year and another $20 billion in the next ten years. He also called for land reform, tax reform to shift more of the burden to those most able to pay, and improvements in housing and healthcare. Kennedy requested that the Latin Americans "formulate the plans, mobilize the internal resources, make difficult and necessary sacrifices if their national energy is to be fully directed to economic development." Regarding the latter, Kennedy and his advisors believed that an additional $80 billion of Latin American internal investment would ensure a 2.5 percent growth per year, and some predicted a 50 percent rise in the standard of living by 1970.

As political scientist Peter Smith observes, "the Kennedy administration was committing the United States to a multi-year, multibillion dollar effort in the Americas. This was utterly unprecedented." With few exceptions, Latin Americans greeted Kennedy's speech enthusiastically. The president's vibrancy, boldness, and Catholicism made him an icon among many in the region. His efforts to promote U.S. public funding and planning in Latin America was, as ECLA director Felipe Pazos noted, "a break with the mentality of an earlier generation which accepted Latin American poverty as a natural consequence of Latin inferiority."

Kennedy soon departed Uruguay to visit other countries and left the U.S. delegation in the hands of Treasury Secretary Douglas Dillon, the Wall Street investment banker-turned-diplomat, who faithfully fulfilled his orders and spurred the Alliance. The only major stumbling block was the Cuban delegation headed by Guevara. Initially, he was courteous and provided suggestions, even asking Dillon about the possible benefits to Cuba. Yet by the end of the twelve-day conference, Guevara went on the offensive to attack the U.S. plan in a rambling two-hour speech. "Many times the promises here have not been ratified up there [in Washington] afterward," he reminded the delegates. He challenged them to meet in 1980 and compare the results of development between Cuba and the other states. The "new age" in Latin America, he told his listeners, was not Kennedy but Castro.

Despite Guevara's denunciations and Cuba's refusal to participate, the delegates completed a charter for the Alliance for Progress. It set a series of economic, social, and political goals and established mechanisms for implementation. Among these were requirements that individual countries develop specific plans that a committee of experts would critique. In many areas, no specific details emerged, only vague, and often ambiguous, plans. Still, most delegates left the conference excited about the expectations for reform and future economic growth. In a concluding address, Brazil's Minister of Finance Clemente Mariani emphasized that "in a gesture of political vision the United States has placed at our disposal the resources which, in conjunction with those of other sources and those we can mobilize ourselves, will be the mainspring of our economic and social development."

La Playa Girón—The Perfect Failure

Despite the great fanfare, Kennedy and the U.S. delegation had traveled to Uruguay under a dark cloud of suspicion about its involvement in Cuba. His criticisms of Eisenhower for being too soft on Castro made it difficult for him to backtrack. Already, he had made it clear that there was "little question that should any Latin country be driven by repression into the arms of the Communists, our attitude on nonintervention would change overnight." Thus, when CIA advisors presented their ideas on how to overthrow Castro in "Project Zapata," Kennedy allowed them to proceed.

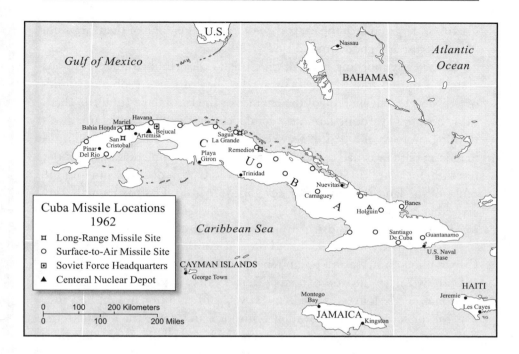

CIA operative Richard Bissell formulated a plan that followed the Guatemalan blueprint. Accordingly, the CIA recruited and began training more than 1,000 Cuban exiles in bases in Guatemala and Nicaragua. Again, the CIA formed a small air force (in this case, composed of B-26 medium-range bombers), piloted mainly by mercenaries. The Cuban exiles would land and establish a beachhead to await a popular insurrection. The CIA wanted to replicate the psychological tactics employed in Guatemala. Bissell concluded "the chance of true success . . . was predicated on the assumption that faced with that kind of pressure, he [Castro] would suffer the same loss of nerve [as had Arbenz]."

Critics of the plan, including Chairman of the Senate Foreign Relations Committee J. William Fulbright, complained that "the Castro regime is a thorn in the flesh but it is not a dagger in the heart." Because Kennedy feared giving Moscow an excuse to attack Berlin, he ordered a scaled-backed version of the invasion plan and tightened rules of engagement to prevent uncovering U.S. complicity. Kennedy even asked Schlesinger, Jr., chair of the SFRC, to write a "White Paper" justifying the invasion. When the CIA requested the green light in April 1961, Kennedy gave it. The operation moved forward, although CIA agents in Cuba refused to inform the anti-

Castro underground of the exact date of the landing, one of them arguing, "I don't trust any goddamn Cuban."

In the early morning of April 17, Cuban exiles climbed in amphibious craft and moved toward Playa Girón, the "Bay of Pigs." Problems immediately developed, as some of the engines of the landing craft failed. Then, those boats still working ran into a coral reef that the CIA had reported was nothing more than a bed of seaweed. Unexpectedly, a lighthouse illuminated the rag-tag armada. The rebels reaching shore immediately fell under fire from local militia. The expected arrival of Cuban dissidents to join the ranks of the landing force never developed. Instead, Castro's regular army arrived and proceeded to pound the rebels. The insurgent air force, having to fly many hours round-trip from bases in Nicaragua, failed to destroy Castro's air force and was unable to provide continuous air cover, allowing Cuban pilots to strafe and bomb rebel positions.

For two days the approximately 1,400 exiles held out. They radioed headquarters begging for U.S. air cover and additional supplies after Castro's air force sank one of their transports and drove the others to the protective cover of U.S. Navy destroyers holding well off shore. Hundreds of the rebels died or surrendered in the nightmarish forty-eight hours. Some tried to escape to the mountains to wage a guerrilla war, but Castro's forces and the rugged terrain surrounding the beachhead blocked them. Finally, most of the invasion force surrendered, although one group floated out to U.S. destroyers holding five miles off the coast, one of the men proclaiming "most of our people feel we were in a way betrayed . . . we were sent in there to get slaughtered."

The Embittered President

The fiasco at the Bay of Pigs greatly affected Kennedy. He publicly admitted to the U.S. role in the event and negotiated with the Cubans for the release of the surviving rebel prisoners by trading U.S. agriculture supplies for their return. Condemnations of the poorly planned and executed action arose throughout the United States and the world. Well-known sociologist Barrington Moore, Jr., called Kennedy's grandiose "New Frontier" a fraud and "a militarist and reactionary government that covers its fundamental policies with liberal rhetoric." C. Wright Mills, a philosopher/sociologist, emphasized that "Kennedy and company have returned us to barbarism. . . . Were I physically able to do so, I would at this moment be fighting alongside Fidel Castro." On the other end of the political spectrum, conservatives criticized Kennedy's handling of the affair as reflective of his inexperience and incompetence in foreign affairs.

Though greatly embarrassed, Kennedy remained defiant. He blamed the CIA and U.S. military for the debacle and ordered a review of the whole plan. His investigating committee, headed by General Maxwell Taylor, concluded that covert operations needed far more development to prevent such horrific failure—not that Washington should avoid intervening in the affairs of sovereign nations in the first place. Soon afterward, Kennedy told newspaper editors "let the record show that our restraint is not inexhaustible . . . if the nations of this Hemisphere should fail to meet their commitments against outside Communist penetration—then I want it clearly understood that this Government will not hesitate in meeting its primary obligations which are to the security of our Nation!"

Years later, Kennedy advisors, led by Schlesinger and Theodore Sorenson, defended their former boss's handling of the Bay of Pigs. They echoed his arguments that he had received poor advice and that the CIA had botched the plans. On the other hand, Kennedy's political opponents and many Cuban exiles accused him of lacking the nerve to order the needed air strikes and properly use the U.S. military to destroy Castro. Most historians and writers focus on the bureaucratic battles that resulted after Kennedy and his advisors blindly rushed into a poorly conceived plan. One of the most damning critiques is that by journalist Peter Wyden, who emphasizes "the Bay of Pigs was a wild gamble. It failed because Kennedy and Bissell [a CIA operative] failed. They failed for altogether human reasons: the drive for gutsy action; the reluctance to cut losses except for the risk of world war. . . . Egos so tall that the eyes and ears can shut out whatever one prefers not to see or hear."

In retaliation for the botched attempt to overthrow Castro, Kennedy and his brother, Attorney General Robert Kennedy, ordered "Operation Mongoose." Headed by General Edward Lansdale, well known for his anti-Communist activities in Vietnam in the mid-1950s, the group picked up where the Eisenhower administration left off in attempting to assassinate Castro and destabilize Cuba's economy. With a budget of $50 million and a full-time staff of more than 300 people who monitored the activities of 2,000 Cuban agents, the organization coordinated attacks on sugar mills, bridges, and oil refineries. It even plotted to create viruses to kill poultry and infect laborers to prevent them from harvesting sugar. At the same time, it tried to assassinate Castro, planning at least eight different attempts between 1960 and 1965. The Kennedy brothers definitely allowed for no accommodation or negotiation. In turn, Castro sought none and decided to adopt all measures necessary to protect his position.

Creating a Latin Camelot

While Cuba sapped much of Kennedy's time and energy, his administration still tried to implement the Alliance for Progress. The president hammered home the point that "those who make peaceful revolution impossible will make violent revolution inevitable." To turn the dream into reality, Kennedy appointed Edwin A. Martin as a special assistant secretary of state and Teodoro Moscoso as U.S. coordinator for the Alliance. Plans flowed in from Latin America, and Congress allocated money, although some believed that problems remained. Senator Albert Gore (D-TN) cogently observed "I am not sure that we will not widen the gap between the very rich very few, and the great mass of the majority."

Despite such misgivings, the White House moved forward on many fronts. On a personal level, Kennedy visited the region three times and consistently devoted time to meeting with Latin Americans. He achieved some successes, including the settlement with Mexico of the disputed Chamizal land in El Paso. Generally, Latin Americans liked the U.S. president, although they remained skeptical of most U.S. businesspersons and politicians.

The approach was multifaceted. In 1961, Kennedy asked his brother-in-law Sargent Shriver to head the Peace Corps. This new organization brought together young Americans to serve as ambassadors of good will for their country throughout the world and reflected an idealism and "humanitarian internationalism" that had characterized various sectors of U.S. society for decades. Kennedy placed a special emphasis on Peace Corps projects in Latin America, telling Shriver in 1962 that "I would like for you to keep in mind the importance of Latin America, which I think should be the primary area."

The Peace Corps emphasized education efforts in Africa and Asia, but in Latin America its volunteers concentrated on community development. According to historian Elizabeth Cobbs Hoffman, the responsibility of the Corps in Latin America was to "identify community needs." Once these needs were classified, "volunteers would help villagers devise creative ways to meet them, whether by building roads, latrines, and schools or by petitioning their municipalities for a greater share of government resources." Like the stated goals of the Alliance, the Peace Corps aimed to raise the standard of living of Latin Americans, especially that of the most disadvantaged.

By early 1962, Peace Corps volunteers started arriving in many nations of the region, although Mexico refused to host any volunteers and Shriver initially refused to place volunteers in Nicaragua. Living with local families, the Peace Corps volunteers eagerly went about their business. By 1969, more than 19,000 young Americans had served in Latin America. They received much praise for their efforts. As one Chilean official stressed, "these young people have brought to us the reality of the generosity of the United States in a way which could not have been done by 15 ambassadors in Santiago."

The Dark Side of Camelot

Alongside the idealistic visions of a Latin American Camelot lurked the administration's decision to prevent vigorously any Communist subversion in the region. Driven by a preoccupation with Castro, the Kennedy administration built upon patterns established in the Eisenhower administration and reshaped military assistance in order "to control mobs and fight guerrillas," as Kennedy put it. Soon after JFK took office, the Joint Chiefs of Staff recommended that U.S. advisors help Latin American militaries move from concentrating on hemispheric defense to developing "the capability of indigenous forces to conduct counterinsurgency, antisubversion, and psychological warfare operations."

The Kennedy administration accepted this advice and adopted several methods to achieve these goals. First, it began reorienting the Latin American military training to combat domestic insurgencies. Believing that it could also liberalize Latin American military officers with indoctrination into U.S. civil-military relations, the administration moved forward without an adequate understanding of the internal realities of most Latin American societies. By 1962, the United States had provided training to more than 9,000 Latin American officers and enlisted men at bases in the School of the Americas in the Panama Canal Zone and military bases throughout the United States. Trained primarily by the U.S. Army's corps of recently established "Green Berets," the Latin American militar-

252 IN THE EAGLE'S SHADOW

ies and police forces received instruction in counterinsurgency tactics that included interrogation techniques, antiguerrilla fighting, and "civic action" programs. To supplement these activities, the Kennedy administration also provided significant training and supplies to Latin American police officers to conduct riot control and surveillance of Communists.

People of the region were quick to criticize the military buildup, a Mexican diplomat characterizing the School of the Americas this way: "give me the names of those first 60 students, and I'll pick your presidents in Latin America for the next 10 years." Senator Morse and others attacked the policy, especially after U.S.-trained Peruvian troops initiated a coup in 1962. Other U.S. officials also urged caution. Undersecretary of State Chester Bowles predicted: "We are failing to build into our training programs for foreign military personnel an understanding of the values and practices of democratic society."

To the Brink

Throughout his short term in office, Kennedy's preoccupation with Castro and the Communists drove most U.S. initiatives in Latin America. Castro recognized the threat posed by the United States. At Punta del Este, Guevara made a capitulatory gesture by promising prominent Kennedy advisor Richard Goodwin that Cuba would not support revolutionary activity in exchange for U.S. guarantees to stop efforts to overthrow the government. Nothing resulted from the informal meeting, as the promise fell on deaf ears in the Kennedy administration. Consequently, Castro began searching for ways to offset U.S. power, the obvious choice being to develop Cuba's relationship with the Soviet Union.

Almost immediately, the Soviets responded to Castro's request. According to recent scholarship by Russian authors Vladislav Zubok and Constantine Pleshakov, Khrushchev became "fervently dedicated" to the Cuban revolution as demonstrating "the victorious march of communism around the globe and Soviet hegemony in the Communist camp." For several years, Mao Zedong had attacked Moscow for betraying Marx's ideas by compromising with the capitalists. Khrushchev desperately wanted to defend his country's honor and saw the Cubans as a test case. Therefore, in the summer of 1962, the Soviets, at the urging of Castro, decided to station nuclear missiles in Cuba. Within a couple of months, forty-two Soviet-made missiles arrived in the Western Hemisphere along with Soviet technicians to operate them.

On October 14, a U.S. U-2 reconnaissance plane on a routine mission photographed the missile sites. After two more days of intelligence gathering, the CIA informed Kennedy, who declared, "he can't do that to me." Immediately, Kennedy formed a group of his best civilian and military advisors into Ex Comm (Executive Committee of the National Security Council). As several observers note, "for the young American president, John F. Kennedy, . . . the encounter represented a supreme test both of will and of prudence." Kennedy asked for policy options. Former secretary of state Dean Acheson and others recommended air strikes to destroy the missiles. The JCS pushed for a full-scale military invasion of Cuba. Meanwhile, a group led by Attorney General Robert Kennedy pressed for a naval blockade, a "quarantine" of Cuba to prevent more missiles from arriving.

After much argument, the president prudently decided on a quarantine. Soon thereafter, U.S. ships encircled Cuba to stop any approaching Russian ships, several more of which, laden with additional supplies and weapons, were en route to the island. Kennedy then took a dramatic step and went on national television to denounce the Soviets. On October 22, he called for Khrushchev to end his "deliberately provocative" action and remove the missiles from Cuba. He promised to maintain the quarantine, even if the Soviets challenged it. Furthermore, he guaranteed massive retaliation against the Soviet Union should any missile be launched from Cuba.

Historian Thomas Paterson calls the ensuing period following the television address as "an international war of nerves." In the end, the Soviets also chose a prudent course. Their ships carrying more missiles turned back. On October 26, Moscow went through private American intermediaries with proposals to remove the existing missiles in return for a U.S. promise not to invade Cuba. The following day, Khrushchev added to the list by asking for the elimination of U.S. Jupiter missiles in Turkey. After some tense moments, Washington agreed. Over Castro's vigorous objections, the Soviets accepted the offer and tensions declined.

The Cuban Missile Crisis took the world closer to the brink of nuclear war than at any time before or since. As Kennedy advisor John Kenneth Galbraith noted: "We were in luck but success in a lottery is no argument for lotteries." The crisis had a chilling effect on U.S.-Soviet relations. Thereafter, Moscow and Washington established a hotline to allow for direct discussions between the U.S. president and the Soviet premier during any future nuclear crisis. Simultaneously, the Soviets began a massive nuclear buildup to prevent having to back down again. In the Western Hemisphere, Castro secured a solid guarantee of no invasion, although U.S. operatives continued efforts to destabilize his government. Cuba would remain an important issue, but never again would it spark an incident the magnitude of that of October 1962.

The Alliance that Lost Its Way

In the aftermath of the Cuban Missile Crisis, the Kennedy administration tried to refocus on the Alliance for Progress, but with mixed results. Several years later, former Agency for International Development (AID) official Jerome Levinson and journalist Juan de Onís characterized the experiment as the "Alliance that Lost Its Way." As historian Mark Gilderhus acknowledges, the rhetoric and goals "always exceeded capabilities and never achieved the mark." Rabe adds that the administration "undoubtedly overestimated their ability to foster change" and "underestimated the daunting nature of Latin America's socioeconomic problems." Even administration officials such as Sorenson admitted that "reality did not match the rhetoric which flowed about the Alliance on both sides of the Rio Grande."

The goals for reducing poverty, illiteracy, and disease were not achieved. On the economic front, Latin American economies grew slowly throughout the 1960s, only 1.5 percent per year. The decline of agricultural wages and lack of industrial development saw the number of unemployed persons rise from 18 million to 25 million. Land redistribution efforts met strong opposition from the landed oligarchy and the U.S. Congress, which all but prohibited using Alliance funds for land redistribution programs. "Taking from the rich and giving to the poor may have sounded good to Robin Hood," Walter LaFeber observes, "but it sounded too much like socialism to Congress." The Latin American elites controlled what reform took place, and by 1965 the disparities remained. For every $100 of new income, the poorest 20 percent received only $2.

Some modest gains occurred in education and healthcare in some countries, but the overall improvement in life expectancy and reduced illiteracy never materialized. Rapid growth in the population, contributed to in large part by a refusal of the Catholic Church to allow artificial forms of birth control, caused many problems. The larger number of people to serve offset gains in the number of schools, hospitals, and other important institutions created. In many areas, child mortality rates remained high and proper sanitation and health care remained a luxury for most Latin Americans, despite the rising expectations pushed by national governments and U.S. propaganda efforts.

On the political front, democracy declined in Latin America rather than flourished. Several democratic governments fell to military control, including that of Honduras, the Dominican Republic, Argentina, and Peru, with Brazil following suit soon after Kennedy's death. In the case of Peru, in July 1962, a Sherman tank given to the Peruvian military by the United States crashed through the gates of the presidential palace. A U.S.-trained Peruvian ranger then awoke President Manuel Prado to inform him that a military junta had replaced his government.

U.S. officials provided little opposition to this military coup or to others that followed, in each case fearing that further involvement in the political turmoil would help the Communist cause. In each case, the United States ultimately extended diplomatic recognition to the military-controlled governments and continued to provide military and economic assistance, arguing, according to Assistant Secretary of State Martin, that "we must use our leverage to keep these new regimes as liberal and considerate of the welfare of the people as possible." Some U.S. officials urged the new governments to hold fair elections, but most simply threw up their hands. After the military overthrow of the El Salvadoran government, Kennedy noted that "governments of the civil-military type of El Salvador are the most effective in containing communist penetration in Latin America." In October 1963, Martin emphasized that the United States preferred democracy to military dictatorship, but that he also understood that limitations existed because "in most of Latin America there is so little experience with the benefits of political legitimacy." He complained that the United States lacked the ability to sustain an elected president in office "when his own people are not willing to fight to defend him." These attitudes remained pervasive among U.S. policymakers throughout the Alliance experiment.

The overall evaluation of the Kennedy administration and its policies in Latin America also remains mixed. While it made an unparalleled effort to promote economic growth, just two years into his presidency Kennedy believed that Latin America was "the most dangerous area in the world." Immediately before his death, he expressed growing concerns about the failure of his policies in the region. The structural limitations imposed by Latin American traditions and elite domination weakened reform efforts. Wealth remained concentrated in the hands of the few, and the poor lacked basic necessities. Military dictators crushed democratic experiments, and hopes for improved human rights and civil liberties faded away. The experiment of the Alliance appeared destined for failure even before Kennedy's assassination in November 1963, although some still believed that the Alliance could succeed and Latin America could emerge from its feudal past. It was left to Kennedy's successor to try to continue the dreams for Camelot in Latin America.

Big Daddy from the Pedernales Takes Over

In November 1963, Kennedy's vice president, the former powerful Senator from Texas Lyndon Baines Johnson, became president. LBJ considered himself an expert on Latin America, although most of his experience related to Mexico and Mexican Americans (he had taught school in South Texas in a predominantly Mexican American community as a young man). Lincoln Gordon, one of Johnson's chief advisors on Latin America, emphasized that Johnson's "emotional concern was concentrated mainly on the Mexican relationship." Another Johnson advisor stressed that the president's "romantic, Tex-Mex view of Latin America . . . distorted his view." Sometimes, racial stereotyping clouded LBJ's perceptions. "I know these Latin Americans," he told reporters, "they'll come right into your yard and take it over if you let them. And the next day they'll be right up on your porch. . . . But if you say to 'em right at the start, 'hold on, just wait a minute,' they'll know they're dealing with somebody who'll stand up. And after that you can get along fine."

In the early 1960s, as Kennedy's vice president, Johnson had supported the Alliance for Progress and the Peace Corps. Shortly after taking office, however, Johnson called JFK's Latin America policy "a thorough going mess." He told Secretary of State Dean Rusk that he recognized Latin America's importance but stressed "it's not the rhetoric that counts, it's the performance." He continued aid programs and added new dimensions of private investment and business cooperation, helping create the Business Advisory Group on Latin America headed by David Rockefeller of Chase Manhattan Bank to counsel the president on private initiatives.

Like his predecessor, Johnson obsessed over Castro and the potential spread of communism. He warned Shriver that he wanted to avoid allowing the "three C's—the Communists, the consumptives, and the cocksuckers" to join the Peace Corps. As historian Joseph Tulchin acknowledges, "U.S.

policy was driven by spasmodic reactions to crises in the Caribbean Basin, . . . and by an overpowering fear that instability would lead to 'another Cuba' in the hemisphere."

A Buck in the Pocket, A Kick in the Ass

Early on, Johnson set the tone for his Latin American policy by appointing Thomas Mann as assistant secretary of state for inter-American affairs and Alliance director. According to one scholar, the bilingual lawyer from Laredo was a "tough anti-Communist and stout defender of U.S. foreign investments." Mann shared some of Johnson's prejudices, once telling someone that "I know my Latinos. They understand only two things—a buck in the pocket and a kick in the ass." Later, he told Johnson to avoid touring the region because Latin Americans lacked "discipline, responsibility, simple Christian charity, respect for law, and dedication to the right values." Despite these misgivings, Mann supported economic development and the Alliance, but worried about the use of "revolutionary" rhetoric and instead favored "orderly evolution." He called Cuba a "cancer" whose only remedy was free enterprise.

Mann immediately left an imprint on U.S. policy. In March 1964, he made a speech to U.S. ambassadors to Latin America in which he outlined four basic ideas that became known as the "Mann Doctrine." They included the promotion of economic growth without emphasis on social reform, no preference for forms of government to avoid charges of intervention, opposition to communism, and protection of private American investment.

Immediately, various groups blasted Mann's statements and worried about their consequences. The *New York Times* ran a headline "U.S. May Abandon Effort to Deter Latin Dictators." The message was loud and clear. The Johnson administration opposed using U.S. economic and military assistance to impose democracy. The point was not lost on Latin Americans, particularly the military leaders.

Former members of the Kennedy administration condemned Mann. Schlesinger called him a "colonialist by mentality and a free enterprise zealot." He added that Mann removed many Kennedy advisors who supported liberal democrats and that Mann believed that "progressive democrats were either wishy-washy liberals or proto-Communists and that the hope for Latin America lay in the businessmen and the armies."

Schlesinger complained that "the Alliance was never really tried. It lasted about a thousand days, not a sufficient test, and thereafter in name only."

The Flag Battle

Even before Mann took over, he had worked to defuse a crisis in Panama in January 1964. For nearly a decade, the Panamanians had pressured Washington to renegotiate the Hay-Bunau-Varilla Treaty. They sought more compensation, guarantees for Panamanian workers, and additional sovereignty. "You in the United States inherited mineral wealth . . . Africa was given gold and diamonds. The Middle East is rich in oil. God gave Panama nothing but a waterway. We must make a living from our resources, as others have from theirs," one Panamanian emphasized. Demonstrations, followed by riots in 1958, led to talks in which Washington promised additional foreign aid and the symbolic flying of the Panamanian flag in the Canal Zone.

The tensions had increased as Johnson began his presidency. Panamanian president Roberto Chiari pushed for more changes while hard-line Americans in the Canal Zone and their supporters in Congress led by Daniel Flood (D-PA) called concessions "Munich in spades" (referring to the appeasement in 1938 of Hitler by France and Great Britain) and complained that negotiations gave away "fundamental American rights." Panamanian students, angry at the failure of talks and the presence of the School of the Americas in the Canal Zone, became more confrontational.

A spark ignited the powder keg in mid-January 1964. American high school students, supported by their parents, refused to raise the Panamanian flag at the Zone's Balboa High School. Panamanians marched to show their flag near the school. As they neared, an American mob attacked them, tearing their flag. The news spread quickly, and 30,000 Panamanians descended on the main avenue approaching the Zone. Shooting began, as snipers poured hundreds of rounds into the U.S. positions protecting the school; the U.S. troops returned fire. At this point, riots erupted, and Panamanians destroyed many American-owned businesses.

President Johnson received immediate training in crisis management. Chiari suspended diplomatic relations, and hard-liners in Congress urged Johnson to respond with force. Congressman Flood argued that Panamanian actions were "part of the audacious, cunning, and far reaching strategy of the Soviets." Senate Republican Minority Leader Everett Dirk-

President Lyndon B. Johnson (right) with Thomas Mann. *Courtesy of LBJ Library, photo by Yoichi Okamoto*

sen emphasized that "we are in the amazing position of having a country with one-third the population of Chicago kick us around. If we crumble in Panama, the reverberations of our actions will be felt around the world."

Johnson faced a terrible predicament. First, he warned Chiari that the United States "cannot negotiate under pressure of violence." Then, he dispatched Mann and Secretary of the Army Cyrus Vance to mediate the dispute, which Johnson blamed on Communists. When Mann met with Chiari, he warned the Panamanian that "Castroites, the Communists, have penetrated high positions" in the Panamanian government. The evidence clearly never supported the argument, and despite the Communist paranoia, Johnson chose negotiation.

After four days of fighting and looting, the Panamanian National Guard reestablished order. Nevertheless, casualties included four Americans dead and eighty-five wounded, and twenty-four Panamanians dead and more than 200 wounded. The fighting caused more than $2 million in property damage, much of it to American businesses.

Although they blamed the Communists, most American policymakers could not ignore the animosity that had provoked the confrontation. In the aftermath, the Chiari government and Johnson administration opened negotiations to address Panama's grievances. Ultimately, Washington agreed to terminate the 1903 treaty in return for granting U.S. control and operation of the canal until 1999. Despite strong public criticism, Johnson submitted the treaty to the Senate in 1967, where it languished as Johnson's attentions turned to Vietnam and internal events in Panama sabotaged acceptance. It would take another Democratic president, over a decade later, to advance Johnson's original ideas.

Trouble Down Rio Way

No sooner had Panama quieted than another crisis arose, this time in Brazil. In the 1950s, that nation had experienced significant growth under the presidencies of Getúlio Vargas, and Juscelino Kubitschek. Import-Substitution Industrialization policies and massive government spending on infrastructure had sparked expansion, creating great optimism that Brazil would emerge as a major power. Yet structural weaknesses and the failure of reform efforts contributed to unfulfilled expectations. This, in turn, created a volatile political climate.

Throughout the 1950s, Washington carefully monitored Brazil's nationalism and any perceived radicalism. When Joaõ Goulart became president in 1961, he initiated reforms that expanded suffrage, promoted unionization, and supported peasant organizing. Goulart's adminis-tration alarmed some Americans when it backed the expropriation of a subsidiary of International Telephone and Telegraph (ITT). Other problems arose when Brazil refused to support Washington's hard line against Cuba. While the Kennedy administration provided Brazil with Alliance funds, the CIA began funneling monies into opposition cam-paigns during important elections in 1962.

In 1963 U.S.-Brazil relations deteriorated. Efforts to address growing economic problems led to extreme austerity measures imposed by U.S. lending agencies. More problems surfaced after U.S. aid to political parties was exposed. In response, Washington withheld aid to Goulart's government, declaring it would only provide assistance to "friendly" governors. The Brazilian president exacerbated tensions when he called for a "solid and cohesive front" of Latin American nations against the United States. According to Michael Weis, he wanted to create "noth-ing less than a new international division of labor, with new standards of production and commerce and just primary goods to stop the 'bleed-ing of our economies.'"

Johnson inherited this volatile situation. Seeing potential extremism in Goulart's government, the administration increased economic pressure by withholding more funds and pressing for loan repayment. U.S. officials in Brazil called Goulart incompetent and urged Washington to promote democratic forces that restrained the president's "extreme leftist and ultranational supporters." More important, the recently announced Mann Doctrine indicated to many Brazilians, especially military leaders, that Washington would recognize any government in effective control. Goulart identified his enemies and sought popular support by announcing plans to expropriate privately owned oil refineries and underutilized lands. Tensions remained high as Brazilians daily expected conflict.

Big Brother Uncle Sam

In late March 1964, the staff of the U.S. Embassy in Brazil, headed by Ambassador Lincoln Gordon and military attaché Colonel Vernon Walters (who had a close relationship with General Humberto Castello Branco, leader of the military plotters), assisted anti-Goulart conspirators. It promised to provide the rebels petroleum, small arms, and ammunition. The Johnson administration also formed a naval task force composed of an aircraft carrier and support ships to play a role in the case of the outbreak of civil war, code-named, "Operation Brother Sam."

The preparations were unnecessary. The military easily seized control on April 1 and forced Congress to name a Supreme Revolutionary Command to rule. Within a week, the Supreme Revolution Command suspended the constitution and began purging the government and the nation of suspected radicals. U.S. officials called the coup a "constitutional" change in government, and Johnson extended his "warmest wishes" to the interim president, Ranieri Mazzilli, whom he praised for having solved the problems "within a framework of constitutional democracy and without civil strife." U.S. officials also sent assistance to the new regime. Massive amounts of aid would flow to Brazil during the five successive military dictatorships that dominated the government until 1985.

While the Johnson administration denied having played any substantial role in the coup, not everyone accepted the official explanation. Historian Phyllis Parker argues that "there is no evidence that the United States instigated, planned, directed, or participated in the execution of the 1964 coup." Yet, efforts by Gordon and Walters "reinforced its support by developing military contingency plans that could be useful to the conspirators should the need have arisen." Washington also contributed to the coup by withholding economic aid from Goulart while providing assistance to governors aligned with the conservatives. The fact that Washington helped replace a democracy with a two-decade-long military dictatorship is undeniable.

Naboth's Vineyard Revisited

The U.S. government's preoccupation with fighting the spread of communism in Latin America remained important after Johnson won reelection in 1964. Massive military assistance and training of army officers and security forces continued. Washington and its Latin American allies won significant victories against Communist insurgencies, reducing the perceived threat. In addition, Washington increased its pressure on Cuba. In mid-1964, the OAS voted 15–4 to sever diplomatic ties and imposed a trade embargo when investigators uncovered Castro's plan to arm Venezuelan terrorists. Within a year, only Mexico failed to comply.

Fighting perceived Communist infiltration remained a cornerstone of Johnson's policies. One of the most visible arenas was the Dominican Republic. Instability had characterized the country since the assassination of Trujillo in 1961. The Eisenhower and Kennedy administrations had assisted the conspirators to demonstrate U.S. opposition to dictators and sympathy for democracy. The decision opened the political process in the Dominican for the first time since the 1920s. Into the vacuum stepped the controversial Juan Bosch, a long-time critic of Trujillo and respected literary figure. He successfully ran for president in 1962, promising land reform and increased Dominican control of native industries.

Problems began from the start. As political scientists G. Pope Atkins and Larman C. Wilson note, Bosch was a "dedicated and honest man" but "a poor organizer and an uncompromising idealist." Over time, "he offended one group after another." In September 1963, Bosch was unseated by a military-led coup. Initially, Washington withheld recognition from the ruling junta. However, when Johnson took over, the Dominicans scheduled elections, after which the administration recognized the military regime headed by Donald Reid Cabral. He cooperated with U.S. officials to implement some reforms, but many points of contention remained.

In April 1965, a major crisis developed. Pro-Bosch supporters, referring to themselves as the Constitutionalists, staged a revolt. The alliance, including leftists, laborers, small farmers, and the poor, called for Bosch to return to complete his term. On the other side, a group headed by General Antonio Imbert took the name of "Loyalists" and backed former president Joaquín Balaguer, a Trujillo crony. The membership of the Loyalists included much of the military, elite, and segments of the middle class. Calling the coup a Communist plot, the Loyalists requested U.S. intervention to foil it. On the other side, the Constitutionalists asked Washington to mediate the dispute, a request denied by the U.S. ambassador to the Dominican Republic, W. Tapley Bennett.

Send in the Marines

As the fighting escalated, the Johnson administration decided to act after the U.S. embassy reported that the Constitutionalist movement had fallen to the "most extremist element." At the request of the Dominican government, 400 U.S. Marines landed in Santo Domingo on April 28. Soon afterward, Jack Valenti, a prominent advisor, warned Johnson that "the choice is: Castro in the Dominican Republic or U.S. intervention." Ambassador Bennett reported that "all indications point to the fact that if present efforts of forces loyal to the government fail, power will be assumed by groups clearly identified with the Communist party." Johnson responded by telling the American people on April 30 that there were "signs that people trained outside the Dominican Republic are seeking to gain control," an obvious reference to Soviet involvement. Soon, U.S. troops led by General Bruce Palmer landed, the number of American soldiers ultimately reaching more than 23,000. The general reported "my stated mission was to protect American lives and property; my unstated mission was to prevent another Cuba and, at the same time, to avoid another situation like that in Vietnam."

The invasion provoked widespread condemnations throughout the hemisphere. Bosch complained that "this was a democratic revolution smashed by the leading democracy of the world." In many Latin American countries, demonstrations erupted against the United States. Various legislative and executive decrees criticized the U.S. intervention, and leading liberals led by Figueres and Betancourt circumvented U.S. officials and tried to fashion a peace in the Dominican Republic that included the Constitutionalists.

The Johnson administration tried to defuse some of the criticism by including the OAS. A special meeting of the Foreign Ministers convened in early May. After much arm twisting, the United States secured a resolution creating an Inter-American Peace Force (IAPF), one ultimately headed by General Hugo Panasco Alvim of Brazil. Soon, six countries sent more than 1,700 troops to the Dominican Republic, the bulk of which hailed from dictatorships. Despite Panasco's title, most IAPF operations remained firmly in Palmer's hands. As Peter Smith notes, "throughout the summer of 1965, as in an earlier era, the Dominican Republic was governed through military occupation by the United States."

Only Here to Maintain the Peace

With the troops in place and OAS support secured, U.S. forces began acting as a buffer between the warring parties in the Dominican Republic. They created a neutral zone and claimed impartiality in the dispute, although many observers, including members of the U.S. press, pointed out that the U.S. troops restricted the movement of the Constitutionalists while allowing safe passage of the Loyalists. As U.S. troops played the role of peacekeeper, the State Department and the CIA tried to produce proof of a Communist conspiracy. Ultimately, they published a roster of fifty-eight names of Dominicans allied with Communists. Critics immediately pointed out that many of the persons on that list were in exile, jail, or ill. Others wryly pointed out that fifty-eight persons in a country of millions failed to pose a dramatic threat.

During the summer, the United States and its OAS allies pushed for a negotiated settlement. U.S. diplomats encountered many obstacles, primarily from Loyalists determined to win a conclusive victory. After many meetings, a peace commission headed by U.S. ambassador to the OAS Ellsworth Bunker succeeded in ironing out an agreement. The parties agreed to a provisional government headed by Bosch's foreign minister, Dr. Héctor García-Godoy, with elections scheduled for the spring 1966. Other components included demilitarization of various zones and amnesty for acts committed during the conflict. U.S. and IAPF forces would remain in the nation in order to administer the agreement, finally withdrawing in 1966 when Balaguer defeated Bosch.

The Dominican intervention had significant ramifications. The action effectively destroyed the last remaining vestiges of the Good Neighbor policy, a point reinforced in the Johnson Doctrine of 1965. In it, the president pledged that the United States would act unilaterally to prevent another

Communist takeover in the hemisphere. The Johnson Doctrine and U.S. intervention in the Dominican Republic also effectively discredited the OAS. Future crises would find Latin Americans skeptical of using the body, and in the eyes of many people, the OAS became a symbol of U.S. imperialism.

The Latin Americans clearly understood the change. Colombian president Alberto Lleras Camargo emphasized that "the general feeling was that a new and openly imperialistic policy in the style of Theodore Roosevelt had been adopted by the White House and that, if there was intervention with Marines in the Hemisphere, against unequivocal standards of law, one could only expect—in Asia, in Africa, and in wherever—new acts of force and, perhaps, the escalation of the cold war to the hot in a very short time."

The Dominican intervention also weakened any future cooperation between the U.S. Congress and Johnson on Latin American issues. During the invasion, Senator Fulbright convened executive sessions of the Senate Foreign Relations Committee to investigate U.S. actions. Over time, Fulbright realized that the Johnson administration had lied about and grossly exaggerated the threat of the Communist menace in the Dominican Republic. In September 1965, the senator publicly blasted the administration for pursuing a policy that sought not to protect American lives, but to maintain an anti-Communist, pro-U.S. regime in power. Within a year, Fulbright had published a biting indictment of U.S. foreign policy, *The Arrogance of Power.* In it, he devoted a chapter to the Dominican intervention and completely dissected the administration's story. "We have made ourselves the prisoners of the Latin American oligarches who are engaged in a vain attempt to preserve the status quo–reactionaries who habitually use the term communist very loosely, in part . . . in a calculated effort to scare the United States into supporting their selfish and discredited aims," he concluded. From this point forward, the administration encountered substantial congressional opposition.

Voices of Dissent

The Dominican intervention and U.S. actions in Cuba and Brazil further fueled the flames of anti-Americanism in Latin America. Books such as Juan José Arévalo's *The Shark and the Sardines* (1961) and Juan Bosch's

Pentagonismo substituto del imperialismo (Pentagonism Substitutes for Imperialism, 1968) strongly condemned Washington's policies. At the same time, the work of a prominent group of Latin American writers gained worldwide recognition, including Mexican Carlos Fuentes's *The Death of Artemio Cruz* (1964) and Colombian Gabriel García Marquez's *One Hundred Years of Solitude* (1967). Both widely read novels included negative portrayals of Americans, especially U.S. businessmen. Throughout Latin America, cultural and political leaders produced a series of stinging denunciations of the United States.

An important academic challenge to U.S. ideals arose in the 1960s from a group of social scientists who became known as the dependency school. Building on ECLA's work, they questioned the basic assumptions of Washington's aid and development programs. In particular, they focused on modernization theory as promoted by economists including Walt W. Rostow in his influential work, *The Stages of Economic Growth: A Non-Communist Manifesto* (1961). An important White House advisor, Rostow examined Western models of development and argued that nations had to meet certain conditions to pass through five stages of progress toward becoming a core nation. His ideas helped shape a whole generation of U.S. policymakers regarding methods of economic development.

The dependency school questioned Rostow's concepts. Its proponents believed in what Andre Gunder Frank characterized as the "development of underdevelopment." Building on the analysis of V. I. Lenin, among others, they argued that imperialist powers forced the periphery to provide raw materials and markets for expensive finished goods, thus slowing growth in the periphery. They challenged modernization analysis by citing the international economy, rather than domestic factors, as the cause of underdevelopment. Theotonio dos Santos wrote: "By dependence we mean a situation in which the economy of certain countries is conditioned by the development and expansion of another economy to which the former is subjected. The relation of interdependence between two or more economies, and between these and world trade, assumes the form of dependence when some countries (the dominant ones) can expand and can be self-sustaining, while other countries (the dependent ones) can do this only as reflection of that expansion." To dependency theorists, the rise of the multinational corporation (MNC) had further accelerated the process, helping undermine many nations' efforts at internal development.

Throughout the 1960s, the dependency analysis gained international attention. Led by Fernando Henrique Cardoso, Enzo Faletto, and Celso Furtado, the dependency school presented a radically different interpretation of Latin America's underdevelopment. As historian Peter Klaren and political scientist Thomas Bossert observe, the dependency school asked: "Why wait patiently for the 'objective conditions' to appear when in fact the Latin American bourgeoisie seemed incapable of bringing about total national capitalist development? If Latin America was indeed doomed to perpetual underdevelopment, the only way to break out of this condition was to mount an immediate revolution with the resources at hand." While accepting the need for change, no consensus existed, although many heralded Cuba as a role model.

Over time, the dependency school came under attack from many quarters. Some people noted a lack of research, pointing out that most of the theory it generated was merely speculative. They also criticized the lack of alternative methods to generate equitable growth in Latin America other than the Marxist model. Despite such shortcomings, the dependency school stimulated intellectual debate and challenged existing concepts, influencing many students and future leaders. It severely criticized U.S. explanations of underdevelopment, thereby empowering Latin Americans.

Stemming the Flow

While most Americans focused on geopolitical issues related to Latin America, another important issue that developed in the 1960s was Latin American immigration to the United States. The United States had not applied the restrictive quotas of the 1924 Immigration Act to the Americas since the Great Depression. Latino workers (documented and undocumented) had flowed into the United States, especially during good economic times in the 1940s and 1950s. Southwestern farmers, ranchers, and employers had opposed efforts to impose sanctions on illegal workers even when powerful groups, including the Truman administration, warned that illegal immigration had a negative impact on the U.S. economy. Each time, congressional blocs defeated efforts to grant the Immigration and Naturalization Service (INS) stronger powers, such as warrantless searches and strong punishment for employers using undocumented workers.

During the late 1950s, attacks on the 1924 Immigration Act intensified, primarily from liberals disillusioned with the discriminatory features in the law that singled out Asians and Eastern Europeans. In 1958, Senator John Kennedy produced a work, *A Nation of Immigrants,* which questioned basic concepts of the exclusionary practices. When he assumed the presidency, he pushed for legislation to replace the national origins quota system with preferences that allocated legal-immigrant status to family members of U.S. citizens, those with high technical skills, and others who could help fill labor shortages in specific industries. Several congressmen led by Clark MacGregor (R-MN) also wanted to end the nonquota status of the Western Hemisphere, arguing it discriminated against prospective immigrants of other nations.

After much debate, Congress passed the Immigration and Nationality Act Amendments of 1965. This legislation repealed the National Origins Quota Act and developed new categories and preferences, including family members and skills requirements. Initially, the Johnson administration opposed imposing restrictions on immigration from the Western Hemisphere, fearing it would hurt inter-American relations. Nevertheless, MacGregor and Senators Sam Ervin (D-NC) and Everett Dirksen (R-IL) imposed an annual limit of 120,000 immigrants

Estimates of the Size and Composition of the U.S. Hispanic Population, 1940–1970

1940	2,142,716
1950	3,558,761
1960	5,814,784
1970	8,920,940

National Origins of Hispanics

	Mexican	Cuban	Spanish	Puerto Rican	Other
1940	1,567,596 (77.5%)	49,938 (2.5%)	150,332 (7.4%)	95,129 (4.7%)	86,636 (4.3%)
1950	2,489,477 (77%)	70,919 (2.2%)	134,659 (4.2%)	326,186 (10.1%)	117,023 (3.6%)
1960	4,087,546 (70.3%)	163,241 (2.8%)	202,822 (3.5%)	1,027,338 (17.7%)	272,972 (4.7%)
1970	5,641,956 (63.2%)	637,931 (7.2%)	248,439 (2.8%)	1,620,777 (18.2%)	704,798 (7.9%)

The numbers do not include a small percentage of people which the researchers could not determine national origin.

from the Western Hemisphere. Despite his disappointment, Johnson ultimately signed the bill.

The new immigration law heightened tensions along the border. The simultaneous end to the Bracero program intensified Anglo mistrust of Mexicans and Mexican Americans. The INS increasingly intercepted and returned undocumented immigrants. From this point forward, the issue of immigration of Mexicans and other Latin Americans (with the exception of the Cubans, still considered as political refugees) became more contentious and a political hot potato as economic downturns in the United States and Mexico increased pressures on both sides.

Johnson's Legacy

Following the Dominican intervention, interest in Latin America diminished dramatically, as the attention of most members of the administration and the American public turned to Southeast Asia. Johnson had committed 500,000 U.S. troops to South Vietnam. Washington also waged a war on poverty in the United States, LBJ's Great Society program. Massive expenditures to fuel U.S. involvement in Vietnam and sweeping domestic programs diminished resources available for the Alliance for Progress. A rapid turnover in the State Department and Alliance offices left efforts regarding Latin American development to private sources, and the region returned to the back burner in U.S. priorities.

Still, as historian Stephen Rabe notes, "although overwhelmed by his war, Johnson had some accomplishments and talked about new approaches in inter-American relations." He successfully helped settle a contentious problem with Mexico regarding access to and the quality of the water of the Colorado River. He backed a treaty for the rehabilitation of the Mexicali Valley and efforts to curb water misuse. The president also sought the creation of a Latin American Common Market. Promising $2.5 billion over five years, he hoped to improve infrastructure and develop regional economic integration. The plan met criticism from Fulbright and Senator Robert Kennedy, who emphasized that it failed to address important social issues, and funding never appeared.

As Secretary of State Rusk emphasized, Johnson left his term in office "disappointed that more was not accomplished for and with our Latin American neighbors." The problems the region had faced when the Democrats took the White House in 1961 remained entrenched. As Robert

Kennedy observed in 1966: "[Latin Americans] will not accept this kind of existence for the next generation. We would not; they will not. . . . So a revolution is coming—a revolution which will be peaceful if we are wise enough; compassionate if we care enough; successful if we are fortunate enough—but a revolution which is coming whether we will it or not. We can affect its character; we cannot alter its inevitability."

Republican Ascendancy

In January 1969, after many years of trying to do so, Richard Nixon took the presidency. Finally arriving in Washington as the nation's chief executive, Nixon claimed foreign policy as his strength. Raised in southern California amidst a significant Mexican American population, he had interacted with Latinos on a daily basis. He had traveled Latin America throughout his vice presidency, which allowed him to claim a special knowledge of the region's people and their needs. As he prepared to run for president, he made a special trip to the region in 1966. Returning home, Nixon called for policy changes. At a news conference, he raised Argentine President Juan Carlos Onganía (head of the military government) as a model, emphasizing that he was "the right man for Argentina at this moment in destiny." "United States-style democracy won't work here," he added, "I wish it would."

The president set the tone for his Latin American policy when he appointed Henry Kissinger as his National Security Adviser. Kissinger shared many of Nixon's convictions about the region. A Harvard University professor of international relations, political scientist, and Jewish immigrant from Nazi Germany, Kissinger had a Eurocentric worldview. This viewpoint meshed well with that of his boss. "Nixon and Kissinger regarded order and equilibrium among the Great Powers as essential requirements," Mark Gilderhus notes. "They disliked utopian designs," he adds, "eschewed idealistic and moralistic abstractions, and favored stability as the road toward peace and predictability in a dangerous world. Their statecraft, seeking *détente,* or relaxation of tension, centered on relations with the Soviet Union, Western Europe, Japan, and People's Republic of China." They believed that all nations wanted stability and that once a working relationship evolved "a community of common interest might result in the containment of Communist expansion by subtle means" rather than confrontation.

The Nixon-Kissinger paradigm created indifference toward Latin America. East-West relations preoccupied Washington, although traditional concerns about Communist infiltration remained. When a Chilean diplomat, Gabriel Valdés, criticized the Nixon-Kissinger model for ignoring Latin America, Kissinger responded: "nothing important can come from the South. History has never been produced in the South. The axis of history starts in Moscow, goes to Bonn, crosses over to Washington, and then goes to Tokyo. What happens in the South has no importance." Valdés responded that Kissinger knew nothing about the region, leading the latter to respond, "No, and I don't care."

The Rockefeller Commission

Although Latin America was not a priority for him, Nixon decided to examine the region. On the advice of OAS secretary general Galo Plaza Lasso, Nixon asked Governor Nelson A. Rockefeller to conduct a fact-finding mission in Latin America and make recommendations on U.S. policy. Rockefeller gathered experts on economics, politics, and development into a commission that made four trips to more than twenty countries, interviewing some three thousand Latin American public and private leaders, although Peru, Chile, and Venezuela refused to host any such visits. Despite the roadblocks, the commission prepared an extensive report within a few months, although it was not made public until late 1969.

The Rockefeller Report was very pessimistic. "The United States has allowed the special relationship it has historically maintained with the other nations of the Western Hemisphere to deteriorate badly," it reported. It blamed many factors, including special interest groups, a lack of a true partnership, "well-intentioned but unrealistic rhetoric," and a "paternalistic attitude." The report warned that "the seeds of nihilism and anarchy are spreading throughout the hemisphere," and "clearly, the opinion in the United States that communism is no longer a serious factor in the Western Hemisphere is thoroughly wrong."

In particular, Rockefeller focused on the inability of the Latin Americans to obtain fair prices for their raw materials. He cautioned that "they find themselves very much in the position which we did at the period of the Continental Congress in 1776, and if you have been to see that play in New York, *1776*, you will feel, as I did, that what we rose up in arms against the British about, we are doing to the other Western Hemisphere nations." Despite recognizing the problem, Rockefeller promoted no significant changes in the Pan American economic relationship.

The commission report instead focused on another solution to the festering problems in Latin America, one that mirrored Nixon's own thinking on the subject. The one feature of Latin American nations that Rockefeller's analysts found as a strong and positive influence was the military. "A new type of military man is coming to the fore and often becoming a major force for constructive social change in the American republics. Motivated by increasing impatience with corruption, inefficiency, and a stagnant political order, the new military man is prepared to adapt his authoritarian tradition to the goals of social and economic progress," the report explained. It added that "without some framework for order, no progress can be achieved."

The commission made several recommendations, including the removal of a $75 million military aid limit placed by Congress in 1967. More important, it called for collaboration with dictators, basing this on the recognition "that the specific forms or processes by which each nation moves toward a pluralistic system will vary with its own traditions and situation . . . the United States cannot allow disagreements with the form or the domestic policies of other American governments to jeopardize its basic objective of working with and for their people to our mutual benefit." Nixon agreed and soon stated that "we must deal realistically with governments in the inter-American system as they are." As Peter Smith notes, "the road toward cooperation with dictators would therefore continue to be a basic element in U.S. policy toward Latin America in years to come."

Only Commies Play Soccer

A major continuity between Nixon and his successors was the preoccupation with Castro. Nixon had strongly criticized the Kennedy administration's handling of Cuba, but the issue had faded to the background during the second half of Johnson's administration. Still, many Americans including Nixon had watched closely Castro's support of revolutionaries, including Guevara's ill-fated efforts in Bolivia in 1966–67. The new president had influential Cuban American friends, including Bebe Rebozo, who fueled his paranoia, and Kissinger even suggested that Nixon had "a neuralgic problem" regarding Castro. Consequently, when Nixon took office, he ordered the CIA to increase efforts to sabotage Cuba and renewed efforts to organize anti-Castro elements.

Castro and his countrymen recognized the significance of Nixon's election. As Mark Gilderhus notes, the Cubans "looked upon the new president, an old enemy, as a fascist. To underscore the point, Cuban propaganda employed a distinctive spelling of his name, replacing the 'x' in Nixon with a swastika." The Cubans also sought more support. While Cuban-Soviet relations had been strained after 1962, the split between the Soviet Union and China played into Castro's hand. Moscow wanted to reestablish leadership in the Communist world, and when Castro asked for assistance, it responded. In early August 1970, a Soviet diplomat approached Kissinger and asked for a reaffirmation of the Kennedy-Khrushchev pledge promising no U.S. invasion. Nixon had a good excuse not to agree, partly because no formal Senate treaty existed. Nevertheless, Nixon secretly reaffirmed it, believing that it strengthened the Soviet commitment not to place offensive missiles in Cuba.

The Soviet role in Cuba appeared momentarily defused. Suddenly, in early September, intelligence agents presented Kissinger with U-2 photographs of construction of a submarine base in Cienfuegos harbor. Kissinger burst into the office of the president's chief of staff, H. R. Haldeman, and showed him pictures that included soccer fields. "Those soccer fields could mean war," he told Haldeman. When asked why, he responded, "Cubans play baseball, Russians play soccer." While incorrect, he properly appraised Soviet plans to build a submarine base. Kissinger warned that such a facility would guarantee "a quantum leap in the strategic capability of the Soviet Union against the United States."

In what historian Stephen Ambrose calls "intelligent and admirable restraint," Nixon moved very slowly and quietly. He ordered Kissinger to pressure Castro to stop construction and develop plans for "trading stock," such as bases in the Black Sea. Privately meeting with the Soviet Ambassador Anatoly Dobrynin, Nixon emphasized that he viewed the base with the "utmost gravity." Without really consulting Castro, the Soviets responded that they would respect the 1962 agreement about offensive missiles. In early October, Nixon sent a note that stated: "the U.S. government understands that the U.S.S.R. will not establish . . . any facility in Cuba that can be employed to support or repair Soviet naval ships capable of carrying offensive weapons . . . armed with nuclear-capable, surface-to-surface missiles." Nixon later claimed that at that point, the Soviets abandoned Cienfuegos.

That was not true. Soviet submarines continued visiting, although no vessels carrying ballistic missiles made port calls.

A Great Danger

One area in which Washington became more active in Latin America was in the interdiction of illegal narcotics. Since the Progressive Era, there had been periodic attempts to stop trade in illegal drugs such as cocaine, heroin, and marijuana. Most such efforts had focused on Asia, but after World War II, Washington increasingly worked with Mexico, Colombia, Peru, and Bolivia to destroy the production of illegal drugs.

During the early 1960s, the emphasis on stopping the drug traffic heightened as consumer demand for narcotics rose in the United States. In 1962, the United States provided Mexico with $50,000 in equipment including aircraft and helicopters to assist a drug-eradication program. Other programs helped the Andean nations find growers and destroy their crops. Problems always persisted, as these efforts often concentrated on small marginal farmers in desperate need of money. Corruption and organized crime also followed the drug trade, and U.S. officials met hostile reactions from many quarters.

During the 1968 campaign, Nixon had promised to crack down on crime and violence. Like many of his counterparts, Nixon blamed the nation's moral decay largely on the use of illegal drugs. He promised a robust campaign against the plague. In September 1969, the Nixon administration launched "Operation Intercept." The three-week, $30 million campaign vigorously prosecuted a war against the drug traffickers in the desert Southwest. The administration called it "the nation's largest peacetime search and seizure operation by civil authorities." Others in Washington called it a form of economic blackmail designed "to get the Mexicans to come around and really start doing something about dope."

At the same time, the heavy-handed nature of the operation alienated Mexico City when U.S. agents overstepped their jurisdictions. Intense negotiations followed, and by September 11, 1969, the two countries signed a binational agreement, "Operation Cooperation." It created a joint anti-drug campaign with increased U.S. assistance for Mexico's interdiction and eradication programs. The work between the Mexicans and the newly founded U.S. Drug Enforcement Administration (DEA) (created in 1973) had some impact. By 1976, Washington issued reports of the destruction of over 56 million square meters of marijuana, 58 million square meters of opium fields, and the arrest of 4,000 people. Still, as U.S. demand for illegal drugs increased, the traffickers became more innovative and the trade boomed. The drug problem would remain a contentious issue in U.S.-Mexican relations, one that expanded to include other countries including nations in the Caribbean, Central America, as well as Colombia, Bolivia, and Peru.

The Dagger Pointed at the Heart of Antarctica

In 1970, a new perceived Communist threat developed in Chile. Since 1964, U.S. intelligence and diplomats there had focused on Dr. Salvador Allende and the Frente de Acción Popular (FRAP) [which became the Unidad Popular in 1969], a combined socialist and Communist party. Its platform denounced imperialism and capitalism and called for a sweeping transformation of Chile's industries to serve the needs of the majority. The CIA warned that "of all the Latin American nations, Chile offers the Communists their best prospects for entering and potentially dominating the government through the electoral process." To prevent this, the Johnson administration funneled massive amounts of money into the coffers of the ultimate victor of the 1964 presidential election, Eduardo Frei.

Under Frei, the Chilean economy and political system did not fare that well. In 1970, despite massive expenditures by the CIA to influence the national elections in Chile, Allende won 36 percent of the vote in a three-way contest among the right, left, and Christian Democrat parties. Soon after the voting, U.S. Ambassador to Chile Edward Korry wrote a report that emphasized: "It is a sad fact that Chile has taken the path to communism with only a little more than a third of the nation approving the choice. It will have the most profound effect on Latin America and beyond; we have suffered a grievous defeat; the consequences will be domestic and international."

Off went the alarms in Washington. Kissinger had once referred to Chile as the "dagger pointed at the heart of Antarctica," but another potential Marxist regime in the hemisphere scared him and others. In the early stages, Washington saw several opportunities to unseat Allende. Since Chilean law allowed the legislature to select the president in the event no candidate gained a plurality, Nixon ordered the CIA "to leave no stone unturned . . . to block Allende's confirmation." As Kissinger mused that summer, "I don't see why we have to let a country go Marxist just because its people are irresponsible."

The CIA followed Nixon's instructions. Its chief operative in Santiago, Henry Hecksher, funneled weapons to help Chilean generals kidnap the chief of staff of the Chilean armed services, General René Schneider. They targeted him for several reasons. He remained nonpartisan (the traditional Chilean military position) while some members of the military opposed Allende. Furthermore, Hecksher hoped to pin the blame on Allende's allies. The conspirators failed in their efforts and the abductors killed Schneider. His death achieved the exact opposite effect: the majority of Chileans blamed the right for the violence, swinging support to Allende and helping ensure his inauguration.

The Ghosts of Interventions Past

After Allende took office, relations between Santiago and Washington deteriorated quickly. The Chileans aggravated Americans by erecting a statute of Guevara in Santiago. In addition, Allende established diplomatic relations with Cuba, North Vietnam, and North Korea and entertained Castro and members of the Puerto Rican Independence Party. On the economic front, the Chilean government nationalized the copper industry (including large U.S. holdings) without compensation, with Allende arguing that previously high profits the companies had enjoyed justified not paying the former owners additional monies. The president also focused on ITT. While the Chilean government offered bonds as compensation, ITT complained that the offer was not "prompt, adequate, and effective." The company enlisted the assistance of President Nixon after contributing significantly to his reelection campaign. Soon thereafter, the CIA and ITT executives began funneling millions of dollars into covert operations against Allende.

The plans to destabilize the Allende government had many levels, especially economic. Nixon told his staff that he wanted to "make the [Chilean] economy scream." In response, the United States implemented an "invisible blockade." It pressured international lending organizations, including the World Bank, the Export-Import Bank, and the Inter-American Development Bank, to withhold funds from Chile. Soon, Washington completely halted U.S. aid to Allende's government and pressured foreign investors to withdraw from Chile.

Nevertheless, Washington continued providing assistance to the Chilean military, a move that created increasingly closer ties between that institution and Washington. Many officers, a high proportion of which came from well-connected and wealthy families, began putting aside traditional attitudes of respect for civilian rule after watching Allende's actions. These activities combined nicely with CIA efforts to undermine Allende by providing money to various anti-Allende groups who began instigating riots, such as that by disenchanted truck drivers who burned tires and imposed roadblocks to express their anger over an inability to set their own freighting charges.

The military ultimately moved against Allende on September 11, 1973, as units surrounded his residence, overpowered the guard, and murdered the president. Soon thereafter, the army began rounding up socialists, Communists, and any suspected sympathizers. It placed them in makeshift prisons within soccer fields located throughout the country. During the bloody aftermath, well over 10,000 of these prisoners perished without having had a trial. The army imprisoned many other people and forced thousands more to flee the country. The new government suspended basic civil liberties and began dismantling recently made reforms.

Washington immediately recognized the new junta headed by General Augusto Pinochet. The United States proceeded to lift sanctions against Chile and release loans and seek credits from the Export-Import Bank for that nation. Nixon, Kissinger, and other U.S. officials applauded the outcome. They denied any U.S. role in the overthrow, although one CIA officer admitted that the operation initiated in 1970 to stop Allende's accession to power "was really never ended." The economic embargo and antagonism between Nixon and Allende had helped persuade the Chilean military officers to act more quickly, although domestic and international businesspersons contributed heavily to Allende's downfall. Like others before it, the Nixon administration clearly shaped the results that ensured a long dictatorship in a Latin American nation.

A Rudderless Ship of State

Nixon remained in office a year longer than did Allende. By August 1974, Nixon's role in the Watergate scandal forced his resignation as president. His replacement, Gerald Ford, had only been in office a short time since

Nixon's first vice president, Spiro Agnew, had resigned after having been charged with accepting bribes. Ford, a former congressman from Michigan, had little international experience. The domestic turmoil over Watergate, protest to the Vietnam War, and a major economic recession undermined Ford's presidency from its beginning.

In Latin America, Ford continued Nixon's policies but devoted little attention to them. Ford turned over most activities to the new secretary of state, Kissinger, who focused on the Middle East and efforts at détente with the Soviet Union. While inattention to foreign policy generally characterized the Ford presidency, some problems arose that required immediate diplomacy and led to confrontation and accommodation.

Perhaps the major international issue during this time was the supply and price of oil. In 1973, the Organization of Petroleum Exporting Countries (OPEC) imposed an oil embargo on the United States following its support of Israel in the October war. The only Latin American nation in the cartel, Venezuela refused to participate in the embargo and continued shipping oil northward. Caracas enjoyed the suddenly massive profits on its exported oil, as did Mexico, another major producer of petroleum that stayed out of OPEC. Nevertheless, the Ford administration decided to punish all of the nations from which the United States imported oil. It withdrew tariff preferences and withheld foodstuffs to OPEC nations. In September 1974, President Ford went to the United Nations and denounced the petroleum producers for price gouging.

The Venezuelans counterattacked. President Carlos Andrés Pérez emphasized: "Great countries have created the economic confrontation by denying equal participation to developing nations who need to balance their terms of trade." Venezuelan Foreign Minister Efraín Schacht Aristeguita complained that "the welfare of one-third of the world is being achieved at the expense of the other two-thirds: one industrial country alone, with only six percent of the world's population, uses, for itself, more than half of the mineral resources of the world."

Despite the rhetoric, the Venezuelans initially took a moderate course of action. Andrés issued a public statement in the United States that Venezuela had not used petroleum as a weapon, and that his country only wanted a fair balance of exchange between raw materials and finished goods. They also distanced themselves from the multinational corporations that had reaped huge profits during the crisis. Ultimately, however, Caracas nationalized the petroleum and iron industries, although with few complaints from Washington. For the moment, the politics of petroleum quieted.

Bananagate

Many Latin Americans had watched the effectiveness of OPEC with much interest. After Watergate, Vietnam, and the OPEC embargo, they recognized that Washington's power had reached its lowest level in the twentieth century. In 1974, Costa Rica, Guatemala, Honduras, Nicaragua, Panama, Colombia, and Ecuador formed the Union of Banana Exporting Countries (UPEB). Building their efforts on UN reports that Latin Americans gained only seventeen cents of each dollar spent by U.S. companies in the region, they demanded more. They settled on an export tax of $1 for each forty-pound box of bananas.

The U.S. companies led by United Brands (formerly UFCO), Standard, and Del Monte refused to recognize UPEB. They wanted to continue to work with individual growers and not a government-controlled cartel and counterattacked the formation of UPEB ferociously. After pressuring Ecuador to withdraw from the cartel, they focused on Costa Rica, where retiring president Figueres had promised to nationalize the industry if they failed to negotiate. Undeterred, Standard officials threatened new Costa Rican president Daniel Oduber, telling him they would dismantle their operations in the country and move elsewhere. The Costa Ricans capitulated and reduced the tax to twenty-five cents per box.

The most nefarious method of breaking the cartel occurred in Honduras. In early 1975, the president of United Brands, Eli Black, jumped from the forty-fourth floor of the Pan American building. In the corresponding investigation, detectives uncovered fraud and mismanagement throughout the company. This included a $1.25 million bribe paid to Honduran president Oswaldo López, who had ruled since 1963. Company officials had promised an additional $1.25 million to guarantee that Honduras would reduce the tax on bananas to twenty-five cents per crate. A national uproar followed, and López resigned. Despite calls for nationalization in the scandal's aftermath, the companies held the line. Ultimately, the cartel collapsed and the banana business returned to usual.

Reigning in the Imperial President

In the aftermath of the Vietnam War, significant challenges evolved relating to the heavy-handed interventions and covert operations of past U.S. presidents. Americans and Latin Americas alike had grown disenchanted with U.S. foreign policy—with past operations in Guatemala, Cuba, the

Dominican Republic, and Chile standing out. To try to prevent further direct interventions, Congress passed the War Powers Act in 1974, which limited the president's ability to deploy U.S. troops, although not significantly. Others wanted more far-reaching changes to U.S. policies.

In the Spring of 1974, the Senate began an investigation of the CIA. Headed by Senator Frank Church (D-ID), a special committee gathered documents and conducted interviews. Immediately, Church and his staff concentrated on CIA involvement in assassinations. "It is simply intolerable that any agency of the government of the United States may engage in murder," the chairman emphasized after meeting with CIA director William Colby.

During the summer, the committee examined more than 110,000 pages of information, conducted 800 interviews, and held more than 250 public and executive sessions. They uncovered the existence of "Operation Mongoose" and CIA assassination plots against leaders throughout the world, including Trujillo in the Dominican and Schneider in Chile. Other findings included the presence of CIA-controlled biochemical weapons, illegal domestic wiretapping, and the opening of mail and the censoring of telegrams. As the proceeding continued, Church referred to the CIA as a "rouge elephant rampaging out of control."

The Church committee ultimately recommended substantial changes in CIA operations, which sparked an outcry from various quarters. The *New York Times* called CIA actions "inexcusable" products of "an amoral secret bureaucracy." One journalist emphasized that the report had "uncovered some maggoty horrors." On the other side, defenders of the agency claimed that the report "left us naked before our enemies." Church received death threats and some newspapers, including one in Missouri, ran headlines declaring, "Sen. Church aids Reds." Nevertheless, his committee's report helped ensure new restrictions on the CIA, including a prohibition against assassinations.

A Man of Morality and Reason

The Church Committee hearings signaled the growing disenchantment with the old ways and a desire for new beginnings. When the Democrats searched for a standard bearer in 1976, they settled on Georgia governor Jimmy Carter as a candidate prepared to make the needed change from business as usual in Washington. A graduate of the U.S. Naval Academy with a degree in engineering, Carter had served in the navy several years before returning to his hometown of Plains, Georgia. A devout Christian, he was known for his honesty and standard of ethical behavior. After starting in local politics, Carter went on to gain the governor's house, where he waged battles against corruption and supported civil rights.

Carter narrowly defeated Ford, and from the outset of his administration, President Carter pushed a different foreign policy. He emphasized that "we've lost the spirit of our nation. . . . We're ashamed of our government as we deal with other nations around the world, and that's got to be changed, and I'm going to change it." He stressed that "a nation's domestic and foreign policy actions should be derived from the same standards of ethics, honesty and morality which are characteristics of the individual citizens of the nation." As historian Gaddis Smith notes, this marked a time "when a fundamental debate about how the United States should behave in international affairs was waged with unusual clarity . . . when an effort was made to think in terms of a lasting world order beneficial to all people rather than to make every decision on the basis of short-term calculation of American advantage over the Soviet Union; when leaders tried consciously and explicitly to discover and apply an effective combination of morality, reason, and power in the conduct of American foreign policy."

The basis of the Carter administration's new approach to foreign policy was an emphasis on human rights. This focus sought to push the United States to work toward a "more humane world order, not simply a position of strength against one adversary," Smith underscores. During the campaign, Carter told a crowd: "We cannot look away when a government tortures people, or jails them for their beliefs or denies minorities fair treatment. . . . We should begin by having it understood that if any nation . . . deprives its own people of basic human rights, that fact will help shape our own people's attitude toward that nation's government." At his inauguration in January 1977, Carter declared that "our commitment to human rights must be absolute."

To initiate the change, Carter created the office of Assistant Secretary of State for Human Rights. Patricia M. Derian, a veteran of the civil rights movement, became the first person to hold that position. Immediately, she began making plans to use economic sanctions against governments guilty of human-rights abuses. The Carter administration, while divided within, made an important first step toward institutionalizing human rights into U.S. foreign policy.

Human Rights and Latin America

The Carter administration devoted more attention to Latin America than had its three predecessors. During the campaign, Carter had emphasized that "we should get away permanently from an attitude of paternalism or punishment or retribution when some of the South Americans don't yield to our persuasion." As one historian acknowledges, Carter "saw in Latin America a special opportunity to apply the philosophy of repentance and reform—admitting past mistakes, making the region a showcase for human-rights policy, seeking to prevent the proliferation of technology which could lead to the production of nuclear weapons, and reducing the level of conventional-arms transfers."

A major component of Carter's new policy was a rejection of his predecessors' excesses. Carter's National Security Council advisor Zbigniew Brzezinski had written "it would be wise for the United States to make an explicit move to abandon the Monroe Doctrine." He noted about the Doctrine that to "most of our neighbors to the south it was an expression of presumptuous imperialism." To demonstrate this new orientation, the Carter administration played up its commitment to human rights. As political scientist Lars Schoultz stresses, "by the end of 1977, it was clear that the United States' efforts to protect human rights were to be concentrated upon Latin America's repressive governments." The historical relationship and perceived lack of a significant Communist threat ensured the change. "Depending on the seriousness of violations, the offending governments would then be approached through quiet diplomacy, subjected to public criticism, or punished with low-grade economic sanctions," Smith writes.

The first test occurred in Argentina, where the military had begun a "dirty war" against its citizens. It suppressed civil liberties and political dissidents began to disappear without a trace. Stories of people, including nuns and priests, being flown out over the sea and thrown alive from airplanes filtered out. Survivors of military torture chambers told of horrific treatment. In Buenos Aires, the "Mothers of Disappeared" began holding vigils in the main plazas. In response, human-rights organizations in the United States and the world decried the repression and began to raise public awareness of the abuses.

Once in the White House, Carter slashed economic and military assistance to Argentina. Publicly and privately the administration criticized the

Argentine military. By the end of the year, the administration blocked loans to Argentina through the Inter-American Association Bank and restricted Export-Import credits. Over time, the sanctions eased in response to Argentine promises to hold fair elections. As Smith notes, "the application of human-rights principles in U.S. relations with Argentina was a compromise, but one weighted on the side of sticks rather than carrots." Some limited benefits accrued, including the release of some prisoners and the opening of visits to Argentina by human-rights groups. Clearly, the Argentine military cheered the results of the 1980 U.S. presidential election and the arrival of a president (Reagan) more concerned with fighting the spread of communism than protecting human rights.

While Argentina received significant attention, the overall response of the United States to repression and human-rights violations in Latin America was lukewarm and inconsistent. In most cases, the Latin American militaries merely ignored Washington, turning to alternative sources, including the Europeans and Israelis, for supplies. They also made many promises to ease restrictions which they later ignored. In addition, prominent Americans within the State Department, Congress, and other groups disagreed with the Carter administration's Latin American policy and undermined efforts to implement it. Finally, as the Cold War heated up toward the end of the 1970s, the Carter administration increasingly returned to a Cold War mentality and began cooperating with anti-Communist allies, despite their human-rights records. A noble idea died as a result.

A Major Test of Carter's Worldview

One of the first goals that Carter made regarding Latin America was the settlement of the Canal Zone debates. Carter believed that a new treaty would ensure "a positive impact throughout Latin America" and "an auspicious beginning for a new era." During his presidential campaign, he had emphasized that "I believe the Panamanians will respond well to open and continual negotiations and the sharing of sovereignty and control, recognizing their rights in that respect."

Once in office, President Carter and his secretary of state, Cyrus Vance, made the canal negotiations a high priority. As Walter LaFeber underscores, "top Carter administration officials . . . viewed the Panama crisis as a key to their entire foreign policy. With a new treaty, they could work out a rapprochement, at least on the economic level, with Latin America. That new relationship might serve as a doorbell to the remainder of the developing nations." Building on negotiations begun by Johnson and continued by Kissinger, the Carter administration plowed forward. It pushed hard for a treaty, dealing closely with Panamanian dictator Omar Torrijos, who had controlled the country since 1968. Tense negotiations headed by Ellsworth Bunker, former U.S. ambassador to the OAS, and Sol Linowitz, a Xerox Corporation executive, continued for nearly a year.

Finally, on August 11, 1977, the parties held a press conference in Panama and unveiled the treaty. It had several parts, starting with the process of returning the canal to Panama by December 31, 1999. Second, the treaty guaranteed the rights of American workers in the Zone through their retirement. Third, it provided the United States with a permanent right to defend the neutrality of the Canal Zone. Lastly, Washington increased its payment for U.S. use of the canal, raising it from $2.3 million to $40 million and promising additional economic and military assistance.

"We Built It, We Paid for It, It's Ours"

The announcement of the new Panama Canal treaty stirred debates in both countries. Since the treaty needed approval by the Panamanian people (as outlined in the Constitution) and confirmation by a two-thirds majority of the U.S. Senate, victory appeared far from assured in August 1977. In Panama, Torrijos pushed through the plebiscite in Panama, although not without opposition. In the United States, the Senate began deliberations in the summer of 1978. President Carter and his staff pushed hard for the treaty, winning the support of diverse groups including the Pentagon (which believed the canal had outlived its tactical purpose) and the Catholic Church, as well as with distinguished former diplomats including Kissinger and Dean Rusk. Over time, Carter won the backing of important senators from both parties including Senate Majority Leader Robert Byrd (D-WV) and Senate Minority Leader Howard Baker (R-TN). With promises of compromise and pork-barrel projects for their states, the pro-treaty Senate group moved forward.

But those who opposed the treaty refused to surrender, as conservative anti-Communist groups including the John Birch Society, the Conservative Caucus, and the American Legion lined up against turning the canal over to the Panamanians. They were led by failed Republican presidential

President Jimmy Carter and General Omar Torrijos shake hands after signing the
Panama Canal Treaty. *Courtesy of the Jimmy Carter Library*

nominee Ronald Reagan, who had emphasized in the primary: "When it
comes to the Canal, we built it, we paid for it, it's ours, and we should tell
Torrijos and company that we're going to keep it." He had added, incorrectly, that the canal was "sovereign United States territory just the same
as Alaska is and as part of Texas that came out of the Gadsden Purchase."
Others in Congress shared this opinion and viciously attacked the treaty
for selling out U.S. sovereignty.

   Throughout the summer of 1978, the foes battled on the floor of the
Senate and in public forums. Carter secured an extra promise from Torrijos
guaranteeing the right of the United States to defend the Canal Zone after
2000, after which the measure won. In March 1978, the Senate approved
the neutrality part 68–32. By mid-April, they approved the other part of
the treaty outlining administration through 2000 by the same vote. Carter,
the Senate leadership, and pro-treaty forces enjoyed a major victory. The
president emphasized that "these treaties can mark the beginning of a new
era in our relations not only with Panama but with all the rest of the world.
They symbolize our determination to deal with the developing nations of
the world . . . on the basis of mutual respect and partnership."

   With the canal treaty, Carter's Latin American policy reached its apex.
It proved a costly victory, for to secure it Carter had expended a lot of

political capital, of which he had a short supply. It also provided the right wing of the Republican party with a potent political issue in the next presidential election, one that Reagan gladly used to demonstrate the growing inability of the United States to maintain its national defenses. Finally, while winning support from Latin Americans for the step forward, Carter failed to translate the action into significant political gains. Although Carter continued to insist that he had ensured changes in U.S. policy, Latin Americans remained skeptical.

A New Cuba Policy?

While the Panama Canal and human rights had been their focus in the first two years of the administration, Carter and his advisors also tried altering U.S. policy toward Cuba. In October 1976, Cyrus Vance, who would become Carter's secretary of state, wrote the president about Cuba: "the time has come to move away from our policy of isolation. Our boycott has proved ineffective, and there has been a decline of Cuba's export of revolution in the region." Vance's view originated from several factors. Other nations, including U.S. allies in Europe, Latin America, and Canada, had normalized relations with Cuba and resumed trading with it. Vance also hoped to use closer relations to reduce Cuban influence in Africa, where Castro had sent troops to help in pro-Communist revolutionaries in Angola and elsewhere.

Carter had hesitated to make statements on Cuba during the election for fear of angering the strong Cuban American population, but once in office he moved quickly. In early 1977, the administration removed restrictions on travel to Cuba, suspended spy flights over the island, and signed a fisheries agreement. In May, the two nations agreed to establish "interest sections" in third-party embassies in Washington and Havana. One U.S. official commented, "this is a step well short of diplomatic relations but one that will facilitate communications between the two governments and make it easier for both to address the many problems we face." Castro responded by releasing some U.S. prisoners and publicly praising the "positive" steps in a television interview with Barbara Walters.

The efforts at a rapprochement lasted only a short time. In late 1978, the Carter administration began complaining about Cuba's presence in Angola, Zaire, and Ethiopia. President Carter stated that the withdrawal of Cuban troops from Africa "would be a prerequisite for normalization [of relations]." Other problems followed, as defense officials leaked information about Soviet delivery of MIG-23 fighter jets to Cuba. With increased pressure from anti-Communist congresspersons, Carter moved back toward a hard line. With the resignation of Vance in 1979, the administration took a hard right with National Security Advisor Brzezinski and his Eurocentric Cold War view. In 1979, the reported discovery of a Soviet Brigade (an army group) in Cuba set off another diplomatic controversy that increased the focus on Cuban activities in Central America (particularly Nicaragua and El Salvador) and the Caribbean. By 1980, the administration had returned to old policies of isolation and containment.

As relations chilled, Washington increasingly denounced Castro's human-rights record. The Cuban leader had the last laugh. Under domestic pressure during hard economic times, Castro suddenly invited Cuban Americans to Mariel to pick up their relatives. A mass exodus of 125,000 Cubans began to depart Cuba in what became known as the Mariel boat lift. Cubans boarded anything that could float and headed northward. Painted into a corner, Carter initially accepted the wave of Cuban immigrants, but over time he restricted its flow. In a final insult, Castro emptied his jails and mental hospitals and put those people on ships bound for Florida as well. When U.S. officials discovered this move, the boat lift ended. A new U.S. president, Ronald Reagan, would inherit the problem.

The Ghost of Sandino

During the last two years of Carter's administration, the president and his advisors increasingly faced problems in Central America. For two decades, small revolutionary movements had survived in Nicaragua, Guatemala, and El Salvador. They had received unlikely support from many areas, including the hierarchy of the Catholic Church. Building a series of encyclicals issued by Pope John XXIII in the early 1960s that stressed human rights and proper standards of living for everyone, Latin American bishops in 1968 had urged support for social justice and denounced "institutional violence." They urged the creation of grass-roots movements to improve lives. In what became known as "liberation theology," Catholic priests (primarily at the parish level) and laymen began forming base communities to address poverty, illiteracy, and human rights. A potent force of change began to swell.

The first major crisis developed in Nicaragua, where the dictator Anastasio Somoza Debayle, second son of the founder of the dictatorship, had ruled since 1966. A graduate of the U.S. Military Academy, he relied on the Nicaraguan National Guard to murder, intimidate, and suppress dissenters and malcontents within his regime. He maintained powerful allies in the United States. Nevertheless, a small group of anti-Somoza revolutionaries had survived and formed the Sandinista National Liberation Front (FSLN) in the 1960s. They received a significant boost in 1972, when Somoza alienated the business community by stealing massive amounts of relief monies after a devastating earthquake, funds he used to rebuild Managua on properties he owned. More people deserted the dictatorship over the next few years and by 1977, the country had plunged into civil war.

The Carter administration's emphasis on human rights created tensions in U.S.-Nicaraguan relations. Pushed by human-rights organizations and congresspersons led by Representative Ed Koch (D-NY) and Senator Edward Kennedy (D-MA), the administration withheld some economic aid. At the same time, dissension developed. Pro-Somoza lobbyists and congresspersons attacked Carter's policy, calling it an assault on a long-time anti-Communist ally. When Somoza made some halfhearted reforms, the administration renewed the economic assistance. "But the crisis soon testified to the contradictions of Carter's human rights policy. As long as the United States stressed opening up the political process and limiting Guard violence, while at the same time doing nothing to redistribute wealth or opportunity, Carter's policy was a recipe for disaster," LaFeber highlights.

The situation deteriorated rapidly in early 1978, when Somoza's henchmen murdered respected journalist Joaquín Chamorro. Mass demonstrations followed, and the National Guard intensified its indiscriminate attacks. A fiery debate broke out in Washington as Somoza's allies attacked efforts to punish the dictator, while human-rights groups denounced giving the Nicaraguan government any further assistance. Carter continued to seek the middle ground by providing aid while pressuring Somoza to reform. Throughout the spring and summer, the administration vacillated as it sought "to constrain Cuban and other communist intrusion in the internal affairs of Caribbean and Latin American countries, and how to encourage freedom and democracy in Nicaragua and minimize bloodshed there."

The fall brought significant changes. A special Sandinista force led by Edén Pastora seized the Nicaraguan Legislative Assembly and several Somoza family members in "Operation Pigpen." The rebels forced concessions and triumphantly boarded a plane at the Managua airport after passing cheering crowds. Somoza responded by turning the Guard loose to bomb towns and massacre people, the force mutilating many of its victims. Amnesty International and an OAS human-rights team documented the crimes against humanity and raised the issue in the United States. Again, Carter searched for a compromise. One commentator lamented that reforming Somoza or finding an acceptable alternative was nearly impossible because "the minimal institutions of a democratic political order do not come easily into being in a country ruled for more than forty years by one family, the sword, the dollar, and every imaginable form of graft and venality."

Swept Away by the Tide

As the situation in Nicaragua worsened in the fall of 1978, the Carter administration made one last attempt to influence the outcome. When Somoza refused to allow OAS supervised elections, the Carter administration terminated military aid, withdrew embassy officials, and cut economic assistance back to only those funds intended to serve "the basic needs of the poor." The action proved unproductive, as Somoza ignored Carter's mandates. The Sandinistas called the response too little, too late. The dictator continued receiving military assistance from Israel and Argentina and ultimately Washington backed an emergency IMF loan to Nicaragua of $66 million. The Carter administration was left without many options.

In late May 1979, the Sandinistas launched their final offensive from bases in Costa Rica. The fighting was brutal, as Somoza's forces continued indiscriminate killing. The worst possible public relations fiasco for Somoza occurred with the murder of Bill Stewart, an ABC newsman. National Guard members took Stewart from his car, forced him to lie down, and then shot him in the back of the head. Another newsman captured the murder on tape and images of the Guard's brutality reached millions of American households that night.

The Carter administration made one final attempt to influence who won control. On June 21, Secretary of State Vance told OAS ministers that there was "mounting evidence of involvement by Cuba and others in the internal problems of Nicaragua. This involvement may transform these internal problems into international and ideological issues, making it increasingly difficult to arrive at a peaceful solution." He presented a plan for an OAS peacekeeping force, the formation of an interim government of national reconciliation, and major investments for relief and reconstruction. The U.S. proposal died immediately, as no other country supported it. Assistant Secretary of State Viron P. Vaky observed that the OAS rejection "reflected how deeply the American states were sensitized by the Dominican intervention of 1965, and how deeply they fear physical intervention."

Despite the bitter defeat in the OAS, Washington continued to push for more moderates in the Nicaraguan government and the prevention of widespread retaliation against Somoza and his forces. In short, the United States pressed for a peaceful transition of power. Such efforts failed miserably. Somoza and his mistress fled the country in mid-July 1979 and settled in Paraguay. Ultimately, Sandinista assassins finished him off when they fired a rocket into his Mercedes. His Guard also disintegrated, running "like rats," according to one mercenary. By early August, a junta ruled Nicaragua.

Accepting the Inevitable

Faced with a government that it consistently had opposed, the Carter administration tried preventing another "Cuba." For their part, the Sandinistas promised not to align themselves with any foreign power and to remain integrated in the international economy. No mass executions occurred, and most National Guard members fled. While the Sandinistas nationalized Somoza's properties and the banking system, the Nicaraguans welcomed U.S. investors including Standard Fruit and Coca-Cola, even suppressing several strikes against the U.S. companies. Such actions won them support. As one U.S. businessman who had worked in Nicaragua told a congressional committee: "Communists are not in control, and unless we democratic and private types concede the issue by default, the chances are against Communism in Nicaragua."

Nevertheless, tensions remained high. Sandinista leaders flew to Havana, where Castro greeted them as heroes (although he warned them against following his model and urged them to maintain a large private sector). Managua also criticized U.S. assistance to El Salvador and failed to support a U.S.-sponsored UN resolution condemning the Soviet invasion of Afghanistan. Still, U.S. Ambassador Lawrence Pezzullo warned Congress that the Sandinistas were "very much a Nicaraguan phenomenon . . . Sandinismo . . . is a Nicaraguan, homegrown movement. Sandino predates Castro. . . . The nature of this thing is such that you have to see it take its own form, rather than make prejudgments about it."

Despite the harsh criticism from American conservatives, Carter allotted $20 million in economic aid to the devastated economy. In autumn 1979, he requested an additional $75 million. State Department officials told Congress such actions demonstrated that the United States could respond positively to revolutions in Central America. In addition, U.S. bankers, fearful of Nicaragua defaulting on $1.5 billion in debt, prodded Congress to accept. For eight months, it debated the request. Several congressional representatives placed poison pills in the legislation, including requirements that 60 percent of the aid go to private sources, and that Managua publicly state that the United States had provided the funds. The junta swallowed its pride and continued negotiating.

By the time Congress finally approved the assistance, relations had worsened, and the Sandinistas asked Moscow for assistance. In a series of agreements, the Soviets provided $100 million in agricultural assistance and power generators. In the meantime, the Sandinistas delayed promised elections, and moderate members of the junta resigned. They also began funneling arms to the El Salvadoran rebels. In response, the Carter administration backed CIA plans to organize former members of the National Guard to interdict the arms transfers. In late 1980, Carter approved additional funds to aid anti-Sandinista members of the press, clergy, labor unions, and political parties. In response to the victory of the rabidly anti-Communist Ronald Reagan in November 1980, the Sandinistas recognized the handwriting on the wall and tightened control by placing new limits on the press and opposition parties. The stage was now set for direct conflict.

The Bloodbath in El Salvador

Complicating Carter's problems in Nicaragua was a hostage crisis in Iran (which made him appear weak) and unrest in El Salvador, where a small oligarchy, supported by the military and hierarchy of the Catholic Church, had dominated the country for many years. In this small nation the person-to-land ratio was the worst in Latin America, and the disparity between the wealthy and poor was extremely high. Boom-and-bust cycles in the coffee industry exacerbated El Salvador's economic difficulties. Throughout the 1960s and 1970s, opposition grew to the ruling junta from urban members of the Christian Democratic Party (CDP) and in rural areas in which priests had organized the peasants. In addition, a leftist movement led by Cayetano Carpio launched a guerrilla war against the military government.

Jimmy Carter, Daniel Ortega, and members of the Nicaraguan Junta, September, 24, 1979. *Courtesy of the Jimmy Carter Library*

As the opposition to it mounted, the oligarchy fought back. Members of the military and the elite organized "death squads" that kidnapped and murdered labor union leaders and other activists. In one case, the military seized CDP leader José Napoleon Duarte, beat him, and placed him on a plane to Guatemala, where they expected the military to execute him. Duarte, however, escaped and fled to Venezuela. Back in El Salvador, no one eluded scrutiny. Assassins killed priests such as Rutilio Grande, a close friend of the Archbishop of San Salvador, Oscar Romero. A pro-government vigilante group known as the "White Warriors" promised to kill all Jesuits. Handouts stating, "Be a patriot! Kill a priest!" began to circulate. On the other side, leftists kidnapped wealthy Salvadorans and held them for ransom, thereby collecting over $50 million to purchase weapons.

The individualized acts of terror in El Salvador became more acute after Carter took office as U.S. president. General Carlos Humberto Romero seized power through fraudulent elections in 1977. Thereafter, he increased the official repression of his opponents. Now, an outcry of support for the Salvadoran people developed in the United States, primarily from the Catholic Church, human-rights organizations, and Congress. Carter responded by blocking an Inter-American Development Bank loan and maintaining an embargo of weapons sales to the Salvadoran government, one begun in 1975 when U.S. officials uncovered Salvadoran arms being sold to U.S. gangsters. The pressure worked somewhat. Romero lifted martial law, and the United States restored economic aid to El Salvador. Still, the death squads continued to operate with impunity, and the leftists continued to gain strength.

The fighting in Nicaragua eventually caused the Carter administration to change its policies in El Salvador. In 1978, an assistant secretary of state for inter-American affairs publicly acknowledged that improving human rights in El Salvador was no longer a priority. "Terror and subversion are the major problems," he reported. In response, the Pentagon dispatched a military mission to train and advise the Salvadoran military in what one U.S. diplomat called a "clean insurgency."

No More Vietnams

The disorder continued in El Salvador. Military officers overthrew Romero, raising some hopes in Washington. The new ruling junta, which included a returned Duarte, announced reforms that included land redistribution, the establishment of a minimum wage, and free elections. The majority of elites balked at the ideas, as did the left, which saw them as too little, too late. Violence increased on all sides, including the brazen assassination of Archbishop Romero by right-wing conservatives during a mass at a cancer hospital after he had announced that "the real power is in the hands of the most repressive sector of the armed forces" and that their "hands are red with blood." He had stressed that "no soldier is obliged to obey an order contrary to the law of God." The OAS investigating team implicated soldiers in the murder, including Major Roberto D'Aubuisson, a top military intelligence officer trained at the International Police Academy in Washington.

Despite Archbishop Romero's murder and the continued violence, the Carter administration continued seeking a middle ground, afraid to involve the U.S. military in another jungle quagmire so soon after the costly and embarrassing war in Vietnam. It therefore followed a policy characterized as KISSSS (Keep it simple, sustainable, small, and Salvadoran") and requested $5.7 million from Congress to "help strengthen the army's key role in reforms," which included land distribution. The efforts failed miserably. Elites sold their lands to the government at inflated

prices or subdivided them among family members to prevent nationalization. Subsequently, they transferred their newly realized funds to Swiss or
U.S. bank accounts. The death squads increased their activities in areas
where peasants sought land and even murdered three land-reform officials,
including two Americans. U.S. officials desperately struggled for an answer
to revolution with reform.

A new sense of urgency arose in El Salvador with Ronald Reagan's
election as U.S. president in November 1980. The Salvadoran left had
read the Republican platform and noted the harsh rhetoric about perceived Moscow-inspired insurgencies in Central America. They decided
to act before Reagan took office, calling for a general uprising "before
the fanatic Ronald Reagan takes over the presidency." They formed the
Farabundo Martí Liberation Front (FMLN), an umbrella military organization of sixteen groups led by members of the Christian and social
democratic groups and Communists. U.S. officials responded slowly.
Carter had already suspended military aid to El Salvador following the
rape and murder of three American nuns and a layperson by death squad
members. Yet when the rebels launched a major offensive in early 1981,
the Carter administration provided additional military supplies to the
Salvadoran military, which helped defeat the offensive. Not long thereafter, Carter was out of office.

Two reporters observed as Carter left the White House that "El Salvador was the stage on which Jimmy Carter would perhaps play his most
anguished version of Hamlet as played by a policymaker." U.S. policymakers had encountered intractable problems with El Salvador. Everything
they had tried had failed. Limited reforms could not contain the inevitable
pressures for dramatic change in a country wracked by social, political, and
economic divisions. Polarization caused by violence led to further conflict.
The process would continue unabated for many years.

El Salvador was a microcosm of the Carter administration's policy in
Latin America. Early in his presidency, Carter had won victories in Panama
and forced some changes by the military regimes in the region regarding
his human-rights policy. But even as Carter neared the end of his presidency, the forces of revolution threatened to sweep the region, especially in
Central America and the Caribbean. His successor would reject his idealism and return to the more simplistic view that Moscow ultimately created
all problems in Latin America, leading Reagan to address a new set of
challenges.

Continuities

During the period 1960 to 1980, the interdependence between the United States and Latin America ebbed and flowed. Early on, the United States had demonstrated an unprecedented interest in Latin America by establishing the Alliance for Progress. While the Europeans and Japanese had become more competitive in the regional markets, by 1960 the United States was clearly the hegemonic power in Latin America, even as new issues such as the drug trade and immigration laws increased the visibility of interdependence. For some Latin Americans, the Alliance represented recognition by the United States of the region's underdevelopment; others saw it as the latest method to strengthen the U.S. position by increasing Latin American dependence on U.S. aid and loans. The buildup of Latin American militaries allied with the United States and armed intervention in the Dominican Republic pushed U.S. power to an apex.

But changes were underway. The admitted failure in Vietnam and the embarrassing fall of Saigon, the Watergate scandal, and the rise of economic competitors in Latin America combined with the increased reliance of the United States on OPEC and strong challenges by the Soviet Union and China weakened U.S. prestige worldwide. Castro remained a thorn in the side of the U.S. government, and new confrontations arose in Chile and Nicaragua. The result was a more compliant and conciliatory United States under President Carter, as the United States found it increasingly difficult to influence hemispheric events.

A major part of the decline in U.S. hegemony was the Latin Americans' increasing ability to challenge the United States. In the economic realm, countries such as Venezuela and Mexico held large deposits of oil. Both nations benefited from the huge drain of resources from the petroleum-dependent United States. Meanwhile, other nations successfully negotiated better deals with U.S. companies for their materials and products. Economic interdependence remained, but the new markets made the Latin American companies more competitive.

Latin Americans also increasingly challenged U.S. political hegemony. Castro was the extreme example, but there were many others, including the Sandinistas, who used violent force to expel a pro-U.S. dictator. They benefited from external alliances, including with the Soviets, Europeans, and fellow Latin Americans. Human-rights groups in the United States such as Americas Watch and the North American Congress on Latin

America (NACLA) underscored the hypocrisy of U.S. support for dictators, and some members of Congress advocated new legislation to cut off assistance to perpetual violators of human rights. Others helped in pushing through the Panama Canal Treaty, one of the high points in the long struggle for Latin American sovereignty.

On the domestic front, the influx of Latin American immigrants, especially from Mexico and Cuba, continued relatively unabated, despite official efforts to stem the tide in the Southwest. As the Latino population grew, so did the recognition of its political and economic influence. Issues regarding immigration, bilingual education, and expanded social services for Latinos gained significance on the national stage. Their influence on U.S. politics and culture, especially in the borderlands, was significant and became increasingly apparent throughout the United States.

SUGGESTIONS FOR ADDITIONAL READING

General works on the Kennedy administration's Latin American policies include Stephen Rabe, *The Most Dangerous Area in the World: John F. Kennedy Confronts Communist Revolution in Latin America* (1999); Richard Walton, *Cold War and Counter-Revolution: The Foreign Policy of John F. Kennedy* (1973); Edwin McCammon Martin, *Kennedy and Latin America* (1994); Elizabeth Cobbs Hoffman, *All You Need is Love: The Peace Corps and the Spirit of the 1960s* (1998); Arthur Schlesinger, Jr., *A Thousand Days: John F. Kennedy in the White House* (1965); Theodore C. Sorenson, *Kennedy* (1965); Milton S. Eisenhower, *The Wine Is Bitter: The United States and Latin America* (1963); Michael Latham, *Modernization as Ideology: American Social Science and "Nation Building"* (2000); and Jeffrey Taffet, *Foreign Aid as Foreign Policy: The Alliance for Progress in Latin America* (2007).

For more on the relationship between Castro and the United States, see Trumball Higgins, *The Perfect Failure: Kennedy, Eisenhower, and the CIA at the Bay of Pigs* (1989); James G. Blight, Bruce Allyn and David Welch, *Cuba on the Brink: Castro, the Missile Crisis, and the Soviet Collapse* (1993); Morris H. Morley, *Imperial State and Revolution: The United States and Cuba, 1952–1986* (1987); William A. Williams, *The United States, Cuba, and Castro: An Essay on the Dynamics of Revolution and the Dissolution of Empire* (1962); Piero Gleijses, "Ships in the Night: The CIA, the White House, and the Bay of Pigs," *Journal of Latin American Studies 27* (February 1995): 1–42; Peter Wyden, *Bay of Pigs* (1979); and Don Bohning, *The Castro Obsession: U.S. Covert Operations in Cuba, 1959-1965* (2005).

For general studies on Johnson, see Robert Dallek, *Flawed Giant: Lyndon Johnson and His Times, 1961–1973* (1998); H. W. Brands, *The Wages of Globalism: Lyndon Johnson and the Limits of American Power* (1995); Paul Conkin, *Big Daddy from the Pedernales: Lyndon Baines Johnson* (1986); and Robert Caro, *The Years of Lyndon Johnson,* two volumes (1982).

Good works on Johnson and Latin America include: Jerome Levinson and Juan de Onís, *The Alliance that Lost Its Way: A Critical Report on the Alliance for Progress* (1970); Robert A. Packenham, *Liberal America and the Third World: Political Development Ideas in Foreign Aid and Social Science* (1973); Julie Leininger Pycior, *LBJ and Mexican Americans: The Paradox of Power* (1997); Joseph S. Tulchin, "The Promise of Progress: U.S. Relations with Latin America during the Administration of Lyndon B. Johnson," in Warren I. Cohen and Nancy Bernkopf Tucker, *Lyndon Johnson Confronts the World: American Foreign Policy, 1963–1968* (1994); and Walter LaFeber, "Latin American Policy," in Robert A. Divine, ed., *Exploring the Johnson Years* (1981).

Good works on the United States and Brazil during the period include W. Michael Weis, *Cold Warriors and Coups d'Etats: Brazilian-American Relations, 1945–1964* (1993); Phyllis Parker, *Brazil and the Quiet Intervention, 1964* (1979); Ruth Leacock, *Requiem for Revolution: The United States and Brazil, 1961–1969* (1990); Martha K. Huggins, *Political Policing: The United States and Latin America* (1998); Jan Knippers Black, *United States Penetration of Brazil* (1977); Alan McPherson, *Yankee No!: Anti-Americanism in U.S.-Latin American Relations* (2006); and Stephen Rabe, *U.S. Intervention in British Guiana: A Cold War Story* (2006).

For more on the Dominican Intervention, reference Piero Gleijeses, *The Dominican Crisis: The 1965 Constitutional Revolt and American Intervention* (1978); Bruce Palmer, Jr., *Intervention in the Caribbean: The Dominican Crisis of 1965* (1989); Abraham Lowenthal, *The Dominican Intervention* (1972); Jerome Slater, *Intervention and Negotiation: The United States and the Dominican Revolution* (1970); and John Bartlow Martin, *Overtaken by Events: The Dominican Crisis from the Fall of Trujillo to the Civil War* (1966).

The Nixon-Ford era is covered in Stephen Ambrose, *Nixon: The Triumph of a Politician, 1962–1972* (1987); Robert D. Schulzinger, *Henry Kissinger: Doctor of Diplomacy* (1989); Richard C. Thornton, *The Nixon-Kissinger Years: The Reshaping of American Foreign Policy* (2001); Jeremi Suri, *Henry Kissinger and the American Century* (2007); Teresa Hayter, *Aid as Imperialism* (1971); Stephen Rabe, *The Road to OPEC: The United States Relations with Venezuela, 1919–1976* (1982); Carla Anne Robbins, *The Cuban Threat* (1983); and Wayne S. Smith, *The Closest of Enemies: A Personal and Diplomatic Account of U.S.-Cuban Relations since 1957* (1987).

For more on Carter and his administration, see Gaddis Smith, *Morality, Reason, and Power: American Diplomacy in the Carter Years* (1986); Lars Schoultz, *Human Rights and United States Policy toward Latin America* (1981); Richard Thornton, *The Carter Years: Toward a New Global Order* (1991); Kenneth E. Morris, *Jimmy Carter, American Moralist* (1996); and Hugo Assmann, ed., *Carter y la lógica del imperialismo* (1978).

The issue of Panama and the treaty are examined in Walter LaFeber, *The Panama Canal: The Crisis in Historical Perspective* (1978); Michael J. Hogan, *The Panama Canal in American Politics* (1986); John Major, *Prize Possession: The United States and the Panama Canal, 1903–1979* (1994); William L. Furlong and Margaret E. Scranton, *The Dynamics of Foreign Policymaking: The President, the Congress, and the Panama Canal Treaties* (1984); George D. Moffett III, *The Limits of Victory: The Ratification of the*

Panama Canal Treaties (1985); Adam Clymer, *Drawing the Line at the Big Ditch: The Panama Canal Treaties and the Rise of the Right* (2008); and John Lindsay-Poland, *Emperors in the Jungle: The Hidden History of the U.S. in Panama* (2003).

For the early U.S. response to the Sandinistas and Central America, see Anthony Lake, *Somoza Falling: The Nicaraguan Dilemma: A Portrait of Washington* (1989); Lawrence Pezzullo and Ralph Pezzullo, *At the Fall of Somoza* (1993); Morris H. Morley, *Washington, Somoza, and the Sandinistas: State and Regime in U.S. Policy toward Nicaragua, 1969–1981* (1994); and Robert Pastor, *Condemned to Repetition: The United States and Nicaragua* (1987).

CHAPTER EIGHT

The End of the Cold War

THE EXPERIMENTS WITH HUMAN RIGHTS AND COOPERATIVE EFFORTS on issues such as Panama's sovereignty declined in the final two years of the Carter administration. With the inauguration of Ronald Reagan, such efforts disappeared completely. U.S. policy returned to having a singular focus on the protection of U.S. economic and strategic interests, especially containing the Communist threat and promoting the free-market model. Within a short period, U.S.-Latin American relations reached their lowest point since the 1920s and the interventionist policies of the Wilson administration. Yet improvements occurred with the end of the Cold War as the Soviet Union dissolved during the presidency of George H. W. Bush. Wars ended in Central America and democracies returned throughout the region. By 1993, a new era of comparative peace and tranquility appeared on the horizon.

Mr. Reagan Goes to Washington

In 1981, Ronald Reagan swept into office after blasting Carter for his vacillation and failure to protect U.S. interests in Iran, Nicaragua, Panama, and El Salvador. Originally, Reagan, the former "B" movie actor, was best known for his supporting roles, including having starred with a chimp named "Bonzo" and for his failed marriage to "A" list actress Jane Wyman. In the 1950s, Reagan made a career move into politics. A one-time New Dealer, Reagan married into the wealthy Orange County, California, family of Nancy Davis and discovered the virtues of conservatism, the Southern Californian brand of which emphasized limited government, reduced taxes, strong national defense, and a virulent anticommunism. In short order, Reagan vaulted from president of the Screen Actor's Guild during the 1950s to the governor of California in the 1960s and to the top of the Republican Party by the late 1970s. Reagan surrounded himself with conservative speechwriters and analysts who provided ideas that he effectively communicated, typically through the television. Promising better times and a return to a strong America, Reagan crushed Carter in the 1980 presidential election.

The new president had little experience or understanding of the complexities of foreign policy. He toasted his hosts in "Bolivia" while visiting Brazil and wrongly believed that the Soviet SS-19 missile was bigger than the SS-18 because it had a higher number. On one occasion, Reagan expressed disbelief that once launched, an Intercontinental Ballistic Missile (ICBM) could not return to base. Early in the administration, Reagan's NSC advisors discovered his lack of knowledge and began relying on public consumption, government-made instructional films to educate him. Often he would simply ask during national security meetings, "What do I have to say?"

Despite his lack of knowledge, Reagan and his advisors clearly articulated a popular message strongly rooted in the anticommunism crusade of the postwar era. During the campaign, he explained foreign problems within a prism remarkably similar to that of the 1940s and 1950s. "Let's not delude ourselves," he told an audience in the 1980 campaign, "the Soviet Union underlies all the unrest that is going on. If they weren't engaged in this game of dominoes, there wouldn't be any hot spots in the world." He informed a fundamentalist minister that the U.S.S.R. was "the evil empire" and later told the British Parliament that "Marxism-Leninism" would end in "the ash heap of history." Additionally, he called on his fellow Americans to stand proud of their nation despite the painful lessons learned in Vietnam and urged a vigorous protection of national interests. This included a massive military buildup and, if necessary, the use of force.

Once in power, Reagan and his advisors indeed signaled a change in U.S. policy toward the non-industrialized world, including Latin America. First, they rejected Carter's human-rights policy. In 1981, Reagan appointed Ernest Lefever as the chief human-rights official in the State Department. Lefever had written that "we cannot export human rights . . . in dealing with Third World countries, their foreign policy behavior should be the determining factor, not their domestic policies." To reinforce this trend, Reagan selected Jeane Kirkpatrick as U.S. Ambassador to the United Nations. During the 1980 election, she had attacked Carter for assisting "the coming to power of new regimes in which ordinary people enjoy fewer freedoms and less personal security than under the previous autocratic regimes, moreover, hostile to American interests and policies." She argued that Washington needed to distinguish between totalitarian regimes like the Soviet Union and pro-American authoritarian governments (such as those of Somoza in Nicaragua and the Shah of Iran), proposing that the latter eventually could make the transition to democracy. Reagan heartily adopted this idea and incorporated it into his foreign policy.

The Sandinista Challenge

Once in office, Reagan immediately focused on Central America and the Caribbean. During the presidential campaign, he had said that the Caribbean was "rapidly becoming a Communist lake in what should be an American lake." Now, several in the administration warned of a "Moscow-Havana" axis spreading the Communist virus, with Kirkpatrick identifying Cuba as "the most important place in the world for us." U.S. national security depended on maintaining Latin American trade routes and protecting the Panama Canal. This required Washington to meet the Soviet challenge without "having to devote the lion's share of our attention and our resources to the defense of ourselves in our hemisphere."

From the start, the Reagan administration focused on the conflict in Nicaragua. The 1980 Republican platform assailed the Sandinistas, calling them a "Marxist" movement, and promised to "support the efforts of the Nicaraguan people to establish a free and independent government." Reagan added that the Sandinistas were a "Soviet ally on the American mainland" and cautioned that Harlingen, Texas, was only a six-day trip by car from Managua. According to Reagan's secretary of state, Alexander Haig, the Soviets had a "hit list" of states in Central America headed by Nicaragua. As political scientist William LeoGrande comments, the White House believed: "A victory in Central America would be Reagan's first foreign policy success and its ramifications would be global. By defeating the Soviet challenge in Central America, the United States would demonstrate to the Kremlin and its Cuban proxies that the new president would not tolerate Soviet adventurism in the Third World. Such firmness would reduce the likelihood of Soviet troublemaking elsewhere."

To combat the perceived Communist menace, Reagan chose covert operations. Several advisors, including Assistant Secretary of State for Inter-American Affairs Thomas Enders, had helped conduct Nixon's secret bombing campaign in Cambodia during the Vietnam War. In November 1981, Reagan approved National Security Decision Directive 17 (NSDD 17) which increased aid to a small army of anti-Sandinista guerrillas (originally funded by the Carter administration) and built on an Argentine military operation already in place. The group, which became known as the Contras, would work out of bases in neighboring Honduras to harass the Sandinistas and interdict arms transfers to the FMLN in El Salvador. Initially, both Reagan and Haig wanted a larger force, but several advisors with experience in covert military activities pushed for limited operations to avoid congressional and media scrutiny.[1]

By early 1982, the CIA had received nearly $20 million to arm and train approximately 500 Contras. While a few White House staff members worried about former National Guard members joining the force and undermining the legitimacy of the movement, the administration decided to let the Argentines run the show. The Argentines showed no concern about who fought, despite warning signs. One former Guardsman observed as he fled in 1979: "there is no way we can defend ourselves against the people. It's not the guerrillas I'm afraid of but the people. I know they hate us and they could overwhelm us." No matter, Somoza's cronies flocked to the Contras and assumed high military positions.

With NSDD 17, a new war began. The Nicaraguan Minister of Agrarian Reform Jaime Wheelock defiantly declared that "Nicaragua has been an appendage of the United States. . . . Our function was to grow sugar, cocoa, and coffee for the United States; we served the dessert at the imperialist dinner table. . . . We have to be against the United States in order to reaffirm ourselves as a nation." To win mass support, the Sandinistas increased land reform, further alienating elites and confirming Washington's suspicions of Communist influence. When the Contra attacks increased, the Sandinistas turned to the Soviets, Cubans, and sympathetic Western European nations to build up their military. As in Cuba in 1960, U.S. policy helped ensure the leftward turn of the revolution in El Salvador.

Keeping a Domino Standing

While the president and his advisors concentrated much energy on Nicaragua, during the first two years of the Reagan administration, El Salvador

---

1 Reagan's chief of staff, James Baker, emphasized that "if we give Al Haig his way, the next thing you know, we'll be carpet-bombing Central America."

was their primary focus, as it supported the military junta aligned with the oligarchy. "It is time the people of the United States realize that under the domino theory, we're the last domino," Reagan told one crowd. Haig warned NATO officials that "a well-orchestrated Communist campaign designed to transform the Salvador crisis from the internal conflict to an increasingly internationalized confrontation is underway." The White House believed that Nicaragua had been lost (momentarily at least) and instead concentrated on containing the Communist contagion in the smallest republic in Central America.

In the process of formulating their containment policy, the administration officials showed little concern for human-rights abuses in El Salvador. As an example, when analyzing the murder of nuns in 1979, Kirkpatrick observed that "the nuns were not just nuns, but political activists" for the FMLN. Haig called the group "pistol-packing nuns" and speculated that "perhaps the vehicle the nuns were riding in may have tried to run a roadblock."

As the conflict raged, the Reagan administration made a significant commitment to the Salvadoran government. In February 1981, it published a "White Paper" that detailed Soviet and Cuban involvement in El Salvador. Soon, the White House approved $25 million in military aid, the majority of which came from special presidential discretionary funds that allowed the appropriation to circumvent congressional oversight. Furthermore, the administration increased the number of military advisors in El Salvador from twenty-eight to fifty-four. In early March, Reagan approved an additional $19.5 million for the CIA to develop new operations to assist the Salvadoran government. Missing was an emphasis on reform, but Reagan argued that "you do not try to fight a civil war and institute reforms at the same time. Get rid of the war. Then go forward with reforms."

Immediately, the administration's policies sparked a controversy. Members of the press dissected fallacies within the White Paper and raised questions about the internal sources of the insurgency, not Moscow's interference. Many people remembered the road to the Vietnam War and warned that Reagan's policies would lead the nation right back into another nation's civil war. Congressional representatives led by Senator Christopher Dodd (D-CT) and Representatives Steve Solarz (D-NY) and Michael Barnes (D-MD) fought to limit and restrict military and economic assistance to the Salvadoran government. Representative Clarence Long (D-MD) called Reagan's policies "gunboat diplomacy all over again," adding, "I wish to God presidents would read a few books. If Johnson had read some, we wouldn't have been in Vietnam. If Reagan would read some, we wouldn't be here now." The battles were fierce and often decided by moderates who straddled the fence, allowing weak legislation that created many loopholes. Still, the battle lines had been drawn, and El Salvador remained a contentious issue.

A Free Market Miracle: The CBI?

The Reagan administration concentrated on military solutions, principally in Nicaragua and El Salvador. However, U.S. officials also developed an economic component to their Latin American policy that became known as the Caribbean Basin Initiative (CBI). Throughout the 1970s, the prices of petroleum and finished goods from the United States, Western Europe, and Japan had risen while payments the Caribbeans received for their exported products had plummeted. Unemployment and inflation skyrocketed, severely straining the limited social and economic welfare systems of the area.

To solve the problem, Reagan encouraged Caribbeans "to make use of the magic of the marketplace." The administration seized on an idea of Jamaican Prime Minister Edward Seaga, who called for a one-way free trade program on selected regional goods. Believing economic downturns in Latin America aided the Communist cause, the White House requested duty-free status for various Caribbean goods as well as developmental loans to the basin. The president won some victories, as several countries gained some ground by exporting fruits and flowers. Over time, however, U.S. labor and business groups torpedoed the stepped-up efforts, especially on products that competed with American-made goods.

Despite the CBI, the gross domestic product of Latin America and the Caribbean Basin declined by 8.3 percent during the Reagan years. Cuts in sugar quotas and higher import tariffs further reduced the productivity of the region. By 1986, U.S. imports from CBI countries sank by 23 percent, even as U.S. imports from other regions increased significantly. Efforts to use free-market capitalism to reform economies had failed miserably because of a basic failure to recognize the extent of the underdevelopment of the region.

A Ticking Time-Bomb: The Debt Crisis

Equally as important as the CBI were the stopgap measures designed to prevent an economic meltdown in many Latin American countries. A pressing problem arose concerning debt payments by Mexico, Venezuela, Brazil, and several other nations in the early 1980s. In Mexico's case, politicians had lavishly spent huge oil revenues on public works projects, to subsidize wages, and to prop up the prices of agricultural products. Graft and corruption also siphoned off huge amounts of monies as the country rode the wave of petrodollars throughout the 1970s.

In the early 1980s, the price of oil bottomed out due to overproduction. As oil revenue dried up, the Mexican government of José López Portillo devalued the peso by 100 percent in 1982. Capital flight followed, and the standard of living of most Mexicans declined. Then, in 1982, Mexico City told Washington that it could no longer service its $83 billion debt. Initially, the Reagan administration was slow to respond, remaining firmly dedicated to the free-enterprise model. Yet when it became apparent that private U.S. banks might collapse if Mexico defaulted on the loans, the White House acted. The Federal Reserve and the IMF provided additional funds to Mexico and restructured the debt. Mexico's economy stabilized momentarily.

Nevertheless, as Dirk Raat observes, "the price of the bailout was high." Mexico agreed to provide the United States with the majority of its oil and natural gas at favorable prices. In political terms, the deal provided the Reagan administration a way to pressure the Mexicans to support U.S. policy in Central America. Before the bailout, President López Portillo (1976–82) had promised to strengthen "links of friendship and cooperation that bind us [Mexico] with the revolutions of Cuba and Nicaragua" and recognized the FMLN as a "representative political force." Yet, when the Harvard-educated Miguel de la Madrid took over from López Portillo in 1982, he moved much slower through the Contadora group, (Mexico, Venezuela, Colombia, and Panama) rather than unilateral efforts to affect events in Central America. The Contadora group, named for the island on which they originally formed, was organized to promote stability in Latin America and also to push economic issues.

Trouble between Allies

In 1982, the Reagan administration encountered challenges in Latin America besides the Mexican debt issue and revolutions in Central America. Foremost, a brewing problem between Argentina and Great Britain exploded into war over the Falklands/Malvinas Islands. It forced Washington to choose sides between two anti-Communist allies and reassess the applicability of the Monroe Doctrine.

In the first year of the Reagan presidency, Washington restored close ties with the Argentines, for the administration appreciated their assistance with the Contras in Central America. On the other side, the Argentine government liked the fact that the Reagan administration had shunted aside human rights and reestablished better relations. But Washington also enjoyed good relations with London, and Prime Minister Margaret Thatcher and President Reagan shared many ideals. The historic ties between the United States and Great Britain remained strong, so the dispute between Argentina and Great Britain put Reagan between a rock and a hard place.

In 1981, the ruling junta in Argentina faced significant economic and political difficulties. They wanted to divert attention from their economic crisis and build national pride. Since the 1830s, the problem of the Falkland/Malvinas had festered and the military thought they had a wonderful issue regarding national sovereignty. The junta concluded that the British lacked the resolve to defend islands 8,000 miles away, home to only 1,800 British subjects. Furthermore, they believed that the United States (based on assurances from several U.S. officials) would support Buenos Aires in return for cooperation with its policies in Central America, that other European nations would remain neutral in the dispute and, if anything, pressure London to recognize Argentina's claim. Finally, Argentina thought other Latin American nations would rally to their cause and provide needed support in international and regional organizations.

Where Have You Gone James Monroe?

With much fanfare, Argentina easily seized the Falklands in early April 1982, defeating a small marine detachment. Its citizens flooded the streets to support the government. The same happened in Great Britain following Prime Minister Thatcher's promise to retake the islands. Caught in between the warring parties, Washington denounced the use of force and called for a cease-fire. Once that appeared unlikely, Secretary of State Haig shuttled for eleven days between Washington, London, and Buenos Aires attempting to fashion a truce. The Argentines remained steadfast, believing that the British could not dislodge them.

The problem became more complex when Argentina went to the OAS and invoked Article 6 of the Rio Treaty calling for hemispheric defense against foreign aggression. Washington disagreed, arguing that the issue should remain in the UN. Nevertheless, the members of the OAS Permanent Council voted 17–0, with the United States abstaining, to support Argentina's claims to the islands. In opposition to U.S. proposals, the OAS called for a cease-fire and negotiations without Argentine withdrawal from the Falklands.

With the United States rebuffed by the other OAS members, President Reagan openly supported the British. On April 30, Washington imposed economic sanctions on Buenos Aires for its aggression in the matter. U.S. military satellites began providing intelligence information to the British, and the United States allowed the British military to use U.S. bases in the Ascension Islands as a staging area. Argentine Foreign Minister Nicanor Costa Mendez bitterly complained. "The Argentine people will never understand or forget that at one of the most critical moments in their history, in contrast to the solidarity that they received from all corners of the hemisphere, the United States preferred to take the side of an extra-hemispheric power."

From the beginning in 1982, the war went badly for the Argentines. A British submarine sank the cruiser *General Belgrano* with heavy losses. Despite scoring some successes against British destroyers with air-to-ship Exocet missiles, the Argentines soon found themselves surrounded on the island by British troops who landed there. After three weeks of fighting in late May and early June, the Argentines surrendered. Soon thereafter, the Argentine junta collapsed, and the new regime announced a transition to civilian rule by 1984. In this light, the war had a positive result.

Nevertheless, the U.S. decision to support London left a bad taste in the mouths of many Latin Americans. Denunciations arose from many quarters. An Argentine-trained leader of the Honduran forces, General Gustavo Álvarez, asked U.S. ambassador John Negroponte: "Where is the Monroe Doctrine? Look at the geography. Is South America part of Europe? Who is the next one you betray?" When Negroponte responded that the United States could not tolerate the use of force, the Honduran reminded him that "one hundred years ago, England used force to take the island."

Americans also attacked Reagan's position. Scholar Robert Leiken told a congressional committee that the United States had abdicated its responsibilities under the Rio Treaty. He added that it was "a betrayal of the spirit of

American unity. . . . And the anger focused on and felt toward the United States, as a hemispheric country, as the promoter of the Monroe Doctrine . . . was infinitely greater than the feelings of antagonism toward England."

A Response to Disasters

While the United States had cooperated with the British in the Falkland War, some friction developed over the former British colonies in the Caribbean. From the moment it took office, the Reagan administration carefully watched leftist movements in Guyana, Grenada, and Suriname (a former Dutch colony). Regarding the latter, the United States urged the Netherlands to depose Lieutenant Colonel Desi Bouterse. The new secretary of state, George Schultz, who took over the position in 1982, had warned that Desi Bouterse "was taking Suriname on a forced march toward Cuba-style Communism." The CIA even proposed hiring a Korean hit squad to assassinate him, but Schultz rejected the idea.

The focal point of U.S. attention during the early 1980s ultimately became Grenada, a small island state of 100,000 people north of Trinidad. In 1979, Grenada's New Jewel Movement overthrew strongman Eric Gairy, a brutal politician who murdered members of the opposition, regularly claimed his own divinity, and lectured the UN on the dangers of UFOs. Prime Minister Maurice Bishop and Deputy Prime Minister Bernard Coard, a self-proclaimed Marxist, led the new government. Bishop and Coard established ties with Cuba and the Soviet Union, leading the Carter administration to withhold assistance to and break relations with Grenada (although no U.S. diplomats had resided there beforehand). When Bishop visited the U.S.S.R. in 1982 and declared that Grenada had joined the international effort to spread communism, Reagan responded: "that country bears the Soviet and Cuban trademark, which means that it will attempt to spread the virus among its neighbors."

The Reagan administration closely monitored Grenada throughout 1983. The construction of a new airport at Point Salines caused concern. When shown aerial photographs of the airport construction site in March 1983, Reagan quipped "Grenada doesn't even have an air force. Who is it intended for?" He answered the Soviets, and warned that the implication threatened "our international commerce and military lines of communication." The British builders of the airport strongly denied the charge, arguing that the facility was intended to boost tourism. The Reagan administration remained skeptical, especially since a Cuban work brigade was present.

TO THE END OF THE COLD WAR

In October 1983, Washington found an excuse for intervention. Coard overthrew Bishop, later killing him and declaring a state of emergency. With the next presidential election less than a year away, a recession plaguing the United States, 241 U.S. Marines having recently died in Beirut, Lebanon, (victims of a suicide bombing attack on October 24), the White House needed an immediate diversion. On October 25, 1,900 U.S. Marines waded ashore onto Grenada as part of Operation "Urgent Fury" to protect American medical students on the island as well as Grenada's neighbors, although Reagan's press secretary Larry Speakes later emphasized that neither rationale really affected the decision to strike.

For six days, fighting occurred as 4,000 more U.S. troops landed to defeat the Grenadian and Cuban resistance. The $75.5 million operation left 18 Americans dead and 116 wounded, as well as 24 Cubans dead and 59 wounded, and an additional 45 Grenadians dead and 337 wounded. The United States expelled all Eastern Bloc persons and Cubans from the island, deposed Coard, and established a pro-U.S. government.

While the invasion sparked widespread condemnation in the international community, the "rescue" of Grenada literally played well on television, with Reagan claiming he had stood tough against communism to the cheers of conservative Americans. The UN Security Council voted 11–1 (Great Britain, Togo, and Zaire abstained) to condemn the unilateral action, but the United States vetoed the condemnation. International opinion hardly mattered to Reagan, who wrote "I probably never felt better during my presidency than I did that day." Schultz described Grenada as the "shot heard round the world. . . . Some Western democracies were again ready to use the military strength they had harbored and built up over the years in defense of their principles and interests." Another person concluded that the United States had "won one for a change."

The victory in Grenada clearly had little to do with protecting the lives of Americans and more to do with helping Americans feel good about themselves and diverting attention from the horrible deaths in the Middle East. After the so-called victory, the United States created a pro-U.S., anti-Communist government in Grenada that proceeded to pull in $110 million in U.S. monies over the following five years. At the end of the Reagan administration, Grenada remained mired in depression and high unemployment. Meanwhile, many worried that the taking of Grenada merely served as a staging ground for the invasion of Nicaragua or the deployment of ground troops in El Salvador.

On the Road to Managua

While the action in Grenada heightened Reagan's popularity, he soon faced serious challenges to his other Latin American policies. The situation in El Salvador continued deteriorating, even after Duarte's election in 1982. Nevertheless, the issue faded into the background, as the White House made defeating the Sandinistas a priority. As hardliners in both countries increasingly controlled policy, direct conflict appeared likely.

Since 1982, the Reagan administration had increased assistance to the Contras. The U.S.-backed Contra force grew to an estimated 4,000 men. The Contras attacked Sandinista targets as well as schools and hospitals in villages sympathetic to the Sandinistas. The leader of the Nicaraguan Democratic Front (FDN—the military arm of the Contras) was former National Guard leader and military attaché to Washington, Enrique Bermúdez. He declared that "we are Nicaraguans and our objective is to overthrow the Communists and install a democratic government in Nicaragua." A congressional outcry arose, led by Congressman Tom Harkin (D-IA) who called the Contras "vicious cutthroat murderers . . . remnants of the evil, murderous National Guard. In the name of all that is right and decent, we should end our involvement with this group."

Congress ultimately placed some restrictions on aid to the Contras in the 1983 appropriations bill, although it fell short of terminating aid to the group, as Harkin wanted. Edward Boland (D-MA), chairman of the House Intelligence Committee, offered a substitute. The first "Boland amendment" to the appropriation bill prohibited the CIA and Defense Department from using funds to overthrow the Sandinistas or promote conflict between Nicaragua and its neighbors, but it permitted continued efforts to interdict the flow of arms to El Salvador. Reagan quickly signed the appropriations bill and promised that "we are complying with the law." In the meantime, a 1982 CIA planning memo predicted the fall of the Sandinista government in Managua by Christmas 1983.

The Challenge from Below

While discontent and skepticism over U.S. policy toward Nicaragua preoccupied Congress and many Americans, a more imposing threat evolved to challenge Reagan's efforts to overthrow the Sandinistas. In January 1983, diplomats from Panama, Mexico, Venezuela, and Colombia met on Contadora, an island off the Panama coast, to discuss Central American issues. Ultimately, they agreed to a twenty-one-point proposal calling for the demilitarization of Central America, the complete withdrawal of foreign advisers, and democratization.

Within the Reagan administration, a mixed response followed. Schultz called it a "breakthrough," although he expressed reservations about ensuring Sandinista compliance. A political moderate, the secretary of state preferred a diplomatic solution to problems in Nicaragua and worried that the policy of openly supporting the Contras damaged relations between the United States and other Latin American nations. On the other hand, conservative anti-Communists in the NSC and CIA denounced negotiations for legitimizing the Sandinistas. Much to their chagrin, the Sandinistas announced that they would sign the agreement and hold elections by 1985.

As historian Walter LaFeber acknowledges: "the United States set out to destroy the Contadora agreement." To poison Contadora efforts, the administration agreed to bilateral discussions with the Sandinistas in Manzanillo, Mexico. There, U.S. officials demanded immediate expulsion of Soviet and Cuban advisors from Nicaragua and a significant reduction of the Sandinista army. In return, Washington promised nothing. The talks ended with no solution, allowing the Reagan administration to blame the Sandinistas for the impasse. To undermine the Contadora plan further, the administration pressured its Central American allies to reject outside mediation. By 1985, Mexico and Venezuela had pulled back from pan regional efforts to focus primarily on domestic economic difficulties caused by the fall of the price of oil.

The Domestic Opposition Heats Up

President Reagan's continued efforts to undermine the negotiations between the various warring factions and build up the Contras, a group he characterized to the press as "freedom fighters" and "the moral equivalent of the founding fathers," only increased domestic opposition. To win support for his policies, he helped organize a bipartisan commission headed by Henry Kissinger to investigate the region. Instead of presenting anything new, the Kissinger Commission merely validated Reagan's anti-Communist policies, although it called for more economic assistance to undermine Communist appeals.

Unlike domestic protest against U.S. involvement in Vietnam, significant opposition having taken many years to develop, U.S. peace groups
mobilized quickly against Reagan's Central American policies. Prominent
members of the American Catholic Church led the charge. Strongly influenced by liberation theology and disgusted with the atrocities committed
by U.S. surrogates, some Catholics spoke out against the Contras and continued U.S. aid and assistance to the Central American militaries. Despite
pressure from virulently anti-Communist Pope John Paul II, who opposed
the Sandinistas, prominent American Catholics marched, wrote letters,
made speeches and sermons, and engaged in other activities opposed to
the Reagan administration.

Other Christian and secular groups joined the Catholics in strong
opposition to Reagan's Central American policies. They included the Sanctuary Movement, Witness for Peace, the Committee in Solidarity with the
People of El Salvador (CISPES), and organizations such as Amnesty International, the Americas Watch, and the North American Congress on Latin
America (NACLA). Sociologist Christian Smith correctly notes, "the U.S.
Central America peace movement was not a unified, monolithic entity."

Despite shared goals, the groups often differed on tactics and emphasis.
Some members lobbied Congress while others published books and articles
outlining the fallacies and hypocrisy of the Reagan administration's positions.
Many practiced civil disobedience by helping Central American political
refugees seek asylum in the United States or by picketing outside the White
House. In one act, more than 60,000 Americans signed a pledge to disrupt
government operations should the United States attack Nicaragua. While
still a minority in U.S. society, these groups remained a constant source of
irritation to Reagan and his advisors, and they consistently presented an
alternative view for public consumption through the media.

Hollywood Versus the Son of Hollywood

One of the most ironic hotbeds of protest against Reagan's Central American policies proved to be Hollywood, as the actor-turned-president faced
much criticism from his former colleagues. Some of the feature-length
releases of the 1980s focused on Central America, including *Under Fire*
(1983), *Salvador* (1986) (nominated for an Academy Award for best screen-
play), *Walker* (1987), and *Romero* (1989) (sponsored by the Catholic
Church). Well-known directors including Roger Spottiswoode, Alex Cox,

John Duigan, and Oliver Stone led the productions, and actors including Nick Nolte, Gene Hackman, Joanna Cassidy, James Woods, Ed Harris, and Raul Julia played parts, usually at reduced salaries.

Each film criticized fundamental ideas regarding past and contemporary U.S. intervention in Central America, particularly by anti-Communist American zealots. In a 1987 interview, Cox emphasized that "Walker was quite mad, but his attitude is totally contemporary. His madness is the madness of Oliver North or Elliot Abrams . . . white guys coming down to small countries thinking they can do anything." While none of the films were blockbusters or received major distribution—with the exception of *Salvador,* which won more attention on video after Stone won an Academy Award for *Platoon*—they challenged many people's opinion of U.S. policy in Latin America and validated the convictions of those already opposed to the policy.

In other ways, popular culture lampooned Reagan's policies. In particular, rock-and-roll musicians lined up against the president. During the 1980s, musicians became politically active, criticizing many Reagan policies regarding apartheid in South Africa, apathy in the face of the spread of AIDS, homelessness, hunger, and intervention in Central America. These activists included megastars such as U-2, Don Henley, and Jackson Browne. U-2 produced songs on its popular album *The Joshua Tree* (1987) including "Bullet in Blue Sky" that condemned an attack on El Salvadoran peasants with bullets supplied by the United States. The band's interviews and concerts focused on such issues, and it rallied people to join organizations such as Amnesty International. Henley sang songs like "All She Wants to Do Is Dance," from the album *Building the Perfect Beast* (1985), which ridiculed American attitudes toward Central Americans. He even developed a music video (a rapidly expanding new medium at the time) that further reinforced the song's ideas. Finally, Browne's album *Lives in the Balance* (1986) denounced Reagan's policy. The title song and music video made significant connections between the quagmire in Vietnam and the potential to repeat the same policies in Central America. Interestingly, the Democrats featured Browne's video on the large screen behind the speakers' podium at their 1988 national convention immediately preceding Michael Dukakis's acceptance speech.

While the exact amount of influence the performers had on the American public is difficult to ascertain, the protest movements certainly garnered attention from the White House, which used the FBI to monitor its opponents. From 1981 to 1988, the FBI investigated more than 13,000 people and 11,000 organizations including nuns, labor union organizers, and college students. Reagan administration officials also employed the Internal Revenue Service (IRS) to harass NACLA and others. In 1988, FBI director William Sessions apologized and temporarily suspended three workers for their roles in illegal wiretapping and searches.

The administration also focused its harassment on cooperative ventures between U.S. and Central American peace groups. It used the Immigration and Naturalization Service (INS) to prevent perceived enemies from entering the United States to receive human-rights awards. This included barring human-rights workers associated with CO-MADRES (Committee of Mothers and Relatives of Political Prisoners Disappeared or Murdered in El Salvador) from receiving the first Robert Kennedy Human Rights Award. The State Department claimed the organization advocated violence, but provided no evidence of it. Interestingly enough, the State Department had no qualms about granting an entrance visa to Roberto D'Aubuisson, leader of the right-wing forces in El Salvador.

A Clash of Wills

As thousands died in Central American civil wars, domestic and international groups pressed Reagan to reformulate U.S. policy. Soon, Congress tried reigning in the CIA and the Defense Department. Revelations that the CIA had helped mine Nicaraguan harbors in clear violation of international law and provided pamphlets that included sections on torture helped liberals in Congress move to restrict aid to the Contras.

The charge this time to limit Contra aid was led by Boland and Clement J. Zablocki (D-WI), chairman of the House Foreign Affairs Committee. While Boland originally was a foreign policy traditionalist willing to follow the president's lead, his position had changed since the first Boland Amendment (Boland I) as the lies and misrepresentations heightened suspicions. The resulting H.R. Bill 2760 (named Boland II) would end funding "for the purpose or which would have the effect of supporting, directly or indirectly, military or paramilitary operations in Nicaragua by any nation, group, organization, movement, or individual." While the bill permitted continued aid to the Contras, no longer could any such shipments include lethal weapons. Consequently, the amendment posed a significant threat to the Reagan administration's policies.

The debate on the amendment created a firestorm. Reagan called the Boland-Zablocki bill "irresponsible," and conservatives in Congress and the press encouraged the president simply to ignore it, arguing that it infringed on his constitutional powers. On the other side, the *New York Times* depicted arming the Contras as mocking "the very principle of non-intervention that the president invokes against Managua and Havana." The *Miami Herald* added that the Contra war was "un-American" and "differs not one whit in principle from what the Soviet Union did when it invaded Afghanistan."

The Reagan administration added fuel to the fire in mid-1983 when it initiated Big Pine II, a six-month military operation involving more than 5,000 U.S. troops, two aircraft-carrier task forces, and the battleship *New Jersey.* Working off the coast of Central America and in Honduras, the troops made mock amphibious attacks while jets swooped overhead providing mock air support. After six months of reassuring allies and attempting to "intimidate" the Sandinistas (according to one Defense Department official, "we're playing a little cat-and-mouse game with them, putting a little squeeze on, making them wonder what's going to happen next") the armed forces withdrew, although they managed to leave behind supplies that evaded congressional oversight. Speaker of the House Tip O'Neill, typically a moderate on foreign policy, condemned the action and observed that Reagan "thinks he's John Wayne. He thinks he can go down there and clean the place out."

By the summer of 1983, Congress was hotly debating the Boland-Zablocki bill, with Boland arguing: "this secret war is bad U.S. policy because it does not work, because it is in fact counterproductive, because it is illegal." The pro-Contra Republicans denounced the bill as aiding the Communists. Newt Gingrich (R-GA) argued that the issue drew the line "between radicals who want unilateral disarmament [of the Contras] and the rest of us." He added that many Democrats believed that "the CIA is more dangerous than the KGB." Ultimately, the House approved the bill 228–195. In the conference meetings, Boland held firm and in October 1984, both houses accepted his bill. The stage for conflict with the White House was set.

Just Say No

While the Contra debate continued, the United States faced other problems in Latin America. Since taking office, the Reagan administration had declared a "war on drugs" and developed education programs based on a "Just Say No" to drugs campaign. The White House pushed for more DEA funding and stiffer penalties for traffickers and users. In response, drug lords in Colombia, Mexico, Peru, and other countries merely intensified their distribution efforts, and the demand for illegal narcotics in the United States remained high. Nevertheless, U.S. efforts to push foreign governments to cooperate with its campaign against drugs met with some successes.

In 1985, a major confrontation developed between the United States and Mexico. Since the early 1980s, Mexico had served as the major pipeline of illegal drugs into the United States, as the DEA had increased its surveillance on Miami and the Caribbean. With Mexican cooperation, the DEA subsequently launched a large undercover operation. In 1985, drug dealers tortured and murdered DEA agent Enrique Camarena. As the Mexican investigation into the murder of Camarena plodded along, the Reagan administration fumed. The U.S. customs director in Mexico, William von Raab, stressed that "the drug situation is a horror history, increasing logarithmically, and Mexico is doing nothing about it." He called Mexican officials "inept and corrupt" and reported that the administration shared his beliefs.

For three years, bashing the Mexicans' antidrug efforts became political sport in Washington. Despite the arrest and prosecution of many drug traffickers by Mexican authorities, including that of Rafael Caro Quintero for the Camarena murder, the White House and Congress continually characterized Mexico City's efforts to slow the drug trade as lukewarm. Threats of refusing to certify Mexico's efforts to combat the problem (thereby denying funding for continued operations) and possible implementation of economic sanctions against Mexico followed. In April 1988, the Senate censured Mexico for its laxness regarding drug trafficking. Mexican officials immediately complained that "no one can take upon themselves the right to certify the conduct of other societies or governments." Another former Mexican advisor on drugs policy, Samuel I. del Villar, wrote that "the 50 million or so American regular drug consumers whose free choice is in fact the real enemy of the war on drugs because they think differently from a transitory majority in the Congress of the United States . . . its [U.S. government] war on drugs was lost from the beginning."

The drug issue remained contentious. During the 1980s, U.S. prisons filled with drug users. Nevertheless, the demand for drugs remained high and the use of cheaper, more addictive drugs, including crack cocaine (distributed in part by a network developed by Contra members to fund their movement and fill their own pockets) reached epidemic proportions. Naturally, an accompanying rise in violent drug-related crime followed. Reagan and his advisors, like their predecessors, won few victories in the "war" on drugs, but in the meantime they further alienated Latin Americans.

The Porous Border

Another perplexing problem remained illegal immigration into the United States. After the passage of the 1965 Immigration and Nationality Act, the issue became more volatile, especially in regard to Mexico. The rate of immigration from Latin America to the United States accelerated in the 1980s, with Mexico's economic decline and the Central American civil wars decided push factors. Millions of undocumented laborers streamed into the United States.

Loud protests over illegal immigration arose in the 1980s from disparate U.S. groups. Racist organizations such as the Ku Klux Klan characterized illegal immigrants as lazy persons coming to the United States to steal jobs from whites and live on welfare; the KKK even offered its services in

Editorial cartoon capturing the resurgence of anti-immigration sentiments in August 1993. *Steve Benson, reprinted by permission of United Feature Syndicate, Inc.*

patrolling the Rio Grande. Others complained that the new immigrants stretched social services of schools and hospitals. Even Chicano civil rights icon César Chavez denounced illegal aliens for undermining attempts to unionize and secure decent wages for U.S. citizens.

Despite the protests, U.S. agencies could not stem the flow of the illegal aliens. Employers in the United States, especially in the agricultural, textile, and service industries, welcomed illegal immigrants because they typically worked for less pay and fewer benefits. The U.S. border with Mexico stretches thousands of miles, and monitoring it fully has never been possible. And even when the Border Patrol agents managed to capture illegal immigrants and returned them to Mexico, they soon crossed in again. As long as jobs existed, so would the efforts of Mexicans and Central Americans to reach the United States.

At the same time, Mexico City made few attempts to stop the flow, the economic downturn and the traditional role of the United States as providing a safety valve to Mexico's burgeoning population providing Mexican officials few incentives to try to do so. In addition, those who went to the United States to work sent a good deal of money home to family members in Mexico, thereby providing the country with much needed capital.

Clamping Down

Under pressure from their constituents, congressional conservatives including Romano Mazzoli (D-KY) and Senator Alan Simpson (R-WY) tried to tighten immigration laws. After several failed attempts and many debates and compromises reflective of the complexities of the issue, the Simpson-Mazzoli Act passed in 1986. The new law allowed for amnesty for undocumented laborers having entered the United States before January 1, 1977, with temporary status granted to those having arrived between that date and January 1, 1980. It imposed fines on employers of undocumented workers, with criminal penalties for habitual violators. Finally, it increased funding and staffing of the INS.

While the Simpson-Mazzoli Act tried new methods to limit immigration, it had limited success. Business owners and farmers in the Southwest continued to hire illegal immigrants, knowing that local authorities were likely to wink an eye at the practice. At the same time, federal officials lacked the ability to enforce existing statutes. The Act also failed to address the major push factors, especially Mexico's feeble economy and violent conflicts in Central America. In short, the United States continued to gain many Latinos.

The Imperial Presidency Falls Hard:
The Iran-Contra Scandal

While illegal drugs and immigration were important issues during the Reagan years, Central America stole the spotlight. The conflict between Congress and the president remained combative. In the final stages of the debate on Boland II, Boland himself warned: "As in Catch-22, if you are engaged in support of the Contras, you are involved in intelligence activities." Yet the administration dismissed Boland II as "partisan politics"; as one senior NSC official put it, "it requires no modification of our plans." Some argued that the NSC fell outside of the scope of the law, leading Vice President George Bush and others to push for "encouraging third parties to help" them continue to arm the Contras. In response, Secretary of State Schultz cautioned that doing so by circumventing Congress was possibly "an impeachable offense."

President Reagan with Caspar Weinberger, George Schultz, Ed Meese, and Donald Regan discussing the president's remarks on the Iran-Contra affair, November 25, 1986. *Courtesy Ronald Reagan Library*

Despite the warnings, Reagan and his advisors placed U.S. Marine colonel Oliver North in charge of raising private funds for the Contras. This heretofore obscure NSC official went about his duties zealously. North managed to pull in significant contributions from the foreign governments of Saudi Arabia ($32 million), the Sultan of Brunei ($10 million), and the World Anti-Communist League led by former U.S. Major General John Singlaub, as well as from celebrities including Pat Boone and Joseph Coors. When a congressional committee asked North about the nature of his activities, he denied having done any fundraising. Later, when Congress got wind of the scheme, investigators requested documents, but the administration invoked executive privilege.

The whole plot began to unravel in April 1986. Despite efforts to put a good face on the group by appointing civilian leaders, the Contras often proved more skilled at putting money in Miami banks than in fighting the Sandinistas. Desperate, North now devised a plan to funnel money to the Contras by using the profits from the secret sale of sophisticated military weaponry to Iran (with whom the United States had no official relations after 1979).

The plan immediately went awry. In October, the Sandinistas shot down a cargo plane—carrying arms purchased by the Contras with the proceeds of U.S. arms sales to Iran—en route to resupply the Contras and captured the pilot, Eugene Hasenfus, uncovering the U.S. role in the activity. Soon afterward, a Middle Eastern newspaper broke the story of an arms-for-hostage agreement between Reagan and the Iranians. The paper trail led to an account at a Swiss bank, where investigators discovered the diversion of cash to the Contras, a clear violation of the Boland Amendment.

A major constitutional crisis followed, one that helped destroy Reagan's Central American policy and severely damaged his presidency. During nationally televised congressional hearings in mid-1987, independent counsel Lawrence Walsh grilled administration members including North, NSC adviser John Poindexter, and Undersecretary of State Elliot Abrams. Before the hearings, Reagan fired North and tried to distance himself from the investigation, a process aided by the death of CIA director William Casey, the most likely direct link between the two men.

North made a huge splash during his testimony, appearing before Congress in full-dress marine uniform. Even in the face of charges that he shredded important documents, he was unrepentant, citing that he had been doing his duty. Soon thereafter, Poindexter, a man known for having a photographic memory, told the committee that "I don't recall" or "I don't remember" more than 180 times during his testimony and protected Reagan by rationalizing that he had kept the whole operation secret from the president because "I simply didn't want any outside interference." At the end of the investigation, a congressional committee concluded "enough is clear to demonstrate beyond doubt that fundamental processes of governance were disregarded and the rule of law was subverted."

The results of the Iran-Contra affair proved unfulfilling for many people. Walsh indicted Poindexter, North, Abrams, and others including Secretary of Defense Caspar Weinberger. He won convictions of North and Poindexter, who clearly had lied under oath, destroyed evidence, and conducted illegal activities. However, courts overturned the convictions on technicalities, and each man secured a presidential pardon. Others, such as Abrams, plea bargained and received light sentences.

Nevertheless, the Reagan administration had suffered a significant blow. Many believed the president lied about his knowledge of the affair. If not, they wondered how the president could have been so out of touch with the doings of his top officials. At the very least, Reagan appeared as a very poor leader. In the larger picture, Walter LaFeber observes that the scandal posed "a dangerous threat" to the country. "Unelected and unaccountable military officers in the NSC worked with key State Department personnel to defy U.S. laws. . . . They dragged the Constitution, U.S. policies in Central America, American reputations and credibility around the world through the mud."

The Mouse that Roared

While the Reagan administration's Central American policy self-destructed, people within the region rushed in to fill the vacuum. In the classic film, *The Mouse that Roared,* a small nation, through a comedy of errors, seizes a doomsday device and forces the United States and other superpowers to declare "peace forever." In 1987, a similar action on a smaller scale took place in Central America. A year earlier, Costa Ricans had elected Oscar Arias Sánchez as president. The erudite son of a wealthy family, Arias ran on a platform of promising to pursue peace in the face of U.S. pressures not to negotiate with the Sandinistas. Arias noted later that "We had to choose between rationality and madness."

When Arias took office, he immediately denounced Contra aid, the Sandinistas, and other warring powers and put forth a peace plan. It called for cease-fires, dialogues between the governments and "unarmed internal opposition," democratic elections, renewed respect for civil liberties, and the creation of commissions of national conciliation to monitor the peace process.

Hardliners in the United States, led by Poindexter and Abrams, denounced it. A former NSC member, Constantine Menges warned: "This is it! The Arias plan . . . is the instrument that will be used for this year's run at a false political statement. . . . Its fatal flaw is that it would have the Nicaraguan armed resistance dismantled today in return for Sandinista promises to have democratic elections in 1990." While moderates within the administration such as Schultz liked elements of the plan, they called for continued aid to Contras to pressure Sandinista compliance.

During internal debates, Reagan sided mostly with the hardliners who set out to undermine the Arias plan. CIA Director Casey flew to San José on a massive USAF Galaxy transport to put pressure on Arias. The Costa Rican refused to meet him at the airport and instead sent several aides, angering Casey who lingered on the tarmac. In response, U.S. hardliners punished Arias by reducing economic assistance and failing to support efforts to restructure Costa Rica's debt.

Arias remained undeterred. He made dramatic speeches at the UN and the European Community Parliament, winning support throughout the world. At the same time, he denied visas to Contra military leaders trying to meet in Costa Rica, closed down a secret hospital and airstrip in northern Costa Rica, and arrested Contras for violating Costa Rica's neutrality. He went on the offensive and succeeded in pushing his fellow Central Americans to agree to discuss his plan. Furthermore, he gained U.S. supporters, including Speaker of the House Jim Wright (D-TX).

Despite pressure from the White House to oppose the proposal, the five Central American nations signed the Arias plan in August 1987. Until that point, Reagan called it "fatally flawed," while Abrams complained that "Communists win these kinds of negotiations." Other conservatives attacked the plan. The *Wall Street Journal* called it "Reagan's Bay of Pigs" and the *Washington Times* warned it was a "peace proposal trap." Until the end, the administration tried to undermine the plan and develop alternatives. The president's special envoy Philip Habib resigned to protest orders that he not negotiate with the Sandinistas. Soon thereafter, the White House requested $270 million for the Contras.

Arias and his allies fought back. In September, he made a rousing speech in front of a joint session of Congress in which he begged: "Let us restore faith in dialogue and give peace a chance." Afterward, he criticized Reagan's request for additional aid to the Contras and contended that Nicaragua needed an opportunity "to comply with all the provisions of the Guatemalan accord [Arias's plan signed in Guatemala]."

Arias received a major boost when he received the Nobel Peace Prize. *Time* emphasized that "the [Nobel] prize both enhances the credibility of the fragile peace process and augments Arias' moral authority as an arbiter of peace . . . at the same time, it further impedes the Reagan Administration's attempts to secure $270 million in new aid for the Contra rebels." On the other side, one State Department official complained "he won the [Nobel] prize for defunding the Contras and taking an anti-American stance." One of Abrams's aides reported that "all of us . . . reacted with disgust, unbridled disgust."

For the remainder of his term, Reagan tried to maintain Contra forces as a viable alternative while pressuring allies to sabotage the peace plan. Nevertheless, the success of the Arias proposal combined with Reagan's loss of credibility from the fallout of Iran-Contra effectively stifled the president. Reagan's requests to Congress for additional assistance went unmet or came only in the form of nonlethal aid to resettle the rebels. The Arias plan proceeded, but with some glitches. As Arias and others recognized, they would not solve the problems overnight. As for Reagan and the conservatives, their time in Washington had neared its end and subsiding tensions in the Cold War, due largely to the rise of the reformer Mikhail Gorbachev in the Soviet Union, removed much of the rationale for intervention in Latin America in the name of fighting communism.

The Legacy of Reagan

During Reagan's two-term presidency, Central America had remained the focus of U.S.-Latin American relations. "The Reagan administration achieved none of its goals in Central America, though it mobilized vast resources and invested a great deal of political capital in pursuing them," historian John Coatsworth observes. "By the time Reagan left office in early 1989 the Sandinista government still ruled Nicaragua, the FMLN insurgents in El Salvador had developed into the most effective guerrilla army in the region's history, the Honduran government was actively seeking a graceful end to its role as the U.S. 'aircraft carrier' on the isthmus," he concludes. "A Costa Rican peace plan opposed by the United States had been signed by all the Central American governments and backed by the OAS and the United Nations," he adds, "Guatemala's first civilian president in 16 years was proving incapable of curbing the excesses of the country's military or ending the insurgency."

The Reagan administration's record in other areas of Latin America also appeared impotent. It had relied on "gunboat diplomacy" in Grenada, had developed selective amnesia in regard to the Monroe Doctrine during the Malvinas Crisis, and had ignored many of the brewing regional socioeconomic problems by emphasizing the free market model.

The new Republican president, George H. W. Bush, inherited many problems from his predecessor, including the issue of unpaid Latin American debts, a never-ending wave of immigration, trade disputes and imbalances, and the continued production, distribution, and demand for illegal drugs. As Bush moved into the White House, antipathy toward the United States was at its highest point in Latin America since the days of Woodrow Wilson. Bush received the task of trying to offset a great deal of ill will. Furthermore, he would need to search for a new model for U.S. relations with the region, as the downfall of the Soviet Union quickly changed the international political climate.

The New World Order

In 1988, George H. W. Bush won the presidency after eight years of having served in Reagan's shadow as his vice president. The Yale-educated son of a senator, Bush had significant political experience, especially in foreign policy. Prior to becoming vice president, he served as U.S. ambassador to the United Nations, director of the CIA, and U.S. representative to China. During the Reagan years, he helped formulate U.S. policy, although at times he remained out of the loop because he tended to be less ideologically conservative and aligned more with Schultz. As vice president, Bush traveled throughout Latin America and came to know the region well.

Bush brought a dramatically different style to the White House. "People say I'm indecisive. Well, I don't know about that," he once quipped. One British journalist observed of Bush "he's not an upfront guy. . . . He doesn't like to lead from the front." Others characterized him as "reactive, ad hoc, adaptable rather than ideologically zealous, conservative, eager to satisfy the right wing in the Republican party while still appealing to moderates, fearful of doing the wrong thing . . . a good manager who liked to deal with facts and not visions, a doer rather than an intellectual, Bush did not seem to think in the long term."

The new president selected a longtime friend, James Baker III, as his secretary of state. The former White House chief of staff and secretary of the treasury, Baker had little experience in foreign affairs but was a skilled politician who admitted being "more interested in the game than in philosophy." One White House official emphasized that Baker "is action-oriented—more so than Bush," adding that Baker "is decisive and no one second-guesses his sense of timing." One journalist commented that the new secretary of state "cultivates international figures and he cuts deals." In addition, Baker and Bush shared a "view of politics—domestic and international—as having very much to do with the art of massage." The new secretary of state and president clearly formed a new vision of U.S.-Latin American relations in 1989.

Peace at Last

One of the first areas on which Bush and Baker focused was Central America. Working with the new assistant secretary of state for inter-American affairs, Bernard Aronson, Baker tried to remove a thorn in America's side. In early 1989, the administration agreed that the Contras were a lost cause and that Washington should support diplomatic initiatives to reject what historian Gaddis Smith calls the "Reaganite obsession with Central America and ritualistic invocation of the principles of the Monroe Doctrine." This allowed the Bush administration to concentrate elsewhere, principally the deterioration of the Soviet Union.

In large part, Baker and Bush responded favorably to Arias's initiative in February 1989 when the Sandinistas agreed to reforms and to hold Nicaraguan elections in 1990. In return, its neighbors pushed to disband the Contras. In marked contrast to the days of Reagan, Baker supported the move. He gambled that the Sandinistas would lose the election if the military pressure dissolved. Simultaneously, Baker won assurances from Soviet leader Gorbachev to stop arms shipments to Managua and to press the Sandinistas to hold free elections in return for a U.S. agreement to end support of the Contras. As LaFeber notes of the Bush officials, "with Soviet help, they corrected one of Reagan's great foreign policy blunders."

The roll of the dice paid off. In the 1990 Nicaraguan elections, inept rule and a ruinous war doomed the Sandinistas and their leader, Daniel Ortega, who lost to the National Opposition Union (UNO) and its leader, Violeta Barrios de Chamorro, wife of a martyred hero. During the campaign, Chamorro received millions of dollars from the U.S. Congress' National Endowment for Democracy. A former member of the Sandinista junta, Chamorro blistered her opponents for Nicaragua's economic woes, corruption, and failed promises. She also received support because many Nicaraguans believed Washington would end its attacks if Ortega lost. All these factors played a significant role in her victory.

While many U.S. conservatives criticized Chamorro's failure to remove the Sandinistas from the military and unions, the transition of power went comparatively smoothly. Bush lifted economic sanctions against Nicaragua in March 1990, and Congress approved aid packages to that nation. Despite the end of its civil war, Nicaragua still faced substantial difficulties. The economy floundered despite new foreign aid and investment. Throughout the 1990s, Nicaragua remained one of the poorest countries in Latin America. The scars of the revolution and counter-revolution ran deep, and they set the country back many years, as poverty, illiteracy, unemployment, and lack of social services remained rampant.

A similar path toward peace took place in El Salvador. Many observers feared the worst when the right-wing ARENA candidate Alfredo Cristiani won the presidency in 1989. Soon thereafter, death squads murdered six Jesuit priests at the Central American University. The fighting between the FMLN and government intensified, as Washington had poured in massive assistance to prevent a collapse of the Cristiani government. Still, war weariness had set in. When a final rebel offensive fizzled, and the government could not effectively counterattack, both sides recognized the futility of continuing.

At that point, Cristiani and the FMLN went to the bargaining table. With much outside assistance, including that of the United States and Soviet Union, the two parties reached a compromise. In return for putting down their arms, the rebels received assurances of the removal of brutal military commanders and recognition of their groups and their demands. The United Nations, with unanimous support in the Security Council, sent a peacemaking force to El Salvador that ultimately numbered close to 1,000 troops. By December 1992, the different sides celebrated at a ceremony marking the formal end of the Civil War.

The dissolution of the Soviet Union and the end of its assistance removed a major obstacle. The Bush administration, tired of the distractions and wanting stability, also bowed out from actively interfering. While comparative peace existed, many problems remained. For example, the Civil War had devastated El Salvador. More than 75,000 persons had died and many more had fled to the United States or refugee camps. As LaFeber underscores, the country "had lost 94 percent of its original forests, 80 percent of its natural vegetation, 77 percent of its arable soil (due to erosion)." And these problems were not unique to El Salvador. For the moment, however, the exhausted parties laid down their arms and sought political means to settle differences.

Public Enemy #1

The Bush administration proved early on that it, like its predecessor, believed force should remain a viable form of diplomacy. During the 1988 campaign, Bush's opponents had characterized him as weak, leading journalists to coin the term "the wimp factor." In the same election, some observers criticized Bush's relationship with Panamanian president General Manuel Noriega during the 1980s when, while vice president, Bush had cozied up to Noriega to assure his cooperation with U.S. policy towards Nicaragua. Both of these factors converged quickly to help form U.S. policy toward Panama.

The U.S. problems with Panama started in the early 1980s following a mysterious plane crash that took the life of Panamanian President Torrijos in July 1981. Noriega seized the opportunity, using his Panamanian Defense Force (PDF) to take power. Once described as a "mean piece of work," Noriega was shrewd and ruthless. When North and Casey had gone shopping for allies against the Sandinistas, they found a willing partner in Noriega. The Panamanian leader (who received an annual retainer of $100,000 from the CIA) allowed the Contras to train in his country and provided hit squads for use against Sandinistas. While rumors about Noriega's ties to the drug trade circulated for many years, U.S. leaders ignored them. In fact, the DEA and Attorney General Edwin Meese sent letters of commendation to the Panamanian dictator. Noriega also regularly received U.S. dignitaries, including Bush, to discuss policy issues.

As the Iran-Contra scandal blossomed and Reagan's credibility suffered, the tales of Noriega's drug ties became more prominent. Senator
John Kerry (D-MA) held hearings in the SFRC Subcommittee on Terrorism, Narcotics, and International Communication that further
substantiated published reports on Noriega's drug-trafficking and money-
laundering operations. Kerry complained that "there has not been a real
war on drugs. And drugs have not been the priority public officials said
they were." As historian William Walker notes, Kerry correctly appraised
the situation when he declared "the line between national security concerns and the implementation of anti-drug programs abroad has become
extremely blurred."

Even conservatives began switching their focus to drug traffickers. John
McLaughlin wrote in the *National Review* in May 1988: "Whereas the
menace in Latin America used to be Marxism, today it is narco-terrorism,
a non-ideological plague." He focused on Noriega as the greatest threat to
U.S. Security, warning that if the Panamanians and Nicaraguans outlasted
Reagan, "Central American leaders will conclude that the Reagan Doctrine
failed in ousting both the Sandinistas and the drug peddler. The result will
be a headlong rush toward geopolitical neutrality and domestic corruption, and an historic loss of U.S. regional influence."

The President and the Dictator

Once Bush became president, he began concerted efforts to deal with
Noriega, building on some late efforts by Reagan. Bush declared early on
in his administration that drugs were "the gravest domestic threat facing
our nation today." The problem became more complicated when a Miami
grand jury indicted Noriega on drug charges in 1988. Bush denied any
knowledge of the dictator's drug-trafficking activities beforehand, although
that appears unlikely given his position as chief of the National Narcotics Border Interdiction Service and the numerous published reports on
Noriega's nefarious activities.

Tensions heightened early in 1989, when Noriega overturned an
election. Publicly, he beat opposition officials. When Bush failed to do
anything about the situation, his critics opened fire. Even when an opportunity presented itself in the form of a coup by disenchanted Panamanians,
the president failed to act. One commentator called Bush's response a "wet-
noodle approach to Panama." Soon thereafter, Noriega defiantly declared a

"state of war" between Panama and the United States, often brandishing a machete at mass anti-American rallies.

With relations deteriorating, Panamanians killed an off-duty marine and the PDF beat an American officer and threatened to rape his wife. Now Bush concluded: "Enough is enough. This guy is not going to lay off. It will only get worse."

On December 20, 1989, the United States attacked Panama with a force of over 20,000 men. The Pentagon employed all the latest weaponry, including Stealth bombers, in the action against Noriega, code-named "Operation Just Cause." One official noted that "we thought if there was a lot of noise outside of the front door, they would go out the back." That did not happen, as hundreds of Panamanian civilians perished in the cross-fire between the PDF and U.S. troops (twenty-three of whom suffered fatal wounds). The fighting inflicted more than $1 billion worth of damage in Panama City; thousands in the poorest areas of the city now found themselves homeless. Noriega evaded capture for fifteen days, but he finally left his sanctuary in the Vatican Embassy, and DEA agents immediately arrested him and put him on a plane to Miami.

Most Americans applauded "Operation Just Cause." As several people noted, "Democrats and Republicans alike cheered; many were simply relieved that an annoyance had been removed; others liked the old-fashioned display of American muscle; some saw the venture as a positive step in the drug war." Congress especially echoed support. "Noriega's bad news is good news for our war on drugs. It proves America won't cave in to anyone, no matter how powerful and corrupt," Senator Bob Dole (R-KS) crowed. On the other side of the aisle, Senator Carl Levin (D-MI) stated: "All Americans rejoice that the United States armed forces have brought this indicted drug-running thug to justice."

Critics also arose, especially in the international community. The United States vetoed an effort by the UN Security Council to denounce the operation. In the OAS, member nations voted 20-1 (with only the United States in opposition) to condemn the invasion. Former senator George McGovern emphasized that it was "ironic that when Mikhail Gorbachev is winning worldwide acclaim for standing clear of other countries' political struggles—even on the borders of the Soviet Union—our government continues to control Central America."

In the aftermath of "Operation Just Cause," the United States installed Guillermo Endara as Panamanian president. Washington poured more money into Panama, but unemployment and poverty remained high there. Some Panamanians complained that "General Noriega has been replaced by General Discontent." In 1994, one of Noriega's cronies, Ernesto Pérez Balladares, won the presidency.

As for Noriega, an American jury sentenced him to forty years in jail without parole, which Bush declared a "fitting punishment." Most observers concluded that despite Noriega's removal, the invasion accomplished little in stopping the drug trade. By March 1990, one State Department expert reported that "our law enforcement people would say that it [drug trafficking] has picked back up to the level where it existed before Just Cause."

The invasion created heightened antagonism toward the United States throughout much of Latin America. Soon after it, Mexican novelist Carlos Fuentes lamented that the Brezhnev Doctrine had ended in Eastern Europe, but that its death was "not being echoed by the demise of the Monroe Doctrine in the other theater of the cold war, the U.S. sphere of influence in Central America and the Caribbean." One Panamanian journalist wrote that "there is a love-hate relationship between Panamanians and North Americans that arose from the very outset of our independence," one comparable to the "love-hate relationship that develops between a teenage son and his overbearing father, there is a rebellious attitude to make your own way." As several observers note "little, it seemed, had changed in almost a century."

A New Political Order

Bush faced other challenges in Latin America, one of the most important of which was the rapid democratization in the late 1980s and early 1990s. Two major catalysts arose. First, the military dictators had proven ineffective managers. During the economic crises of the 1970s and 1980s, debts had risen, creating high inflation and unemployment. Unable to develop effective models of development for their respective nations, the military officers stepped aside. Second, the end of the Cold War changed geopolitical realities. Washington began withdrawing its support of dictatorships as the Soviet threat subsided. U.S. officials had tired of the repression and often the statism of the totalitarian regimes. They believed that civilian leaders would better promote democracy and free-market capitalism.

During the 1980s and early 1990s, Argentina, Brazil, Peru, and the Central American states all evolved into democracies. One of the most interesting cases occurred in Chile. Relations with the dictator Pinochet had been strained during the Carter administration, which suspended arms sales and banned exports to Chile because of human-rights violations there. Reagan, however, overturned the embargos and praised Pinochet's anti-communism, free-market model. Indeed, he warmly received the Chilean foreign minister, René Rojas Galadames, in 1981, while the State Department denied a visa to Allende's widow in 1983. As Gaddis Smith notes, it appeared Pinochet was "a permanent friend and fixture of the Reagan administration."

By the mid-1980s, however, relations began to deteriorate. The hard-liners like North, Kirkpatrick, and Casey began leaving office at the time Pinochet declared a state of martial law. Schultz took the lead and appointed a moderate career diplomat, Harry G. Barnes, Jr., as U.S. ambassador to Chile. In July 1986, Barnes attended a funeral for a U.S. citizen, Rodrigo Rojas di Negri, whom Pinochet's security forces had burned alive during a demonstration. Ultraconservative Senator Jesse Helms (R-NC) of the SFRC denounced Barnes for having "planted the American flag in the midst of a Communist activity," but the State Department supported Barnes. Washington increased its public denunciations of Pinochet's regime and requested that the UN Human Rights Commission censure Chile.

Ultimately, the efforts of domestic and international opponents doomed Pinochet. Washington stepped up efforts to force him to open the political process and reduce the violent repression of his political opponents, consistently condemning his brutality and imposing further economic pressure. This led to Pinochet holding a plebiscite on extending his rule in 1988 (two years ahead of schedule). Fifty-five percent of the voters wished him to step down, with Pinochet's opposition having employed U.S. media consultants to formulate a television campaign. By 1990, Pinochet allowed free elections in which Christian Democratic leader Patrício Aylwin (a former opponent of Allende) won with the support of seventeen centrist and left-of-center groups. Much to the delight of Washington, none of the left-wing groups won a single seat in Congress. While Pinochet maintained control of the army for several years and still posed a threat to the stability of the government, democracy had returned to Chile.

Going Uncle Sam's Way

The democratization movement and the economic malaise of the 1980s combined with the delegitimization of the Communist model pushed newly elected officials to look northward for economic development paradigms. Leaders such as Argentine president Carlos Saúl Menem declared in 1990 that "we want to be part of the first world, the only possible world. . . . I don't want to belong to the Third World. Argentina has to be in the First World, which is the only world that should exist." To accomplish this, many Latin American leaders (a significant number of whom had been trained in U.S. and British universities) pushed the U.S. model and rejected statism. In this process, they also moved away from government responsibility for socioeconomic opportunity and equality.

The Bush administration quickly backed the efforts to develop free-market economies. In 1990, Bush announced the Free Enterprise Initiative for the Americas, in which he promised U.S. economic assistance and the negotiation of free-trade status on commodities in return for Latin American reciprocity. Over time, free-trade zones began appearing in Latin America, and U.S. businesses took advantage of the opportunities for cheaper labor and government incentives by moving some operations there.

At the same time, Bush used the debt issue to promote free-market ideas. With few exceptions, Reagan had virtually ignored the problem. Nevertheless, crushing debt had caused problems throughout the region, as in the case of Brazil and Mexico, where the sum exceeded $100 billion. The administration agreed to help renegotiate debt and reduce immediate payments, driven largely by the fear of what would happen to U.S. bankers should it fail to act. Washington, however, expected something in return. The Latin Americans had to implement austerity plans that reduced social services and public subsidies to state-owned businesses and utilities. Consequently, government budgets declined, and the economies typically stabilized, but they did so at a significant social cost, especially to the poor and working class. With the left in disarray and the government enjoying strong support from the middle class, little opposition developed.

A Giant Sucking Sound

The best example of the U.S. influence in the economic affairs of Latin America was the negotiation of the North American Free Trade Agreement (NAFTA) between the United States, Canada, and Mexico. In 1990, the new Mexican president, Carlos Salinas de Gortari, declared that "we want Mexico to be part of the first world." He decided to participate in discussions on NAFTA, a plan overseeing the gradual removal of tariffs between the three partners. As political scientist Peter Smith and historian Thomas Skidmore acknowledge, "this idea entailed a total repudiation of the protectionist strategies of import-substituting industrialization, and it discarded the nationalist tradition of keeping a suspicious distance from the 'colossus of the north.'"

For two years, Salinas and his advisors (many of whom were educated at Harvard, MIT, Yale, and Stanford) worked with U.S. and Canadian negotiators on the details of NAFTA. Finally, in October 1992, Salinas, Bush, and the Canadian Prime Minister Brian Mulroney signed the pact in San Antonio, Texas. It committed each signatory nation to eliminating trade barriers and tariffs over a fifteen-year period. More important, in the eyes of Salinas, NAFTA made foreign investment in his nation easier by allowing U.S. banks and securities firms to establish offices in Mexico. In addition, NAFTA created a Trade Commission to mediate disputes. With the treaty in hand, the three leaders returned to their respective legislatures for approval.

For the most part, approval in Canada and Mexico went smoothly despite criticism from small business owners and intellectuals condemning U.S. imperialism. In the United States, newly elected president Bill Clinton heartily backed the pact. Still, significant U.S. opposition lined up to oppose the approval of NAFTA. Labor unions and Texas billionaire Ross Perot denounced the treaty, warning that "a giant sucking sound" would arise as U.S. jobs went to Mexico. Others worried about the effects NAFTA would have on the environment, as Mexico's environmental protection laws remained underdeveloped. Despite the vigorous opposition to it, the House approved the treaty 234-200; the Senate by a vote of 61-38. NAFTA went into effect in 1994.

The impact of NAFTA was immediate. U.S. and Canadian investment flowed southward, helping jumpstart the Mexican economy (along with a U.S. bailout in 1995), especially in Mexico's northern states. Simultaneously, NAFTA created new problems in Mexico, as Indian nationalists, the Zapatistas, in the southern state of Chiapas rose in revolt. The Zapatistas highlighted the lack of uniform benefits for Mexican citizens, especially for natives.

NAFTA also pushed other countries toward integration into regional groups, as Chile and others sought membership in NAFTA as well. Still others responded with their own plans. In 1991, Argentina, Brazil, Paraguay, and Uruguay created a customs union with a joint tariff system, with further commitments to establish a common market. The rapid acceleration of regional integration marked a significant turning point in economic development, although the social and political ramifications remained unanswered.

Continuities

The signing of NAFTA highlighted an accelerated interdependence developing between the United States and Latin America and highlighted the need for improved cooperative relations, particularly in economic matters—and by extension cultural and environmental concerns.

This interdependence extended to managing debts that threatened important economies in Mexico, Argentina, and Brazil. The United States and world leaders recognized that these expanding societies teetered on the brink of chaos, one that threatened to affect the global economy.

Other issues such as narcotics drew the countries further into interdependent relations. The U.S. efforts to cut off the great demand for drugs in the United States caused a massive expenditure of monies and energies to destroy the supply. Countries such as Mexico, Panama, Colombia, Peru, and Ecuador developed closer relations, partly driven by their own problems developing from the drug trade, principally the crime and corruption that the industry generated, which undermined their civil societies. U.S. DEA agents and local officials collaborated in crop-eradication programs and labored to stop ships, airplanes, and other means of transportation for the contraband cargo. Despite their efforts, the demand for drugs remained high and the supply steady.

With the decline of U.S. power in the wake of the Vietnam War and Watergate scandal and with the growing economic strength of Europeans and Japanese in Latin America, the Reagan and Bush administrations continuously battled challenges to American primacy in the region, both real and imagined. Like no period since the 1920s, in the 1980s and early 1990s the United States utilized military force, specifically in Grenada and Panama and through surrogates in Nicaragua and El Salvador. Millions of dollars of American military assistance flowed to pro-U.S. regimes, often accompanied by U.S. advisors.

Washington also employed other methods of coercion, including economic levers. Loans and grants flowed southward through programs such as the CBI to promote economic growth and stymie the rise of anti-American socialist and communist movements. The Reagan administration in particular used economic aid to reward its allies and punish those who challenged its positions.

As they had traditionally, Latin Americans never passively accepted U.S. efforts to strengthen its hegemony in the region. In the political realm, Nicaragua and Cuba as well as others directly confronted the United States, often forging alliances with other nations to resist U.S. efforts to force compliance. In Nicaragua, for example, the Sandinistas used ties to the Soviet Union and the Eastern Bloc to secure weapons to fight the Contras and economic assistance to circumvent U.S. efforts to destroy their economy. They also relied on others, including groups such as the World Court and the Contadora group to challenge the legitimacy of the U.S. attempts to overthrow their government. In the face of such extreme pressures, the Sandinista survived more than a decade and remained a political power in the country even after losing power in 1990.

In addition to the heated struggle within the region, the 1980s and early 1990s saw the arrival of a great many more Latinos into the United States. Central Americans as well as more people from the Caribbean fleeing political turmoil flooded into cities such as New York, Los Angeles, San Antonio, and throughout the country. To the great consternation of those Americans who worried that so many newcomers would strain and adversely affect U.S. society, the efforts at immigration reform in 1986 resulted in a massive infusion of Latinos into the mainstream American economy and political system.

SUGGESTIONS FOR ADDITIONAL READING

For a good overall review of the period, see Gaddis Smith, *The Last Years of the Monroe Doctrine, 1945–1993* (1994) and Alan McPherson, *Intimate Ties, Bitter Struggles: The United States and Latin America since 1945* (2006).

U.S.-Central American relations during the 1980s have received a lot of attention, especially during the period and its immediate aftermath. Good works include Robert Kagan, *A Twilight Struggle: American Power and Nicaragua, 1977–1990* (1996); William M. LeoGrande, *Our Own Backyard: The United States in Central America, 1977–1992* (1998); E. Bradford Burns, *At War in Nicaragua: The Reagan Doctrine and the Politics of Nostalgia* (1987); Cynthia J. Arnson, *Crossroads: Congress, the President, and Central America, 1976–1993* (1993); Christian Smith, *Resisting Reagan: The U.S. Central America Peace Movement* (1996); Ross Gelbspan, *Break-ins, Death Threats, and the FBI: The Covert War Against the Central America Movement* (1991); Donald E. Schulz and Deborah Sundloff Schulz, *The United States, Honduras, and the Crisis in Central America* (1994); Martha Honey, *Hostile Acts: U.S. Policy in Costa Rica in the 1980s* (1994); Jack Child, *The Central American Peace Crisis, 1983–1991: Sheathing Swords, Building Confidence* (1992); Dario Moreno, *The Struggle for Peace in Central America* (1994); Robert Pastor, *Condemned to Repetition: The United States and Nicaragua* (1987); Suzanne Jonas, *The Battle for Guatemala: Rebels, Death Squads, and U.S. Power* (1991); Roy Gutman, *Banana Diplomacy: The Making of American Policy in Nicaragua, 1981–1987* (1988); Richard White, *The Morass: United States Intervention in Central America* (1984); R. Pardo Mauer, *The Contras, 1980–1989: A Special Kind of Politics* (1990); and Jonathan Feldman, *Universities in the Business of Repression: The Academic-Military-Industrial Complex and Central America* (1989).

For more information on the Falklands/Malvinas War, see Barry Gough, *The Falkland Islands/Malvinas: The Contest for Empire in the South Atlantic* (1992); Max Hastings and Simon Jenkins, *The Battle for the Falklands* (1983); and David Pion-Berlin, *Through Corridors of Power: Institutions and Civil-Military Relations in Argentina* (1997).

Good books on the debt crisis include Barbara Stallings, *Banker to the Third World: U.S. Portfolio Investment in Latin America, 1900–1986* (1987); and Paul W. Drake, ed., *Money Doctors, Foreign Debts, and Economic Reforms in Latin America from the 1890s to the Present* (1994).

Other good works on U.S.-Latin American relations during the 1980s include Thomas Carothers, *In the Name of Democracy: U.S. Policy toward Latin America during the Reagan Years* (1991); Robert A. Pastor, *Whirlpool: U.S. Foreign Policy toward Latin America and the Caribbean* (1992); Howard J. Wiarda, *In Search of Policy: The United States and Latin America* (1984) and *Finding Our Way: Toward Maturity in U.S.-Latin American Relations* (1987); Margaret Daly Hayes, *Latin America and the U.S. National Interest: A Basis for U.S. Foreign Policy* (1984); and Kevin Buckley, *Panama*.

For more on the drug control issues, read William O. Walker, *Drug Control in the Americas* (1989); William O. Walker, ed., *Drugs in the Western Hemisphere: An Odyssey of Cultures in Conflict* (1996); Elaine Shannon, *Desperados: Latin Drug Lords, U.S. Lawmen, and the War America Can't Win* (1988); John Dinges, *Our Man in Panama: The Shrewd Rise and Brutal Fall of Manuel Noriega* (1990); Peter D. Scott and Jonathan Marshall, *Cocaine Politics: Drugs, Armies, and the CIA in Central America* (1991); and Bruce M. Bagley and William O. Walker, eds., *Drug Trafficking in the Americas* (1994).

CHAPTER NINE

The New World Order

THE END OF THE COLD WAR significantly affected U.S.-Latin American relations. With the decline of the Soviet threat, American policymakers increasingly focused on domestic issues such as health care and jobs. With their political and economic power unchallenged globally, most Americans paid little attention to Latin America outside of economic relations and typically only responded to crises such as those that arose in Haiti in 1994, continuing problems in repaying debts, and as regarded issues that directly affected the United States, such as illegal immigration. The process continued unabated and intensified at the turn of the twenty-first century, despite early efforts by President George W. Bush. When Islamic terrorists attacked the United States on September 11, 2001, many Americans turned their attention toward the Middle East. By 2008, the United States remained comparatively unengaged with Latin America, with its attention fixed almost fully on the wars in Iraq and Afghanistan and its own huge economic woes.

New Faces, Same Issues

In 1992, as the U.S. economy floundered, the American people elected Democrat Bill Clinton. Presidential analyst Fred Greenstein has characterized Clinton as having "energy, enthusiasm, intelligence, and devotion to policy," which he combined with "absence of self-discipline" and "hubristic confidence in his own views and realities." The former Arkansas governor had little international experience and announced he wanted to "keep foreign policy submerged" while he concentrated on the domestic economy, health care, and taxes.

Still, Clinton made some good choices for foreign policy advisors, including Warren Christopher as secretary of state and Anthony Lake as

President George H. W. Bush, Canadian Prime Minister Brian Mulroney, and Mexican President Carlos Salinas participate in the initialing ceremony of the North American Free Trade Agreement, 1992. *Courtesy of the George Bush Presidential Library*

national security adviser. Veterans of the Carter administration, both men proceeded cautiously and meticulously to avoid past mistakes. In Latin America, they concentrated on trade, debt issues, and helping ease the nations' transition toward democracy.

The end of the Cold War allowed Clinton to focus on domestic issues and brought to power others with similar concerns on internal affairs. By 1995, the Republicans had majorities in both houses of Congress. One diplomat characterized the Republican party leaders as having a "very strong element that is anti-internationalist, unilateralist, even isolationist—very xenophobic, extremely touchy." The contentious relationship that developed between president and Congress hamstrung U.S. foreign relations at important junctures throughout much of the Clinton administration.

While a shift in emphasis to domestic concerns occurred, major issues remained in U.S.-Latin American relations. The move toward open markets was still a U.S. priority. The Clinton administration successfully pushed for the approval of NAFTA in the face of opposition by important Democratic constituents, primarily organized labor. In other areas, it focused on stabilizing Latin American economies through rearrangement of debts, continuing the Bush administration's policies of imposing austerity plans and opening new markets. Finally, stemming the drug trade remained a high priority, as drugs from Latin America continued to flow into the United States at an alarming rate. Ultimately, direct assistance trickled to virtually nothing outside of the drug-control efforts. As Peter Smith notes, this occurred largely because by the 1990s, "extrahemispheric influence in the Americas virtually vanished . . . the United States had finally realized its ambition of the 1790s: to create a zone of uncontested influence within the Western Hemisphere."

It Isn't as Easy as It Looks

While Clinton and his team focused on economics, several crises developed in Latin America. A spotlight shone on Haiti. For most of the Cold War, the Duvalier family had ruled Haiti as their virtual fiefdom. Reliant on force as well as more subtle means of manipulation, the family and their cronies grew rich while the country remained the poorest in the hemisphere. Most administrations looked the other way since Duvalier and company were staunch anti-Communists. The Carter administration had attacked the Haitians' human-rights violations, securing some cosmetic changes from Jean-Claude "Baby Doc" Duvalier. Nevertheless, conditions remained horrible for most Haitians.

Poverty and political repression caused an exodus of refugees from Haiti, many of whom boarded rickety boats and fled to the United States during the late 1970s. At a time when the United States welcomed hundreds of thousands of persons from Cuba and Southeast Asia, Washington rejected the Haitian refugees. Since few of these Haitians had marketable skills and political leaders in South Florida viewed them as a burden, the Carter administration arranged a deal with the Duvalier government to deport any Haitian refugees. Not everyone agreed with the policy. Richard Celeste, director of the Peace Corps, argued that "regardless of diplomatic and domestic pressures, I believe we must be at least as generous to those refugees as we are to Southeast Asians, Cubans, Eastern Europeans, and Russians. . . . We can, should, set an example of what should be done by a country of first asylum. This, I believe, is the least we can do for those Haitians who flee to our shores."

The Reagan administration continued the policy of returning would-be Haitian immigrants. Problems worsened after 1986, when Duvalier fled Haiti in the face of pressure from domestic and international groups who demanded he step down. For four years, various generals and cliques fought for control of Haiti. In December 1990, a brief period of hope dawned as a thirty-seven-year-old priest, Jean-Bertrand Aristide, won power. Strongly influenced by liberation theology and nationalism, he once told a group

of Americans: "I cannot forgive what your country has done to Haiti."
Immediately, he implemented controversial reform policies that alienated
the military and the elite. In September 1991, military officers drove Aristide into exile and installed General Raoul Cédras, who ruled through a
series of puppet presidents.

The international community, including the United States, condemned
the action, although some members of the CIA considered Aristide emo-
tionally unstable and dangerous. For its part, the OAS imposed a trade
embargo and pressured Cédras to resign. The armed forces responded violently, driving more Haitians to flee. At first U.S. officials took this wave
of Haitian refugees to a safe haven at Guantánamo Bay (site of the U.S.
military base in Cuba) and granted additional requests for asylum. As the
number of refugees increased, Bush ordered U.S. sailors to return immediately all the Haitians at Guantánamo to Haiti. Remarkably, he defended
this decision against Clinton's criticisms during the presidential campaign
by stating: "We're not trying to starve the people of Haiti and we're not
trying to freeze them or cook them or do anything of that nature."

In 1993, when Clinton took over as president, he found the issue more
complex than he had anticipated. Intelligence sources informed him that
200,000 Haitians planned to flee; public sentiment in the United States
clearly opposed welcoming those persons into the country. In addition to
the lack of marketable skills, the extremely high incidence of HIV among
Haitians was underscored by the American media. As fear and racism
drove policy, Clinton responded that he would continue Bush's policy, one
described by an Aristide aide as a "floating Berlin Wall."

The Immaculate Invasion

Throughout 1993, negotiators from the OAS and UN continued pressing Cédras to resign and let Aristide return. In July, the concerned parties
accepted a proposal that included general amnesty and new leaders. In
early October, 200 U.S. and Canadian peacekeepers steamed into Port-au-
Prince to implement the plan. Upon their arrival, however, Cédras's allies
brandished machetes and threatened to turn Haiti into another Somalia
(referring to a recent massacre of U.S. peacekeepers in Africa). The ship
withdrew amid charges that the Americans had turned tail and run. Cédras
retained power and became even more defiant.

For nearly a year, the Clinton administration sought compromise. Many
U.S. officials wanted to dump Aristide and find an alternative. But influ-

ential African Americans led by human-rights activists and members of the Black Congressional Caucus pressured President Clinton to continue to support Aristide. By the summer of 1994, tensions reached a fevered pitch. When Haiti expelled its UN human-rights monitors, U.S. Ambassador to the UN Madeline Albright warned the Haitian government: "You can depart voluntarily and soon, or you can depart involuntarily and soon." Despite opposition from Republicans and much of the American public, the Clinton administration moved forward. In a first step, Clinton made speeches that emphasized that "the message of the United States to the Haitian dictators is clear: Your time is up. Leave now, or we will force you from power."

In spite of the rhetoric, Clinton allowed one last-ditch diplomatic effort. Jimmy Carter and former chairman of the Joint Chiefs of Staff Colin Powell left for high-level talks with Cédras in mid-September. The Haitian junta proved uncompromising until news reached it that U.S. planes loaded with troops had left the ground. Then, President Émile Jonaissant announced "we'll have peace, not war." While Cédras initially refused to sign the agreement, U.S. troops landed in "Operation Uphold Democracy." Within a week, 15,000 U.S. troops were in place. They met little resistance. Journalist Bob Shacochis described the whole episode as "the Immaculate Invasion."

For a year, U.S. troops acted as peacekeepers in Haiti, serving as police officers, medics, and engineers. Often caught between rival parties, the Americans periodically found themselves squelching violent conflicts. Nevertheless, as promised, in April 1995 the U.S. forces withdrew. Throughout the invasion, the media and Clinton's enemies skewered him. One emphasized: "Never before has the United States gone to war to stop refugees from coming to our shores." Another observer stressed that Clinton took action "less [from] his concern about human rights or democracy, than his belated assessment that the only way to keep refugees away from Miami is to stop the murders in Haiti." At the end of the U.S. occupation, little had changed. Limited economic aid flowed to Haiti and its economy and social structures remained mired in chaos. One U.S. peacekeeper summed the situation up concisely, if bluntly: "We're still gonna have a shitload of people in boats wanting to go to America."

The Old Thorn in the Side

The fear of an exodus of Caribbean islanders to Florida also played a substantial role in U.S.-Cuban relations. Despite the end of the Cold War, relations between the United States and Cuba remained tense, although Castro had seen the writing on the wall foretelling the failure of communism and tried to make certain concessions. By 1992, he withdrew his troops from overseas, announced that Cuba would provide no additional assistance to revolutionary movements, and initiated some free-market reforms. Nevertheless, the Bush administration moved timidly, fearful of aggravating the politically powerful Cuban American voting bloc during an election cycle. Indeed, Bush signed the Cuban Democracy Act of 1992, strengthening the trade embargo and punishing companies investing in Cuba, although it normalized relations with Vietnam. This act required open elections, constitutional reforms, and free markets before allowing improved relations.

After the election, Clinton continued the policy, following the precedents established by his eight predecessors. The result was the flight of more persons from the devastated Cuban economy, which, without Soviet subsidies now lay in disarray. Thousands of refugees, including Castro's daughter and granddaughter, fled Cuba. A crisis developed when some Cubans hijacked boats on which to flee, leading Castro to plan to allow 35,000 refugees to leave. Clinton responded quickly, consulting with anti-Castro exiles and Florida governor Lawton Chiles. Clinton negotiated with Havana to increase legal immigration in return for Cuban prohibition on illegal immigrants. Washington also announced it would immediately return all future refugees to Cuba. In return, Clinton promised to try to restrain anti-Castro congresspersons, and for the moment, tensions decreased.

Problems resurfaced in February 1996, as a Cuban exile group, Brothers to the Rescue, began to fly over Havana and drop propaganda leaflets from their airplanes. Despite repeated warnings to cease and desist by Cuban officials, they continued their missions. Ultimately, Cuban MIG jets shot down two of the planes, killing four people. A political outcry arose. Secretary of State Madeline Albright vigorously stated: "This is not *cojones,* this is cowardice." In addition, Senator Jesse Helms (R-NC) and Congressman Dan Burton (R-IN) pushed a law through congress allowing U.S. citizens to sue foreign businesses using confiscated Cuban lands and barred the easing of U.S. Sanctions against Cuba until democratic elections occurred there.

Many complained that the Helms-Burton law made it easier for Castro to control dissent. "If you want to let light into the island, then don't keep trying to keep all its windows shut," one human-rights activist warned.

Indeed, Castro continued to rely on anti-Americanism to explain Cuba's economic failures. Ultimately, the Clinton administration suspended parts of the Helms-Burton act because the European Union complained that it violated rules of the World Trade Organization. By 1999, the Clinton administration eased other restrictions by allowing more American flights to Cuba, permitting Cuban Americans to send a modest sum of $1,200 per year to their families in Cuba, and easing restriction on the transfer of food and medicine through nongovernmental agencies.

Still, the rhetoric remained strident. The Elían González episode in 1999–2000 proved the volatility of the issue. The young boy, found at sea after the boat on which he and his mother traveled sank, was brought to the United States and placed in custody of family members. The father sought the return of the boy to Cuba, but hardliners in the Cuban American community, especially in South Florida, fought the idea. After a deadlock, U.S. Attorney General Janet Reno ordered federal officials into relatives' Miami home to take the child and return him to his father, who had flown to the United States to pick up his son. The action enraged many Cuban Americans and most likely contributed to the defeat of Al Gore in Florida during the disputed 2000 presidential election.

With such intense emotions evoked, it appeared unlikely that U.S.-Cuba relations would thaw with the election of George W. Bush as president. Bush needed the support of the Cuban American community in the electoral rich state of Florida. Also, his brother, John Ellis "Jeb" Bush, the governor of Florida, faced a strong challenge to reelection in 2002. The Cuban American community promised retribution on both politicians should they move toward conciliation with Castro.

Green Diplomacy

While immigration, drugs, and trade dominated U.S.-Latin American relations, a new issue arose during the 1990s, as increasing numbers of persons focused on the environment. Building on the grass-roots movements in Europe and the United States in the 1960s and 1970s, in the 1980s, environmentalists began to consider the destruction of ecosystems in the developing world. Working through the UN and environmental activist organizations such as Greenpeace, environmentalists worldwide began to decry deforestation, the population explosion, and global warming. Dire predictions of an impending catastrophe were born of new research.

During the 1980s, the Reagan administration resisted efforts to support birth-control programs, limit fishing, and take other environmental actions. Pressure mounted from groups such as the "Grateful Dead" and other activists who held concerts to raise consciousness and money for environmental issues. These organizations often cited the massive environmental destruction in Latin America, especially that of the rain forests of Brazil and Central America, in which loggers, ranchers, and farmers cleared huge tracts for profit (40 million acres of forests disappeared each year during the decade). In an effort to halt the wholesale destruction of the Latin American rainforests, a vital supplier of the Earth's oxygen, activists organized boycotts of restaurants such as McDonald's, which bought Brazilian beef, and recruited businesspersons such as ice-cream magnates Ben Cohen and Jerry Greenfield to promote reforestation and the protection of endangered species. Hollywood also featured the issue in films like *The Emerald Forest* (1985), *The Medicine Man* (1992), and *The Burning Season: The Chico Mendes Story* (1994). Many agreed with Worldwatch Institute's Lester R. Brown who warned, "we do not have generations. We only have years in which to turn things around."

Even with the Cold War over and despite continued pressure from concerned groups, Washington was slow to act on environmental issues. Some victories occurred in the United States, as Congress passed the Clean Air Act of 1990 to reduce the incidence of acid rain. Still, President Bush hesitated to take an active role on the preservation of the environment in the Western Hemisphere. In 1992, he spoke at the Earth Summit in Rio de Janeiro, arguing that environmental rules cost jobs. Furthermore, he refused to sign the UN-sponsored Biodiversity Treaty designed to protect many endangered species. This was due in no small part to Republican reliance on big corporations and pro-business practices during a U.S. recession that undermined most attempts to foster environmental concerns.

In 1992, environmentalists strongly supported the presidential candidate Bill Clinton. "Our natural security must be seen as part of national security," President Clinton would later emphasize. Accompanying Clinton was Vice President Al Gore, whose 1992-bestselling book, *Earth in the Balance,* heightened awareness of global warming. Clinton signed the Biodiversity Treaty and forwarded it to the Senate. Still, his efforts were lukewarm. Always the centrist, Clinton feared aggravating large business interests. He also wanted to avoid being saddled with the label, "Green," which was synonymous with "liberal," a tag Clinton eschewed with zeal.

He also encountered strong opposition from the Republican majority in Congress, which developed in the midterm elections of 1994. Strongly pro-business and anti-regulation, the new congressional majority attacked environmental legislation on all fronts.

Nevertheless, Clinton and Gore ultimately proved more supportive of environmental issues than had their predecessors. More than 166 countries, including the United States, joined together in Kyoto, Japan, in 1997 at a conference on the environment. With Gore pushing the U.S. delegation, the attendees signed the Global Warming Treaty calling on all the developed signatory nations to reduce their production of carbon dioxide, methane, and other greenhouse emissions by 6 to 8 percent of the 1990 levels. Although a signatory, the United States is not bound by the Kyoto Protocol because it had not ratified the agreement as of 2009. Critics, however, pointed out that most such gains would be offset by increases in non-industrialized pollutants. Still, some countries in Latin America, especially those already concentrating on environmental issues, looked on the treaty as an opportunity. To advance internationalism the treaty allowed for the sale of clean-air credits to the industrialized world, building on other efforts by private and government groups that provided debt relief for the creation of national reserves. Nations like Costa Rica began negotiating with the United States and Europe for clean-air credits that it might cash to receive aid monies. Still, most environmental issues remained unsolved, and they will continue to influence U.S.-Latin American relations.

Building the Great Wall of America

Throughout the 1990s, the issue of illegal immigration and incorporating new (legal and illegal) immigrants into U.S. society was a political hot potato. Despite increased enforcement by the border patrol, which seized and expatriated more than 1 million undocumented workers per year, the exodus from Latin America continued. The same concerns that had characterized immigration debates for 100 years remained: the emphasis on the overwhelming of governmental social services, increases in divisions in U.S. society, and immigrants taking jobs from old-stock Americans and depressing wages.

Other concerns drove efforts to limit immigration, especially from Latin America. Most Latinos voted Democrat—by a margin of three-to-one—and resided in important electoral states including Texas, California,

New Jersey, New York, Florida, and Illinois. Conservative Republicans, many from states with few Latino residents, renewed efforts to control illegal immigration in the Southwest.

One of the leaders of the drive to tighten immigration policy was Patrick Buchanan, a former member of the Nixon White House and conservative commentator. In 1992, he complained "I think God made all people good, but if we had to take a million immigrants in, say Zulus, next year, or Englishmen, and put them in Virginia, what group would be easier to assimilate and would cause less problems for the people of Virginia?"

Such sentiment pervaded the border states, especially California. In 1994, its citizens passed Proposition 187, which denied most state benefits to illegal aliens, including access to a public education. California also began lawsuits against the federal government, seeking reimbursement for having provided social services to illegal immigrants. Elsewhere, attacks began on bilingual education and advocates of "English-only" became vocal and well organized.

When conservative Republicans took control of the House in 1994, the issue of immigration heated up. While many people supported allowing additional well-trained and skilled laborers into the United States to help staff high-tech industries and the medical fields (strengthened by a new immigration reform act in 1990), most attacked the porous nature of America's borders. The Clinton administration found itself seeking the middle ground and ultimately signed the Illegal Immigration Reform and Immigrant Responsibility Act of 1996. It funded the hiring of new Border Patrol and INS agents, instituted an entry-exit database for enforcement verification, created new tamper-proof border-crossing cards and employer verification materials, and sped up the removal and detention process.

Despite such efforts, legislating immigration has done little to stop the flow of Latin Americans, principally Mexicans, into the United States. The booming U.S. economy of the 1990s required more labor; U.S. unemployment remained low while Mexico's economy stagnated. The need for more agricultural workers and unskilled laborers even led to calls for a return of the Bracero program by governors in the Southwest.

Still, immigration remained a divisive issue. Many politicians and members of the public remain vehemently opposed to the changes in U.S. demographics. As a candidate for the Reform Party in 2000, Buchanan announced at the Nixon Library: "In too many cases, the American melting pot has been reduced to a simmer . . . America is Balkanizing like never before." "A country that cannot control its borders is not sovereign," he told the audience, sparking exuberant applause. Many agreed with him. A Mesa, Arizona, man wrote an editorial in the *Arizona Republic* in February 2000: "With the tab for border patrol already in the millions and increasing annually but not enough, why not build a wall?" "Without some total commitment similar to this approach," he added, "we are not serious about stopping the flow."

Latino America

Despite all the complaints and longing by some Americans for a return to bygone days when Latinos were a small minority with little power in the United States, the fact is that Latinos are and will become an increasingly powerful force in American society. They have shaped and will continue to shape the American political, social, cultural, and economic landscape. By 1999, there were more than 31 million people of Latino origin.[1] Many experts correctly predicted that within the first ten years of the twenty-first century, Latinos would become the largest minority in the United States, surpassing African Americans. Latinos have disparate voices caused by differences in nations of origin, but each group brings unique ingredients to the cultural mix of the United States.

In politics, Latinos already play a significant role. Leaders such as Federico Peña, Bill Richardson, Mel Martínez, Loretta Sanchez, Henry Bonilla, Ilena Ros-Lehtinen, have paved the way for future Latino leadership at the local, state, and national levels. With Latinos concentrated in important positions, politicians from both parties have developed strategies to win the support of Latino voters. While remaining underrepresented, especially at the national level, the trend will not likely continue, as Latino politicians gain more voice in American politics and force parties to focus on issues of immigration, jobs, bilingual education, racism, and the family.

The Latino influence on American culture increases daily. The trend is especially evident in popular culture. Most major metropolitan areas support Spanish-language newspapers, and Spanish-language radio and television shows fill the airwaves. Many Latino actors and singers have

---

1 Of that number, the breakdown in percentage terms is: 65.2 percent Mexican American; 9.6 percent Puerto Rican; 4.3 percent Cuban; 14.3 percent from Central and South America; and 6.6 percent other.

"crossed over" into mainstream society, led by pioneers such as Rita Moreno, Desi Arnaz, Anthony Quinn, and Rita Hayworth, to the new generation of Carlos Santana, Edward James Olmos, Cheech Marin, Salma Hayek, Jimmy Smits, Hector Elizondo, Raul Julia, Jennifer Lopez, Cameron Diaz, Andy Garcia, America Ferrera, George Lopez, and Carlos Mencia. Movies featuring the stories of Latinos, such as *My Family, Born in East L.A., El Norte, Lone Star,* and *The Perez Family,* have been successful. In the music business, Carlos Santana, Selena, Jennifer Lopez, Ricky Martin, Marc Anthony, Gloria Estefan, and Christina Aguilera have won huge followings among American and international audiences. In each case, they bring Latino traditions into the cars and homes of millions of Americans, challenging stereotypes and promoting the Latino culture.

This trend has shaped American views of the world. More Americans speak Spanish as a first or second language and Anglos increasingly turn their back on the study of other European languages to learn Spanish to enhance their ability to participate in the new economic realities. Added to these patterns is a new respect for the history and literature of Latin America, with Carlos Fuentes, Gabriel García-Marquez, and Isabella Allende having become common names to many American readers. This also carries over into secondary and college classrooms, wherein increasing numbers of students study Latin America. Since the 1960s, Latin American studies programs have popped up throughout the country.

Despite the negative publicity associated with illegal immigration and the pervasiveness of stereotypes of Latinos in the popular consciousness of many Americans, the Latino influence will only grow in strength and popularity in the twenty-first century. The southwestern United States already demonstrates the trend, which continues as the North and South American cultures increasingly blend. While the entire country might not undergo a similar transformation, important strides toward a new understanding already have been made.

The Decider Takes Over

As the United States ushered in the twenty-first century and continued blending Latinos into the culture, the country experienced political upheaval, one ultimately affected by Latinos. The Republican presidential nominee, Texas Governor George W. Bush, son of the former president, squared off against Vice President Al Gore. On the night of the election, the country watched early reports that Florida had fallen to Gore, despite the efforts of Florida Governor Jeb Bush, brother of the Republican nominee, and the conservative Cuban American population, but then, experts wavered, as electoral irregularities and challenges to the vote count in Florida developed. By the next day, Gore held a lead of more than a half million in the national popular vote and only needed one more electoral vote to win. Still, the outcome in Florida remained too close to call.

For more than six weeks, Democrats and Republicans fought in the courts and on the ground to secure Florida's electoral votes and victory. The nation watched anxiously as officials debated how to handle "butterfly ballots" and "hanging chads." After starting and stopping recounts that gave Bush victory by less than 700 votes, the Republican dominated U.S. Supreme Court ultimately ended the process by a clearly partisan vote of 5–4. Gore soon conceded and Bush became the forty-third president of the United States.

The new president had little experience in foreign policy despite the obvious advantages of having a father who had served as chief liaison officer to the People's Republic of China (before formal normalization of relations), CIA Director, vice president, and president. Yet Bush the younger had rarely traveled out of the United States and in 1997 declared: "I don't have the foggiest idea about what I think about international foreign policy."

During the 2000 campaign, Bush consistently avoided discussing foreign policy issues and answered questions by arguing that he would create a skilled team of advisors. He did, however, sustain an active interest in one country: Mexico. Largely because of his West Texas roots, where Mexican Americans played a significant role in the economy and society and his time as governor of Texas (1994–2000), he developed an understanding of border issues and the importance of Mexico to Texas, and by extension to the American economy and culture. Some of this interest spilled over into other parts of the region such as Venezuela, with its oil industry. When Bush entered the White House, he felt comfortable with those matters more than other areas.

Two Cowboys Hit It Off

As promised, Bush surrounded himself with an experienced foreign policy team that comprised many former members of the Reagan administration including John Negroponte, Elliot Abrams, John Poindexter, and later Otto Reich. Most important, he tapped General Colin Powell as secretary of state. The new leader of the diplomatic corps sustained a strong interest in America's southern neighbors, partly because of his Jamaican roots, his experiences during the Reagan and Bush administrations in the region, as well as his activities as a private citizen during the Haitian crisis in 1994.

When Bush took over, he concentrated primarily on domestic issues including education and tax cuts. In the foreign policy realm, which received little attention from the Bush administration before September 11, 2001, many of his closest advisers concentrated on the Middle East or China. Still, Bush, Powell, and a few others looked south. The primary focus remained on Mexico, where events unfolded that made the U.S. relationship with that nation reach its highest point in the modern era.

A major catalyst proved the election of Vicente Fox, who won the Mexican presidency in 2000. The tall, charismatic former governor of Guanajuato, known for his cowboy boots and big belt buckles, had strong ties to the United States. His grandfather left Ohio for Mexico in the late 1890s, and his father maintained American citizenship. After attending the Universidad Iberoamericana, he went to work for Coca-Cola. Starting as a route manager, he ultimately became company supervisor for Mexico and then all of Latin America. Over time, he entered politics, rising to take a major leadership role in the National Action Party (PAN), one of the most significant challengers to the long-term power of the Institutional Revolutionary Party (PRI).

Fox won a hotly contested presidential contest in 2000, effectively breaking the eight-decade-long stranglehold of the PRI. Immediately, he implemented changes in Mexico including its foreign policy, where his secretary of foreign affairs, the respected academic Jorge Castañeda, took charge. Fox pursued a much more activist foreign policy that included seeking and gaining for Mexico a temporary seat on the UN Security Council and promising more international and regional engagement on issues of human rights, free trade, and democratic reforms.

Bush and Fox entered national leadership with many commonalities. They shared experiences as governors of important states less than 1,000 miles apart; they loved the modern cowboy lifestyle (although Fox referred to Bush as a "windshield cowboy" because of his aversion to horses), and had similar views on free markets. They built a good friendship, visiting each other's ranch in Crawford, Texas, and San Cristóbal, Guanajuato. At times, they attended church together and liked to trade cowboy boots and hats. It was a relationship unlike any between an American and Mexican president in the history of the two nations.

In addition to their affability toward one another, the two men shared common positions that shaped the U.S.-Mexico relationship. They agreed on basic concepts regarding immigration reform and the threats of Castro in Latin America. In 2001, Fox asked the Cuban leader to leave a summit in Monterrey, Mexico, before President Bush arrived. Later, when Venezuela sought a seat on the UN Security Council, the Mexicans supported the pro-American Guatemalan candidate instead. These actions led groups such as the Council on Hemispheric Affairs to characterize Fox's policy toward the United States as "overtly submissive."

Nonetheless, the Mexicans continued providing reliable support for the United States especially after the devastating terrorist attacks of September 11. They joined the majority in the region and the world in condemning the assault on the World Trade Center and Pentagon and promised to back the United States in their war on terror. For one of the few times in American history, Latin Americans, including Mexico, lined up in huge numbers to back the efforts of their northern neighbors.

The Cowboy and Caudillo

Despite the generally good relations between the United States and Latin America early in the Bush administration, the White House refused to budge on easing any restrictions and opening any dialogue with Castro, a process aided by the role that Cuban Americans had played in his campaign in Florida in 2000. While elderly and increasingly feeble, Castro and his failed economic policies made him relatively toothless, on the horizon another more highly threatening figure arose in the form of the Venezuelan leader Hugo Chávez.

In 1998, Chávez easily won the presidency in Venezuela. Born in a mud hut in 1954 of mixed Indian, Spanish, and African descent, he chose an unlikely path for the son of schoolteachers. Graduating from the Venezuelan Academy of Military Sciences in 1975 with a degree in engineering, he later studied political science at Simon Bolívar University, where he developed an interest in the political ideas of Bolívar as well as socialism and communism.

Over time, Chávez rose up through the ranks to lieutenant colonel, earning the reputation as a fiery speaker and vocal critic of Venezuelan elite society. He organized a group of young military officers who committed to the principles of "Bolivarian socialism." In February 1992, he won national

Presidents of Nicaragua, Daniel Ortega, left, of Bolivia, Evo Morales, second from left, of Venezuela, Hugo Chávez, third from left, and Cuba's vice president Carlos Lage, right, wave beside a woman holding a 1970's picture of Fidel Castro and late Chilean president Salvador Allende, during a meeting at the alternative Integration of the Iberoamerican countries' summit in Santiago, Saturday, Nov. 10, 2007. *(AP Photo/Claudio Santana)*

recognition when he led a coup against the democratically elected government of President Carlos Andrés Pérez in response to perceived economic mismanagement and austerity measures. The coup failed miserably. On national television, Chávez told his forces to lay down their arms but noted that he only had failed *"por ahora"* (for now).

His coup attempt landed him in jail, but Chávez felt vindicated when the legislature impeached and removed Pérez from office. Soon thereafter, Chávez received a pardon (in 1994). Now he sought power by more traditional means. With a base of primarily the poor and working class, Chávez promised revolutionary change and an end to the corruption of Venezuela's elites and traditional politicians. In 1998, he won the presidency handily with more than 56 percent of the vote.

When Chávez took over power, few predicted the impact his presidency would have on U.S.-Venezuelan relations. In his first speech regarding the United States, he emphasized that our struggle "is not against the United States. Our struggle is against corruption and against this government . . . . We believe that the United States would not interfere with our project because it is not openly at odds with [U.S.] foreign policy." In one of his first interviews on the topic, he stressed that his administration promoted "no anti-imperialist or anti-*yanqui* discourse, which, in event, went out of fashion in the era of the 1960s."

Despite his enormous influence on the flow of Venezuelan petroleum into the United States, the Clinton administration gave the new leader very little attention. In part, Clinton found himself distracted by his impeachment, among other issues. When Chávez visited Washington in January 1999, Clinton met with the Venezuelan for only fifteen minutes, this in the office of a national security adviser. Relations soured over the next year and Chávez's rhetoric began to grow decisively anti-U.S. Still, the U.S. Ambassador John Maisto argued, "look at his hands, not his mouth," in explaining that Chávez sustained good relations with the oil companies and relied on the U.S. market for the sale of nearly three-fourths of his petroleum exports.

Relations deteriorated further when the Bush team took over. A Clinton holdover in the State Department, Peter Romero allied with Roger Noriega (assistant secretary of state for Western Hemisphere affairs), and later Otto Reich (the White House special envoy to Latin America), other hardliners, and Cuban Americans to develop a tough policy toward Chávez. Others joined the choir including Venezuelans led by a former head of the Petróleos de Venezuela Sociedad Anónima (PdVSA) [whom Chávez had fired], Luis Giusti, who had strong ties with members of the Bush administration and its close friends in the oil business.

For his part, Chávez angered Americans by condemning the U.S. invasion of Afghanistan and associating with anti-American leaders like Libyan leader Muammar al-Qaddafi, Iranian president Mahmoud Ahmadinejad, and the FARC rebels in Colombia. More important in the eyes of many of the old Cold Warriors in the Bush administration, Chávez developed a close relationship with Castro. During one speech, he called Cuba a "bastion of Latin American dignity, and that is how she should be seen, that is how she should be nurtured." He often praised Castro and provided large quantities of oil to the socialist state. His actions infuriated U.S. conservatives, particularly those within the Cuban-American community who saw Chávez as an extension of Castro and increasingly focused their attention on him, a process aided by people with strong ties to the oil industry who had significant investments in Venezuela. Chávez also used his increasing oil revenues to try to win support in the region to fulfill his Bolivarian dreams by supporting new "leftist" leaders such as Evo Morales in Bolivia.

The confrontation between the United States and Venezuela peaked in April 2002. The opposition to Chávez had grown in many sectors of

Venezuelan society, particularly the elite and middle classes who feared his march toward Bolivarian socialism. Protests led by military officers and labor unions broke out to denounce the firing of management boards in the national petroleum industry. On April 11, gunfights erupted between pro-Chávez supporters and the opposition that ultimately led to a coup in which conspirators asked for Chávez's resignation, which he reportedly gave. A government under the leadership of Pedro Carmona took over, but two days later, the pro-Chávez forces quickly defeated the conspirators and returned their man to power.

Great controversy swirled around the reported Bush administration's complicity in the coup, although the White House denied any role in it whatsoever. In the weeks preceding the ouster, Carmona and other dissidents visited Washington and met with Reich, Abrams, and other U.S. officials. One senior Bush administration official noted that "they came here to complain . . . our message was very clear: there are constitutional processes." A Defense Department official noted, however, that "we were not discouraging people. We were sending informal, subtle signals that we don't like this guy. We didn't say, 'no, don't you dare,' and we weren't advocates saying, 'Here's some arms; we'll help you overthrow this guy.'"

Other contacts between U.S. Officials, including members of the U.S. military and CIA, reportedly occurred in Venezuela during the run-up to coup. In addition, the National Endowment for Democracy (NED), the non-profit, often conservative-dominated, congressional-supported organization that supported expanding democracy, had increased its flow of resources into the Venezuelan opposition in the months preceding the coup.

The administration further raised suspicions when it immediately recognized the Carmona government in violation of the Rio Treaty, which prevented member nations from formally extending recognition to those having seized power by force. Nevertheless, the White House rationalized that Chávez had resigned voluntarily, and therefore the treaty lacked applicability. This occurred despite the fact that every nation in the region with the exception of Chile, many meeting in Costa Rica for a conference, universally condemned the action and refused to recognize the Carmona government. White House press secretary Ari Fleischer added fuel to the fire when he expressed that the administration favored Chávez's departure. "The government suppressed what was a peaceful demonstration of the people [that] led very quickly to a combustible situation in which Chávez resigned."

The Bush administration immediately backpedaled when the coup collapsed. White House officials intensified their efforts to distance themselves from the plotters, denying any knowledge of the coup or its support of the conspirators. Democrats in the Senate led by Christopher Dodd (D-CT) requested an investigation of the U.S. role, which led to a report that emphasized, "U.S. officials acted appropriately and did nothing to encourage an April coup against Venezuela's president." Another investigation by the State Department stressed "U.S. assistance programs in Venezuela, including those funded by the National Endowment for Democracy (NED), were consistent with U.S. law or policy." Despite the official findings, the circumstantial evidence of U.S. complicity mounted over time, and Chávez intensified his accusations that the Bush administration cooperated in the overthrow of his democratically elected government. The full story, however, remains unclear and will only develop over time.

If anything, the coup and perceptions of U.S. involvement in it discredited the opposition and allowed Chávez to exploit the long-simmering anti-Americanism in his country and the region. He emerged stronger and more vocal in his denunciations of Bush and the United States. For its part, the Bush administration backed off as the invasion of Iraq drained U.S. energy and resources, although critics argued that the administration replicated its actions in the removal of Aristide in Haiti in 2004.

Nonetheless, U.S.-Venezuelan relations remained tense in the aftermath of the 2002 coup, with Chávez bragging at one point, "I would like to place a bet with Mr. Bush to see who lasts longer, him in the White House or me in Miraflores (the Venezuelan equivalent)." At another juncture, he called Bush the "devil" during a speech at the United Nations and at government rally yelled out that Bush was a "pendejo" (loosely translated "dumb ass"). Such statements combined with increasing efforts to socialize Venezuela's economy infuriated many conservatives in the U.S., including televangelist Pat Robertson, who in August 2005 used his national show, the *700 Club,* to observe that Chávez "thinks we're trying to assassinate him, I think that we really ought to go ahead and do it." He added, "it's a lot cheaper than starting a war. And I don't think any oil shipments will stop." Other tensions arose over a U.S. arms embargo and when Colombian forces raided Ecuador in 2008 and discovered information linking Chávez to the FARC rebels.

By 2008, U.S.-Venezuelan relations remained strained but the war in Iraq continued to limit U.S. options, with many U.S. officials choosing to ignore Chávez and focus instead on sustaining economic relations as oil prices skyrocketed to well over $100 a barrel. Also, many Americans recognized that Chávez had been contained on one front by the Brazilians under Luiz Inácio Lula da Silva and on another by Colombians under Álvaro Uribe, as well as by others not willing to submit to Venezuelan leadership. The Venezuelan did have allies among relatively weak regional leaders such as Morales, Daniel Ortega in Nicaragua and Rafael Correa in Ecuador, but overall the region remained democratic and capitalist and his calls for unification in opposition to the United States often fell on deaf ears. In addition, the Venezuelan opposition handed Chávez a significant defeat on a referendum to extend his presidency in December 2007.

Nonetheless, with the price of oil at an all-time high, Chávez sustained an enviable position vis-à-vis the United States and, as predicted, outlasted Bush in office. While he has made some efforts to soothe feelings by calling for an end to the fighting by the FARC in Colombia and eased some of the rhetoric on using oil as a weapon, Venezuela's relationship with the United States remains combustible.

The Arrogance of Power

Even as the United States confronted Chávez, the most important issue for the Bush administration centered on the war on terrorism. The attacks of September 11 changed the international dynamics significantly. While the Bush administration had originally shown more interest in Latin America than had its predecessor, that focus shifted quickly to the Middle East, with Latin America becoming a peripheral issue to most Americans and their leaders as Muslim terrorists became public enemy number one.

The change in focus had two important ramifications. The lack of attention to Latin America from senior members of the Bush administration and members of Congress allowed the vacuum to be filled by diplomats and lower level officials with an interest in Latin America and others associated with nongovernmental organizations such as the International Republican Institute and the NED. As the power shifted downward, conservatives within the White House, State Department, and Congress increasingly devoted time and effort to attacks on historical enemies like Castro and Aristide and new ones like Chávez. The politics of confrontation took center stage over the policies of accommodation and cooperation that had characterized the Clinton years and the first half of the Bush administration.

While Mexico, Venezuela, and Cuba remained concerns within the administration, the majority of Latin America received much less attention. Promises of cooperation on trade, immigration, and drug enforcement often fell by the wayside as Washington remained preoccupied elsewhere. Washington paid attention only to Colombia, where U.S. officials tied the FARC to global terrorism, or the Iron Triangle in the corner of Paraguay, Brazil, and Argentina, where Middle Eastern terrorists linked to groups like Hezbollah worked. While positive feelings toward the Unites States skyrocketed in Latin America immediately after September 11, the subsequent inattention and the U.S. invasion of Iraq in 2003 eroded all such good feelings.

After September 11, an arrogance and single mindedness developed in the Bush administration, as hard-liners such as Paul Wolfowitz, Don Rumsfeld, Richard Perle, John Bolton, Douglas Feith, and the powerful vice president, Dick Cheney, took center stage in developing policy largely supplanting moderates such as Colin Powell. Emboldened by the power ceded the president by Congress and the judiciary branch in the wake of 9-11, the war hawks aggressively and ambitiously pushed forward with a plan to use American power to battle terrorists globally.

The ultimate manifestation of the new policy, although one with strong roots in the traditions of American foreign relations, was the Bush Doctrine. Presented in a National Security Council document "National Security Strategy of the United States" in September 2002, it committed the United States to the use of preemptive military strikes to depose regimes considered dangerous to U.S. interests. In addition, it argued that the United States had to promote democracy to undermine the cultural and political institutions that bred terrorists, especially in the Middle East, which harbored the majority of enemy soldiers.

The new reality manifested itself in many ways. One Bush administration official emphasized to a journalist: "We're an empire now, and when we act, we create our own reality. And while you're studying that reality—judiciously as you will—we'll act again, creating other new realities, which you can study too, and that's how things will sort out. We're history's actors . . . and you, all of you, will be left to just study what we do."

Critics immediately attacked the fundamental concepts of the statement, particularly the preemptive intervention concept as violating international law and destroying systems of cooperation. They characterized the Bush Doctrine as a dangerous break with the past and harkened back to other instances in which the United States had tried to impose its will on other countries, primarily Vietnam. Latin Americans joined the chorus, unpleasantly reminded of the unilateral preemptive interventions such as in Nicaragua and Haiti during Wilson's time or 1965 in the Dominican Republic. They remembered Wilson's promises to teach them to elect good men. To them, the Bush Doctrine sounded eerily familiar.

Despite the criticisms, the Bush administration pushed its vision forward. Domestically, it attacked anyone who disagreed with its policies, such as the disabled Vietnam veteran Senator Max Cleland (D-GA) who faced an onslaught after speaking in 2002, complete with attacks on his patriotism. In Latin America, Chávez and Aristide increasingly came under fire, and over time, even close allies such as Fox faced intense scrutiny.

The lead up to the invasion of Iraq highlighted the changes in U.S. policy. In 2002, the calls for war with Saddam Hussein increased. Some like Secretary of the Treasury Paul O'Neill argued that people within the White House had been determined to displace the Iraqi dictator well before September 11. After the invasion of Afghanistan and the toppling of Taliban rule there, the administration turned its attention toward Iraq. Now members of the administration began to charge Hussein with trying to secure weapons of mass destruction, of aiding the 9-11 terrorists, and letting Iraq serve as a base of operations for radical Islamists groups such as Al Qaeda. Their rhetoric positioned Iraq at the center of the war on terrorism, then they called for actions stronger than the existing UN economic sanctions against Iraq for Hussein's continuous lack of cooperation with UN Nuclear inspectors.

Caught in the middle were Vicente Fox and Ricardo Lagos, president of Chile. At the time of the run up to war, Chile and Mexico retained two of the temporary seats on the UN Security Council. Fox in particular found himself under great pressure because of his closeness to Bush, complaining that "from the start, Bush tackled the selling of the Iraq war with the air of a man who already had his mind made up." U.S. officials hinted that work on immigration would suffer "if Mexico opposes the U.S. in its time of need."

Despite the pressure, Fox emphasized that "there was no way that Mexico was going to authorize the invasion of Iraq without more evidence of [Iraq having] WMD (weapons of mass destruction) than anyone had shown us yet." He deemed Secretary of State Powell's presentation in February 2003 at the UN as having a "few fuzzy photographs and a sophomoric PowerPoint presentation." He added that "as a nation we knew firsthand what it was like to be occupied" and that "no true son of Mexico could ever back the invasion of a sovereign country unless that nation was a danger to the rest of the world."

Ultimately, the vote in the Security Council never occurred, as the United States could not secure a majority. Fox recognized that he paid a price, both with Bush and hardliners in the United States who thought he betrayed his friend in the White House. Initially, the war went well for the United States, as U.S. forces quickly dispatched what little resistance the Iraqi military offered and captured Hussein and most of his lieutenants and strongmen. On May 1, 2003—less than two months after the invasion had commenced—President Bush, dressed in a full navy flight suit, swaggered across the deck of an aircraft carrier at sea and proudly announced the end of major combat operations in Iraq under a huge banner that read "Mission Accomplished."

Yet, events unfolded that appeared to vindicate Fox as U.S. forces found no WMDs or evidence of Hussein having ties to Al Qaeda. Instead, they found themselves embroiled in a civil war between warring religious and political factions that appeared as intractable as some of the Latin American interventions. Fox concluded that "on Iraq, I think that George W. Bush did what he deeply believed was right. The sad thing is that he was so deeply, deeply wrong."

The unilateralism and arrogance that had culminated in the invasion of Iraq stirred up many negative images of the United States in Latin America. The spirit of cooperation that existed after September 11 dissipated quickly and public approval of the United States among Latin Americans plummeted. More anti-American voices led by Chávez, Morales, Ortega, and others including Andrés Manuel López Obrador in Mexico were heard. Increasingly at conferences and international and regional organizations tensions arose although reliable allies like Colombian president Uribe and others continued to cooperate on issues like drug interdiction and free trade. Many in the region waited for the end of the Bush presidency and hoped for a new start.

The Battle of the Border

A victim of the war on terrorism was the efforts to create comprehensive immigration reform in the United States. Bush had shown a great understanding of the value of the issue, both in economic and political terms, as he proved a very skilled campaigner among the growing Latino population in the United States. However, he found himself swimming against an ugly backlash after September 11 directed against all foreigners, especially those of color who spoke different languages and had contrasting cultures.

The increased presence of Latinos in the United States further stoked the fears of blatantly anti-immigrant groups in the United States. The demographics had continued to change significantly since the last major effort at immigration reform in 1986. The number of Latinos grew by 58 percent in the 1990s, becoming 13 percent of the total population. The largest minority group in the nation, Latinos lived in every part of the country and remained significant economic and political forces, especially in the electoral-rich states of Texas, Florida, and California. By the early 21st century, six of the twenty-five most common surnames in the United States were Latino with García #8, Rodríguez #9, and Martínez #11. This corresponded with the rise of the largest cities in America. Whereas in 1900, the biggest urban areas were primarily in the Northeast, by 2008 the major cities are found in the Southwest, including San Antonio, Los Angeles, San Francisco/San Jose, and San Diego (with their original Spanish names) as well as Phoenix, Houston, and Dallas. The other two were Chicago and New York City, both with significant Latino communities.

The shifting demographics sent a chill into the spine of those afraid of the decline of the position of Anglos in society and provided a perfect wedge issue in American politics for those willing to manipulate the topic, often drowning out moderates who expressed legitimate concerns about the impact of illegal immigration on schools, neighborhoods, and hospitals, but otherwise had no nativist or racist feelings toward Latinos. Political commentator Pat Buchanan and conservative talk show hosts like Bill O'Reilly, Rush Limbaugh, and Lou Dobbs of CNN were the loudest anti-immigration leaders. Others created grass-roots organizations such as Chris Simcox and James Gilchrist who initiated the Minutemen Project to patrol the border and report the activities of illegal immigrants to Border Patrol agents as well as start building a fence to block them. The rhetoric heated up as politicians such as Tom Tancredo (R-CO) and Duncan

Hunter (R-CA) took the lead in pushing for enforcement-only solutions such as immediate deportations, long walls and other barriers along the border, and severe punishment of employers who knowingly hired illegal immigrants.

The right-wing leaders had significant successes over time in changing the debate in the country. In October 2006, human-rights groups organized massive demonstrations of millions in May 2007 to support immigrant rights and demand reform of immigration policies. Nonetheless, President Bush signed a law authorizing the construction of a 700-mile fence along the U.S.-Mexico the border. While one reporter noted that the "action . . . conflicts with his own stated vision of immigration reform," the president faced intense pressure from fellow Republicans who encountered significant challenges in congressional elections in 2006 and desperately sought a way to divert attention from the floundering U.S. economy, corruption in their ranks, and the ongoing quagmire in Iraq that was costing the nation nearly $4 billion a month and the lives of many brave U.S. soldiers. The House Majority Leader John A. Boehner (R-OH) proudly called the fence-building legislation "a major victory in Republicans' efforts to make a real difference in securing our borders."

More important, in 2007 the hardliners undermined the Comprehensive Immigration Reform Act. Supported by Bush and other prominent Republicans including presidential nominee John McCain, who worked in tandem with Edward Kennedy (D-MA), the legislation eased the process of securing green cards and in essence created a guest-worker program. Its opponents believed the act opened up a way to citizenship for the millions of illegal immigrants. Immediately, the hardliners attacked the president and his allies on the Internet, radio, and television for creating an "amnesty bill" for those who had violated the law. Some argued that the influx of new citizens would further erode enforcement and reward illegal activities as well as dramatically shift the political balance in favor of the Democrats, who, as mentioned, typically received the majority of Latino votes. Ultimately, the rebellion within the president's own party killed the bill and all efforts at comprehensive reform died, the issue languishing at the national level and individual states becoming the battlegrounds.

Not everyone in the Republican party and the conservative movement embraced the anti-immigrant forces, including President Bush, who worried about their effect on the future of the GOP. Prominent conservative Barry Goldwater, Jr., personally denounced the activities of many of the hardliners in Arizona, which became ground zero for many of the anti-immigrant groups. In one case, Goldwater attended a rally for those who wanted severe sanctions against those businesses employing illegal immigrants. Amid the chants of "deportation, deportation, deportation," Goldwater watched speakers, including a cousin of his, whip the crowd into a frenzy. "Speeches soaked with hateful, angry racist tones and dialogue," he reported, "eyes closed, listening to the roar of inflammatory rhetoric and sermonizing, I could have easily mistaken myself to be at one of David Duke's Ku Klux Klan rallies."

He lamented that the principles of conservatives like his father and Ronald Reagan, who had rejected racism, had been subverted and that "conservative leaders today have fallen from these principles and become ensconced in the polarized political spectrum" and had "tarnished the image of the Republican Party with the extreme hysteria and rhetoric." He added that hardliners "are targeting, in a way that is neither fair nor reasonable, a group of people who have been coming here for a long time." He concluded "this hysteria has to stop. We all walk this world as human beings, and we should all seek to understand and help one another. . . . We need to urge our lawmakers to practice tolerance and fairness, to become more involved in working a for a comprehensive solution that will be just to all."

Those outside of the United States also had negative views of the enforcement-only groups and the harsh anti-Latino rhetoric. The polarization negatively affected U.S.-Latin American relations at a time when U.S. prestige in the region had suffered a severe setback from the Iraq War. Many Latin Americans, especially among the poor and working class, looked to leaders such as Chávez, Morales, Ortega, Rafael Correa in Ecuador, and Obrador in Mexico who spewed anti-Americanism that often evoked the negative images of the immigration debate. The hardliners in the United States merely fueled the fires with their anti-immigrant rhetoric that seemingly focused exclusively on people from Latin America.

Vicente Fox, despite being the most pro-American president in Mexican history, proved an extremely vocal critic of the enforcement-only group. While acknowledging Mexico's responsibility for not providing sufficient economic opportunities to stem the flow of people northward to the United States, he particularly denounced "America's Berlin Wall" and pointed out that Bush's ordering of the National Guard to the borders had signified a giant lack of respect afforded Mexico. He added that the "idea of building an American Berlin Wall gave ammunition to Hugo Chávez and his allies, who pointed to the wall as the symbol of U.S. hatred for Latin America." He concluded "all around the world, people saw the border wall as a monument to the indifference of Bush's wealthy United States to the plight of poor and downtrodden of 'have-not' countries."

The anger and resentment oftentimes took strange twists. In El Alberto, Mexico, an entrepreneurial indigenous community known as, the Hñahñu, which had lost many members of its community to the United States, set up an adventure park with an unusual twist. Mexicans paid $18 to simulate a border crossing, complete with a booming voice in English screaming over a loudspeaker while searchlights crossed the sky, "Hello, this is the border patrol. . . It's too dangerous to cross the river. Remember your kids and families at home." For five hours, tourists walked in mud, sprinted across cornfields and walked precariously along ledges and across rivers, huddling near tunnels in the dark of night. Paid actors posing as border patrol agents waited in the night. At one point, they caught a group of the tourists, yelling, "We have you surrounded! We will let out the dogs." At one point, one even fired a gun into the air amid the threats of deportation. While some critics of the park argued that it served as a training ground for those preparing to head north, one of the founders noted it honored those who had to leave and go north to support their families and that the point of the park "is misunderstood. This is so my neighbors prosper, so that no one else is forced to go."

The immigration debates in the United States negatively affected the perceptions of the United States in Latin America. It divided Americans and raised tensions, particularly in areas where the immigration fights played out daily. The presidential candidates in the 2008 election, Barack Obama (D-IL) and John McCain (R-AZ), walked precariously around the issue, fearful of upsetting various constituencies even though the souring economy and Iraq pushed the issue into the background anyway. Nonetheless, Latin Americans as well as Latinos in the United States watched the debate, and while immigration reform temporarily ground to a halt during the election cycle, it remained a potent issue for future leaders of the nation to address.

Continuities

The end of the Cold War significantly affected U.S.-Latin American relations for at least a decade. For the first time since World War II, the United States faced no major perceived foreign threats in Latin America, or for that matter globally. U.S. policymakers responded with less interest in a region that had become increasingly democratic and stable, at least on the surface.

Nonetheless, interdependence continued to develop as more countries such as Chile and Colombia sought free trade agreements with the United States as its economy grew significantly in the 1990s and early twenty-first century. Other nations also tried to replicate U.S. advances in telecommunications, pharmaceuticals, and other growing industries related to the new technologies. While gaps remained, zones in Latin America including northern Mexico and countries with an educated workforce such as Costa Rica increasingly developed closer economic ties to the United States.

These economic efforts corresponded with other efforts to address issues such as the drug trade and tied closely with the ever-expanding growth of the influence of North Americans in popular culture and education. Technological advances such as the Internet accelerated the process, which included more debate over human rights, social justice, management of natural resources, and a growing concern over the environment that ranged from the destruction of native species to global warming.

The lack of threats to the preponderant U.S. position in the region combined with the democratic tidal wave outside of Cuba to create a sense of complacency, particularly during the Clinton administration. In the 1990s, Washington focused on domestic issues and hotspots in the world including the Middle East, the Balkans, and some areas of Africa. Outside of the episodes in Haiti, the tensions with Cuba, and the economic bailouts, most Americans and their policymakers paid little attention to Latin America.

Things improved momentarily with the administration of President George W. Bush, with several advisors focusing on the region, principally trade, drugs, and immigration. The events of September 11, 2001, however, changed the dynamics and distracted the administration from its early positive efforts. The U.S. invasion of Iraq and the heavy-handed dealing with Chávez in Venezuela created animosity among many Latin Americans. As Bush prepared to leave office, the United States, weakened by the adventures in the Middle East and significant economic problems at home, found itself hitting a low point in the post–Cold War era. Powerful forces have rushed to fill the vacuum, although in reality U.S. influence in the region remains high.

While the 1990s saw few conflicts between the United States and Latin America, by the beginning of the twenty-first century, new challenges appeared on the horizon in the form of new economic powers including China and the European Union and regional leaders such as Chávez who increasingly returned to rhetoric that challenged American development models and Washington's political hegemony. Empowered by sky-high petroleum prices that allowed him to try buy influence in the region, the Venezuelan proved a vocal critic, the loudest since Castro in the 1960s. Others joined the chorus and anti-Americanism peaked after the invasion of Iraq in 2003.

One of the most important trends during the nearly two decades after the end of the Cold War has been the explosion of the Latino population in the United States, which has surpassed African Americans as the largest ethnic minority in the country. With augmented numbers, Latino social, cultural, and economic power has increased substantially. Tens of millions of Latino consumers have changed regional and even national shopping and advertising patterns. Increasingly in music, film, and other forms of popular culture Latinos play increasingly important roles, which extended into areas that just twenty years before had very few Latino residents from Iowa to North Carolina to Michigan.

In the political realm, Latinos have determined the outcomes of many local and state contests as well as the presidential election in 2000 and affected the outcomes in 2004 and 2008. They will likely do so in the future, daring the vast majority of politicians to ignore issues relevant to Latinos at their own risk. This creates some challenges, as the Latino voting bloc is hardly uniform—conservative Cuban Americans, for example, differ dramatically in many ways from their southwestern Mexican American counterparts. Nonetheless, despite the ugly rhetoric and anti-immigrant attitudes present in various areas of the United States, no major candidate can afford to pander to those exclusionist groups in the face of the potent voting bloc.

SUGGESTIONS FOR ADDITIONAL READING

For more on the 1990s and the future, reference Abraham Lowenthal, *Partners in Conflict: The United States and Latin America in the 1990s* (1990); Jonathan Hartlyn, Lars Schoultz, and Augusto Varas, *The United States and Latin America in the 1990s: Beyond the Cold War* (1992); Albert Fishlow and James Jones, eds., *The United States and the Americas* (1999); Harold Molineu, *U.S. Policy toward Latin America: From Regionalism to Globalism* (1990); Guy Poitras, *The Ordeal of Hegemony: The United States and Latin America* (1990); and Bob Shacochis, *The Immaculate Invasion* (1999) and Philippe Gerard, *Clinton in Haiti: The U.S. Invasion of Haiti* (2004).

A lot more work remains to emerge on environmental issues, but several good books are Susan E. Place, ed., *Tropical Rainforests: Latin American Nature and Society in Transition* (1993); Sterling Evans, *The Green Republic: A Conservation History of Costa Rica* (1999); Bruce Rich, *Mortgaging the Earth: The World Bank, Environmental Impoverishment, and the Crisis of Development* (1994); Roger D. Stone, *Dreams of Amazonia* (1985); Susanna B. Hecht and Alexander Cockburn, *The Fate of the Forest: Developers, Destroyers, and Defenders of the Amazon* (1989); Evan Ward, *Packaged Vacations: Tourism Development in the Spanish Caribbean* (2008); and Richard P. Tucker, *Insatiable Appetite: The United States and the Ecological Degradation of the Tropical World* (2007).

To read about the immigration issues, see Frank D. Bean, Jurgen Schmandt, Sidney Weintraub, eds., *Mexican and Central American Population and U.S. Immigration Policy* (1989); and James G. Gimpel and James R. Edwards, Jr., *The Congressional Politics of Immigration Reform* (1999).

For more on Latinos in America, reference Rodolfo Acuña, *Occupied America: A History of Chicanos* (sixth edition, 2006); David G. Gutiérrez, ed., *Between Two Worlds: Mexican Immigrants in the United States* (1996); Peter Skerry, *Mexican-Americans: The Ambivalent Minority* (1993); Alejandro Portes and Robert L. Bach, *Latin Journey: Cuban and Mexican Immigrants in the United States* (1985); Alejandro Portes and Rubén Rumbaut, *Immigrant America: A Portrait* (1990); Lyn MacCorkle, *Cubans in the United States* (1984); Maria Cristina Garcia, *Havana USA: Cuban Exiles and Cuban Americans in South Florida, 1959–1994* (1997); Feliciano Ribera and Matt S. Meier, *Mexican Americans/American Mexicans: From the Conquistidors to Chicanos* (1993); F. Arturo Rosales, *Chicano! The History of the Mexican-American Civil Rights Movement* (1996); Lester Langley, *Mexamerica: Two Countries, One Future* (1988); and David E. Lorey, *The U.S.-Mexican Border in the Twentieth Century* (1999).

Good books on the foreign policy of George W. Bush include: James Mann, *Rise of the Vulcans: The History of Bush's War Cabinet* (2004); Robert G. Kaufman, *In Defense of the Bush Doctrine* (2007); Robert Jervis, *American Foreign Policy in a New Era* (2005); Ivo Daalder, *America Unbound: The Bush Revolution in Foreign Policy* (2005); Alexander Moens, *The Foreign Policy of George W. Bush: Values, Strategy, and Loyalty* (2004); Bob Woodward, *Plan of Attack* (2004).

For more on George W. Bush and Vicente Fox, reference: Vicente Fox and Rob Allyn, *Revolution of Hope: The Life, Faith, and Dreams of a Mexican President* (2007).

For more on the U.S. relationship with Chávez and the Bush administration, reference: Richard Gott, *Hugo Chávez and the Bolivarian Revolution* (2005); Cristina Marcano and Alberto Barrera Tyszka, *Hugo Chávez* (2007); Nikolas Kozloff, *Hugo Chávez: Oil, Politics, and the Challenges to the United States* (2006).

Epilogue

Political scientist and former Carter advisor Robert Pastor describes U.S.-Latin American relations thusly: a "Latin American whirlpool that draws the United States into its center, where it spins us in perilous eddies and then, just as suddenly, releases us to drift to the rim, where we forget the region and deal with other matters." He also adds that just when the United States thinks it has escaped the whirlpool, "the vortex retains it pull."

In 2008, the United States found itself preoccupied elsewhere, principally the Middle East, where it was bogged down in complex and intractable conflicts in Iraq and Afghanistan. Yet Latin America remains a priority in many quarters of the country. The economic integration remains a constant source of the interest of U.S. companies as well as European and Asian ones. The huge oil reserves recently discovered in Brazil alone could alter the power base of the international petroleum community and ease American dependence on the Middle East even as it thrusts Brazil's rapidly growing economy further into the limelight. The presence of nearly half a billion consumers for American products combined with a desire for Latin American goods ranging from coffee to wine to fruits firmly integrates the economic systems of the neighbors, especially as countries like Colombia and Chile try to become free-trade partners with the United States.

Yet many problems continue to plague the region. Poverty, unemployment, and a lack of opportunity remain prevalent in most nations. The deficiency of good systems of public education ensures a lack of skilled workers for the global technology revolution sweeping the planet. Many of the citizens go without jobs, proper housing, and health care. These push factors force a migration northward to the United States. Others seek income by conducting illegal activities such as the growing and trafficking of narcotics, fomenting a culture of violence and corruption that undermine efforts to create stable societies where sound investments, both domestic and foreign, can generate more opportunities.

For the United States, its relations with its southern neighbors remains troubled. Long-term animosities often caused by the history of interventionism and elitism fuel long-standing reservoirs of anti-Americanism in Latin Americans. The United States finds a region in 2008 increasingly integrated with other global economic and political systems as China, the European Union, and the United States compete for primacy with traditional regional powers including Mexico, Brazil, and Venezuela. U.S. hegemony in the region peaked in the 1990s, but the economic stagnation caused by huge government deficits, high oil prices, overextension in the housing industry, and the costly wars in the Middle East has forced Americans to reevaluate their relations in Latin America.

Nonetheless, many encouraging signs exist for the United States in the region. Democracy dominates in every country outside Cuba where Raúl Castro has succeeded his brother Fidel, although with varying degrees of success. A country like Colombia appears poised to become a major player on many levels as it emerges from forty years of civil war under the success of Plan Colombia, partly facilitated by the more than $6 billion in American military and economic assistance. The Uribe government has reigned in the right-wing paramilitaries and marginalized the rebels. Colombians, tired of the incessant cycle of violence and its negative impact on the economy and society, have rejected both extremes and worked hard to create a stable society. While many challenges remain, it appears likely that the path toward peace will continue.

Other positive indicators regarding the future of U.S.-Latin American relations include the fact that huge energy resources recently uncovered in the region may shift U.S. oil dependence outside of the tumultuous Middle East and toward its southern neighbors. Mexico and Venezuela already provide significant amounts of the valuable commodity. Adding Brazil's large reserves as well as other energy sources in countries such as Bolivia may allow the United States to further extricate itself from the morass in the Middle East.

Furthermore, the wars in Iraq and Afghanistan may also have laid the foundations for a neo-isolationism in which Americans follow long-held traditions and retreat internally after failures in far off lands. Not only will Washington shift its priorities inward, but it will most likely invest more time and energy in improving relations with its regional partners.

While points of contention remain on issues such as immigration and drugs, the economic and political integration of the democratic societies appears to be moving forward. Furthermore, new changes appear on the horizon as Cuba will likely have a significant change in its leadership in the next decade, possibly ending the four-decade-long confrontation that has undermined relations between the United States and Latin America.

The focus southward also will continue to grow with the increase in the Latino population. Like African Americans who historically have focused U.S. attentions on predominantly African-influenced nations such as Haiti and Liberia, Latinos have continued to call attention southward to Cuba, Mexico, and other Latin American countries, a trend likely to intensify. The presence of Latinos has been increasing and will continue in the diplomatic corps, business community, and military. These often bilingual and bicultural Americans will help the process of integration and ease some of the long-standing racial and cultural tensions that so often tarnished the past.

In 2008, the United States is treading water on the rim of the whirlpool. Yet the future looks brighter. Perhaps the next time Washington develops an overarching interest in Latin America, the vortex will not be the swirling morass of periods such as the 1980s but one of more cooperation and collaboration. Major obstacles remain in the form of anti-Americanism and, often, what one must term U.S. arrogance and greed, but with the inauguration of Barack Obama in 2009 things look better at this moment than at any time in the past five years.

Index

In the Eagle's Shadow: The United States and Latin America
Developmental editor and copy editor: Andrew J. Davidson
Production editor: Linda Gaio
Indexer: Susan Schmid
Proofreader: Claudia Siler
Cartographer: Jane Domier
Typesetter: Bruce Leckie
Printer: Versa Press